THE
Atlantic Monthly
1 8 5 7 — 1 9 0 9

THE
Atlantic Monthly
1857 – 1909

Yankee Humanism
at High Tide and Ebb

ELLERY SEDGWICK

University of Massachusetts Press   Amherst

Copyright © 1994 by
University of Massachusetts Press
All rights reserved
Printed in the United States of America
First paperback printing 2009
LC 93-34629
ISBN: 978-1-55849-793-1
Designed by David Ford
Set in Adobe Minion by Keystone Typesetting, Inc.
Printed and bound by Thomson-Shore, Inc.

Library of Congress Cataloging-in-Publication Data
Sedgwick, Ellery, 1942–
    The Atlantic monthly, 1857–1909 : Yankee humanism at high tide and ebb / by Ellery Sedgwick.
    p. cm.
    Includes bibliographical references (p.   ) and index.
    ISBN 0-87023-919-8 (cloth : alk. paper)
    1. Atlantic monthly (Boston, Mass. : 1857)   2. New England—Intellectual life.   I. Title.
PN4900.A7S43   1994
051—dc20   93-34629
                                                                                                                      CIP

British Library Cataloguing in Publication data are available.

This book is published with the support and cooperation of the University of Massachusetts at Boston.

Portions of this book have been previously published in journals as follows: "The Early Years of the *Atlantic Monthly*," *American Transcendental Quarterly* (Dec. 1985), 3–30; "Walter Hines Page at the *Atlantic Monthly*," *Harvard Library Bulletin*, Fall 1987, 427–49; "Henry James and the *Atlantic Monthly*," *Studies in Bibliography*, 1992, 311–32.

To my wife, Robin, with gratitude

Contents

      List of Illustrations   ix

      Acknowledgments   xi

      Introduction: Overview, 1857–1909   1

1   The Founding of the *Atlantic* (1857)   21
      Boston's High Tide

2   James Russell Lowell (1857–1861)   45
      Yankee Humanist

3   James T. Fields (1861–1871)   69
      The Publisher as Editor

4   William Dean Howells (1871–1881)   113
      Editorial Realist

5   Thomas Bailey Aldrich (1881–1890)   161
      Editorial Aesthete

6   Horace Elisha Scudder (1890–1898)   201
      Missionary of Yankee Culture

7   Walter Hines Page (1898–1899)   245
      Progressive Editing

8 Bliss Perry (1899–1909) 275
   Liberal Humanist in the Progressive Era

Notes   319

Works Cited   323

Index   329

Illustrations

Francis H. Underwood   20

James Russell Lowell   44

James T. Fields   68

William Dean Howells   112

Henry Oscar Houghton   126

Thomas Bailey Aldrich   160

Horace Elisha Scudder   200

Walter Hines Page   244

Bliss Perry   274

Acknowledgments

If much of writing is solitary, much is also communal. I am grateful for the assistance of those who helped in the realization of this book. Austin Chinn and Cecilia Tichi gave early encouragement and dialogue that helped to define approaches. Cullen Murphy, current managing editor of the *Atlantic*, helped me to understand the magazine's functions, past and present. I am especially indebted to Ellen Ballou, author of *Building of the House: Houghton Mifflin's Formative Years*, for her exhaustive research, her decisive style, and her balanced insights into the relationship between literature and the publishing business, all of which have served as models I aspire to but do not expect to achieve.

Longwood College provided me with a sabbatical in 1988–89 during which the majority of the manuscript was written. John McKernan mercifully shredded an initial draft and suggested useful tactics for improving it. My colleagues Michael Lund and Gordon VanNess helped me rework portions of later drafts. Craig Noll's editing repeatedly saved me from my own mental lapses while Ashley Warren was efficient and effective in checking accuracy and documentation in the final stages. I am obliged to Paul Wright of the University of Massachusetts Press for taking much of the anxiety out of the process of bringing the manuscript to publication, and to the anonymous reviewers who both understood what I had attempted and helped me to articulate it more fully. My greatest debt of gratitude is to my wife, Robin, for making labor on this book both possible and meaningful.

THE
Atlantic Monthly
1 8 5 7 — 1 9 0 9

Introduction: Overview, 1857–1909

This book is a history of the first half century of the *Atlantic Monthly* magazine, from its founding in 1857 through the end of Bliss Perry's editorship in 1909. The *Atlantic* still thrives, but its first half century marked the period of its greatest cultural influence, particularly in literature. Those years also reflect most fully its expression of the humanist tradition of the New England cultural elite and the dialectic between that tradition and the developing democratic mass culture.

The history of the *Atlantic Monthly* during the nineteenth century is partly the story of its first seven editors: James Russell Lowell, James T. Fields, William Dean Howells, Thomas Bailey Aldrich, Horace Elisha Scudder, Walter Hines Page, and Bliss Perry. The *Atlantic*'s editors are worth the attention of readers of nineteenth-century cultural history because it was their business to be unusually sensitive to the intellectual currents of their times. Their editorial decisions dramatize major American cultural values and conflicts. They are of further interest because each has had an authoritative voice in shaping what was published and read, what authors and ideas gained influence among a significant cultural minority of Americans. Each has impressed his own personality, values, and vision of the magazine's purpose on his incarnation of the *Atlantic*.

Editors, however, like politicians, are supposed to be simultaneously leaders and surrogates for their public's values. Emerson declared at the *Atlantic*'s founding that its editors must be ready to defy the public and accept only what they believed to be of permanent worth, and nineteenth-century *Atlantic* editors took their function as cultural leaders seriously (*Journals* 14: 167). But most were also pragmatists, attuned not only to the intellectual currents of the time but also to the tastes and values of their readership. Their sensitivities to their public and their ability to articulate and represent the responses of relatively educated, middle-class nineteenth-century readers make them of further interest.

In addition to evaluating the *Atlantic*'s editors, and through them its readership,

Introduction 1857–1909

this book also provides information on the publishing history of a broad range of nineteenth-century American authors. During the magazine's first fifty years, it published major work not only by many traditionally canonical authors such as Emerson, Holmes, Hawthorne, Longfellow, Lowell, Stowe, Thoreau, Whittier, Howells, James, and Jewett but also by a large number of authors who have received renewed recognition during the past twenty years such as Rebecca Harding Davis, Rose Terry Cooke, Charles Chesnutt, W. E. B. DuBois, Zitkala-Sa, Mary Austin, and Abraham Cahan. Inevitably, too, the researcher into *Atlantic* history, surveying with mixed melancholy and relief the legions of forgotten authors, manuscripts, and passions that have passed into near oblivion in the volumes gathering dust in library stacks, encounters many writers who deserve at least brief memorial and perhaps further scholarly attention.

Several decades ago, William Charvat proposed new approaches to literary and cultural history, recognizing that authors should be studied not in isolation but as part of a triangle of relationships, the other two points being the reader and the publishing trade. The lines of cultural influence, Charvat suggested, are reciprocal between all points in the triangle (*Authorship* 284). In 1986, Michael Anesko, in his excellent book on Henry James's dialectic with the literary marketplace, repeated Charvat's claim that while the publishing trade in America "has had a positive and dynamic function in the world of literature" for at least two centuries, its influence has been little studied (7–8). With a few notable exceptions, this deficiency remains although there are now clear signs of increasing interest in publishing history.

Throughout the nineteenth century the *Atlantic* was owned by major Boston publishing houses, most notably Ticknor and Fields and Houghton Mifflin. *Atlantic* editors, representing both readers and publishers, significantly influenced many authors, remembered and forgotten, particularly in the formative early stages of their careers. For many writers, including Howells, James, Jewett, and Chesnutt, the *Atlantic* was the first major source of recognition, providing the first contact with an audience and with the literary marketplace. Often it became a consistent source of publication. Editors influenced writers by articulating the responses and demands of the *Atlantic* audience and, to a degree, of the publishers, as well as by articulating their own intellectual and aesthetic criteria for acceptance. They also initiated new work by actively soliciting it, gave writers generative suggestions for topics and treatments, acted as censors, engaged in ideological and stylistic arguments, and participated in negotiating financial rewards with the publisher.

Critics from Malcolm Cowley to John Tomsich and Richard Brodhead have argued that the so-called quality magazines, particularly the *Atlantic*, the *Century*, *Harpers'*, and *Scribner's*, most accurately and fully represented middle- and upper-middle-class American culture in the second half of the nineteenth century. Although the *Atlantic* had a smaller circulation than the others, it often carried greater intellectual prestige and represented an influential, relatively highbrow portion of that culture. The *Atlantic* and all of the other quality magazines contained in varying proportions not only literature but also commentary on politics, science, economics, art, and current social issues. Some cultural scholarship, like Tomsich's *Genteel Endeavor*, has selectively mined these sources. Too often, however, attention has focused narrowly on literary fiction, particularly its genteel limitations as judged by modern tastes, and has ignored the larger context. The only comprehensive study of the ideology of these magazines, beyond Mott's pioneering surveys, is Arthur John's informative book *The Best Years of the Century*.

The broader purpose of this history, therefore, is to examine the *Atlantic* as an institution that represented a significant voice in American "high" literary or intellectual culture. The book aims to define the mainstream within the magazine's literary, social, and political values and to comment on the relationship between high literary culture and American political and social democracy. It examines the extent to which the *Atlantic*'s editors, writers, and readers, most of whom represent an elite cultural minority, were democratic or antidemocratic, sympathetic or opposed to social and political trends, engaged in or alienated from the broader American culture. It traces changes in their values in response to larger changes within American society, such as the rise of industrial capitalism, increasing ethnic pluralism, their waning influence as a high-cultural elite, and the dominance of mass culture.

In defining the *Atlantic*'s literary, social, and political ideology, this book also examines the degree to which the magazine, and by extension the high-culture tradition it represents, has been canonically broad or narrow, the degree to which it has identified itself with an established body of authors and texts, as well as the degree to which it has encouraged, tolerated, marginalized, or suppressed divergent ideas and new voices. In writing about the nineteenth-century quality magazines, of which the *Atlantic* is perhaps the archetype, Richard Brodhead has commented that "the version of literary culture that they strove to establish has been known since the turn of the century as 'genteel' and to the extent that it has been discussed at all, it has been dismissed without further curiosity as a kind of institutionalized insulation system, an attempt to keep the literary field clear of references to disturbing social or sexual subjects" (472). I have tried to supply a balanced analysis of the canonical scope, accomplishments, and limitations of high literary culture as represented by the *Atlantic* and to suggest the range of ideas and values to which it exposed educated middle-class readers.

The *Atlantic* was founded in 1857 by Francis Underwood, an assistant to the publisher Moses Phillips, and a group of New England writers including Emerson, Holmes, Lowell, and Stowe. Its founders wished to expand the market for the publication, distribution, and recognition of the relatively new American literary culture, particularly that which had developed in and around Boston during the

New England renaissance. The magazine was to provide mutual profit for its publisher and writers by supplying a continuous, short-term outlet for publication, regular income and publicity for established writers, a way for new authors to develop a public, and a means for stimulating a broader readership. The *Atlantic* soon became the leading periodical publishing mainly American writing and an important part of the post–Civil War rise of the quality magazines that created a substantial, new, national market for American literature and made authorship an economically viable profession in the United States. As Michael Anesko demonstrates, for many authors in the second half of the century, the magazine market became far more financially remunerative than book publication (168).

The Yankee humanists who initially founded, edited, and contributed to the *Atlantic* intended it to be more than a market. With the important exception of an uncompromising opposition to slavery, they did not project that the magazine would advocate explicit editorial positions. But they did intend it to be a missionary agent for propagating their own cultural values. With an evangelical zeal that Daniel Howe attributes to their Protestant heritage, the mid-nineteenth-century New England cultural elite who initiated the *Atlantic* took as their secular mission, and their profession, the propagation of high ethical, aesthetic, and intellectual values in the American republic (508, 516). At a time when orthodox religion was waning rapidly, they sought to develop and transmit values through a humanistic culture.

Thomas Wentworth Higginson, himself a minister turned writer, as well as a frequent contributor and sometime assistant editor of the *Atlantic*, wrote: "The New England authors ... saw if not themselves—for they were not self-conscious—at least their profession, as having a Promethean role to play. They were teachers, educators, and bringers of the light with a deep and affectionate feeling of obligation towards the young republic their fathers had brought into being. That New England was appointed to guide the nation, to civilize it, to humanize it, none of them doubted" (*Cheerful Yesterdays* 167). The *Atlantic*, Higginson acknowledged, was a focal point of this cultural mission.

The New England authors, editors, and publishers who exerted a formative, enduring influence on the *Atlantic* were more socially and ideologically diverse than most commentators have recognized. In a broad sense, however, they did represent a Yankee cultural elite. They were largely Anglo-Saxon, middle-class, liberal Protestant, and, in politics, Conscience Whig, Free Soil, and Radical Republican. Commentators from Oliver Wendell Holmes to Stowe Persons and Lawrence Buell have noted that many of them came from relatively privileged socioeconomic backgrounds, often from middle-class families with a history of intellectual interests.[1] Holmes as well as many modern commentators have noted that Yankee teachers, writers, and intellectuals, like Emerson, Lowell, and himself, frequently came from old ministerial lines and that those who had formerly professed religion now increasingly professed humanistic literary culture.

The cultural elite itself, however, was far more a meritocracy than a hereditary gentry. In Werner Sollors's terms, it was a grouping based mainly in individual "consent" rather than genealogical "descent." Stowe Persons, who misleadingly calls them a "cultural gentry," specifies that "their position was not a birthright, either in theory or in practice" but a result of intellectual character and personal choice (2). As Bronson Alcott, Francis Child, James Fields, Howells, Whittier, E. P. Whipple, and many others demonstrated, the New England cultural and intellectual elite was open to those from varied, less privileged backgrounds. Conversely, most privileged individuals did not become members of the cultural elite. That position was achieved mainly by choice of profession. Furthermore, as Lawrence Buell accurately points out, many of these writers and intellectuals, including Emerson, Hawthorne, and Lowell, in varying degrees rejected inherited social position, values, and material advantages in choosing the profession of authorship and evolving their own ideologies (390).

Holmes, Persons, Buell, and others all demonstrate that the nineteenth-century New England cultural elite, including those who founded and sustained the early *Atlantic*, were, despite some overlap (as in the case of Holmes), distinct from the dominant social and economic elites. This distinction became increasingly marked and frequently turned to opposition as the century progressed and industrial capitalism produced new socioeconomic elites. Persons notes that the values of the cultural elite emphasized intellectual and moral development, as opposed to the manners, fashion, and money of the social and economic elites (44–59). They were further distinguished by their social function, the transmission of culture. They tended to enforce not social and economic but intellectual and moral hierarchies. They were teachers, scholars, ministers, lecturers, editors, and writers, often practicing two or three of these professions simultaneously to earn a relatively modest livelihood by serving as creators and communicants of social, ethical, religious, and aesthetic ideas.

As reflected in the antislavery stand of the Yankee humanists, their ideas by no means always supported a comfortable social and economic status quo. In addition to their function as cultural evangelists and the value they placed on the life of the mind, the cultural elite were also distinguished from the social and economic elites by their generally progressive values. Buell, for instance, demonstrates that the major New England writers of midcentury were distinctly liberal and nondogmatic in religion, a large majority holding convictions somewhere between Unitarianism and Emersonian transcendentalism. He notes also that most were both considerably more politically active and more politically progressive than the norm (389–91). Several, such as Emerson, Higginson, Thoreau, and Whittier, were particularly radicalized by their opposition to slavery. These liberal values in politics and religion were clearly reflected in the early *Atlantic*.

As David Hall demonstrates, the Yankee humanists who formed New England's midcentury cultural elite, like English liberals such as Mill, Arnold, and Leslie Stephen, with whom they had extensive contacts, attempted to reconcile social democracy with cultural authority and adherence to a hierarchy of cultural values. They were democratic in a genuine but limited sense. Virtually all affirmed a belief that the social and political organizations of the United States were a further stage in the evolution of civilization beyond the quasi-feudal and aristocratic orders of Europe because they gave more scope to the intellectual, moral, and spiritual development of individuals. The democracy that constitutionally protected the rights of the individual was sacred to them. Most of them sincerely believed that these rights should apply equally to all without reference to property, race, or privilege. The sincerity of their commitment was reflected in their advocacy of civil disobedience, even war, as a remedy for the denial of these rights by slavery. But toward the other major tenet of American democracy—majority rule—they were deeply ambivalent, particularly in matters of intellect, aesthetics, and morality. In these matters, they believed, as Emerson repeatedly asserted in the *Atlantic* and elsewhere, that "the truth, the hope of any time must always be sought in the minorities" ("Aspects of Culture," Jan. 1868, 90). The educated minority had a moral obligation to resist resolutely the cultural tyranny of the majority and the leveling pressures of conformity while simultaneously seeking to educate that majority.

This resistance to the democratic principle of majority rule in intellectual, aesthetic, and ethical issues and the attempt to reconcile social democracy with an authoritative hierarchy of cultural values were reflected in the *Atlantic* throughout the nineteenth century and beyond. In general, particularly in the early period, a spirit of liberal optimism concerning the educability and fundamental integrity of the American majority prevailed. An Emersonian faith in the divinity within, the inherent worth of individuals, and their potential for moral and intellectual growth increased the elites' sense of the importance of their own cultural mission. Since democracy offered greater scope for individual development, the stimulation and guidance of that development became more crucial. Later, particularly during the eighties and nineties with the rapid development of industrialization, class and ethnic divisions, and mass culture, the *Atlantic* reflected strong undercurrents of doubt about the direction and potential of the American majority. By the turn of the century, however, a spirit of progressive optimism, characteristically stronger in social than in literary matters, again set the dominant tone.

The Yankee humanists of the New England cultural elite which sustained the early *Atlantic* clearly shared, then, a hierarchical and hegemonic rather than a modern and relativistic concept of cultural values. Partly because of their Calvinist religious tradition, they believed that in higher cultures the primary purpose of life itself, as of education, was not social prestige, entertainment, sensual experience, power, or even promoting social welfare but specifically the development of intellect and moral character in the individual. This hierarchical idea of culture, like the related ambiguity toward majority rule in intellectual and ethical matters, created tensions between the cultural elite and the developing industrial mass culture, tensions that became increasingly manifested in the *Atlantic* later in the century.

But if the Yankee humanists believed that some forms of culture were better than others because they developed more highly the moral and intellectual potential of the individual, they did not believe that that hierarchy was or should be static. Before Herbert Spencer formulated his theories of social evolution, Emerson and the New England cultural elite had a sanguine faith in the progressive moral and cultural evolution of both individuals and civilizations. Emerson, Lowell, Higginson, and later Howells and Scudder, among others, saw America as yet culturally underdeveloped but potentially capable of leading the progress of civilization through broad, democratic participation in a high ethical culture. Their function, most believed, was to develop and propagate that culture and thus promote progress, not, as critics such as Vernon Parrington have suggested, to enforce a static social hierarchy (435–41). They explicitly rejected the notion that "culture" was a means of denoting and enforcing social status, viewing such an idea as a corrupt European, particularly British, practice from which they as Americans distinguished themselves.

The Yankee humanists further believed that the written word and its tradition were major sources of moral and intellectual development. Most were educated in the traditional canon of Western humanism and believed that a knowledge of that body of work could greatly enrich individual development and public discourse. But they also shared a conviction that American literary culture, now at a critical stage in its formation, while being conversant with that tradition, must develop its own forms and values appropriate to American conditions. In early volumes of the *Atlantic* Lowell, Emerson, Higginson, and others explicitly advocated American intellectual independence. While sometimes quite critical about the accomplishments to date of their American high literary culture, they were nevertheless certain of the value of what it would produce and were unembarrassed in asserting their own standards of intellectual quality and their desire to spread their culture as broadly as possible.

While most of the Yankee cultural elite believed that the intellectual and moral development of the individual was primary, they also had strong convictions advocating the social responsibility of the educated individual. As noted above, their political and social values were distinctly liberal and reformist compared with those of the American mainstream. Parrington, among others, describes the New

England culture, even at midcentury, as essentially conservative, disengaged, and dryly scholarly. This was not true of most Yankee humanists. It was particularly untrue, as Buell points out, of the generation that established the *Atlantic* four years before the Civil War, in part to speak against slavery. They believed that American high literary culture and those steeped in it should be actively engaged in American social and political as well as cultural life. The American scholar, Emerson had announced, must engage in social action as well as reflection. In the eighteenth century, the high-culture elite had exercised considerable political influence. By the middle of the nineteenth century, their influence was reduced but still potent, particularly in antislavery politics. Later, during the 1870s, their political power continued to wane; though many continued to speak for civil service reform and to criticize laissez-faire capitalism, some lapsed into cynical conservatism or refocused their social commitment on explicitly cultural issues. But the response of the Yankee cultural elite to the progressive movement around the turn of the twentieth century demonstrated again that their essential tradition was a moderate, socially engaged liberalism.

These values, then, were generally shared by the New England cultural elite who established the essential character and traditions of the *Atlantic*. The *Atlantic*, like the lyceum movement supported by the same group, was one expression of the Yankee humanist's sense of mission to civilize and humanize America, to promote high culture as a source of values, to encourage public knowledge of both the traditional canon and contemporary writing, to debate and establish intellectual and moral standards in American politics and social life as well as in literature, to resist with vigilant criticism the erosion of these standards by commercial forces, to propagate these standards through education, and to stimulate further cultural production. The magazine's history is in some measure a record of the accomplishments and limitations of Yankee humanism in fulfilling these tasks.

While the general assumptions defined above unified the Yankee humanists who established the *Atlantic*, several factors both inside and outside their tradition worked to diversify viewpoints among the New England cultural elite in general and within the magazine in particular. This diversity increased over time and was later crucial in allowing the magazine to adapt and survive the decline of the New England tradition and the rise of mass culture.

First, even in the *Atlantic*'s early years, New England's cultural elite, contrary to the popular image of the effete, socially exclusive Brahmin guardian of culture, was no closed patrician circle. Of the *Atlantic*'s first four editors, only Lowell was either born in the environs of Boston or educated at any college, much less Harvard. The other three—James T. Fields, William Dean Howells, and T. B. Aldrich—were all self-educated young men from the provinces with strong literary ambitions who achieved central positions in the New England literary culture. Furthermore, both the social and the intellectual homogeneity of the *Atlantic*'s early circle of contributors have been considerably exaggerated, initially through the conscious, commercially motivated promotions of the magazine's second editor and publisher, Fields. Even among the early core group, Lowell and Emerson, Holmes and Whittier, Fields and Mrs. Stowe shared a general faith in the power of literary culture, but their lives and their values on many issues were quite different.

More important still in terms of diversity, the Yankee cultural elite shared a respect for intellectual individuality and a tolerance for dissent. They admired Emersonian individualism and self-reliance. Most were conscious of being a cultural minority and were outspoken dissenters from the majority on such central issues as religious orthodoxy and political compromise with slavery. They founded the *Atlantic* not so much as an editorial organ for promoting particular doctrines, except in opposition to slavery, as a platform for individual intellectual debate and literary expression.

Furthermore, the humanistic concept of culture articulated by Emerson and others held specifically that intellectual cultivation liberated a person from provincialism, irrational prejudice, ethnic and egotistic narrowness, giving a breadth of view and an ability to see issues whole. It "redresses his balance . . . revives the delicious sense of sympathy and warns him of the dangers of solitude and repulsion" (R. Emerson, "Culture" 343). By this widely held measure, the intellectual integrity of editors, writers, and readers could be judged by their freedom from self-interested prejudice, their breadth of perspective, and their willingness to encounter new ideas. Certainly the *Atlantic* often fell short of this ideal (as Emerson did in his customary usage of the masculine pronoun), but its tradition of intellectual tolerance was strong.

The tolerant liberalism of Yankee humanism itself, then, inclined the *Atlantic* toward a relative diversity of views. In addition, from early on, increasing economic pressures influenced several editors, especially Fields, Howells, and Page, to diversify the magazine beyond the waning elite audience which initially composed its major readership. These financial pressures to expand the audience unquestionably sometimes led to censorship and compromise of literary/intellectual standards through attempts at popular appeal. But in the case of the *Atlantic*, they sometimes led also to a greater range of voices and contents intended to attract a wider range of readers. Thus, if the editors' conservative emphasis on "high standards" tended to limit the magazine's pluralism, the Yankee respect for individualism and dissent and later economic pressures to reach a larger audience tended to push the magazine toward diversification, change, and adaptation.

The *Atlantic*'s formative first quarter-century under Lowell, Fields, and Howells constituted the golden day of liberal Yankee humanism, and the magazine reflected this optimistic creed in a relatively pure form. The headier utopianism and transcendental enthusiasms of the early New England renaissance were past. But the *Atlantic* demonstrated some of the moral convictions of the later reform phase of transcendentalism, the mellowed spirit of a moderate dissenting individualism, the speculative bent of enlightenment rationalism, and an expansive optimism about the potential of the American nation, once free of the curse of slavery, for social, material, and cultural progress. The New England Indian summer was at the full; its fruits, including the writings of the Olympians, seemed still maturing. Signs of slow decay were visible only in retrospect.

The *Atlantic*'s fondness for Emersonian philosophy and Holmes's rational skepticism soon gained it a reputation for breadth of individual speculation and theological liberalism that angered the orthodox and spurred its denunciation in the pulpit and religious press. The *Atlantic* carried the first major American exposition and defense of Darwin, by Asa Gray; despite Agassiz's counterarguments, the essential tenets of Darwinism were well entrenched in the magazine by the 1870s. During these years, the *Atlantic* also spoke for social and political reform. This was clearest in its strong abolitionist stand, its rejection of political compromise on slavery, and its postwar leadership in proposing radical Republican Reconstruction measures. But it also spoke for greater social, intellectual, and economic opportunities for women, as well as for progressive reforms in both public and higher education. Fields and Howells introduced, as well, some of the earliest American descriptions and discussions of the damaging social consequences of postwar industrialism.

The early *Atlantic*'s major contributions were in literature, and there also its tendency was liberal. *Atlantic* writers advocated a specifically American culture and literature, not chauvinistically rejecting European culture (in fact, drawing the best from Europe), but adapting it to American circumstances and actively supporting American authorship, language, forms, and values. The magazine lent strong support to the rise of local color regional writing, much of it produced by and identifying with women, beginning with Harriet Beecher Stowe and including Rose Terry Cooke, Mary Murfree, Elizabeth Stuart Phelps, Celia Thaxter, Constance Woolson, and Sarah Orne Jewett. Much of the earliest development of American realism also took place in the pages of the *Atlantic* during its first twenty-five years. Lowell and Fields both showed themselves sympathetic to a limited realism. Howells developed much of his own realism while editing the *Atlantic* and made the publication and critical support of a new generation of realistic writers, including Henry James, H. H. Boyeson, John DeForest, Sarah Jewett, and Mark Twain, a major aim of his editorship.

During the *Atlantic*'s earliest years most writers and readers were from New England, and the New England influence dominated. During the postwar expansion in territory and transportation, however, Fields and particularly Howells broadened its geographical scope, and by its twentieth year both authorship and circulation were genuinely national, though retaining a New England flavor.

From the beginning, the magazine's emphasis was solidly on supporting contemporary American writing, but Lowell and others believed that a place should be reserved for discussion of traditional humanistic texts. Homer, Horace, Dante, Shakespeare, Goethe, and others were not the exclusive province of the academy but should be a part of literate public discourse. Discussion of the great works, they believed, would stimulate and enrich, rather than displace or inhibit, production of first-rate contemporary work. Lowell and Howells believed also that critical reviewing would help to establish high standards for American writing, expose the shoddy, and stimulate the good. Howells in particular established an authoritative reviewing department that satirized didacticism and sentimentality while promoting realism.

During the magazine's first twenty years, the critical and popular reputations of many of the writers identified with the *Atlantic* remained high. Beginning in the seventies, however, the magazine lost writers—and readers—to more middlebrow illustrated "quality" magazines. The founding of *Scribner's* (later renamed the *Century*) in 1870 marked rising competitive pressure from increasingly popular magazines flaunting increasingly large circulations and paying increasingly large authors' fees. Still, the *Atlantic* had established itself as an authoritative voice on literary and cultural issues and a source of support for good writing. It also reflected an essential optimism on the part of the cultural elite about the broad acceptance of their culture as a literary and intellectual standard and a source of national values.

By the 1880s and 1890s, however, during the editorships of T. B. Aldrich and Horace Scudder, Yankee humanism was rapidly losing its liberal optimism in the face of massive American social changes, including industrial capitalism, class politics, and the rise of mass culture, all of which challenged the magazine's values and its function. In the *Atlantic*, this shift in tone and mood was generally moderate. The magazine's pages during these years show that even in its most conservative phase, the New England tradition was not as reactionary, narrowly self-insulating, or impervious to democratic America as its many critics have claimed. But there was clearly a decline from a progressive liberal humanism to a retrospective, idealistic genteel tradition. The ideals of the recent past congealed into prescriptive dogma, its living authors into canonical figures, and its individualism into conformist concern for social cohesion. There was some refusal to acknowledge disturbing social realities, some defensive reaction to change, some narrowing of sympathies, and considerable loss of the old expansive optimism about the potential of the American majority and the leadership role of the cultural elite.

Although he did not reduce the magazine to his views, T. B. Aldrich in some ways typified the most conservative political, cultural, and literary attitudes. Reactionaries like Aldrich, Charles Eliot Norton, Barrett Wendell, and Henry Adams expressed alienation from the mainstream of American life, sardonic cynicism about the democratic electorate and popular taste, anger at finding themselves superfluous in a nation that refused to respect their cultural leadership, bitterness at a perceived dispossession of the Yankee race by a flood of immigration, and increasing shrillness in their prophecies of American cultural decline. Such views were sometimes represented in the *Atlantic*, but the magazine's characteristic tone in these years was typified more by Aldrich's successor, Horace Scudder. With a patient, gentle idealism, Scudder dedicated his life to preserving and propagating the high-minded values of Yankee humanism in an age of rapidly developing industrial mass culture. Scudder possessed a sensitive social conscience and an awareness of cultural change, but his mission, and much of the emphasis of his magazine, was trying to preserve the gains his predecessors had won over the past thirty years, not to strive for further progress.

During the editorships of Aldrich and Scudder the *Atlantic* largely steered the course of literary high culture and continued to lose circulation, writers, and influence. Still admired by many for its intellectual integrity, it was praised more than read. It was widely considered old-fashioned and stolidly highbrow, particularly in contrast not only with the illustrated quality monthlies like the *Century*, now achieving circulations over 200,000, but even more with the newer, cheaper, advertising-based, mass-circulation magazines of the nineties such as *McClure's* and *Ladies' Home Journal*, which quickly achieved circulation near a half-million. Literary production was now much more geographically diverse; the national center of gravity in publishing, and to an extent in intellectual life, had moved to New York, leaving Boston to eulogize its past. The *Atlantic*'s publisher, Henry Oscar Houghton, and his editors, by refusing to illustrate the magazine or to escalate authors' fees, largely rejected competition with the New York magazines for writers and audiences and acquiesced in accepting a modest economic niche as an exponent of traditional high culture.

In keeping with this function, Aldrich, Scudder, and some writers in the *Atlantic* during these years conducted an Arnoldian campaign to preserve traditional high culture against the barbarians and philistines of the rising commercial and democratic mass culture. Like Arnold, they saw the traditional works of Western humanism fading from the realm of public discourse, and they wished to resist this erosion. Aldrich and Scudder, therefore, continued to publish frequent articles discussing the major texts and authors of the Western canon. Their *Atlantic* was one of the last general periodicals to carry extensive commentary on the Greek and Roman classics and to defend the study of these works. Both the discussions and the classical works themselves were rapidly becoming banished to the limbo of the academy, soon to be followed by the other major works of Western humanism. Within twenty-five years, more progressive *Atlantic* editors would consider these works unpromising subjects for which the magazine's audience had neither interest nor sufficient background knowledge.

Another effort at cultural preservation was the attempt to canonize the New England writers who had helped to establish the *Atlantic*'s reputation. Since Fields's time, because of their commercial and personal connections with the magazine, the Olympians had been spared some, though not all, of the frank and incisive criticism given to others. Now, as they died during the 1880s and 1890s, they were eulogized in the *Atlantic*, and Scudder labored successfully to continue and broaden their influence by embalming them in anthologies and school curricula.

In the treatment of contemporary literature, too, the *Atlantic* of 1880 to 1895 attempted to preserve the status quo rather than advocating progressive change. Mainly because of Horace Scudder, who wrote a vast number of reviews, the magazine generally continued to support a moderate Howellsian realism in its literary criticism and selection of fiction. Scudder, however, unlike Howells, could not enthusiastically support the next generation of grimmer and grittier realists like Garland and Upton Sinclair. There were also signs of reaction. The *Atlantic* gave voice to some who hoped for a resurgence of romance and published an increasing quantity of romantic fiction. Aldrich was a literary as well as a political Tory, insisting on strict orthodoxy in poetic form, loathing dialect, and favoring lapidary, classical treatment of self-consciously beautiful subjects. He saw himself as a defender of high aesthetic culture against lowbrow incursions. It was indicative that he both despised the sentimental literary populism represented by James Whitcomb Riley and published far more of Henry James's work than any other American periodical editor did during the eighties.

Atlantic political attitudes during this period lacked the liberal advocacies of the magazine's earliest years and reacted against the social instability caused by industrialization by emphasizing social cohesion. The major political issues of the period involved the conflict in a rapidly industrializing society between labor and capital. The magazine, sustaining its role as a forum for intellectual debate, published advocates and critics of both sides. Most *Atlantic* writers, however, represented a cultural elite whose influence and values were threatened equally by a capitalist plutocracy (America's version of Arnold's barbarian aristocrats) and by a largely uneducated, increasingly foreign-born labor force. While sometimes inclined to think the plutocrats easier to civilize, they were highly critical of the increasing political power, the class antagonism, and the intellectual indifference of both. In this period of rapid, unstable, divisive industrial growth, they advocated the values of an earlier, smaller, organic society based on universal acknowledgment of their own code of moral responsibility and hierarchy of cultural values.

Most *Atlantic* commentators were also naturally sympathetic to increasing the political role of an educated intellectual meritocracy through a professionalized civil service. Accordingly, during this period, the *Atlantic* disengaged itself from

Introduction 1 8 5 7 – 1 9 0 9

what seemed a morally bankrupt Republican party, attacked the political spoils system and corruption in both parties, advocated mugwump independence, expressed fear of labor violence, and supported civil service reforms. Some of the reform impulse of Yankee humanism remained, but it was much more moderate and self-protective. Horace Scudder began a modest increase in coverage of social issues in the early nineties, but throughout this period the *Atlantic* remained very heavily literary.

Scudder, while committed to the *Atlantic*'s high-culture literary tradition, deserves credit for partly recognizing that to maintain readership and influence, the magazine had to establish closer contact with contemporary American social realities, including changes in the literary marketplace. It had to become less belletristic and intellectual and had to add more popular fiction and journalistic reportage of the kinds promoted by the new mass-circulation magazines like *McClure's*. Scudder himself was too committed to the preservation of high literary culture to accomplish these changes, though he saw the need for them. But Scudder's dynamic successor, Walter Hines Page, represented a new generation with progressive ideas about politics, literature, and publishing.

In the closing years of the nineteenth century, Page began in earnest an editorial transformation that would deeply modify the *Atlantic*'s high-culture literary tradition by integrating it with what Christopher Wilson has called "progressive journalism."[2] Page left the *Atlantic* partly in impatience at its pace of change, but his influence was disproportionate to his brief tenure (1895 to 1899, the last two years as editor) because he recognized that the magazine must either adapt to the new realities of American culture and publishing or die. Page's successor, Bliss Perry, while more politically liberal than Page, was more attached to high literary culture and the old Yankee humanism. Still, he saw clearly the necessity for Page's policy of increasing journalistic reportage and popular fiction while decreasing high literary culture, and he moderately pursued this policy. Both Page's and Perry's editorships were characterized by gradual adaptation to the new, less literary, magazine journalism which would divide the magazine's twentieth-century incarnations from its nineteenth-century past. The full editorial commitment of the *Atlantic* to its own brand of progressive journalism, however, was accomplished only after the magazine became independent of Houghton Mifflin in 1908. Ellery Sedgwick, who bought the magazine and became its editor and primary owner for nearly thirty years, would complete the transformation before World War I.

The editorships of Page and Perry, from 1898 to 1909, as well as the early years of Sedgwick's editorship, were marked not only by gradual shift in editorial inclination toward journalism and away from literary high culture but also by distinctly more progressive social values than during the previous twenty years. During this time, and in fact well into the 1920s, the genteel idealists and the retreating defenders of traditional high culture continued to fight rearguard actions against social change and literary modernism, particularly in commentaries on the literature, morals, and manners of the age. Gradually, however, there was a clear renewal of intellectual breadth, energy, and liberal faith in the magazine. Its dominant spirit through the First World War, particularly in politics and social issues, was progressive and moderately liberal.

The causes of the *Atlantic*'s editorial and cultural adaptation were both commercial and ideological. Unquestionably, money was a powerful force for increased cultural democracy. Every *Atlantic* editor from Scudder on felt a strong economic incentive to popularize the substance of the genteelly impoverished magazine and modify, though not destroy, its high-culture image. In effecting the gradual transformation of the *Atlantic* from genteel to progressive, Page in particular was motivated by the desire to increase readership and turn financial loss to profit, as well as to regain an influence and a relevance to contemporary life that he felt the magazine had lost. Page (like Sedgwick, who would later complete the transformation) was a professional editor with a background in newspaper and magazine publishing rather than a literary figure or scholar, as were most of the other nineteenth-century editors. He was acquainted with and involved in the financial as well as the editorial side of the business. He had learned the strategies of progressive publishing around the turn of the century in New York, where mass-market magazines edited by the likes of S. S. McClure, Edward Bok, Frank Munsey, and John Brisbane Walker were starting to generate circulations over a half-million and displace the old "quality" magazines like *Harper's* and the *Century*. He knew that while the *Atlantic* could never achieve anything near this kind of circulation, it could be resurrected by finding a broader readership without alienating its traditional audience.

The second driving force of change was the fact that Page and Perry represented a new generation. Their progressive ideology was an affirmative response to new social conditions. They had more antecedents in the optimistic and engaged liberal humanism of the 1850s and 1860s than in the disengaged aestheticism and cultural retrospection of Aldrich and Scudder. *Atlantic* editors after 1895 were conscious in their career choices and in editorial policy of a strong tension between traditional literary culture and the social, economic, and political realities of contemporary American life. They experienced directly the split in American culture that George Santayana was to define in 1911 between a retrospective, idealistic, timid, "genteel tradition" that ruled in literature, manners, morals, and religion, and the forward-looking, pragmatic, often ruthless spirit of "aggressive enterprise" that drove American industry, politics, technology, and social organization (39–40).[3] Page and Perry had been raised in the old, high literary culture and felt affectionate respect for it. But each was more or less impatient with its

Introduction 1857–1909

defensive isolation from American political and social life. Each began as a teacher or scholar but entered journalism and publishing because these professions offered greater engagement in contemporary affairs. Their political heroes, also in several cases personal friends and contributors, were moderate, progressive liberals such as Cleveland and particularly Roosevelt and Wilson, the latter two both scholars turned politician.

Page and Perry, like Sedgwick later, consciously set out to make the *Atlantic* span the culture gap, to synthesize literature and journalism, the humanistic tradition and contemporary American life. To bridge this gap, they very substantially increased the coverage of social and political issues, including national and international current events, and often reduced the space devoted to literature, literary criticism, and discussions of the canon of Western high culture. In defining their audience and selecting subjects, approaches, and styles, the editors of the *Atlantic*'s progressive period seemed conscious of at least two readerships, generally corresponding to the two sides of Santayana's culture gap. They could not afford to alienate the *Atlantic*'s traditional readers, whom their predecessors had defined as the cultivated classes, readers with heavily literary and intellectual interests, including many women, academics, and older readers attached to the cultural past. But in their shaping of subject and style, they now concentrated on interesting a somewhat younger and certainly broader range of professional, middle-class elites, including those active in business and politics.

Atlantic editors from Lowell to Scudder had thought of their magazine as essentially a monthly book in which they ideally hoped to publish literature and intellectual discussion of permanent worth which could be preserved in volumes and read with profit decades later. Page and his successors felt that a monthly magazine should be mainly a report and commentary on the contemporary world with an active life of thirty days. In style, as in subject, they particularly valued journalistic immediacy, directness, relevance, and impact and correspondingly devalued leisurely reflection, philosophizing, aesthetic elegance, or excessive intellectual subtlety.

Related to his emphasis on a journalistic style and increased coverage of social issues, Page further sought to close the culture gap by deemphasizing "Literature with a capital *L*" and blurring the distinction between formal fiction and the direct reportage of personal experience. His motives were at least partly commercial, and he received enthusiastic encouragement from the *Atlantic*'s business manager, MacGregor Jenkins, who was trying desperately to shed the magazine's highbrow image. But Page himself shared a middlebrow taste for the directly human and personal and an impatience with the aesthetic or academic concerns of previous editors such as Aldrich and Scudder. The first casualty of this shift in editorial taste was Henry James; unquestionably the *Atlantic* now carried less distinguished fiction than in the past. Its nonfiction, however, presented a broader spectrum of American experience reported realistically from firsthand observation, thus in some ways accomplishing the aims of literary realism.

Under Page, Perry, and later Sedgwick, the high literary culture—expressed in fiction, poetry, and literary criticism—that had long been the main source of the *Atlantic*'s prestige generally declined in volume, importance, and often quality, with several notable exceptions. In their selection of fiction, these editors were influenced more than their predecessors by a frank commercial appeal. For instance, while the *Atlantic* was still one of the few general magazines to publish serious poetry, it increasingly reflected the prejudice of its readership against poetry that was too long, irregular in form, or not transparent on the first reading. These prejudices severely limited the magazine's encouragement of early modern poetry.

Beginning in the early nineties, the literary judgments of *Atlantic* editors were strongly influenced by anxiety about what would sell, as well as by anxiety about offending genteel sensibilities and by editorial tastes in conflict with modernist aesthetics. All three of these causes, particularly commercial appeal, account for the sharp increase in the *Atlantic*, as in the other "quality" magazines, of serialized historical romances after 1890. While the *Atlantic*'s literary criticism continued to represent a range of perspectives, here also there was a clear current of resistance to deterministic naturalism and proletarian realism, and a sympathy with the idealistic reaction that saw literature as a model of moral free will and defended romance for showing the world as it might be.

Not only commercial concern and the lingering influence of genteel idealism but also the editors' own progressive temperaments combined to limit their sympathy with the directions in which modern literature was developing. Page, like Teddy Roosevelt, who shared his contempt for Henry James, believed that introspection, the dissection of internal states of feeling, was debilitating and decadent in literature as in life. Perry, who admired Whitman, criticized poets and writers who wallowed in the dissection of personal pain, and he looked in vain for the resurgence of poets who would speak with a loud, affirmative voice about liberal American ideals. Both editors were aware of their audience's limited tolerance for depressing literature and restricted the magazine's quotient of literary tragedy.

If the prevailing attitudes in much *Atlantic* literature and literary criticism of the turn of the century tended to resist the future, the prevailing attitudes in politics and social issues seemed to take a more progressive stance. Not only did the magazine become more engaged in a broader spectrum of American social and political life, but this engagement generally reflected a renewal of the old liberal optimism about the national future and even some return of the reform impulses that had marked the social involvement of the magazine's early years. The political ascendency of moderate reformers drawn from an educated elite—most prominently Roosevelt and Wilson, both of whom wrote for the *Atlantic*—brought renewed optimism about the social function of the intellectual, who could bring the values of high culture to bear on public life. Not only was America becoming a world power, but it was relying heavily on the intellectual elite, many of them *Atlantic* contributors, to conduct its political affairs.

Despite some major political differences between the two editors, the *Atlantic* under Page and Perry was moderately liberal on most social issues. While Page was a pure, pragmatic progressive, Perry's liberalism derived partly from the older principles of Yankee humanism, though without the genteel illusion that it was possible or desirable to return to a preindustrial, small-town America. Both editors were essentially committed to broadening economic development, education, and political participation. Both insistently raised issues of racial equity at a time when this was not a popular topic and solicited well-documented essays exposing social or industrial abuses and calling for government regulation.

There was a clear tendency during these years also to broaden the ideological, social, and ethnic diversity of contributors to the magazine. The *Atlantic* had always considered itself accessible to talent from any quarter and had always accepted unsolicited material from diverse sources. But now its editors were actively soliciting diversity, spurred partly by a progressive editorial philosophy that sought broader contact with American social realities, encouraged more controversy, and appealed to a wider audience. The late nineties saw the beginning of extensive first-person accounts of immigrant experience by writers such as Abraham Cahan, Jacob Riis, and later Mary Antin. Page and Perry solicited not only Booker T. Washington but also Charles Chesnutt and W. E. B. DuBois, among others, to describe and comment on black experience, including some sardonic indictments of white majority culture.

Page and Perry, then, initiated a new evolution in the *Atlantic* (later completed by Sedgwick), one driven partly by economic survival. Both in the selection of fiction and in the increased coverage of current affairs, these editors aimed less at a cultural and intellectual elite and more at a broader, educated middle-class audience than had their predecessors. But the evolution was motivated also by the desire of the magazine's editors to reengage it in contemporary life and to bridge the gap they perceived between an ineffectual, retrospective high literary culture and the social, economic, and political realities with which they felt that culture was in danger of losing touch.

Editorially, Page and Perry tried to address readers on both sides of Santayana's culture gap, attempting to reconcile or at least balance the old literary culture and the new progressive journalism. While decreasing the magazine's literary component and increasing its reportage and analysis of social issues, they actively promoted diversity and sometimes debate. In their editorial attempt to bridge the culture gap, the magazine itself tended to mirror the split between a conservative idealism in literature and a moderately liberal, progressive spirit in social, economic, and political issues. The *Atlantic* of 1909, then, retained much of the Yankee humanism of its origins, modified to survive and maintain its diminished influence into the twentieth century.

Francis H. Underwood, who initiated the idea of the *Atlantic* and served as Lowell's assistant from 1857 to 1859 (from John T. Trowbridge, *My Own Story* [Boston: Houghton Mifflin, 1903]).

1

The Founding of the Atlantic

(1 8 5 7)

Boston's High Tide

"The founding of the *Atlantic Monthly*, in 1857," according to Van Wyck Brooks, "marked [the] high tide of the Boston mind" (*Flowering* 483). In that year, Boston, with its outlying towns of Cambridge and Concord, was the capital of literary culture in the United States, a status it enjoyed only a generation. Until 1850, American literary and intellectual taste had been dominated by the writers, editors, and publishers of the New York–Philadelphia axis, and by 1880, the tide had begun to shift back toward New York (Charvat, *Literary Publishing* 37). But in the fifties, literary production, intellectual activity, and institutions for the publication and distribution of books combined to make Boston the major influence in a literary culture that was just beginning to be national as well as regional. The literate American public had not yet apotheosized the Olympians of the New England pantheon. But the relatively new rail lines through the Berkshires were carrying their works west, giving them a fully national audience, and from Cincinnati to San Francisco, as well as in London, they were beginning to be read with an enthusiasm and respect not often given to American authors. During the preceding decade, many of the writers living in and around Boston, including Emerson, Hawthorne, Longfellow, Lowell, Thoreau, Whittier, and the historians Prescott, Parkman, and Motley, had published major works, and most had achieved significant recognition. They, like posterity, were conscious of an "increasing volume, solidification, and diversity amid centralization" of New England literary and intellectual production centered in Boston (Buell 20).[1]

These and lesser-known writers within what has been loosely called intellectual

Boston were much more socially and ideologically diverse, much less a coherent literary movement, than they have seemed to outsiders, then or now. There were indeed social and intellectual ties between many. Lowell, Holmes, and, oddly, Emerson were particularly sociable, and institutions such as the *Atlantic*, the publishing firm of Ticknor and Fields, the Saturday Club, and Harvard College provided important connections and opportunities for intellectual exchange. But the image of a homogeneous group of New England authors is a fiction compounded from the self-interest of several parties. The *Atlantic*'s early publishers, James T. Fields and Henry Oscar Houghton, successfully promoted the idea that the New England writers formed a single Olympian literary society represented by the magazine and by the Fields and Houghton publishing houses. Envious contemporaries from other regions also tended to view the New Englanders as monolithic and impervious to outsiders. Later, modernist critics reduced many of these writers to simplistic homogeneity in order to dismiss them as fireside poets or genteel, pharisaic Brahmins. But the New England writers living in and around Boston were more varied in their social backgrounds, contacts, and values than these images suggest (Brooks, *Flowering* 482).

The transcendentalist movement of the thirties and forties had its locus in Emerson's Concord and was derided by the Boston rationalist Holmes and the scholars of Cambridge, although its fever had infected some of their young, including Lowell. A modified transcendentalism lived on in Concord's Walden Walking Society. On Sunday mornings, Emerson and Ellery Channing, descendants of old New England ministerial lines, walked out into the Concord countryside with Thoreau, the son of a pencil maker, and Bronson Alcott, the Yankee peddler turned educational philosopher. They agreed in preferring nature to a tedious sermon but enjoyed arguing about virtually everything else. Only Emerson, now fifty-eight, kept significant contacts with Boston or Cambridge. Nor did the depressed and reclusive Hawthorne, when he returned in 1860 from roaming Europe to the Wayside House in Concord, add much to the intellectual cohesion. He and Emerson, while socially polite, found each other's works misguided, even morally damaging, and stimulated each other by opposition rather than agreement.

Cambridge had a social and intellectual center in Harvard College, but its inhabitants still ranged widely in interests and ideology. Longfellow, already at fifty enshrined in popular affection as the unofficial national poet laureate, had just given up the Smith Chair in modern languages and literature at Harvard to devote himself entirely to poetry. Lowell, thirty-eight, had just assumed the same chair to teach Spanish grammar to undergraduates. But the elder generation of scholars mistrusted Lowell's flippant wit manifested in his "Fable for Critics" and his earlier radical activism as a writer and editor in opposition to the Mexican War and to slavery. Charles Eliot Norton was a close friend and later literary executor not only of Lowell but also of Ruskin and of Clough, a fastidious scholar of the fine arts and organizer of a night school and model lodging houses for the poor. Francis Child, a collector of ballads, was the son of a Boston barkeeper, one of Harvard's first distinguished scholars, and cultivator of rare roses. Cornelius Felton, a robust and hearty classicist, would soon become president of the college. Also at Harvard were the Swiss immigrant Louis Agassiz, an ebullient naturalist with a boundless zeal for propagating his enthusiasms, and Asa Gray, botanist and friend of Darwin, soon to publish in the *Atlantic* a defense of Darwin's theories that would set him at swords' points with Agassiz. In a few years, Henry James, Sr., that strange enthusiast of Swedenborg, Fourier, and other intellectual radicalisms, would, after traveling the world, find Cambridge the most intellectually congenial place to settle and to educate his adolescent children.

The elder James, inclined to mysticism, could have agreed on little with Oliver Wendell Holmes, Bostonian exponent of enlightenment rationalism. Holmes, the intellectually irreverent son of a Calvinist minister, was professor of anatomy and physiology at the Harvard Medical School and soon to begin a second career as a founder and major contributor to the *Atlantic*. But in midcentury Boston, one did not need to agree in order to admire, and James declared that Holmes was "intellectually the most alive man I ever knew" (Brooks, *Flowering* 358). In 1857, the witty, gregarious little doctor was one of the few members of "intellectual Boston" actually to live in what he called, characteristically satirizing his own provincial pride, "the Hub of the Universe." His publisher, James T. Fields, had recently married the beautiful Annie Adams and moved to the house on the water side of Charles Street that would become famous as a literary salon. But, unlike Holmes, Fields had not come to Beacon Hill, the hub of the Hub, as a Harvard-educated descendant of a prominent Boston family with Copleys in their drawing room. Fields, the son of an impoverished widow from Portsmouth, New Hampshire, had come to Boston at thirteen as a bookstore clerk, had largely educated himself at the Mercantile Library, and had worked and charmed his way to junior partnership in the publishing firm of Ticknor and Fields. Similarly, Fields's oldest Boston friend, E. P. Whipple, had come from Salem as a bank clerk, also educated himself through the Mercantile Library, and by 1857 had become, after Poe and Lowell, probably the best-known American literary critic as well as first reader for Ticknor and Fields. John Greenleaf Whittier, a farmer's son, after an itinerant career in the radical antislavery movement, had permanently settled in Quaker simplicity at Amesbury, thirty miles north of Boston. Paradoxically one of the shyest but most politically active of the authors later associated with the *Atlantic*, Whittier had begun as a cobbler and come to journalism, then literature, as a protégé of William Lloyd Garrison. The New England antislavery movement itself was socially and intellectually diverse, encompassing farmers and artisans, as both Whittier and Garrison originally were, as well as many associated with the liberal Protestant ministry, such as James Freeman Clarke, David Wasson, and Harriet

Beecher Stowe, and the younger generation of Cambridge intellectuals such as Lowell and Thomas Wentworth Higginson. In 1850, Whittier had nominated Higginson, a minister in Newburyport, Massachusetts, to run for Congress on the antislavery Free Soil ticket. The bid was unsuccessful but alienated Higginson from his conservative congregation, and by 1857, Higginson was minister to the highly unorthodox Free Church of Worcester, west of Boston. He was soon to become colonel of the first black regiment in the war and later a reformer and *Atlantic* essayist. In his youth he had been swept away by the "newness" of transcendentalism, and he was now actively engaged in a lifelong commitment to moral reform causes including not only abolition but also women's rights, temperance, and labor law.

The individuals within intellectual Boston and its suburbs were not homogeneous in either social background or narrowly defined ideology. For this reason, they often stimulated each other by irritation as well as by support. They did, however, share important common values, interests, and webs of social contact. It was these shared interests that led to the founding of the *Atlantic* and the shaping of its early character.

Collectively, these Yankee humanists—writers, scholars, and intellectuals—formed a New England cultural elite who shared an interest in developing and disseminating an American literary and intellectual culture. The purpose of this culture was not just aesthetic, although aesthetic values were important to them, but the creation and transmission of American ethical values and ideals. They hoped that this culture would have a broad and direct influence on the conduct of personal, social, and political life. As Higginson wrote, they saw themselves as teachers and educators whose mission was to civilize and humanize a new nation. During the 1850s, the waning influence of religion, the increasing vulnerability of sectarian dogma to rational skepticism, the increasing critical mass of intellectual activity in New England, and the rapid expansion in population, transportation, and geographic area gave them a sense that this was a crucial moment in the nation's cultural life.

Since political independence and before, American intellectuals had talked bravely of a national literature that would propagate explicitly American cultural values. But in the 1850s, particularly in and around Boston, many felt that this hope was becoming (or had become) a reality. Boston's idea of a national literature, unlike the strident literary nationalism associated with the *Knickerbocker Magazine* in New York, was not narrowly chauvinistic. Lowell, for instance, while expressing high hopes for the national literature, felt that a forced nationalism was more likely to subvert than to develop great art (Duberman 167). Furthermore, many of the Boston writers were scholars, learned in and attached to the traditions of Western humanistic culture. Most had studied, traveled, even lived in Europe, particularly in England and Italy, and several maintained close personal ties with writers such as Carlyle, Mill, Macaulay, Ruskin, Arnold, and Clough.

Although they were anxious to receive European ideas, most believed that as American institutions, geography, social philosophy, and character were different, so must American literature and culture be different. Emerson's insistence on intellectual independence, his prophecy, expressed in his "American Scholar" address of 1837, that "our day of dependence, our long apprenticeship to the learning of other lands draws to a close," had often been reiterated even by cultural conservatives such as Holmes and Longfellow (*Works* 81). The works published since by Emerson, Hawthorne, Thoreau, Longfellow, Lowell, Whittier, Parkman, and others not only presented American ideas, settings, customs, and characters but also created a visible body of American literature.

Boston writers during the fifties, then, were conscious of new prospects for developing a literary culture capable of adapting the best of European tradition to the circumstances of the New World, yet expansively independent and rejecting imitation. But even the most liberal and optimistic of them, like Emerson, foresaw problems confronting the propagation of a high humanistic culture in a democratic society professing egalitarian principles, particularly when the energies of that society were so much absorbed in territorial expansion and the production of wealth. In the 1850s, liberals such as Emerson agreed with conservatives such as Norton that the initiative must be taken by an educated elite whose obligation was to place ideas and principles above wealth and self-interest, and whose function was to create, inspire, arbitrate, and propagate high culture. Emerson had articulated precisely this vision of a cultural elite, which he called "the cultivated classes," in his "American Scholar" address in 1837 as he would again in later Phi Beta Kappa addresses published in the *Atlantic*.

This sense of cultural responsibility, which had led many of the Yankee humanists to become not only writers and scholars but also lyceum organizers and lecturers, contributed significantly to the founding of the *Atlantic*. After attending several meetings at which the *Atlantic* was proposed and finally established, Emerson wrote in his journal:

> A journal is an assuming to guide the age—very propre [*sic*] and necessary to be done, and good news that it shall be so. But this Journal, is this it? His solar eye looked over the list, without much comfort... Has Apollo spoken? In this the sentiment of freedom is the sting which all feel in common. A northern sentiment the only tie; & the manifest conveniency of having a good vent for such wares as scholars have.
>
> ... And the best the Editor can do, is, to see that nothing goes into the Book but important pieces. Every piece must have something sterling, some record of real experiences. It suffices that it be weighty.... Great scope and illumination ought to be in the Editor, to draw from the best in the land, & to defy the public, if he is only sure himself that the piece has worth and is right. Publics are very placable and will soon find out

when they have a Master. The value of capital is to be able to hold out for a few months, and go on printing, until the discerning minority of the public have found that the Book is right, and must be humbly and thankfully accepted, and abandon themselves to this direction, too happy that they have got something good and wise to admire and to obey. (*Journals* 14: 167)

The others involved in founding the *Atlantic* generally agreed with Emerson's view that the democratic age indeed needed intellectual, moral, and aesthetic leadership and that the magazine should contribute to that cultural leadership by addressing itself to the "discerning minority," which in turn could educate the tastes of the broader majority.

Since the days of the Puritan ministers, the New England cultural elite had not constituted a remote scholarly caste but had been actively engaged in the social, ethical, and political issues of the times. To the Boston mind, intellectual culture had never been merely a matter of scholarship or aesthetic taste but rather one of moral and social action. Emerson's "American Scholar" was a student not primarily of books but of life. Literature and politics, ethics and aesthetics, thought and social action were parts of an inseparable unity: "Man Thinking." Parrington's long-lived image of nineteenth-century New England intellectuals as permanently lost in the stacks and serenely unruffled by the great issues of the day sacrifices truth to cultural prejudice (2: 435–39, qtd. in Cary, *Genteel Circle* 5). As Buell demonstrates, the generation reaching maturity in the forties and fifties was both particularly engaged in social issues and particularly progressive in their views (389–90). Much of the force behind contemporary social reform came from the intellectual community, and much of the literature of that community had a social purpose. In 1857, the year after "bleeding Kansas" and the year of the Dred Scott decision, the major political and moral issue that moved intellectual Boston was slavery. Opposition to slavery to the point of civil disobedience was one ideological tenet that most shared. The desire to have a forum where recognized writers could regularly publicize their antislavery views was, as Emerson's journal reflects, a major impulse that brought the *Atlantic* into being.

Reformers, scholars, and literary artists, liberals and conservatives from Boston, Cambridge, and Concord—diverse as they were—in the 1850s shared a heightened sense of their opportunities and obligations for cultural leadership. As Emerson's *Journal* suggested, they shared also an interest in finding a "good vent" for their wares, expanding their market, keeping their work more frequently before a larger public, and generating more regular income than was offered by the limited methods of book publication and distribution before the Civil War. Most book publishers were still small, relatively unstable operations, and most of them had only recently grown out of retail bookstores. Only a very few writers could support themselves mainly as literary professionals, and even these had taken a long time to become established. Most continued to derive their principal income from editing, lecturing, journalism, or teaching. As Hawthorne and others had discovered, it was very difficult for young writers to gain exposure to an audience, even for works on which they had labored for years. Until after the Civil War, the average book sold only 1,500 copies and, even when the author was well known, rarely sold as many as 30,000 (Tebbel 390). The average monthly magazine, on the other hand, circulated 12,000 copies every month (Mott 2: 10). A successful magazine might circulate over 50,000 copies or even, like *Harper's*, 100,000 and could offer writers regular exposure, thus developing an audience for their books.

But Boston, while increasingly the center of literary, intellectual, and reform activity, in 1857 had no major comprehensive magazine. Some Boston authors contributed occasionally to New York's *Putnam's* or the *Knickerbocker Magazine*, but these contacts were irregular, and both magazines were about to expire. Many attempts had been made to establish Boston magazines. In 1853, Thoreau wondered in his journal whether a magazine could survive in Boston because so many had failed (*Journals* 5: 506). Even when they had succeeded, they were too narrowly focused to draw from a significant range of New England writers and ideologies or to develop a significant readership, although they did provide coherence and impact for particular groups that would later be drawn together in the *Atlantic*. Since 1815, the scholars of Cambridge and Harvard College had contributed to making the *North American Review* respected if not widely read. From its founding, the *Review* had been critical, not literary. It was modeled on the English intellectual quarterlies and saw itself as a scholarly but readable arbiter of literary and intellectual standards. Despite its prestige, it had never circulated more than about 3,000 copies (Mott 2: 231). By 1857, the conservative "Old North" still had intellectual authority but had acquired a reputation, in Lowell's phrase, as a "literary megatherium"—antiquated, ponderous, and of sluggish circulation.

The *Liberator*, a crusading, radical abolitionist weekly, had been founded in 1831 by William Lloyd Garrison, then twenty-five, who continued to edit it with unflinching integrity until 1865, when he felt its mission was accomplished. As narrow as it was righteous, the *Liberator* continued on the one hand to have an influence disproportionate to its circulation of only about 3,000, but on the other to exclude both as readers and writers many, even in New England, sympathetic to the cause.

Between 1840 and 1844, the Concord transcendentalists had produced the *Dial*, edited first by the formidably energetic Margaret Fuller and later by Emerson. Despite its minuscule circulation of at most 300 copies and its short life span, the *Dial* had been influential in defining and defending the Concord enlightenment. Like the *North American* and the *Liberator*, however, it had certainly not represented New England intellectual culture as a whole, brought together the region's various factions, or developed a significant readership.

Since the 1830s, however, there had been interest in having a broader, Boston-based magazine that would represent no narrowly defined ideology but draw the best New England writing from all circles and give it wide circulation. In 1831, Joseph Buckingham, editor of the *Boston Courier*, and his son Edwin had established the *New England Magazine*, a literary monthly that published Longfellow, Whittier, Hawthorne, Holmes, and others before they had gained wide recognition. But in 1833, Edwin Buckingham, the editor, died at the age of twenty-three. The magazine, its vital impulse gone and its circulation poor, languished for two years before it too expired.

In 1843, another young enthusiast, James Russell Lowell, with his friend Robert Carter as partner, founded the *Pioneer*. Their aim was to take a position of leadership in encouraging the production and circulation of American literature, in upholding high critical standards, and in promoting progressive political reforms. The ambitious, youthful idealism of this venture was reflected in the magazine's prospectus:

> The contents of each number will be entirely original, and will consist of articles chiefly from American authors of the highest reputation. The object of the Subscribers in establishing the *Pioneer*, is to furnish the intelligent and reflecting portion of the Reading Public with a rational substitute for the enormous quantity of thrice-diluted trash, in the shape of namby-pamby love tales and sketches, which is monthly poured out to them by many of our popular magazines—and to offer instead thereof, a healthy and manly Periodical Literature, whose perusal will not necessarily involve a loss of time and a deterioration of every moral and intellectual faculty. (Qtd. in Scudder, *Lowell* 99–100)

The brave assumption of the *Pioneer*'s editors that literary merit would quickly be recognized by a grateful public and generate a sustaining circulation, removing the need for substantial capital, soon proved unfounded. The magazine, although it published such writers as Hawthorne, Poe, Whittier, Jones Very, W. W. Story, and Elizabeth Barrett, never sold even the 500 copies printed monthly. Suddenly and mysteriously, Lowell's eyesight failed, and he was forced temporarily to abandon both writing and editing. The distributors abrogated the contract, and the intrepid *Pioneer* folded after publishing only three numbers.

Although saddled with a debilitating $1,800 debt, Lowell had not lost faith in the idea of a Boston-based magazine standing for literary excellence and progressive politics. Emerson retained a similar interest in establishing a first-rate journal, although after the collapse of the *Dial* he carefully evaded further entanglement in editorial duties. In 1850, Emerson wrote to a friend that "the measles, the influenza, and the magazine appear to be periodic distempers" among Boston intellectuals and characterized his own case and Lowell's as "chronic" (to Samuel Ward, 24 Feb. 1850, qtd. in E. Emerson 10).

Throughout the decade preceding 1857, the magazine virus was often in the air. Diverse as they were, writers in and around Boston at this time also increasingly shared a consciousness of a New England literary renaissance, a desire to further an explicitly American literature, a sense of the potential for cultural leadership, an awareness of the opportunities and dangers facing high culture in a developing democracy, and a rising opposition to slavery, as well as a hope to expand their publishing market and readership. From the cohesion created by these common interests, the *Atlantic* was shaped. Higginson later wrote of its founding:

> The new era of American literature was at hand, but the Transcendentalist movement of itself could not directly have created it.... Fortunately, in the natural progress of things a new combination effected itself, and those who like Holmes had ridiculed the earlier movement, found themselves ready within twenty years to unite themselves with those who, like Emerson, had produced it; that first impulse thus forming by cohesion a well defined circle of contributors who held for a time the visible leadership of American letters. (*Cheerful Yesterdays* 167)

Higginson's comment accurately suggests that the *Atlantic* was founded by its potential contributors. The fact that professional writers contributed so substantially to founding the magazine, editing it, and establishing its early policies gave it a much different tone from other general periodicals such as *Harpers'* that were initiated and often edited by their publishers. Still, a catalyst was needed to precipitate the cohesion, not only between the New England writers with their common interests and diverse ideologies, but also between these writers and publishers with the capital to finance a magazine. This catalyst was an energetic and idealistic young publisher's assistant named Francis Underwood.

Underwood shared the New England vision of good literature in the service of moral progress, particularly in opposing slavery. Born in rural western Massachusetts in 1825, he was "a typically self-made American . . . the best part of him developed and trained in the usual hard struggle of a poor but ambitious New England boy striving to better his condition" (Trowbridge, "Author of Quabbin" 109). Through an ungraded public school and self-instruction he had prepared himself to attend Amherst, but he dropped out for lack of funds. Considering the ministry but deciding he could not endorse the dogma, he taught school and studied law in Kentucky, where he developed a revulsion for the South's "peculiar institution" of slavery. Returning to Massachusetts in 1850, he had joined the Free Soil party and through this affiliation become clerk of the state senate in 1852.

By 1853, at twenty-eight, he had conceived a scheme for a magazine that would "bring the literary influence of New England letters to aid the anti-slavery cause" (Underwood 48). He presented the idea to John P. Jewett, the proprietor of a small publishing house which had just had the good fortune to bring out the immensely popular *Uncle Tom's Cabin*. Jewett not only had proved himself willing to risk publishing antislavery literature but had found that the risk could be profitable. In doing so, he had gained both the capital and the confidence to take on a new venture. He tentatively agreed to finance the project, if Underwood could show evidence of support for it among established writers. Underwood, anticipating him, had sent letters soliciting blessing and manuscripts from antislavery men such as W. L. Garrison and Wendell Phillips, liberal ministers such as Theodore Parker and T. W. Higginson, and men of letters sympathetic to the cause, including Lowell, Emerson, Thoreau, and Whittier.

The response was moderately encouraging, and by December Underwood had enough manuscripts to constitute an initial issue to appear in February 1854. In the meantime, however, the combination of overexpansion and a recession brought the small firm of Jewett and Company from boom to bust. Before the new year, Jewett was forced to abandon not only the projected magazine but the publishing business altogether. James Russell Lowell, an acquaintance whom Underwood particularly cultivated, and who had seen similar hopes of his own similarly dashed, sent the would-be founder a generous letter of condolence and encouragement: "There are as good fish in that buccaneering sea of Bibliopoly as were ever caught, and if one of them has broken away from your harpoon, I hope the next may prove a downright kraaken on whom, if needful, you can pitch your tent and live" (Scudder, *Lowell* 1: 356).

Underwood apparently had every intention of continuing the quest that was to establish the *Atlantic*. He soon left his position as clerk of the senate for literary employment as a reader in the substantial Boston publishing house of Phillips, Sampson and Company, a position that offered greater acquaintance with the men of letters whose allegiances he wished to secure for his idea. By 1856 he had organized a group of writers including Lowell, Holmes, Emerson, E. P. Whipple, and others who met sporadically at the Parker House in Boston to discuss the possibilities of creating a "literary and anti-slavery magazine" (E. Emerson 11). More certain than ever of support, Underwood proposed the idea to his employer, Moses Phillips. Phillips was reluctant—not unreasonably so, in view of the fate of previous Boston magazines. Underwood did not feel that he could push the matter further himself, but with characteristic perseverance he enlisted the aid of the firm's junior member, William Lee, and its most popular author, Harriet Beecher Stowe, who now published with Phillips, despite his earlier rejection of *Uncle Tom's Cabin*. Both of these laid siege to Phillips—Lee quietly, Stowe with her habitual, voluble enthusiasm—and by the spring of 1857 the publisher was so convinced that he almost believed the idea had been his own.

On May 5, 1857, Phillips convened another dinner at the Parker House that proved to be the birth of the new magazine. The event, the company, and the undisguised satisfaction Phillips felt in finding himself a member of it are recorded in a letter to his niece:

> I must tell you about a little dinner party I gave about two weeks ago. It would be proper, perhaps to state that its object, first, was to confer with my literary friends on a somewhat extensive literary project, the particulars of which I shall reserve till you come. But

to the party: my invitations included only R. W. Emerson, H. W. Longfellow, J. R. Lowell, Mr. Motley (the "Dutch Republic" man), O. W. Holmes, Mr. Cabot and Mr. Underwood, our literary man. Imagine your uncle at the head of such guests. The above-named were the only ones invited, and they were all present. We sat down at three P.M. and arose at eight. The time occupied was longer by about four hours and thirty minutes than I am in the habit of consuming in that kind of occupation, but it was the richest time intellectually by all odds that I have ever had. Leaving myself and "literary man" out of the group, I think you will agree with me that it would be difficult to duplicate that number of such conceded scholarship in the whole country besides.... They seemed so well pleased they adjourned and invited me *to meet them* again tomorrow, when I shall again meet the same persons, with one other (Whipple, the essayist) added to that brilliant constellation of the philosophical, poetical and historical talent. Each one is known alike on both sides of the Atlantic, and is read beyond the limits of the English language. Though all this is known to you, you will pardon me for intruding it upon you. But still I have the vanity to believe that you will think them the most natural thoughts in the world to me. Though I say it that should not, it was the proudest moment of my life. (Qtd. in M. Howe 14–15)

As it turned out, Phillips's frank pride in his association with his brilliant constellation of literary guests at the Parker House dinner proved important. The severe recession of 1857, unforeseen in May, brought his publishing house close to collapse before the magazine's first appearance in November and almost caused a repetition of Underwood's disappointment with Jewett in 1853. Possibly the publisher's vanity and his reluctance to back down on the agreements made with those eminent reputations amid the ample dinner, good champagne, and better conversation were all that kept his resolve firm in the face of financial uncertainty. The *Atlantic* may have been launched by vanity and champagne.

At any rate, planning for the magazine went ahead vigorously during the summer of 1857, despite the recession. At the Parker House dinner in May, Underwood had continued to play a modest but essential role in the realization of his idea by nominating Lowell to be the editor of the still nameless magazine. Emerson in particular had felt that Lowell was the right one to "defy the public" and had probably lobbied Phillips to hire him. "My confidence in success," he wrote Lowell, "is . . . based mainly on your accepting the responsibility of editor, with as much and as various aid as you please" (17 May 1857, *Letters* 5: 78). Whether or not he knew of his impending nomination as editor, Lowell had already been actively soliciting support for the project among his friends for weeks before the May meeting. He soon accepted the unanimous nomination on the condition that all of the founders, and Holmes in particular, would promise their support and their manuscripts.

Lowell at this stage in his career was a logical choice and fully sympathetic with the spirit in which the magazine was founded. He had been born in 1819 the youngest son of Charles Lowell, a "liberal New England minister, optimistic, benign, rational, moralistic" (Duberman 5). He belonged by birth to that Brahmin caste, first described by Dr. Holmes in the *Atlantic*, which was distinguished not by wealth or social prestige but by a tradition of liberal intellectual and moral leadership and a respect for learning. Howells and others noted in Lowell a lifelong conflict between deeply held democratic principles and what Lowell himself called a "toryism of the nerves." During his lifetime, from 1819 to 1891, as the nation changed from a largely homogeneous, socially hierarchical, stable, agrarian republic of small towns to an urbanized, ethnically diverse, socially polarized, unstable, industrial mass culture, his politics underwent a transition from radical activism to a conservative disillusion with democracy. But he is too often remembered by hostile critics mainly for his last years, after the hardening of his political arteries, after the corruption by excessive deference, after the affectation of the ambassadorial top hat and gloves, after the bitterness of finding himself sharply criticized and finally alienated from the dominant mass culture of the nation he had earlier served and loved.

In 1857, when he began his four-year editorship of the *Atlantic*, Lowell was thirty-eight and still essentially progressive in both his political and his literary values. As a young man, he had consistently shown a Byronic tendency to rebellion and irreverence that sometimes manifested itself in "challenges to authority and good breeding" (Buell 45). Having attended Harvard as his forefathers did, he had been elected class poet for 1838 but was rusticated for disobedience before the performance. During his young manhood in the forties, he had been activated by the fervors of transcendentalism and reform, particularly through the ardent social idealism of his first wife, Maria White, a former pupil of Margaret Fuller. Under these influences, he had achieved before the age of thirty a considerable reputation in several fields. His first series of "Biglow Papers," attacking the Mexican-American War and manifest destiny as a betrayal of grass-roots American principles, established him as a brilliant political satirist and spokesman for liberal American values. His "Fable for Critics" revealed him as an incisive American critic, unafraid to deflate large reputations, while "The Vision of Sir Launfall" suggested his promise as a lyric poet. He was also, however, deeply engaged in the abolitionist movement and in 1848 had largely forgone literature to write for, then to edit, a major abolitionist journal, the *Anti-Slavery Standard*.

In the late forties and early fifties, the Lowells had lost three children to childhood diseases, and in 1853, Maria White Lowell, always frail, had succumbed to tuberculosis. After a long, paralyzing depression, Lowell's old humor, high spirits, and generosity began gradually to reappear. He regained his balance, remarried, and accepted the Smith Chair in languages at Harvard. By 1857, his youthful radicalism was largely spent, but his principles were essentially the same, and he was reengaging the world. Though an appreciative scholar who genuinely loved the classical texts of Western humanism and a sympathetic teacher who regularly invited students to his house, he was not content with teaching French and Spanish grammar or retreating permanently into the book-lined study at Elmwood, his family's home in Cambridge. Howells would note that even later in life, Lowell was far more observant than most Cambridge intellectuals of the diversity of human life and more open "to contact with the commoner life" (*Literary Friends* 229). Lowell, as René Wellek comments, often referred to himself as a bookman, but he was also "a man of the world and its strife" whose "learning was worn lightly and always served a humane purpose" (200). His acceptance of the *Atlantic* editorship reflected a renewed, active commitment to a larger contemporary world both in literature and in politics.

In many ways, Lowell was the archetype of the Yankee humanist of his period, and many of his qualities would be reflected in the *Atlantic* through the nineteenth century. His biographer, Martin Duberman, defining the traits Lowell shared with his more conservative friend Charles Eliot Norton, noted that both had "a love of letters and scholarship, a belief in the utilitarian nature and moral purpose of art, an insistence that what men achieved was less important than what they were, a confidence in rationality coupled with a commitment to ideality, a disgust with the pursuit of money and possessions, a large curiosity and intelligence, and a belief that although the individual was sacred, he developed within and owed responsibility to his society" (195). In middle age, Lowell was at times melancholy, unable to work efficiently, erratic in judgment or insensitive, and on occasion highhanded or timidly conventional. But his editorship also reflects his generous capacity for friendship and support, his abundant wit and good humor, his social commitment, and his insistence on principle in issues he felt to be matters of intellectual or moral integrity.

Several practical considerations made Lowell a logical choice for the *Atlantic* editorship. The publisher Phillips wanted an experienced journalist with wide literary connections and an impressive reputation to launch the risky venture, Underwood wanted someone strongly committed to opposing slavery, and Emerson wanted an editor with high standards and intellectual integrity. Lowell was the first choice of each. For fifteen years, he had shown an active interest in establishing a first-class literary periodical in Boston. He had also had experience in literary journalism while writing for the *Pennsylvania Freeman* and editing the *Anti-Slavery Standard* as well as his own abortive *Pioneer*. He not only was active in the Anti-Slavery League but possessed a proven capacity to express his political convictions both in poetry and in editorial prose—a capacity on which the magazine was to rely heavily. He had the familiarity with both literary and antislavery circles necessary to enlist support for the magazine. Equally important, he possessed, at thirty-eight, a substantial reputation among both writers and the reading public that would give credibility and distinction to the new enterprise.

True, Lowell's editorial duties would have to share his attention with his professorship and his own writing. But in the mid-nineteenth century editorial positions were as often as not shared with other occupations, and he was to have the conscientious Underwood as his office assistant. He had, as he often claimed, a temperamental antipathy toward systematic work. But the proposed salary of $2,500 a year was a generous supplement to the $1,800 he drew from his chair at Harvard. He anticipated (inaccurately, as it turned out) that the editor's burden would not be heavy. Moreover, he felt a faith in the new magazine's potential benefits to American culture reminiscent of his hopes for the *Pioneer*. It would monthly put serious literature and the best current thought, expressed with style and wit, before a public habituated by a scarcity of alternatives to third-rate romances and travel sketches. It would offer writers of literature, cultural critics, and scholars a wider and more regular readership and source of revenue than was available before. In both literature and politics, it would apply high-minded principles and would teach its public to do so. Unlike most other American magazines, which were timidly nonpartisan, it would "have opinions of its own and not be afraid to speak them" but would nevertheless remain "scholarly and gentlemanlike" in tone (Lowell, letter to C. E. Norton, 23 May 1857, qtd. in Norton 579).

Activated by these expectations, Lowell set about soliciting and reviewing manuscripts during the summer of 1857 with energy and enthusiasm. At a subsequent Parker House dinner, Holmes had proposed to christen the new ship the *Atlantic*, perhaps because of the intellectual trade it was intended to carry between the New World and the Old. To this end, Underwood was dispatched in June to England to gather material there. By fall, Lowell had been able to accumulate and sift enough to constitute a respectable first issue of 128 pages and to lay the groundwork for several to follow it.

Emerson might well insist in the privacy of his journal that the *Atlantic* editor should defy the public and establish himself as its master rather than its bondservant. But Lowell was on the firing line, responsible for building and sustaining a readership and avoiding the waste of Moses Phillips's capital. Lowell wholeheartedly shared Emerson's sense of the necessity for cultural leadership and was to prove his commitment to that idea repeatedly throughout his editorial term. But he was more of a pragmatist than Emerson, and he had learned from his misadventure with the *Pioneer* and from observing the failure of a long line of idealistic but narrowly conceived Boston literary and antislavery periodicals that a magazine must attract and hold readers before it could enlighten them. Lowell, like all of his successors in the *Atlantic* editorship, was faced with determining the degree to which literary high culture was economically self-sustaining and the compromises or balance of material necessary to make it so. In composing his initial issues, he recognized the need to establish the *Atlantic* as a source of literary and intellectual credibility without making it pedantic, dry, or humorless.

The first number of the *Atlantic* was ready for distribution before 1 November

1857, amid much public and private speculation about its character and chances of survival. A perceptive reader could have discerned much about the nature of the magazine and its subsequent history from perusing the issue. The plain buff brown cover bore the title of the new journal, advised prospective subscribers that it would be "Devoted to Literature, Art, and Politics," and prominently designated Boston as its place of origin. The main ornamentation, a small engraving of John Winthrop, the distinguished Puritan founder of the Massachusetts Bay Colony, reinforced an impression of New England moral earnestness and of a dignity that was above alluring readers by elaborate decoration or illustration.

The inside front cover set forth in rather cautious language the magazine's editorial principles and subjoined a list of "literary persons" interested in the new enterprise. The statement of principles, while emphasizing that the magazine would maintain high intellectual standards, was appropriately respectful rather than defiant toward its prospective public. The contrast in tone with Lowell's earlier manifesto in the *Pioneer* was striking. The twenty-four-year-old Lowell's tone in the *Pioneer* had been the brash, satiric idealism of youth; the thirty-eight-year-old Lowell's tone in the *Atlantic* was the principled but moderate voice of middle age. The *Atlantic* was in some sense born middle-aged. If this heritage sometimes added a note of moderation and caution, it also partly accounted for the magazine's modest success and long survival while numerous other ventures either failed upon launching or began brilliantly and later foundered.

Literature was to be the first consideration, and the sponsors promised, in a carefully balanced phrase, that "in Literature . . . while each number will contain articles of an abstract and permanent value, it will also be found that the healthy appetite of the mind for entertainment in its various forms of Narrative, Wit, and Humor, will not go uncared for." They affirmed also that although "they will not hesitate to draw from the foreign sources at their command," "native writers will receive the most solid encouragement, and will be mainly relied upon to fill the pages of the *Atlantic*." The impressive list of "literary persons" who had been solicited and promised support suggested that native writers would indeed form the majority of contributors, but this "native" meant mainly those living in New England.

If literature was primary, the other arts were not to be neglected. The *Atlantic*, its sponsors announced, would comment on "the whole domaine of aesthetics . . . without any regard to prejudice, whether personal or national." Finally, they declared: "In politics, the *Atlantic* will be the organ of no party or clique, but will honestly endeavor to be the exponent of what its conductors believe to be the American idea. It will deal frankly with persons and with parties, endeavoring always to keep in view that moral element which transcends all persons and parties, and which alone makes the basis of a true and lasting national prosperity. It will rank itself with no sect of antis." This pronouncement was characteristic in identifying moral principle as the foundation of the *Atlantic*'s political ideology, but the suggestion of nonpartisanship was more politic than frank, considering the strong antislavery views of its editors, publishers, and major contributors.

The November 1857 issue of the *Atlantic* gave the curious reading public an ample taste of the monthly banquet that Lowell would set during his three and a half years as editor. As was the norm in American magazines during the fifties, all pieces were anonymous, a policy that lasted through Lowell's tenure but was terminated by the editor-publisher Fields, who was highly conscious of the advertising power of names. "The names of contributors," Emerson had insisted, "will be given out when the names are worth more than the articles" (M. Howe 25). To Phillips, however, the names were worth a great deal in publicity value, and he had unobtrusively leaked them to the Boston newspapers before commencing publication. Thereafter, the identities of *Atlantic* contributors were something of an open secret (Scudder, *Lowell* 1: 422).

Slightly over half of the 128 pages in the first number were devoted to essays. Emerson's "Illusions" fulfilled the pledge of "articles of abstract and permanent value," while Holmes's "Autocrat of the Breakfast Table" fed the appetite for humor and entertainment. Both brilliantly represented the old-fashioned humanistic essay characteristic of the *Atlantic* through the nineteenth century, whose aim was not information but moral wisdom, not analysis of a current issue but broad-ranging reflection and the development of a personal philosophy. Other essays characteristically balanced a humanistic interest in past and present and reflected the magazine's international scope. Lowell ran a scholarly piece by Motley on Florentine mosaics, Norton's appraisal of the recent Manchester exhibition of painting, and a posthumous assessment of a minor British writer, Douglas Jerrold, by his compatriot James Hannay.

If the *Atlantic*'s first number contained humanistic Yankee philosophy and scholarship, it also reflected an intellectual culture actively engaged in political and economic issues. Parke Godwin, a New Yorker who had recently drafted the first Republican party platform, had been contracted to supply regular articles on politics. Godwin's department was to occupy the final position in the body of the magazine because that position could be held open longest by the printers, giving the writer optimum chance to include late developments. Godwin's first article was on the severe recession of 1857 that had almost, for the second time, scuttled the *Atlantic* before it set sail. The magazine's interest in foreign affairs was reflected in another political piece examining the origins of the bloody revolt of 1857 in British India.

Fiction was the only field in which women contributed to the first issue, but in this they contributed a substantial 50 percent—a proportion that was roughly to hold through the rest of the nineteenth century. Stowe, perhaps the most popular writer of fiction in America at the time, had promised a serial but, overwhelmed by the recent drowning of her son, had thus far sent only a grim little story titled "The Mourning Veil." Lowell had accepted three other pieces of fiction by largely unknown young authors: Rose Terry's "Sally Parson's Duty"; a serial portrait of New England village life by a new Connecticut author, Calvin Philleo; and John T. Trowbridge's "Pendlam," an excellent satire on religious fads. All of these works contained elements of the local color regional realism that was to become the magazine's staple, and all were set in rural New England of the present or recent past. All were written by New England authors, but clearly young aspirants as well as established writers were given "solid encouragement" to contribute.

Poetry was more often written by members of the magazine's inner circle and clearly intended to be a major feature. Later issues usually contained four to six poems, but Lowell lavished nine on the first number. Four were by Emerson, including "Days" and the much-parodied "Brahma." Longfellow and Whittier both contributed less opaque poems characteristically affirming that high holiness lies in good works—the moral burden of many *Atlantic* poems to come, many by the same poets. Interestingly, however, Lowell himself contributed an amusing satire on the soporific properties of didactic verse, probably inspired by his new obligation as editor to peruse so much of it. Even the most righteous versified morality, it warned contributors, was not thereby poetry.

The magazine's end section, in print even more villainously fine than the body, contained a seven-page department headed "Literary Notices." Here, as in the body, the focus was on literature broadly defined, but the range of intellectual interests was broad. Works on politics, history, economics, and science were candidates for review. Nor were reviews limited to works in English, but they covered important publications in all major European languages, suggesting again that while the *Atlantic* was to be written by Americans, its intellectual scope was international. Lowell believed that frank literary criticism, in contrast to the commercially and personally motivated reviews typical of the time, could educate public taste and set high standards for American literature. As a result, *Atlantic* criticism and reviews, written by Norton, Whipple, and Lowell himself among others, were generally acknowledged from the beginning as more substantive and influential than those in other periodicals.

The November 1857 issue foreshadowed many of the essential elements of the *Atlantic*'s character. It was a reflection of the New England literary renaissance and of mid-nineteenth-century Yankee humanism. Born of a culture that admired books, it was not only suffused with discussion of books, but much of it was aimed at attaining the permanency of a book rather than settling for the ephemerality of a magazine. Some of it even succeeded. (In fact, many subscribers later had it bound into volumes for their library shelves.) Much of it aimed not to inform the busy or to amuse the tired but to engage the reader in reflection, in a consideration of basic principles and the application of these principles to the conduct of life.

It earnestly promoted the development of the reasoning intellect, the aesthetic taste, and the ethical conscience. The *Atlantic*'s intellectual interests were broad. It sought to stimulate specifically American literary production, among both established and unknown authors, and to articulate high critical standards to encourage the best and expose the shoddy. Significantly, most of the fiction had an aura of regional realism, and about half was by and about women. While the emphasis was strongly on literature, it was politically engaged, analyzing political issues at home and abroad and having an editorial voice. While it had a very strong regional flavor, its interests were national and international. It valued the past partly as a context for understanding the present, and it reserved a portion of its space for scholarly appreciation of the great works of Western civilization and the events of history. But its editor, Lowell, himself had a sense of humor as well as a clear understanding that the magazine would survive only if it had a range of tones and appeals. As promised, humor, entertainment, and satire were "given their due."

The most successful monthly in the nation in 1857 was *Harper's New Monthly Magazine*, and its contrast with the new *Atlantic* was striking. *Harper's* had been initiated in 1850 not by a group of writers or literary enthusiasts but directly by its publishers, the brothers Harper. In fact, although Henry Raymond was nominally managing editor, Fletcher Harper himself retained direct editorial control almost until his death in 1877 (Mott 2: 391). His guiding editorial principle was to publish "what would be intelligible, interesting, and useful to the average American" (Exman 77). Harper later wrote: "If we were asked why we first started a monthly magazine, we would have to say frankly that it was as a tender to our business" to draw both authors and readers for Harpers' books (Mott 2: 383). An advertisement in the flyleaf of the first volume announced the hope to give the magazine an unequaled popular circulation through offering "the great mass of the American people an immense amount of useful and entertaining reading matter." Accordingly, from its lavish pictorial covers to the fashion illustrations of its end pages, *Harper's* appealed to a much lighter, more popular, broader middle-class taste.

The contrast between the small, severe portrait of the Puritan Winthrop on the *Atlantic*'s plain cover and the elaborately decorated, bubble-blowing flower-strewing putti on *Harper's* forecast much of the story. From the beginning until well into the twentieth century, the *Atlantic* obdurately refused illustration to focus solely on the printed word. After 1880, as the technology for reproducing illustrations and the public taste for them developed, this policy became an increasing liability that limited the *Atlantic*'s appeal. *Harper's*, in contrast, in 1857 already used about fifty woodcuts per issue and, like others later, found illustration an immensely popular and valuable part of the magazine.

While fiction in the *Atlantic* was regional and almost entirely American, British fiction, usually pirated (in the absence of an international copyright law), was for a long time *Harper's* major staple. In the early years, it carried about three times as much fiction as the *Atlantic*, and while some of it had elements of realism, one or two stories in each issue were inevitably selected to please a highly romantic and sentimental taste for what Lowell had called "namby-pamby love tales." *Harper's* published about half as much verse, much of it frankly light, amusing doggerel.

Another major staple in *Harper's* was the illustrated travel and adventure article. In the issue corresponding to the first *Atlantic* in November 1857, four of six *Harper's* essays, including the two leads, were of this type, while the remaining two discussed the education of women (endorsing education for domestic duties and cultivated recreation) and the history of "Club Men," topics and treatments considerably less intellectually ambitious than those in the *Atlantic*'s essays. Seven "departments" occupied *Harper's* end pages. These included "Literary Notices," which confined itself to a single paragraph per book and did not attempt criticism; an "Editor's Table" essay; and "Editor's Drawer," containing humorous anecdotes from subscribers' letters. In politics, *Harper's Weekly* supported Buchanan's compromises on slavery, but the *Monthly* was carefully nonpartisan, partly for fear of losing its southern circulation. The "Record" department in *Harper's* listed contemporary events without commentary. The final two departments featured a cartoon sequence and fashion plates.

Over the next century, these two long-enduring American periodicals, compelled by market forces and competition between them, would increasingly grow to resemble each other, eventually in the twentieth century becoming so alike that each worried about preserving its identity. But in the early years, despite some overlap in fiction, they clearly had different editorial policies and audiences. Little wonder then that, despite surface civility, partisans of *Harper's* sometimes looked on *Atlantic* writers as an excessively cerebral, solemn, and self-congratulatory coterie of overstuffed reputations, or that Lowell and other *Atlantic* sympathizers looked on the editors of *Harper's* as pious literary pirates or mercenary "Scribes and Pharisees" interested mainly in profitable entertainments for the fashionable and monied mob.

In 1850, *Harper's Monthly* had met with an immediate success that astonished its publishers. Within six months it was printing 50,000 copies of each issue, and within a decade its circulation had climbed steadily to 200,000 (Mott 2: 390–91). Lowell and Phillips knew that their enterprise would not generate these numbers. In fact, they mainly hoped to avoid the fate of their Boston predecessors and the one really comparable New York venture, *Putnam's*, which had succumbed to the recession of 1857 in the same month that the *Atlantic* began publication. But the *Atlantic* did achieve success on its own terms. Selling at twenty-five cents per issue, or three dollars per year—*Harper's* price and the standard for a monthly at the time—its first numbers sold out editions of 20,000, and by 1860 it had more than 30,000 subscribers (Duberman 179). Assuming that most copies went to families and that many were lent by individuals or lending libraries, this would have given the magazine a probable readership of well over 100,000.[2]

The *Atlantic* was by nature more an earnest, high-minded provincial than a charming and fashionable cosmopolitan like *Harper's*. But it appealed immediately to certain types of readers, preserved most of those it won, and grew gradually but steadily during its first decade until it ran into competition with a new crop of New York illustrated monthlies in the 1870s. The *Atlantic* appealed, as Lowell intended, to a cultural elite more than, as *Harper's* did, to a broad middle-class audience including the socioeconomic elite. But this cultural elite definitively did not consist mainly of Brahminic Bostonians. The writers and scholars around Boston read the magazine, and it remained a significant forum for many of them, although the most intellectually purist among them such as Emerson and Norton soon found it too popular and gradually lost interest. Its essential appeal, however, was to the broader, national segment of the middle class who cared for the life of the mind, enjoyed literature, opposed slavery, were liberal and nondogmatic in religion, and wished to stay in touch with the intellectual currents of the times. Many of these were engaged in professions involving the transmission of cultural values. It was indicative of the *Atlantic*'s target audience that teachers, postmasters, and clergy received a discount of one-third on subscriptions. Some were liberally educated, but many were largely self-educated. A later *Atlantic* editor, Bliss Perry, affirmed that throughout most of the nineteenth century the lyceum system had a much more major influence than colleges in developing an audience for the magazine (letter to T. W. Higginson, 26 July 1907). Certainly the lyceum system promoted the broader geographic distribution of the magazine, in part because several of its major writers, such as Emerson, regularly undertook extended lecture tours.

In 1859, with a total circulation a little over 29,000, some 5,800 copies went to Boston, 5,400 were "mail subscription," and 18,074 were designated as foreign, apparently meaning that they were distributed out of state (Ellery Sedgwick to Frank Crowninshield, Feb. 1929, in the *Atlantic* archives, quoting a document that then adorned the walls of the editor's office). Many, though probably not the majority, of these "foreign" readers lived in New England. James Parton later noted satirically in the magazine itself: "Go where you will in New England, you can never get far beyond the meerschaum pipe, white kids, lessons on the piano and the *Atlantic Monthly*" ("The Mean Yankee at Home," Jan. 1869, 74). As Parton's comment suggests, the magazine became for some, particularly in remote villages, a form of cultural accomplishment and a badge of polite civilization. But for many readers it was more. To Emily Dickinson in Amherst, the *Atlantic* was "a temple" which she visited regularly (Brooks, *Indian Summer* 6). Like Dickinson, many inhabitants of small towns found it a crucial link with the larger world of literature and intellectual life impossible for moderns to understand, with our plethora of printed sources and electronic media.

This was nowhere more true than in the Midwest. In Hamilton, Ohio, the young William Dean Howells read the *Atlantic* avidly, as did neighbors such as James Garfield. Reading the magazine and discussing it with friends led Howells to begin imagining a literary career, and he began that career by sending his poems for Lowell's editorial scrutiny. Even further afield, T. W. Higginson, a frequent contributor, traveling on lecture tour into remote areas of Minnesota, noted how strange it was "to dip down into these little western towns and find an audience all ready and always readers of the *Atlantic*, so glad to see me.... One man there told me of a village [Casper, Iowa] with fifty houses and a club of twenty-five subscribers to the *Atlantic Monthly*" (qtd. in M. Higginson 265). Often these houses contained portraits of Emerson, Longfellow, or Lowell similar to the prints later distributed by Ticknor and Fields with subscription renewals. The monthly arrival of the magazine carrying the newest work by these authors was an anticipated event. It was read after dinner in family circles and became not just a link with the larger world but also a source of shared ideas and an occasion for intellectual exchange within small communities.

From the beginning, then, the *Atlantic* had a clear literary and intellectual identity, and certain kinds of readers identified themselves with it. This attachment in turn produced a stable readership and, relative to other magazines, a high rate of subscription renewals. This sense of identity exerted a conservative influence—for better or for worse—on subsequent editors, who felt reluctant to attempt substantially popularizing the magazine and thus risk alienating the traditional readership in uncertain hopes of gaining a broader new one.

Beyond establishing a modest but sustaining circulation, the *Atlantic* achieved another kind of success. It was quickly recognized, by writers and readers alike, as an instrument for the stimulation, distribution, and recognition of a substantial development in American letters. Higginson later spoke with lingering enthusiasm of seeing "a literature actually forming before my eyes" (*Cheerful Yesterdays* 18). The *Atlantic*'s quality and significance were felt as far as England. The dour and crusty Charles Reade, while refusing to submit his work for editorial judgment, wrote to Underwood: "Let me congratulate you on the circulation and merit of your monthly. It is a wonderful product at the price.... [T]he stories are no worse than *Blackwoods* and *Frazers*, etc., etc. and some of the other matter is infinitely beyond our monthly and trimesteral scribblers, being genuine in thought and English in expression.... After twenty five years of these rotten old cabbage stalks ... I turn my nose to such papers as your 'Autocrat of the Breakfast Table,' etc. with a sense of relief and freshness" (10 Oct. 1858, qtd. in Perry, "Editor" 671).

Even in the tempered retrospective judgment of Frank Luther Mott, the historian of American magazines, the *Atlantic* became "immediately, so far as belles-lettres were concerned, the most important magazine in America" (2: 33).

While most writers and critics of the time readily acknowledged the *Atlantic*'s literary importance, many accused it of rank provincialism. It represented, they claimed, not America but New England. The percentage of *Atlantic* authors published from the various regions in fact tended to diminish in direct relation to their respective distance from Boston. Among the fifty-four authors represented in the first volume, thirty-five were from New England, ten from New York, six foreign, two from the South, and only one from west of the Mississippi. During the magazine's first fifteen years, fully two-thirds of its contributors were New Englanders (Mott 2: 495).[3]

Some authors from other regions, most notably from New York and the South, felt that the *Atlantic* was a closed club designed for the propagation of New England letters, a mutual admiration society whose members puffed each other and blackballed the earnest efforts of the nonelect. Even if such authors were disposed, like most of the reading public they coveted, to admire the New England writers whose names were habitually associated with the magazine, the sense of being excluded from the circle rankled. The New York poet Edmund C. Stedman wrote to Bayard Taylor: "The Boston house, naturally, drive apace every steed that wins a heat. But when a man's pace is slow, though sure, they don't make much of him unless he is 'in their midst.' . . . They never ask me for anything and have declined what little I have sent them. I have this week hit upon a magnificent subject, but when done, I shall not have the courage to send it to the *Atlantic*" (qtd. in Mott 2: 497). This sense of exclusion was as much defensive perception as actual editorial treatment. Underwood and Lowell had explicitly solicited contributions from quite a few New Yorkers, including among others Herman Melville, who promised to contribute but failed to send anything; G. W. Curtis, who demurred because of other commitments; Richard H. Stoddard, who did contribute; and Parke Godwin, who agreed to become the regular political commentator. In fact, even Stedman later acknowledged Lowell's "genial & unexpected interest" in his work (letter to Lowell, 24 May 1866, in Duberman 166).

While Lowell did publish occasional poems by Paul Hayne and several other southerners, the *Atlantic* received few contributions or subscriptions from the South. But the reason had little to do with literary snobbery. A month after the *Atlantic*'s first publication, the *Southern Literary Messenger* commented: "It is not likely that many Southern men will subscribe to the 'Atlantic Monthly'; their sense of self-respect would forbid the direct encouragement of a work engaged in a systematic defamation of everything southern" (Bagby 472).

The *Atlantic*—at least as far as literature was concerned—had not been consciously founded in a spirit of sectionalism. In fact, its editors and publishers, perhaps aware of suspicion from other regions, prominently announced in its pages that "the *Atlantic* has never been and will never be a sectional journal" and that all manuscripts would be welcomed and fairly considered (Feb. 1860, back cover). Still, most submissions continued to come from New England. And consciously or unconsciously, the magazine had been brought into being largely to gather the fruits of the flowering of New England. Why should Lowell, busy as he was, forage far afield when he lived in a New England orchard that filled his monthly basket amply? If two-thirds of the contents of the *Atlantic* originated in New England, was it not a fact that just about that proportion of the best writing in the country in the late fifties originated there also? Even Howells, consistently a champion of western writing and writers, acknowledged that "the editors of the *Atlantic* had been eager from the beginning to discover any outlying literature" but that "there was in those days very little good writing done beyond the borders of New England" (*Literary Friends* 115). Most literary culture before the Civil War was essentially regional, though this regionalism faded rapidly with the development of transportation in the sixties and seventies. The other regions had magazines of their own. In New York, *Harper's Monthly*, like the *Atlantic*, aspired to be national, but the old *Knickerbocker*, as its name suggested, was a strongly local product; *Sartain's* was the repository for the Philadelphia writers; and the South had *DeBow's* and the frankly sectional *Messenger*.

Undoubtedly, Lowell's habitual circle of acquaintance, his lack of a systematic and energetic policy of soliciting outside it, the literary abundance of New England, the scarcity of writing from the West, rising tension and war with the South, and the defensive diffidence among many outsiders to attempt to publish in the *Atlantic* all conspired to make the magazine less than fully representative of the nation as a whole. But its partiality for New England writing gave it a definite flavor and coherence and did not prevent it from becoming in its early years, both in reputation and in fact, the best literary magazine in the country. Provincial complacency and self-conscious worship in the cult of New England letters did not become substantial dangers until the 1880s, after substantial literary production developed in the South and West and after New York had become the nation's literary capital.

James Russell Lowell, age thirty-eight, in 1857, the year he became editor of the *Atlantic*. By permission of the Library of Congress.

2
James Russell Lowell
(1857–1861)

Yankee Humanist

As a result of the *Atlantic*'s immediate reputation, Lowell, who in June of 1857 had felt that his editorial duties would be light, by late November found himself inundated with manuscripts. Not long after the publication of the first issue, he lamented humorously to Emerson: "You have no notion how hard bestead we are. Out of 297 manuscripts only at most six accepted. I begin to believe in the total depravity of contributions" (19 Nov. 1857, Scudder, *Lowell* 1: 416). A month later he was complaining in earnest to his friend Norton: "For a lazy man I have a great deal to do. A magazine allows no vacations. What with manuscripts and proofs and what not, it either takes up or breaks up all one's time" (31 Dec. 1857, *Letters* 1: 280–81).

Lowell was not a lazy man. For extended periods of time he worked up to fifteen hours a day. As editor-in-chief, he had responsibilities that in the twentieth century would be delegated to a large professional staff.[1] In addition to setting editorial policy, he had to read and make all final decisions on manuscripts, determine the makeup of issues, write literary notices or arrange for them, correspond with authors, be ombudsman for questions from the press, and even read proofs of all manuscripts except Holmes's—all in addition to his full-time teaching duties at Harvard (Lowell to J. W. Palmer, 17 Apr. 1860, in Duberman 178).

But if Lowell's editorial exertions were sometimes intense, they were seldom systematic. He worked at home in Cambridge, leaving the job of "office editor" to his assistant, Francis Underwood. A tardy and apologetic letter to Robert Grant White pictures the chaos that sometimes reigned in his Cambridge study:

> I used to be able to answer letters in the month during which I received them, but now they pile up and make a jam behind the boom of my occupations, till they carry

everything before them, and after a little confused whirling float placidly down to the ocean of Oblivion.... I am afraid that at this moment there are at least a hundred and fifty unanswered letters in and on and round my desk, whose blank [looks] seem to say "how long?" (6 Apr. 1859, Scudder, *Lowell* 1: 441)

The deluge of manuscripts and inquiries that flooded Lowell was partly a result of the relative liberality with which Phillips underwrote his magazine. Later the *Atlantic* would have difficulty competing for authors with the large-circulation illustrated monthlies of New York, but in Lowell's time, it was one of the very few American magazines that offered reliable and substantial payment. Its average rate for prose was about six dollars per page, while distinguished contributors like Emerson received ten. Poems brought between ten and fifty dollars, depending on their length and the reputation of their authors. Both scales, although lower than those of the most popular weekly story papers like Robert Bonner's *Ledger*, were almost double the norm among pre–Civil War monthlies (Mott 2: 19–25, 506). The *Atlantic* was expanding both the audience and the remuneration for good writing, and the response among authors was more than the inefficient Lowell had expected or could handle.

Once, while Lowell was walking between Cambridge and the Phillips and Sampson office in Boston, his hat, stuffed with manuscripts, blew off into the Charles and sank. The incident was characteristic. Occasionally manuscripts were lost in the shuffle; frequently they languished for months at the bottom of growing heaps. Even accepted pieces were sometimes shelved for up to two years. Lowell was seldom so much as a month in advance in composing his issues, and his notes on the magazine's makeup, scribbled in last-minute haste on scraps of waste paper, must have been a tribulation to its printers, Henry Oscar Houghton's Riverside Press.

Underwood was an enthusiastic and willing assistant; he solicited contributions, handled some correspondence, and rough-sorted manuscripts, bringing the best to the attention of his chief. As first reader, he had unlimited power of rejection over unsolicited manuscripts. But the major responsibility, both for the magazine's editorial policy and for the realization of that policy in its content, was Lowell's.

Despite Underwood's help, Lowell sometimes felt buried under the weight of his work. Once he submitted his resignation but was persuaded to withdraw it. In fact, his already substantial workload was frequently compounded by his lack of organization on the one hand and by a scholarly rigor, even fastidiousness, on the other. The result was periodic strain on his relationships with authors. Some authors found him arbitrary, even arrogant, alternately disorganized and nitpicking. Others found him a source of generous encouragement.

Lowell was often exacting in matters of literary technique. The editorial changes he suggested usually benefited the works in question and were often accepted by the authors with equanimity. Whittier, and even Emerson, gracefully acknowledged the validity of corrections he proposed in their diction and meter. Higginson, however, felt that Lowell was editorially high-handed, particularly with younger authors. "I wish to be understood," he objected on one occasion, "as giving a suppressed but audible growl at the chopping knife which has made mincemeat of my sentences. It isn't pleasant to think that my sentences belong to such a low order of organization that they can be chopped in the middle and each half wriggle away independently" (to Francis Underwood, n.d., in M. Higginson 158).

Lowell's propensity to take editorial liberties became more serious when it involved ideology rather than style, and it lost the magazine at least two very valuable contributors: Thoreau and the political essayist Parke Godwin. In April 1858, Lowell, encouraged by his publisher Phillips, felt free to append to Godwin's criticism of the Buchanan administration four pages of his own editorializing condemning political compromise with slavery in a much more radical tenor. A blank space was left between the two portions, but there was no other indication that the editorial came from two hands, and Godwin was given no advance warning of Lowell's intentions. Godwin was too irate to write Lowell directly, but in a scathing letter to Underwood, bristling with regional enmity, he severed his connection with the magazine:

> I did not hope to satisfy the "fervid" Abolition sentiment of New England; nor to write sensation articles for the news vendors: but I did hope to make the magazine gradually a power and an authority in the best minds of the country. It seems that I have made a mistake: and that my considered sentences are unsuited to the "fervid" atmosphere of Boston. . . . I am . . . a writer and not a "thunderer" as the gentleman who attempts to supply my deficiencies is. . . . Fred Cozzens and I had arranged to go and eat a dinner with you on Saturday, but as we are afraid that we should be found very cold and dull clods amid the fervid and glowing wits who surround the Maga, our prudence has got the better of our valor: we shall instead warm up our heavy clay with some less Olympian brewages. (26 Mar. 1858, in Perry, "Editor" 673–74)

Lowell's addition clearly demonstrated his intention that the magazine should aggressively oppose political accommodation with slavery, but it was shoddy treatment of his contributor.

Yet if Lowell, especially when caught in the rush of deadlines and a deluge of work, could be insensitive or high-handed, he could also be extremely generous with his time and encouragement. Before the first number was issued, Lowell and Underwood sent out letters to a large number of authors announcing the magazine and inviting contributions; those who promised contributions were listed in the first issue to entice subscribers. After this initial round, Lowell does not seem to have solicited much, mainly because he found his desk piled high without soliciting and also because he could make many requests in person. Still, he proved himself extraordinarily willing to spend time discussing literature with younger writers who sought him out. "The encouragement conveyed by a simple chat with

Lowell was enormous. It was an encouragement given openly and freely. Even the most famous Brahmins made themselves available to almost anyone with the slightest pretensions to a literary career" (Tomsich 21). The younger writers who benefited from Lowell's genial attention included his own assistant Frank Underwood, Rose Terry, Louisa May Alcott, Harriet Prescott Spofford, John Burroughs, Thomas Bailey Aldrich, and William Dean Howells. Lowell's treatment of Aldrich and Howells, both virtually unknown, both from beyond Boston—and both later themselves editors of the *Atlantic*—was indicative.

Towards Howells particularly, Lowell showed sincere interest and affection from the beginning. When Howells's poems arrived from Columbus, Ohio, unsolicited and unrecommended, Lowell recognized a talent, unripe but substantial. In fact, one poem seemed so good that he suspected it to be translation of Heine, but upon finding it an original, he published it. Several more acceptances followed, initiating a correspondence in which Lowell counseled Howells, among other things, to be less imitative, to find his own voice, and to "sweat the Heine out of you as men do mercury" (qtd. in Lynn 79). When the young Ohioan's first book of poetry came out, the editor took the trouble to write a generous but unpatronizing *Atlantic* review praising the "Western flavor" of some poems, recognizing "a fresh and authentic power" and predicting even better work in the future ("Review of *Poems by Two Friends*," Apr. 1860, 511).

When Howells himself appeared in Cambridge in 1860, Lowell welcomed him heartily. Lowell spent long hours in his study with the ambitious young aspirant, talking both poetry and practical strategies for a literary career. In fact, he tried to help Howells initiate that career immediately by arranging for him to dine in a small reserved room at the Parker House with Lowell, Holmes, and James T. Fields, who had just purchased the magazine, to explore the possibility of Howells's being hired as Lowell's assistant. At that time, Fields had to reserve the place for his partner's son, but he would later remember Howells when he himself became an editor in need of an assistant. In the meantime, Lowell made sure that Howells had a chance to meet the major New England authors whom the Ohioan was reading in the *Atlantic*. In a letter of introduction to the saturnine Hawthorne he wrote:

> My dear Hawthorne, I have no masonic claim upon you except the community of tobacco, and the young man who brings this does not smoke.
> But he wants to look at you, which will do you no harm, and him a great deal of good.
> His name is Howells, and he is a fine young fellow and has written several poems in the *Atlantic*, which of course you have never read.... If my judgment is good for anything, this youth has more in him than any of our younger fellows in the way of rhyme....
> Therefore let him look at you and charge it to, yours always, J. R. Lowell. (5 Aug. 1860, *Letters* 1: 305–306)

While Lowell, like the young poet himself, did not foresee the literature Howells would write and champion over the next fifty years, he clearly recognized literary talent far beyond the Boston circle—at least when it showed up in his manuscript pile or on his doorstep. And he acted with extraordinary generosity to develop that talent. His literary advice, encouraging Howells to find his own voice and develop the western note, was essentially liberating rather than prescriptive, and he continued to play a very important part in launching Howells's professional career, both as writer and as editor.

If Lowell as an editor, then, was sometimes disorganized, arbitrary, or insensitive to the rights of contributors, he not only brought in good material through personal contacts but was often generous in supporting unknown young writers. He also established editorial policies that had a long-lasting effect on the magazine. These policies, reflecting the Yankee humanism from which the magazine derived, emphasized a reasonably broad scope for intellectual inquiry; a relatively realistic, ethical fiction opposed to overt sentimentality and didacticism; an interest in the Western cultural tradition combined with an emphasis on developing an explicitly American literary culture; and an active political engagement based on moral principle, particularly in opposition to slavery—in short, high culture combined with moderately liberal social policies. Like most editors, Lowell sometimes compromised with the demands of his readers and publisher. But these high-minded policies were generally realized in the contents of his magazine.

Inevitably there was some tension between Lowell's high-culture aspirations for the *Atlantic*, on the one hand, and, on the other, the tastes of prospective readers and the desire of the publisher for larger circulation. This tension has been a dynamic force throughout the *Atlantic*'s history; the magazine's editors have always had to try to determine the degree to which high culture is economically self-supporting. At the founding dinner in May 1857, Phillips, despite his awe at the company, had given a speech indicating the role he would play. "Mr. Cabot," he had said, "is much wiser than I am; Dr. Holmes can write funnier verses than I can; Mr. Motley can write better history than I; Mr. Emerson is a philosopher and I am not; Mr. Lowell knows more of the old poets than I; but none of you knows the American people as well as I do" (qtd. in M. Howe 15).

If the other founders were to exert their influences on behalf of literature, history, and philosophy, sometimes, as Emerson had suggested, in defiance of popular values, Phillips, like subsequent publishers, was to exert his on behalf of the public taste. On some issues, like slavery, Phillips was not afraid of radicalism; on others, like religion, he was sensitive. Generally, he gave his editor a respectful measure of independence. Still, Lowell felt from the publisher "a constant pressure ... to 'popularize' the magazine." This he accurately claimed to "resist without clamor" and with general success, but it did encourage in him a sense of strategic restraint and an instinct to balance more esoteric material with the popular (Lowell to unknown addressee, qtd. in Scudder, *Lowell* 1: 424).

Both the moderate pressure exerted by Phillips and Lowell's resistance to it were probably healthy influences, as were some of the tensions evident later in the nineteenth century between market forces and the high-culture inclinations of editors such as Aldrich and Scudder. The publisher's influence, supplementing Lowell's own editorial experience, prevented the magazine from expressing too much academic antiquarianism, ideological narrowness, or abstruse philosophizing and thus becoming another *Dial, Pioneer,* or *North Atlantic Review.* Lowell always made sure that each issue had some leavening or popular element in it. But he was not always forced to choose between the popular and the substantive as some later editors felt forced to do. As Lawrence Levine has suggested, there seemed less of a split between highbrow and lowbrow at midcentury than there would be later, and Lowell was fortunate enough to have major contributors such as Longfellow, Whittier, Holmes, and Stowe, whose work was considered both popular and substantive.[2] Holmes and Stowe were not only Lowell's most popular contributors, but also his most prolific. Their monthly serial installments of "The Autocrat of the Breakfast Table," *Elsie Venner* (originally "The Professor at the Breakfast Table"), and *The Minister's Wooing* fueled much of the magazine's initial circulation success.

In addition, Lowell's sympathy with Emerson's ideas of cultural leadership and defiance of popular taste guaranteed that his *Atlantic* would have a relatively high level of intellectual debate and inquiry. While in Lowell's *Atlantic,* as later, fiction often served as a popular balance to weightier material, the high end of the magazine's intellectual range was reflected in the essays of Norton on the arts, Whipple on literature, Asa Gray on evolution, C. C. Hazewell on foreign affairs, T. W. Higginson on social reforms, and Emerson on the conduct of life. Lowell's cultural elitism also reserved a place in the magazine for some rarefied literary works and for readable scholarship. In accepting a complex thirty-page sequence of poems by Arthur Hugh Clough which he serialized under the title "Amours de Voyage," Lowell expected that it would be "caviare to the Generals (of whom, you know, American society is largely made up) and ought to be so" (15 Feb. 1858, Duberman 165). To a contributing Shakespearean he asserted: "I don't care whether the public are tired of the Divine Villiams or not—a *part* of the magazine, as long as I have anything to do with it, shall be expressly *not* for the Mob (of well-dressed gentlemen who read with ease)" (to R. G. White, Scudder, *Lowell* 1: 423).

The Yankee humanists whom Lowell and his *Atlantic* in some measure typified were deeply attached to the major figures of Western literature and history. They found in reading and reflecting on the lives and works of Aristotle, Euripides, Caesar, Chaucer, Dante, Shakespeare, Johnson, Voltaire, Goethe, and their like some of the intellectual, moral, and spiritual values that their forefathers had found in religion and the profound insights into human nature for which many readers today look to psychology or the social sciences. Lowell, the college professor and Cambridge bookman, was editorially committed to perpetuating discussions of literature and history. Typically the papers he selected dealt not with academic minutia of purely scholarly interest but with broad issues of meaning and values. But even in his time, he was aware that such pieces spoke to a restricted audience and competed for space with more immediate issues. Most *Atlantic* editors throughout the nineteenth century continued this commitment to history and to the major texts of the Western canon, while the broader cultural relevance of that history and canon declined in the face of mass culture, and the "great works" were eventually relegated to the academy.

If Lowell's elitist tendency to resist popular taste led him to accept some bookish pieces, it also led him to take some other editorial risks that the editors of more popular magazines would not take, particularly in political commentary but to a limited degree also in controversial topics such as women's education and religion. Lowell's consciously elitist resistance to the specter of public taste and opinion that haunts most editors unquestionably limited the *Atlantic*'s potential circulation. During the nineteenth century, it never achieved even a quarter of the readership of *Harper's*. But it also initially helped to give the *Atlantic* an intellectual authority, range, and incisiveness lacking in the early *Harper's* and its imitators.

Lowell's editorial policy and the contents of his *Atlantic* consciously aimed at a fairly high level of intellectual culture. But they explicitly rejected traditional European, particularly British, models of high culture and advocated a more American form. If their American model still implied cultural hegemony and an educated elite, that elite was to be a meritocracy whose function was not to preserve their own privilege but to educate the broad populace, to be evangelists of literary culture. Following the lead of Emerson's "American Scholar," most *Atlantic* writers implied that the aim of high culture was not to produce academic scholars or a self-perpetuating elite of witty and erudite clubmen for whom literate culture was a mark of status. Rather, it was to produce independent, thinking individuals who would stimulate the cultural development of the society as a whole. They implied that in Europe the aim of high culture was to enforce a static hierarchical social order. In America, on the contrary, the purpose of high culture was ideally to stimulate a fluid, evolving civilization offering all individuals freedom for intellectual and moral development.

Despite their respect for the great works of Western culture, author after author in the *Atlantic* advocated independence from the European past and expressed an expansive, even visionary optimism about the evolution of American culture and values. Most had extensive personal ties with Europe, were steeped in its literature, and distrusted a crude kind of cultural chauvinism. But they were nevertheless clearly proclaiming cultural independence. In an 1860 *Atlantic* essay titled "Culture," Emerson anticipated ideas of social evolution developed later by Herbert Spenser and saw America potentially at the forefront of that evolution. Humankind, according to Emerson, was an unfinished species evolving through higher moral and intellectual stages, propelled partly by the leadership of individual genius and partly by the meliorative effects of a shared intellectual culture. He felt that Americans, because of the freedom their society offered individuals, could lead this progress if only they would "extract this tapeworm of Europe" from their brains.

In "The New World and the New Man" (Oct. 1858), the transcendentalist minister David Wasson celebrated the American character, of which he chose Emerson as the archetype, for its instinctive intuition of moral principle, its social openness and tolerance, and its freedom from European precedent and tradition. Matthew Arnold, who was provoked to several skirmishes by the *Atlantic*'s aggressive Americanism, called Wasson's article an example of American "tall talk." In a later *Atlantic* article, "On a Certain Condescension among Foreigners," Lowell himself acidly countered another Arnoldian criticism, by suggesting that the English were incapable of understanding American culture and democracy because they were themselves antidemocratic, and that Americans must therefore "disinfect ourselves of Anglicanism" (Jan. 1869, 82–94).

Even the rationalist Holmes waxed rapturous with the same evolutionary vision of American potential as Emerson and Wasson:

> Never since man came into this atmosphere of oxygen and ozone, was there anything like the condition of the young American of the nineteenth century, . . . heir of all old civilizations, founder of the new one which if all the prophecies of the human heart are not lies, is to be the noblest, as it is the last; isolated in space from the races that are governed by dynasties whose divine right grows out of human wrong, yet knit into the most absolute solidarity with mankind of all times and places by the one great thought he inherits as his national birthright; free to form and to express his opinions, . . . he seems to want nothing for a large, noble, wholesome, beneficent life. ("Professor at the Breakfast Table," Dec. 1859, 751)

Within fifty years, Holmes, Lowell, and many other early *Atlantic* contributors would be dismissed by literary critics, even in the magazine they had founded, as essentially derivative from British literary and cultural models.[3] By that time, these early *Atlantic* writers would represent the tradition from which the later cultural critics had to extricate themselves, even as in the 1850s, England represented a tradition from which Emerson, Holmes, Lowell, and others wished to distinguish themselves. The fact remains, however, that collectively the *Atlantic*'s early contributors were a potent force for intellectual independence and encouraged America to see itself as culturally distinct, particularly in its democratic individualism, freedom from tradition and authority, moral conscience, and broader social tolerance.

The desire to develop a distinctively American culture was reflected in Lowell's selection of literature for the *Atlantic*. Several years before assuming the *Atlantic* editorship, Lowell had written that Americans "may fairly demand of our literature that it should be national to the extent of being free from outworn conventionalities and as thoroughly impregnated with humane and manly sentiment as is the idea on which our political fabric rests.... Let it give a true reflection of our social, political, and household life" ("Nationality in Literature," *North American Review* 69 [July 1849]: 209). While the reflection of the nation in *Atlantic* fiction was only partial, this explicitly American, essentially realistic literature remained Lowell's goal.

Despite the strong metaphors of tapeworms and disinfectants, perhaps inevitable in any claims for independence, Lowell and the other founders never had any intention to exclude English literature from the magazine. In fact, Holmes's name for the magazine had implied intellectual commerce between Europe and America, and before publication of the first issue, Underwood had been dispatched to England to make contacts and gather manuscripts. But from the beginning, as the editorial statement in the inaugural issue had specified, American authors were to be the main staple. In the event, the trunk containing most of the manuscripts garnered by Underwood and Norton, who was just returning from England, mysteriously disappeared from the pier and was never rediscovered. As a result of both accident and policy, then, the literature in Lowell's *Atlantic*, in clear contrast with *Harper's*, relying heavily as it did on pirated British fiction, was almost entirely by Americans and about American life.

From a modern or postmodern perspective, Lowell's tastes and editorial judgment in literature were clearly circumscribed by certain moral and aesthetic standards specific to the mid-nineteenth century. But if his judgment lacked the sophisticated irony, the pure aestheticism, and the ethical relativism on which modern taste has long congratulated itself, he did more than any contemporary editor to hold the line against the prevailing literary sins of the time: excessive sentimentality and moral didacticism. It was Lowell's accomplishment that *Atlantic* fiction "went counter to the general honeyed stickiness with its very first numbers" (Mott 2: 173). And although he had reservations about some aspects of realism, Lowell and his *Atlantic* played an important role in developing New England local color realism, which aimed to depict explicitly American conditions and character.

Lowell believed, as he stated in an *Atlantic* review praising Hawthorne's *Marble Faun*, that the highest function of literature was not simply to mirror external realities but to give "a thorough conception of the world of moral realities" (Apr. 1860, 509). With Emerson, he believed that the greatest works revealed ethical principles operative in the world and were universal rather than particular. He also predictably found certain kinds of realism distasteful. Articulating a Victorian reticence that later inhibited the success of the Jamesean psychological novel, he condemned "keyhole realism" that stooped to pry into the private passions played out behind decently closed doors. Not only sex but even death scenes he felt should be veiled rather than exploited. Having a Victorian sense of the beautiful, he also found certain kinds of physical description distasteful. For instance, he persuaded a reluctant Walt Whitman to drop from the *Atlantic* publication of his poem "Bardic Symbols" the characteristically graphic lines:

> See from my dead lips the ooze exuding at last!
> See the prismatic colors glistening and rolling!
>
> (Mott 2: 501)

In general, however, neither Lowell's ethics nor his aesthetics were prudish. At a 1859 dinner for the religiously conservative Stowes, Lowell, fortified with some surreptitiously served liquor, spent much of the evening trying to convince Harriet Beecher Stowe that Fielding's *Tom Jones* was the greatest novel in English, while the provocative Dr. Holmes enjoyed proposing to Calvin Stowe that the pulpit was responsible for most profanity (M. D. Howe 24).

Concerning realism, if moral realities were for Lowell the highest aim of literature, he insisted that those airy realities became literature only when given a local habitation and a name. There must be a realistic "adaptation of the world of sense and appearance to the purposes of art"; higher truths must be convincingly embodied in plausible human life (Apr. 1860, 509). To Harriet Beecher Stowe, Lowell wrote, "My advice is . . . to stick to nature, and to avoid what people commonly call the 'Ideal.' . . . Don't I feel it every day in this weary editorial mill of mine, that there are ten thousand people who can write ideal things for one who can see, feel, and reproduce nature and character" (4 Feb. 1859, qtd. in Mitchell 367).

In his own writing, his editorial advice, and his editorial judgment, Lowell was a great lover of the local, accurately observed and realistically recorded. His "Biglow Papers" aimed to articulate essential moral principles, but in response to specific American political events. These principles were embodied in grass-roots rural Yankee characters who spoke distinct New England dialects. Their speech, actions, and social contexts were all exactly observed. Nor was Lowell's love of the local limited to New England, as his encouragement of a distinctly "western flavor" in Howells's early work indicates.

Lowell's insistence that moral realities must be fully and accurately embodied in observed local fact lay at the root of his opposition to didacticism, which he shared with Howells and later realists. The disembodied idea, he felt, lacked the power of art. Not that he could excuse shoddy morals, even in literature of aesthetic merit. One young contributor, John T. Trowbridge, discovered this moral stringency when, to his irritation, Lowell rejected his narrative poem, previously accepted and in proofs, upon noticing that its protagonist borrowed money from his father "as might befit the scamp of a piece, but not its hero" (Trowbridge, "Recollections" 583–84). Ethical values were necessary to good literature but were not sufficient to create it; the aesthetic sense must be given its full due. In fact, Lowell's own first

Atlantic poem was a satire on those who used literature as a vehicle for moral uplift. Didacticism began, Lowell said, when the maiden goddess Minerva, "Queen of Prudes," had set about writing "po——, no verses":

> And full they were of pious phrase
> So extra-super moral,
> For sucking Virtue's tender gums
> Most tooth enticing coral.
>
> ("The Origins of Didactic Poetry," Nov. 1857, 110)

Lowell's opposition to didacticism and sentimentality, his insistence on aesthetic qualities beyond ethics, and his advocacy of accurate realistic observation influenced many contemporaries through his reviews, editorial advice, and selections in the *Atlantic*. The guidance he offered to Harriet Beecher Stowe during a period of self-doubt she went through in the writing of *The Minister's Wooing* was characteristic. She was discouraged and complained of difficulty making her moral clear. After receiving the first installment of the work in progress, Lowell wrote to encourage her New England realism, discourage her didacticism, and renew her confidence. "What especially charmed me in the new story," he wrote enthusiastically, "was, that you had taken your stand on New England ground. You are one of the few persons lucky enough to be born with eyes in your head—that is, with something behind the eyes which makes them of value." Lowell suggested that *Uncle Tom's Cabin*, despite its righteous influence, had won "cheap sympathy with sentimental philosophy" and suffered from intrusive moralizing. This book would need no moralizing intrusions because it had a true "perception of realities without which the ideality is impossible. . . . Let your moral take care of itself, and remember that an author's writing desk is something infinitely higher than a pulpit." "No one," he concluded, "appreciates your genius more highly than I. . . . Don't read any criticisms of your story; believe that you know better than any of us. . . . The native sod sends up the best inspiration to the brain and you are as sure of immortality as we all are of dying—if you only go on with entire faith in yourself" (F. Wilson 442–43 and A. Fields 249–50).

Lowell encouraged other writers in similar ways, with the result that his *Atlantic* carried considerable relatively realistic fiction. Rose Terry Cooke was another early New England regional realist who benefited from Lowell's influence. In a generally sympathetic *Atlantic* review, he criticized some of her poems as suffering from the abstractness and melancholy he felt plagued much modern poetry, but he praised those that had "the true game-flavor of the border" (Mar. 1861, 382). He encouraged this same New England game-flavor in her fiction and published many of her earliest stories.

Harriet Beecher Stowe, particularly in *The Minister's Wooing* and her later "Oldtown" series, and Rose Terry Cooke were the vanguard of a long tradition of New

England regional realism, primarily written by and about women. In describing that tradition, Josephine Donovan affirms that "the school's original theoretical underpinnings, or justifications, were laid down by the early editors of the *Atlantic Monthly*: namely James Russell Lowell . . . James T. Fields . . . Howells . . . Aldrich . . . Scudder. These men through theoretical statements (mainly Lowell and Howells), editorial selections, and personal encouragement of the women authors deserve credit for the early growth of the movement" (6). This tradition, sustained by writers such as Elizabeth Phelps, Celia Thaxter, Mary E. Wilkins Freeman, Sarah Orne Jewett, and Alice Brown, continued to be a major current in *Atlantic* fiction for almost fifty years until it died out around the turn of the century, subverted by commercial romanticism on the one hand and gritty urban naturalism on the other. The New England regional fiction written by these women was explicitly and consciously realistic. It developed partly in opposition to both the romantic and the sentimental-domestic traditions of most popular contemporary fiction by and about women. This intentional antiromantic bent was clear, for instance, when Rose Terry Cooke, who delighted in a conscious subversion of the conventional heroine, asked the reader's forgiveness "if I offer you no tragedy in high life, no sentimental history of fashion and wealth, but only a little story about a woman who could not be a heroine" ("Miss Lucinda," Aug. 1861, 141). A good many of the women in *Atlantic* stories were not heroines in the conventional sense, and their histories raised significant questions about conventional romantic ideas of love, marriage, women's roles, and fulfillment. Before the publication of the *Atlantic*'s first number in 1857, the misogynistic Thoreau wondered in his journal whether "the new magazine which all have been expecting may contain only another love story . . . without the slightest novelty in it" (*Journal* 10: 228). If he had bothered to read the fiction by women in the *Atlantic* over the next few years, he might have found much of it original, particularly in encouraging women to be self-sufficient.

Lowell's own opposition to conventional romanticism was clear in his reviews as well as his editorial selections. In a review of George Eliot's first major work, *Scenes from Clerical Life*, he blasted the romancers who "failed to copy Nature faithfully and heartily" and praised Eliot for making her story read like a "reminiscence of real life" without falsifying literary effects (May 1858, 891). He encouraged and published other attacks on "the numberless prose romances that occupy the present generation of readers," dismissing them as silly, byzantine, and frivolous (W. L. Symonds, "Carnival of the Romantic," Aug. 1860, 129). The contemptuous Thoreau and the scholarly Norton had their doubts about *Atlantic* fiction, especially that written by women. Norton warned Lowell that he heard the *Atlantic* roundly abused in some academic circles for publishing second-rate love stories (Duberman 174). In truth, there were some conventional stories on the Cinderella pattern. But Lowell knew very well that not only a major portion of the magazine's readership but also about half its contributors of fiction were women. He knew too that several of these authors were among the best. He encouraged and published relatively realistic fiction treating contemporary issues by young men, including Underwood's serial novel condemning stock speculation, stories by the early realist John DeForest, and satires on contemporary spiritualism by Bayard Taylor and John Trowbridge. But Lowell found in the writing of several women, particularly Harriet Stowe and Rose Terry Cooke, an effective alternative to the usual thin, sentimental conventional commercial romance, an alternative that had the flavor of an authentic realism rooted in American life.

Despite some limitations, Lowell's literary taste and the substantial influence he exerted as the *Atlantic*'s first editor cannot be dismissed as merely scholarly, conventional, imitative of the British tradition, or conventionally idealistic. In fact, Lowell's editorial influence strongly supported the early development of American realism. As Fred Pattee recognized, he "was attracted by the genuineness and truth to life in a tale, be it high life or low, and he rejected without hesitation the mechanically literary, the artificially romantic, and the merely sentimental. With the advent of *The Atlantic Monthly*, a healthy realism for the first time decisively entered American fiction" (168). In her analysis of the *Atlantic*'s nineteenth-century literary criticism, Helen McMahon confirms Pattee's judgment of both Lowell and the magazine. "From the beginning of its history," under Lowell, McMahon concludes, the *Atlantic* "played a not inconsiderable role in encouraging the rise of realism . . . through its insistence on believable patterns of experience" (100).

If Lowell's *Atlantic* was progressive in supporting the development of realism, it was progressive too in its political values and, despite clear inhibitions, in its discussion of religious issues and science. The ideal of Yankee humanism, inherited from the drafters of the first amendment in the Bill of Rights and reinforced by iconoclastic Emersonian individualism, was rational tolerance and open intellectual inquiry.

Like most magazines, Lowell's *Atlantic* never achieved this ideal, but it came closer than virtually any of its contemporaries. Beyond the unconscious limits imposed by cultural ethnocentrism, Lowell faced the conscious limits imposed by Victorian reticence, by a sense of social responsibility, and by the simpler fear of alienating subscribers. Magazines have always been more vulnerable and therefore more sensitive to public displeasure than books, and Lowell's was no exception. First, while most books were bought and read by an individual, general magazines like the *Atlantic* were considered "family reading." In the middle-class nineteenth-century American family there was a wide discrepancy between what was deemed appropriate for men and women and younger folk. Second, magazine subscribers have on-going control over their purchase and can choose to terminate at any point. This gives them a sense of proprietary power, and many will write letters to the editor criticizing a decision while they would not think of complaining to a publisher or author of a book. For these reasons *Harper's* and most other major monthlies of the time carried no political editorials and carefully avoided religious controversy. But if Lowell's *Atlantic*, like that of his successors, was far from immune to public pressure, its range of intellectual tolerance was broadened by its elitist Emersonian belief that truth is often articulated by individuals or minorities opposed to the conventions accepted by the majority.

Emerson himself, who gave the magazine some of its initial intellectual breadth, was widely admired in some circles but still highly controversial in others. Socially and financially powerful conservatives not only parodied his vatic utterances like "Brahma" but considered his individualism socially disruptive. The religiously orthodox, a powerful and vocal group, considered him a subverter of faith.

Holmes, then in his late forties, was both a more controversial and a more prolific contributor to Lowell's *Atlantic*. Like Lowell, the indefatigably curious doctor lived long enough to be astonished and stung to find himself typed by posterity as a stuffy and conservative advocate of the status quo (Gilman 715). He was similarly dismayed to find the unworldly, "harmless, inoffensive aristocracy" of socially and financially modest teachers and ministers, whom he christened in the *Atlantic* the "Brahmin class," misunderstood as a bloated socioeconomic elite who used culture as a weapon of snobbery (Brooks, *Flowering* 493). Holmes himself was neither modest nor unworldly; neither was he a smug, versifying celebrant of social convention and the intellectual status quo. In medicine, he significantly advanced understanding of puerperal fever, saving an unknowable number of lives, and he anticipated many later developments in psychology. In literature, like Lowell, he gave frank criticism, generous personal attention, and practical professional guidance to many younger writers, including later *Atlantic* editors Aldrich and particularly Howells. Harriet Stowe, who met him at a dinner for *Atlantic* authors, found in him, despite their extreme difference in ideology, "the most valuable friendship of her life" (F. Wilson 439). The well-traveled Henry James, Sr., pronounced Holmes without a peer for sheer intellectual vitality. And the iconoclastic Emerson admiringly credited Holmes's *Atlantic* writings with monthly throwing "buckets of Greek fire against acres of paunch and bottom" and threatening to "throw out of employment all the dunces, . . . all the respectabilities and professional learning of the time" (*Journals* 9: 227).

Holmes was not profound, but he was provocative. His essays, poetry, and novels made readers observe afresh and challenge unexamined convictions. Almost all of his literary work was first published in the *Atlantic* from 1857 until near his death in 1894, the best during the first ten years. In the fifties and sixties particularly, the Doctor's voice in the *Atlantic* carried on the tradition of enlightenment rationalism. In the witty personae of the Autocrat and the Professor, he satirized myriad small, pious self-delusions and modeled a healthy frankness with ourselves and with others. He also condemned the more serious inhumanities committed in the name of moral or religious orthodoxies. In his "medicated novels" particularly, he attempted to demonstrate the classical liberal idea that the moral will of individuals is sometimes determined by environment and heredity and that transgressors may merit sympathy and assistance rather than condemnation. Interpreters have found in these works significant anticipations of not only the psychology of Freud and Jung but also the ideas of Darwin and Marx (Brooks, *Flowering* 498, and Oberndorf 1–19).

Holmes's best shafts were reserved for the stringent Calvinism with which he had grown up and which was still potent in antebellum America. In the second issue of the *Atlantic*, he initiated a frontal attack, asserting that Calvinist dogma and the Puritanical repression of instinct were bound to cause neurosis in the healthy mind: "Any person ought to go mad, if he really holds such and such beliefs.... Anything that is brutal, cruel, heathenish, that makes life hopeless for the majority of mankind and perhaps for entire races—anything that assumes the necessity of extermination of instincts which were given to be regulated ..., if received, ought to produce insanity in every well-regulated mind" ("Autocrat," Dec. 1857, 181). Holmes subsequently attacked the inhuman logic of Calvinism and celebrated its subversion in every form from the scholarly monograph to the amusing satire "Deacon's Masterpiece; or, The Wonderful One Hoss Shay."

It was soon clear that many of Holmes's shafts scored hits. Harriet Beecher Stowe, who was very familiar with orthodox circles, observed that "Dr. Holmes has stung and irritated them by his sharp, scathing irony and keen ridicule" (F. Wilson 530–31). The orthodox struck back, belaboring Holmes and the *Atlantic* both from the pulpit and in the evangelical press "almost without intermission" during Lowell's editorship (Holmes to J. L. Motley, 16 Feb. 1861, in Morse 2: 156).

Throughout the long fray, Lowell not only supported Holmes but welcomed him to continue submitting theological dogma to humanistic reason. On reading one contribution, he warned: "The religious press (a true sour-cider press with bellyache privileges attached) will be at you, but after smashing one of them you will be able to furnish yourself with a Samson's weapon for the rest of the Philisteri" (19 Dec. 1858, *Letters* 1: 289). Holmes persisted; so did the theological bellyaching. Phillips was concerned and cautioned Lowell to avoid unnecessarily provoking religious controversy. This sensitivity prevailed when Thoreau's narrative of life in the Maine woods was being prepared for publication in the spring of 1859.

Although Lowell thought Thoreau a self-advertising, romantic egotist, he nevertheless had several times encouraged Emerson to ask Thoreau for contributions to the *Atlantic*. Thoreau had responded by sending "Chesuncook," "the subjects of which," he wrote, "are the Moose, the Pine tree, and the Indian" (to Lowell, 23 Jan. 1858, *Correspondence* 504). Lowell accepted the piece as a three-part series. Among the casualties of the editorial vermilion pencil, however, was a sentence of pantheistic homage to the pine tree that read: "It is as immortal as I am, and perchance will go to as high a heaven, there to tower above me still" (*Maine Woods* 122). Thoreau, meticulous with his proof as with everything important to him, noticed the deletion and indicated that he wanted the passage retained. But on scanning the July *Atlantic*, he discovered that this notation had not been honored.

With characteristically icy indignation, Thoreau wrote Lowell:

> I have just noticed that that sentence was, in a very mean and cowardly manner, omitted. I hardly need to say that this is a liberty which I will not permit to be taken with my MS.... I do not ask anybody to adopt my opinions, but I do expect that when they ask for them to print, they will print them, or obtain my consent to their alteration or omission....
>
> I am not willing to be associated in any way, unnecessarily, with parties who will confess themselves so bigoted and timid as this implies. I could excuse a man who was afraid of an uplifted fist, but if one habitually manifests fear at the utterance of a sincere thought, I must think that his life is a kind of nightmare continued in broad daylight. It is hard to conceive of one so completely derivative. Is this the avowed character of the Atlantic Monthly? I should like an early reply. (22 June 1858, *Correspondence* 515–16)

No reply by Lowell exists; no notice of the omission appeared in the August *Atlantic* as Thoreau had requested, and he was made to wait several months for payment. Probably the failure to honor Thoreau's notation was a conscious act on Lowell's part. Certainly his handling of the aftermath was shabby. The incident shows Lowell at his worst—high-handed and subject to personal pique. The quarrel with Thoreau also shows that Lowell and Phillips were reluctant, as later editors and publishers would be, to engage too often in religious controversy. Still, the welcome Lowell gave to theological radicals associated with transcendentalism and social reform such as Emerson, David Wasson, Theodore Parker, James Freeman Clarke, and T. W. Higginson, as well as the sallies of Holmes, continued to identify the *Atlantic* in the public mind and the religious press as an exponent of a liberal humanism that many felt was overtly antagonistic to orthodox religion.

Lowell's liberal humanism, the range of his interests, and his general willingness to support intellectual speculation even when it challenged religious orthodoxy were demonstrated in his treatment of science in the early *Atlantic*. Science had not yet been added to literature, art, and politics in the magazine's subtitle, but Lowell covered that branch of human inquiry more thoroughly than most of his successors did. Humanistic naturalism, precise observations of and reflection on the natural environment, was to become a staple of the *Atlantic* throughout the nineteenth century. Thoreau's "Chesuncook" began the tradition in the *Atlantic*, and in 1860 Lowell accepted an early piece by another young transcendentalist/naturalist, John Burroughs, who with John Muir and others was to continue this tradition for the next fifty years. But Lowell, unlike most subsequent editors, also showed a clear interest in hard science and technology, running articles not only on calculus, precise measurement and meteorology but also on the telegraph, stereoscope, and screw propulsion, articles with a technical sophistication that today would place them in *Scientific American* rather than the *Atlantic*.

At least once, Lowell was forced to admit that the technicality of the article outstripped his own ability to judge it. After publishing D. W. Bloodgood's paper on meteorology as a lead article, Lowell was greeted by a howl of protest from scientists attacking its accuracy. In a published retraction he confessed that the "aesthetic editor" stood convicted of scientific ignorance and was justly sentenced for the next month to eat corncobs and read Sylvanus Cobb or, worse, his own works ("July Reviewed," Sept. 1860, 378–80).

Lowell was not, however, ignorant when he accepted a highly controversial three-part series defending the theories of Darwin by Darwin's earliest American exponent, the Harvard botanist Asa Gray. Lowell knew that Darwin had been challenged by the bishop of Oxford and that the same debate between religion and science was heating up in America, because his uncle J. A. Lowell and his friend Alexander Agassiz, both professors of science at Harvard, had led the American attack against Darwin. Despite these personal connections, Lowell gave a prominent place to Gray's articles, which were both a direct refutation of J. A. Lowell and Agassiz and an unequivocal commitment to Darwin's ideas of evolution and natural selection, although they speculated noncommittally that these ideas might not inevitably exclude a divine plan. Darwin himself was delighted with the *Atlantic* series, thanked Gray profusely, and reprinted the articles in England as a rebuttal to the bishop of Oxford (Dupree 295–96). In his old age, Lowell lamented the impact of Darwinism while admitting it as truth. But as a forty-year-old editor, he clearly supported free intellectual debate on the issue and provided an authoritative platform and large circulation to the most important early American defense of Darwin's ideas.

Lowell's editorial treatment of religion and science demonstrated that the Yankee humanism represented by the early *Atlantic* valued intellectual speculation and tolerance. Within limits quite liberal for the time, it generally upheld the right of individuals to read, reflect, and decide for themselves. In the realm of politics, however, as sectional tensions over slavery were strained past the limit, intellectual tolerance was opposed by the claims of New England conscience. The magazine's political views were liberal and progressive, but the emphasis was on clearly defined moral principle and social responsibility, not intellectual speculation.

In the Yankee humanism that flourished in the 1850s and 1860s, the same ethicism fundamental to literature was fundamental to politics. In the *Atlantic*'s first issue, Lowell had announced that the magazine's political appeal would be to "that moral element which transcends all persons and parties." He and the other founders shared the conviction stated in Emerson's *Atlantic* essay titled "American Civilization" that "the end of all political struggle is to establish morality as the basis of all legislation" (Apr. 1862, 509).

For better or worse, the morality of those who conducted the *Atlantic* was explicitly a product of New England, and the magazine became as much an organ for the export of New England conscience as for New England literary culture. At this time, the moral sense of intellectual New England, influenced by liberal Christianity and the still-recent fervors of transcendentalism, placed human rights unequivocally above property rights, and the obligation to act on conscience above law and even social stability. Many of those most closely associated with the *Atlantic*—Lowell, Underwood, Whittier, and Stowe among others—had long belonged to the Anti-Slavery League of New England. In spite of the initial declaration that the magazine would "rank itself with no sect of antis," Lowell and others clearly meant it to take a forceful, principled stand against slavery and political compromise with the South.

Underwood's original motive in initiating the magazine had been "to give the active support of letters to the anti-slavery cause" (48). After perusing the second issue of the *Atlantic*, George William Bagby, editor of the *Southern Literary Messenger*, decided that it was succeeding all too handsomely. "This magazine has appeared before the world," he wrote, "challenging the patronage of all lovers of polite learning by articles of the highest excellence in point of style and sentiment . . . all enlisted in making attractive a work the object of which is to wage war on Southern society" (472).

The *Messenger*'s editor had not exaggerated greatly. The article that prompted his lament—"Where Will It End?"—was written by Lowell's radical abolitionist friend Edmund Quincy in response to the recent Dred Scott decision and combined a virulent sectional antagonism with a high moral appeal to conscience over law. Quincy, positing the moral and cultural superiority of the North, had characterized the southern leadership as "an oligarchy as despicable as it is detestable." Northerners, he insisted, should practice civil disobedience rather than submit to federal laws perpetrated by a political entity so barbaric and morally corrupt. "That the intelligent and civilized portion of a race should consent to the sway of their illiterate and barbarian companions in the commonwealth . . . is an astonishment that should be a hissing to all beholders everywhere" (Dec. 1857, 242). This and subsequent pieces demonstrated that the *Atlantic* stood solidly against any compromise with "the slave power," was morally contemptuous of the South, encouraged its readers to disobey the fugitive slave laws, and encouraged its writers to express their opposition in strong language.

Parke Godwin, while still chief political contributor, devoted all but one of his series to condemning the extension of slavery into the territories. His articles were forthrightly critical of the floundering Buchanan administration's concessions to the South. Lowell, however, had felt them too moderate. In his letter of apology for his zealous additions to Godwin's essay, he wrote that the magazine must be "aggressive to make an impression" (Duberman 175).

After Godwin's resignation, Lowell undertook to write the *Atlantic*'s political commentaries himself. One result was that these articles soon began to appear sporadically rather than monthly. But when they did appear, they were appropriately aggressive and bore the same tone of militancy as the antislavery journalism he had written in his mid-twenties. Aware that the *Atlantic* could exercise considerable political influence within New England and relatively little outside, Lowell selected local targets and named names in his initial attacks: the Boston-based American Tract Society and Massachusetts "compromise Democrats" such as Caleb Cushing. The basis of his argument was both justice for the enslaved black and the prevention of an insidious moral rot in the nation as a whole, in both its institutions and its individual citizens. Slavery if unchecked would corrupt the entire American body politic, North as well as South. The victims whom slavery degraded to less than human were both black and white. Evidence that this degradation had already gone far was apparent in the hypocritical compromise of the northern Democrats and the Buchanan administration, who set expediency and prosperity above conscience and sought to hold the nation together with "quack cement" and to establish its politics on the quicksand of complicated and empty legalities, rather than the granite foundations of moral principle, humanity, and justice.

After writing three militant articles in late 1858, Lowell found himself unable to continue them on a regular basis, despite the encouragement of Phillips and of Emerson, who termed them brilliant. Between December 1858 and September 1860 the *Atlantic* was without a strong and consistent voice on political issues. The crucial presidential election of 1860, however, brought Lowell back into the arena. The Republican party, formed in 1854, had seemed to him too moderate in endorsing only nonextension of slavery rather than outright abolition. But he had found in it the only genuine hope of politically countering the powerful "southern oligarchy." Now that hope seemed about to be realized. "This election," he wrote more prophetically than he knew, "is a turning point in our history" ("The Election in November," Oct. 1860, 494). It would answer a permanent yes or no to the corruption of American moral and political principles. The election of Douglas or Breckenridge would mean "that labor has no rights which Capital is bound to respect— that there is no higher law than human interest and cupidity" (493). Lowell admitted that he had originally supported the more radical Seward for the Republican nomination, but he now praised Lincoln as a moderate who would check slavery in the territories without inflammatory attempts to abolish it in the Deep South, where it was already becoming economically unprofitable and would die a natural death. As for the recurrent southern threat of disunion, he felt now, as he had two years ago, that it was "an old scarecrow," the tantrum of a spoiled child.

As secession rapidly turned from threat to reality after Lincoln's election, the *Atlantic* published a series of commentaries by Lowell condemning the Buchanan administration's appeasement of "the treason against the ballot box." "We do not," he wrote in January 1861, "underestimate the gravity of the present crisis and we agree that nothing should be done to exasperate it; but if the people of the Free States have been taught anything by the repeated lessons of bitter experience, it has been that submission is not the seed of conciliation, but of contempt and encroachment" ("The Question of the Hour" 120). In June 1861, Lowell criticized Lincoln's March inaugural address as a futile gesture at conciliation and his initial hesitance to use full force against the rebels for fear of alienating the undecided border states as a harmful delay. Now that the president had begun acting with necessary decisiveness, however, he foresaw rapid victory for the Union and "a radical change in the system of African slavery" ("The Pickens and Stealin's Rebellion" 763).

Lowell's article of June 1861 was his last as editor of the *Atlantic*. Moses Phillips, who had liberally underwritten the magazine during its first two years and established it on a reasonably sound financial basis, had died suddenly in August 1859 at the age of forty-six. His older partner, Sampson, died soon after, and the assets of the publishing house, including the *Atlantic*, were to be sold. In the fall of 1859, the continuance of the magazine seemed in doubt, although Lowell claimed that it was now a paying venture and felt confident that it would be sustained in some form.

Accounts of the sale and the degree of interest shown by publishers vary considerably. Lowell's biographer, Horace Scudder, himself a later editor of the *Atlantic*, claims that there was a "lively competition among publishers" and even a rumor that *Harper's* wished to buy it to bury it (*Lowell* 1: 450). But as the Boston lawyer Alexander Rice, Phillips and Sampson's assignee, later told the story, he had received not a single bid by the morning of the deadline date in October 1859, although he had notified twelve publishers of the sale. Hoping at the last minute to interest at least one buyer, he strolled from his Beacon Street offices over to the Old Corner Bookstore on School Street, the offices of Ticknor and Fields. James Fields, the younger partner of the house, was in Europe, but William Ticknor was in, and Rice, mentioning nothing about the lack of bids, set about trying to convince him that the *Atlantic* not only would bring prestige to the house but was a profitable property in its own right. Ticknor remained uneager. Confident, however, that his bid would not take the field, he obligingly scribbled a figure, sealed it, and bid Rice good day. Rice, according to his story, returned to his offices and at the ring of twelve unsealed the single bid—$10,000. When he returned to congratulate the surprised Ticknor on his purchase, the publisher's first response was, "Pray let no one know what I bid, for my friends would think me crazy" (Perry, "Editor" 716).

Rice's story was not entirely accurate; there had been at least one other bid. Francis Underwood, the man who had originally conceived the *Atlantic*, had rallied financial support among a group of friends loyal to himself and to Lowell. Although Lowell had not encouraged the idea, Underwood was enthusiastic at the prospect of establishing the magazine as an independent entity, responsible not to a publisher but only to those who loved literature for its own sake. Immediately after the sale was announced, however, he wrote disappointedly to the magazine's proofreader, George Nichols: "Ticknor and Fields have it. . . . The new arrangement will probably leave me out of a place" (Oct. 1859).

Underwood's supposition that he would be cut out was correct; he was replaced as assistant editor by Ticknor's son Howard. Through his political affiliations, Underwood soon gained a place as clerk of the superior court and later as consul to Glasgow. But the rest of his life seemed to him a rather bitter decline. His *Atlantic* acquaintances—especially Lowell, Whittier, and Holmes—continued to treat him with a friendly kindness, not unmixed with pity, and he spent much of his later life writing adulatory biographies of them and remembering earlier and happier days.

Lowell confided to Norton that he was privately glad to see the magazine "in the hands of a practical publisher," rather than a group of amateur enthusiasts, "for we should be in danger of running aground." But he also expressed uncertainty about his own position:

> As friend to friend, I may say that I think it just the best arrangement possible, though I did not like to say so beforehand too plainly. I did not wish in any way to stand in [Underwood's] light, but it is much better as it is. Whether T[icknor] will want *me* or not, is another question. I suppose that he will think that Fields will make a good editor, beside saving the salary, and F. may think so too. In certain respects he would, as the dining editor for example, to look after authors when they came to Boston and the like. I shall be quite satisfied, anyhow,—though the salary is a convenience, for I have done nothing to advance my own private interest in the matter. (Oct. 1859, Scudder, *Lowell* 1: 450–51)

Lowell was genuinely of divided mind about retaining the editorship. The prospect of having more time for his own study and writing was attractive, but he did exert some influence, at least indirectly, to keep his job. Apparently Lowell had asked Emerson, who was just then transferring his own important account to Ticknor and Fields, to persuade the magazine's new publishers that a continuity was needed, for the moment anyway, both in the *Atlantic*'s editorial policy and in its editorship. On finding that continuity assured, partly through Emerson's influence, he wrote the latter: "My heartiest thanks. I saw Ticknor yesterday and he says he wants the Mag. to go on as it has gone on" (Oct. 21, 1859, J. R. Lowell papers).

The *Atlantic* did go on through the cataclysmic year 1860 approximately as before. But despite a relatively amicable working relationship between Lowell and his publishers, there were unresolved tensions. On his return from Europe, Fields, whom Lowell accurately estimated to be the dominant partner, began contributing to the magazine himself and supervising it rather more closely than Phillips had done. His ideas on what should go into it did not always coincide with Lowell's, and on such occasions Lowell chafed a bit. A letter that Lowell wrote to Fields in June 1860 suggests that the editor was not so concerned about retaining his position as to be timid about avoiding conflict with his publisher and supporting his personal standards:

> Cambridge,
> St. Headache, 1860
>
> My Dear Fields,
> ... Mr. Nichols tells me that you sighed a little over heavy articles and instanced that on Roger Bacon. All Ham connection is at a discount in these secession days—but I think you are wrong—not merely about that article which seemed to me as interesting as it was thorough—but on the general question.... If we make our Mag. merely entertaining, how are we better than those Scribes and Pharisees the Harper's? We want to make it interesting to as many classes of people as we can, especially to such as give tone to public opinion in literary [matters], if there be any such in America. (*New Letters* 99)

Fields's impatience to take his own turn at the *Atlantic* helm became increasingly apparent over the next year, and in May 1861 Lowell, seeing the handwriting on the wall, submitted a characteristically frank and good-natured letter of resignation:

> My Dear Fields,
> I wish you all joy of your worm.... I was going to say I was glad to be rid of my old man of the sea. But I don't believe I am. I doubt if we see the finger of Providence so readily in the stoppage of a salary as in its beginning or increment. A bore, moreover, that is periodical gets a friendly face at last and we miss it on the whole....
> Well, good-by, delusive royalty! I abdicate with what grace I may. I lay aside my paper crown and feather sceptre....
> You will be surprised before long to find how easily you get on without me, and wonder that you ever thought me a necessity. It is amazing how quickly the waters close over one. He carries down with him the memory of his splash and struggle, and fancies it is still going on when the last bubble even has burst long ago. Good-by. Nature is equable. I have lost the *Atlantic*, but my cow has calved as if nothing had happened. (23 May 1861, *Letters* 1: 310)

Lowell had always felt some ambiguity about his editorship. If he had, at times, genuinely enjoyed wearing the paper crown of literary authority and felt some satisfaction in wielding the feather scepter on behalf of literary merit and political morality as he conceived them, he had also been restless under the burden of editorial duties and felt that they dissipated his creative powers. At any rate, the separation was friendly enough. Lowell, involuntarily freed to the muses, continued contributing regularly to the *Atlantic* throughout Fields's editorship—now mainly poetry rather than essays and reviews as before.

T. W. Higginson, later arguing Fields's superiority to Lowell as an editor, wrote, "It is my impression that [the *Atlantic*] would have died under Lowell from his want of method and business habit; and it certainly took great start in Fields' hands" (letter to Horace Scudder, Dec. 1876, attached to inside front cover of the copy of Scudder's *Index to the Atlantic Monthly* held by the Boston Athenaeum). Perhaps Lowell's replacement was fortunate for the growth of the magazine; there were indications that neither its circulation nor his inclination to expand its circle of writers had increased much during his last two years. Still, his contribution as the *Atlantic*'s first editor had been decisive in establishing the character of the magazine, which later editors and cultural conditions would modify but not fundamentally change until after the turn of the twentieth century.

Lowell had, with the help of Phillips's capital and a loose network of distinguished literary acquaintances from the Boston area, established the *Atlantic* as the leading American general literary and intellectual magazine of the time. He had given it a cultural authority that came not from narrow prescriptions but from the quality of the material it published, a quality acknowledged even by those who defensively resented the magazine's regionalism. While giving regular national exposure mainly to writers of the New England renaissance, Lowell's *Atlantic* spoke for an explicitly American culture and literature reflecting American values and conditions. In his reviews, editorial advice, and selection, Lowell had encouraged the development of a regional realism. Much of this indigenous early realism was written by and about women, and some of it consciously challenged the conventional values of popular literary romance. While sometimes inefficient or insensitive to the rights of contributors, Lowell was more often generously encouraging to authors both old and young. He was not active in soliciting new work, but he often gave extraordinary personal attention to younger literary aspirants who sought him out, particularly if they came, like Howells, from beyond the Boston circle.

If Lowell's *Atlantic* did not overthrow certain Victorian aesthetic and ethical decorums and, in Thoreau's case, flinched from religious controversy, it was conspicuously ahead of most contemporary magazines in its encouragement of intellectual speculation and debate. This debate included humanistic and scientific challenges to religious orthodoxy that angered many. Lowell also deserves credit for the magazine's engagement in political and social issues and for the unusual radical decisiveness of its political stand. That stand against compromise with slavery, often articulated by Lowell himself, gave credence to the magazine's profession that politics should be founded on moral principle. Lowell had, in short, established the *Atlantic* as an eminent exponent of a liberal Yankee humanism that remained, despite some later conservative reactions to American social and cultural transformations, fundamental to its tradition and character.

James T. Fields, publisher of the *Atlantic* and its editor, 1861–1871. By permission of the Boston Athenaeum.

3
James T. Fields
(1 8 6 1 – 1 8 7 1)

The Publisher as Editor

James Thomas Fields came to the *Atlantic* editorship through quite a different route than Lowell. Lowell had been born a Cambridge Brahmin in Holmes's original sense, a descendant of a line of New England scholars, judges, and ministers. Fields had come to Boston at thirteen as a poor apprentice bookstore clerk from the provinces. His subsequent rapid rise, like that of his successor Howells, demonstrated that the mid-nineteenth-century Boston cultural elite was far less a hereditary class than a meritocracy with diverse routes of access. While Lowell had come to the editorship mainly as a poet, critic, and scholar, Fields, although he had once aspired to being a poet, continued to write, and genuinely loved literature, came to it mainly as a publisher and man of business.

Both contemporaries and later critics have been divided in judging Fields's influence on Boston literary culture, and specifically on the *Atlantic* in his dual role as editor and publisher. He has been accused both then and now of allowing mercenary motives and promotion too much influence over editorial policy, particularly in arranging favorable reviews of his firm's books, favoring light literature over more serious work, intellectually diluting the magazine's contents, and creating the first promotional literary celebrity system. Martin Green has said that for all his genial good fellowship and sympathy with authors, Fields was in a basic sense a fraud who profited by bloating the reputations of the New England authors beyond their worth, thereby not only misleading the public but preventing a healthy mutual or self-criticism among the writers themselves (115–18).

Those authors, however, while generally viewing Fields's promotions with irony, were genuinely grateful, as Lowell had written to Norton, to have their books and the *Atlantic* placed in a stable, well-capitalized publishing house conducted by a practical man of business sympathetic to literature. Many agreed with Emerson when he called Fields "the guardian and maintainer of us all" (Tryon 323). Most found Fields very fair, even liberal in his financial dealings, active in searching for both new markets and new writers, sympathetic as an audience, appreciative and reasonably discriminating in his literary taste, and an engaging social companion. Fields shared their optimism, encouraged by both profit and principle, that good literature could become widely popular and that they and the *Atlantic* could play an important role in spreading literate culture and New England values across America. Several subsequent commentators have confirmed that Fields, his publishing house, and his *Atlantic* not only were central to the development of the New England literary movement in its golden age but contributed importantly to the development of new audiences for literature and to establishing the profession of authorship in America (Austin 17, Tomsich 20, Tryon 167).

Fields's editorial record at the *Atlantic* indicates some truth in both judgments. On balance, however, he not only was a more effective editor than Lowell but also added breadth and liveliness to the magazine. He had replaced Lowell both to save the salary and because he felt Lowell's tastes were often too esoteric. From the beginning, he intended to popularize the magazine moderately, promote it, and seek a somewhat broader audience. In some cases, this popularization was intellectually corrupting, especially in reviews and fiction. But other forms of popularization such as the increase in reportage and attention to women's issues were a generally healthy redress to the magazine's scholarly tendencies and represented useful attempts to bridge the gap between highbrow and middlebrow culture.

Fields, however, did not change the *Atlantic* radically—nor did he wish to do so. His publishing career had been built on the premise that writing of a high quality could sell, and he had a convert's respect for the Boston culture that had shaped his own tastes. The magazine's value to his firm lay in its reputation for literary excellence rather than any prospect of mass circulation. While he personally lacked some of Lowell's idealism, his *Atlantic* continued to embody the same New England culture and to advocate the same essential liberal Yankee humanism as Lowell's.

Fields was born in 1817, the son of a Portsmouth, New Hampshire, sea captain who was lost at sea when Fields was three. The family was impoverished, and Fields was apprenticed at thirteen, through the kind offices of a relative, to Messrs Carter and Hendee, proprietors of the Old Corner Bookstore on Tremont and School streets in Boston. Fields had attended school in Portsmouth but was largely self-educated. Through long nights of reading and discussion at the Boston Mercantile Library after long days of work, he had developed a love of literature and a taste for literary quality. Equally important, his days as a clerk at the Old Corner Bookstore had made him a shrewd judge of literature as a commodity. He had gained a reputation among his fellows for being able to predict not only what books would sell but even what book each customer entering the store would buy.

As a young man, Fields had felt that he might himself be destined for the revered profession of authorship, and he had produced literary essays and sentimental, occasional verse that were sometimes printed in the Boston newspapers. Throughout his career he continued to write poetry, discursive essays, and anecdotal recollections of his relationships with authors. Maturity, however, and his rising business fortunes convinced him that his literary talent was minor and that his contributions to literature and contact with writers would be made mainly as a publisher.

Intelligent, handsome, good-humored, and efficient, he rapidly made himself indispensable to the firm, and when it was purchased by William D. Ticknor in 1834, he was retained as a valuable asset. During the next two decades, Fields not only rose to full partnership with Ticknor but took a decisive part in developing the business from a small, eclectic retail operation to a major publishing house with a highly distinguished list of English and particularly American authors. He believed that a large potential market existed in America for good writing by Americans and made it a policy of his firm to discover, encourage, and publish the best. By 1861, when Fields became editor of the *Atlantic*, the firm's American list included Emerson, Longfellow, Lowell, Hawthorne, Whittier, Bayard Taylor, Charles Sumner, Thoreau, Julia Ward Howe, Paul Hayne, Richard Stoddard, E. C. Stedman, and Harriet Stowe. The English list offered, among others, Tennyson, Browning, Barry Cornwall, Leigh Hunt, Charles Kingsley, Thackeray, Thomas DeQuincey (whose complete works Fields himself was the first to collect and edit), Arnold, Charles Reade, Coventry Patmore, and Owen Meredith.

These authors were drawn to Ticknor and Fields because the firm had carefully built and consciously nurtured a reputation as liberal and effective publishers of first-rate literature who treated their authors well. An international copyright law was not established until 1890, and during the mid-nineteenth century English writing was habitually pirated by American publishers, who paid the authors nothing. Ticknor and Fields, however, won the allegiance of many English authors by giving them 10 percent. Browning had gratefully saluted Fields as "more righteous than the Law" (qtd. in Austin 400). With his American authors also, Fields had a reputation for liberality; Lowell and Hawthorne even protested occasionally that they were overpaid. Furthermore, once Fields had accepted a book, he generally took pains to assure it the widest possible distribution through his nationwide contacts with booksellers and to publicize it by placing both advertisements and sympathetic reviews in a carefully selected network of newspapers. He was one of the first American publishers to recognize the potential of systematic promotion, which he used to benefit both his authors and himself.

Beyond his efficiency and imagination in business and his reputation for liberality, Fields was personally charming. Large, handsome, hearty, and sanguine, he was, in the words of his biographer, the "total extrovert" (Tryon 97). With his attractive younger wife, Annie, he turned his Charles Street home into a salon that long remained the social center of literary Boston. He loved literary talk and was an amusing anecdotalist as well as an appreciative and responsive listener. Lowell had pegged him, accurately if disparagingly, as the consummate "dining editor."

To many authors Fields was not only an entertaining and attentive host but a solicitous friend. Writers prone to self-doubt and melancholy—as many of the species were then as now—seemed particularly drawn to Fields's healthy and sociable high spirits. Several, and among them established authors as well as young aspirants, seemed to depend on his advice and reassurance to bolster their confidence. To Longfellow, Fields served not only as publisher and business manager but also as a close companion of long walks, vacations, and travels. In 1849, Fields had sought out Hawthorne in his Salem solitude and cajoled the reluctant author into revealing the manuscript of a long short story titled "The Scarlet Letter." The publisher's friendly enthusiasm and certainty that it would sell if expanded to a novel helped to induce Hawthorne to complete this work, one that immediately established his reputation. Thereafter, Hawthorne not only relied heavily (perhaps too heavily) on Fields's judgment as a publisher but also relied on his support as a personal friend, though one whose enthusiasm and compliments he often took at a steep discount.

For all of Fields's accomplishments and his humane good nature, there was in his relationship to literature and to authors an admixture of the entrepreneurial spirit that influenced his conduct of the *Atlantic*. His literary judgments were almost always circumscribed by a sense of what could sell widely enough to be remunerative. He was a successful publisher partly because his literary instincts were sympathetic with those of a sizable public. Although his tastes had a reasonable range, he had a personal and professional preference for light fiction, an agreeable, sociable literature that was not depressing, harsh, or overly critical.

Fields's treatment of literature as a commercial product was perhaps clearest and most corrupting in his attitude toward literary criticism. Especially in his early years as a publisher, he systematically used reviews, some of which he wrote himself, some of which he hired others to write, as a means of advertising. "All is well," he had written a friend, "the pills are puffed, and pills thus puffed will sell" (Tryon 85). He shared the opinion of most publishers of the day that the main use of reviewing was the manufacture of reputations and the sale of books.

In Fields's relationships with authors also there was a good deal of puffing. Even T. W. Higginson, who admired him, found him "a bit of a flatterer" (*Cheerful Yesterdays* 187). This flattery of authors was not entirely a deliberate business manner but seemed natural to Fields. Even in his friendships there was an element of adulation, a note of self-conscious amazement at finding himself admitted to intimate terms with great literary figures, which precluded criticism or objective assessment. He loved to act both as a source and as a conduit for compliments; more than anyone, Fields earned the Boston literary circle a reputation as a smug mutual admiration society. He was also more responsible than anyone else for promoting the "cult of New England letters," the public perception of a close-knit celebrity circle of "Atlantic authors," and for apotheosizing these authors as the Olympians of American literature. His house on Charles Street became not only a literary salon but a shrine hung with relics of the great figures, before which the visitor was expected to be properly worshipful—as indeed Fields was himself beneath all his hearty, confident good fellowship.

Fields, then, was essentially a publisher, and a resourceful one. Although he found a place at the center of the Boston literary world and exerted a powerful influence on it, he was a self-made provincial entrepreneur. He shared the Boston vision of a national high culture implicit in the founding of the *Atlantic* but was motivated more directly by profit and prestige, less by personal idealism, than were Lowell and others. While he assiduously and effectively promoted New England leadership in American letters, he did little to encourage the intellectual integrity, the vigorous idealism, the self-critical temperament, the moral individualism, and the strong sense of social responsibility which for thirty years had justified that leadership.

But despite Fields's personal lack of idealism, these New England values remained relatively strong during the 1860s with their turmoil and test of moral fiber. And Fields, through his publishing house and his *Atlantic*, did as much as anyone to ensure their wide distribution and influence. He also did as much as any American to make authorship a profession that was both respected and also financially feasible. In the words of his biographer, "He was at once the patron of letters and the huckster of the product. . . . He set out to manufacture reputations shamelessly and to make money. He ended by setting American literature on its feet and providing the reading public with the finest writing in the English language" (Tryon 167).

It was a sign of Fields's astuteness as a publisher that the transition between Lowell's editorship and his own was virtually imperceptible to readers of the magazine. Changes occurred, but they were subtle and were introduced gradually. While Fields was ambitious to expand circulation, he was fully aware that the magazine's essential appeal, the quality that differentiated it from others, and much of its advertising value for his firm lay in its reputation as an organ of American high culture. Sudden attempts to dilute its intellectual and literary standards in order to broaden its readership would be resented by many of its present readers. For these reasons, the changing of the editorial guard at the *Atlantic* has always, at least publicly, emphasized continuity rather than change.

Fields's essential editorial strategies were threefold. First, he intended to build on the magazine's established reputation as the forum for New England's major writers. This he would do by maintaining, expanding, and publicizing a circle of "Atlantic authors" identified exclusively with the magazine. Second, he would actively scout, or have his assistants scout, for new writers who might be tested on the public and brought to the firm through the magazine. Third, through editorial selection and guidance to authors, he would moderately lighten the magazine's tone, broaden its appeal, and thus increase its direct profitability. The first two activities were to receive high visibility; the third was to be accomplished without fanfare.

Fields and his elder partner Ticknor had profited from the principle that good literature properly publicized could be good business and had expended considerable effort to identify the house with the names of the best American and English authors. Fields intended to maintain the magazine on the same principle. To this end, he took pains to sustain and promote a central circle of well-known writers and to fix them in the public mind as "*Atlantic* authors." This task was relatively easy, since he had inherited such a group from Lowell, including, besides Lowell himself, Emerson, Higginson, Holmes, Longfellow, Stowe, and Whittier.

Creating the *Atlantic* circle was made easier still by the fact that after the collapse of Phillips and Sampson, Ticknor and Fields were the publishers for most of the important writers in New England, as well as many beyond its pale. The "courtesy of the trade," strong during Fields's time, though it gradually waned through the rest of the century, mandated that publishers would not initiate bidding wars to lure authors already attached to another publisher unless the author voluntarily showed an inclination to change. This protocol did not specifically extend to magazine solicitations, but since magazines were often feeders for publishing houses, editors of magazines attached to publishing houses, like the *Atlantic* and *Harper's*, were inhibited from soliciting authors strongly associated with magazines published by other houses lest they be considered raiding. This arrangement gave the *Atlantic* a clear sphere of influence over Ticknor and Fields authors. With several, Fields also negotiated for exclusive magazine publication.

Fields's most important addition to the group of regular *Atlantic* contributors was Hawthorne. In 1857, Fields had written Hawthorne advising him, as a friend and business manager, that there could be no profit in contributing to Phillips and Sampson's new monthly. In 1859, however, Fields wrote the author in England announcing his own firm's purchase of the *Atlantic* and asking for a contribution. Hawthorne replied with wry amusement: "I cannot but admire your wishing me to write for it, after all your friendly advice to the contrary. However, I will—that is, after I get home" (17 Nov. 1859, Austin 210). As a result, fourteen pieces by Hawthorne appeared in the *Atlantic* during Fields's editorship, including a series drawn from the novelist's notebooks after his death in 1864.

In addition to recruiting Hawthorne, Fields won back Thoreau and published seven of his essays, several posthumously, between 1861 and 1864. Furthermore, in his attempt to moderately popularize the magazine, he added to the *Atlantic* regulars a group of essayists who represented the best of a new, more brisk and topical style of professional magazine journalism, including James Parton and Gail Hamilton (pseudonym of Mary Abigail Dodge).

Fields, then, not only retained the magazine's old inner circle but added two major trophies and some smaller game to it. His systematic efforts to identify these writers exclusively with the *Atlantic* were usually successful, especially during the early period of his editorship. In addition to trade protocol, regional identity, and personal cajolery, Fields gained these exclusive rights through a combination of financial incentives, effective publicity, and a paucity of serious competition.

Fields maintained a reputation, generally if not always deserved, for paying well, relative to the rates offered by other magazines. The *Atlantic*'s prewar rates for prose had been between $5 and $10 per page, depending on the fame of the author. To compensate for the rapid wartime inflation, in 1863 Fields raised this continuum to between $5 and $15 or even $20 per page, the top of the scale reserved for a few writers such as Hawthorne, Holmes, and Parton. If a particularly valued author such as Stowe suggested that he or she was tempted by other offers, Fields would pay a premium for exclusivity to the *Atlantic*. Fiction was paid at a slightly higher rate than essays, and by 1866 relative unknowns were receiving $100 for a ten- to fifteen-page story, while more influential names, such as Stowe, drew $200 or more. Similarly, the prewar rate for poetry, between $10 and $50, was gradually raised to between $25 and $100, while Longfellow regularly received $150 for his poems (Mott 3: 13; Tryon 265).

Fields augmented his reputation as a fair paymaster by instituting the practice, unusual at the time, of paying on acceptance rather than on publication. He also earned the gratitude of several authors, usually impoverished young women, by even paying in advance in cases of particular need. For regular authors, Ticknor and Fields functioned as a bank, maintaining a royalty account against which they could draw or request transfers at their convenience. The firm took every opportunity to ensure that their authors felt liberally treated in financial matters. William Dean Howells later remembered with amusement the ceremony with which $100, not in inflated greenbacks, but in solid gold coin, was impressively counted into his hand in payment for several *Atlantic* poems (*Literary Friends* 33–34).

Throughout his editorship, from 1861 to 1871, Fields managed to hold together most of the core group of authors who gave the *Atlantic* its reputation and much of its substance. But he had considerably more trouble preserving the loyalties after the war than before it. First, the war itself created a rapid inflation, and although the *Atlantic* rates rose, they often did not keep pace. Authors were aware that they were receiving less in real value for their contributions during the late sixties than they had been when the magazine was founded. Furthermore, Hawthorne's widow, Sophia, feeling cheated at being paid less for the novelist's posthumous pieces than her husband had received when he was alive, was encouraged by Gail Hamilton to bring a suit against Fields. Although settled out of court, the suit was widely publicized and damaged the publisher's reputation for generosity.

A still more important challenge to the loyalty of both *Atlantic* writers and readers was the postwar development of several competing magazines. Significantly, all of these magazines were based in New York, which suggested that the center of national literary activity was already beginning to shift away from Boston in the years immediately following the war, a momentum that would soon accelerate.

Since the founding of the *Atlantic*, authors in regions other than New England, particularly New York authors, had felt slighted by its editors. Their alternatives had been limited, but the situation was changing, and competition among "quality" magazines was clearly on the increase during the late sixties. The old *Knickerbocker* had terminated in 1859 after a long decline during which contributors were paid with increasing irregularity. The first series of *Putnam's*, designed to be a high-class New York–based literary magazine, had expired in 1857 after four years of publication. It was briefly resurrected in 1868 under Charles Briggs, E. C. Stedman, and Parke Godwin, then collapsed again in 1870. *Harper's*, in contrast, was increasingly successful, and Fields's moderate popularization of the *Atlantic* placed the two in more direct competition. But *Harper's* still published relatively little American fiction and was felt by some serious writers to be lightweight.

With the establishment of the *Nation*, however, in 1865, New York gained a periodical of considerable intellectual authority. Edited by the English journalist E. L. Godkin and largely supported by Boston shareholders, including Charles Eliot Norton, the *Nation* was founded, like the *Atlantic*, to be an arbiter of high culture and an organ of liberal politics, particularly in the postwar Reconstruction. Although it was issued weekly rather than monthly and carried no prose fiction, it competed with both the *Atlantic* and the *North American Review* for contributors and probably for readers as well. Within a year or two, it had dealt such a blow to the scholarly old *North American* that Fields, whose firm now owned that hoary periodical, was embarrassed that it might die on his doorstep like an old beggar (Tryon 328). Among the *Atlantic* contributors who appeared in the *Nation*'s early numbers were Lowell, Norton, Henry James, Sr., Henry James, Jr., Howells, John Fiske, and Asa Gray. Emerson, apparently like Norton, disappointed with Fields's inclination to follow rather than guide public taste, asserted the *Nation*'s "superiority to any other journal we have or have had" (Mott 3: 338). The *Nation* clearly challenged the *Atlantic*'s standing among the culturally influential, although its intellectual weight and limited circulation (6,000–12,000) prevented it from supplanting Fields's *Atlantic* among the educated general public.

In the same year that the *Nation* was founded, 1865, Fields's junior partner, James Osgood, caught a rumor of another challenge to the *Atlantic*, this one with more popular potential. Thomas Bailey Aldrich, then in New York but later to become an editor of the *Atlantic*, investigated and reported that "this magazine is to be a New York establishment: it is to have on hand the most famous American and English authors (dead or alive) and is expected to dry up the *Atlantic* in about two calendar months" (letter to Osgood, 2 June 1865). This upstart was the *Galaxy*, a literary monthly edited by Williams and Francis Church. In the words of the *Nation*, it was "born of a divine discontent with the *Atlantic Monthly*" on the part of New York (Mott 3: 361). Apparently this discontent was shared by authors in other sections as well. Rebecca Harding Davis, a novelist from Wheeling, West Virginia, then living in Philadelphia, whose first works had been published in the *Atlantic* by Fields, wrote the *Galaxy*'s editors encouraging their creation of "a national magazine in which the current of thought in every section could find expression as thoroughly as that of New England does in the *Atlantic*" (Mott 3: 391). The *Galaxy* began with a circulation of about 6,000 and rose to a peak circulation of about 23,000 by the time of Fields's retirement in 1871. Its average rate of pay was always somewhat lower than the *Atlantic*'s and its payments sometimes uncertain. But if it failed to dry up the *Atlantic*, it did offer an alternative source of publication and a substantial New York audience. Accordingly, it attracted contributions from several important younger authors who before its birth had appeared mainly in the *Atlantic*, including Rebecca Harding Davis, John DeForest, and Henry James.

The *Atlantic*'s competition from New York was clearly increasing. But it was not until the 1870s with the development of the lavishly illustrated *Scribner's* (later the *Century*), *Harper's* new focus on American literature, the aging of the *Atlantic*'s major authors, and the rise of a more professional and independent new generation of authors that the competition became intense and Boston lost ground rapidly to New York. In the 1860s, Boston remained a cultural and publishing center, while Ticknor and Fields and the *Atlantic* continued to exercise a prestige that drew young authors and editors like Fields's successors Howells and Aldrich. Both of these young literary aspirants emigrated from New York to join Ticknor and Fields in 1866, and both felt in Boston an intellectual stimulation absent in New York.

Despite increasing competition, then, the *Atlantic*'s prestige and its inner circle held during Fields's editorship, partly as a result of his exertions. Fields actively promoted the image of his publishing house and magazine as the focal points of that circle. Naturally the successful promotion of this image compounded the existing resentment on the part of less established writers in other sections of the country. In fact, however, although the proportion of contributions from New England remained at about two-thirds, Fields did make a more active effort to attract young writers, often from other regions, than Lowell had. Unlike Lowell, he frequently solicited manuscripts. As a publisher, he had wider contacts with authors beyond Boston, and he used the publishing house as a feeder for the magazine as well as the magazine for the house. He also particularly encouraged his younger assistants on the magazine to cultivate new contributors.

Fields's first assistant on the *Atlantic* was his partner's son, Howard Ticknor, who had been appointed to replace Underwood as Lowell's assistant as soon as Ticknor and Fields took possession of the magazine. Fields had a thinly disguised dislike for Howard Ticknor and a low estimate of his abilities, and he entrusted him with little more than routine correspondence and office work. A second office assistant added in these days was Susan Francis, the first of several women who gave a considerable part of their lives to the *Atlantic* without advancing to positions of major editorial responsibility. Francis, having begun during Fields's time, was still sifting the sludge pile of unsolicited manuscripts for Bliss Perry nearly fifty years later. She shared with Jessie Fremont, wife of John C. Fremont and an acquaintance of Fields's, the credit or blame for calling his attention to a young Californian named Bret Harte, which led to the *Atlantic*'s publication of an early Harte story in 1863 and a disappointing later contract during Harte's triumphal eastern tour in 1870. But throughout her long years at the *Atlantic*, Susan Francis was largely relegated to the task of shucking mountains of oysters while passing the occasional pearl higher up the editorial chain for "discovery."

A far more influential, albeit unofficial, assistant was T. W. Higginson. Although Fields asked him to take over the department of literary reviews, Higginson declined. Apparently he never drew an editorial salary, but he later referred to Fields as "my old boss," and during the early years of Fields's editorship, his influence was substantial. Higginson had contributed frequently during Lowell's time, but his ties with the magazine were greatly strengthened by the succession of Fields, whom he considered both a superior editor and a more congenial man. In July 1861, he had written to his mother: "You ask about the *Atlantic*. Fields will edit it, which is a great thing for the magazine, he having the promptness and business qualities which Lowell signally wanted. . . . Fields' taste is very good and far less crotchety than Lowell's, who strained at gnats and swallowed camels, and Fields is always casting about for good things, while Lowell is rather disposed to sit and let them come" (T. Higginson, *Letters* 111).

During the ten years of Fields's editorship Higginson contributed a prolific total of eighty pieces, including thirty-six essays and stories, a serial novel, and thirty-eight reviews. He also frequently proffered frank and critical editorial advice, to which Fields listened and sometimes responded. Higginson's chief editorial function, however, was to do some of Fields's "casting about for good things." He was to keep an eye open for young writers of ability, solicit manuscripts, review them, and send the best to Fields.

One result of this arrangement was Higginson's 1862 *Atlantic* essay "Letter to a Young Contributor," written at Fields's request. As an early advocate of feminism,

Higginson addressed this open letter to "young ladies" as well as "young gentlemen" and encouraged both to aspire to publication but not to expect it until they had served a disciplined apprenticeship. Shortly after its publication, he wrote to Fields: "Since that 'Letter to a Young Contributor' I have had more wonderful effusions than ever sent me to read with requests for advice, which is hard to give" (Apr. 1862, *Letters* 115).

The most famous of these "effusions" came from thirty-two-year-old Emily Dickinson. Dickinson had read the *Atlantic* regularly since its inception, was familiar with Higginson's work, and considered him a fit judge to tell her whether her work was "alive," whether it "breathed" (15 Apr. 1862, *Letters* 272). Higginson's immediate reply was a sincere but qualified yes: it breathed quite deeply, but rather irregularly for his tastes. In his first letter he advised her to delay publication and polish her form. But during the later correspondence, which lasted until her death in 1886, he did encourage her to publish and apparently approached editors (perhaps *Atlantic* editors) with her poems (A. Wells 50). Neither Miss Dickinson nor the editors seemed willing. Four years after her death, Higginson coedited the first volume of her poetry, which rapidly went through six editions in its first year. For his substantial voluntary labors as one of her earliest encouragers, "Dear Preceptor," and posthumous editor, Higginson has generally been rewarded with the contempt of her later admirers, who reverence her safely enshrined in a reputation that he belatedly helped to establish.

Higginson's relationship with Emily Dickinson was characteristic of the patient encouragement and advice he gave to a number of young women. Donovan notes that Higginson deserves considerable credit, along with Lowell, Fields, and Howells, for his support of women's local color writing through both his critical articles and his personal influence (Donovan 6). Several other women whom he encouraged not only were less reluctant than Dickinson to publish but wrote in a manner more amenable to the editorial tastes of the time. Largely through his contacts with Lowell and Fields, Higginson lent substantial support to the early careers of Rose Terry, Harriet Prescott, Charlotte Hawes, Celia Thaxter, and Dickinson's friend Helen Hunt, all of whom became popular writers of the period, published extensively in the *Atlantic* and other magazines, and then, with Higginson himself, began their inexorable retreat into obscurity just as Emily Dickinson began to emerge from it.

Higginson continued to promote the contributions of younger authors throughout Fields's editorship. But by 1866, Fields felt the need of more immediate and practical editorial assistance. For this purpose, he hired an ambitious young man from the hinterlands of the Midwest named William Dean Howells. When the young Ohioan had made his first pilgrimage to Boston in 1861, Lowell had arranged a small Parker House dinner to introduce him to Fields and Holmes and probably to propose taking him on as assistant at the *Atlantic*. Fields had declined, but

Howells, on returning from his Venetian consulship in 1865, had renewed the contact and inquired explicitly about the possibility of an *Atlantic* assistantship. Fields again demurred but promised to remember Howells if he found himself in need of an assistant. Lowell, with whom Howells had also renewed contact, had written Fields to see what he could do for Howells, who he believed would make his mark in literature. When Howard Ticknor was transferred to another Ticknor and Fields magazine the next year, Fields passed over several applications from "Boston men" and offered the position to Howells, who was then working, through the intervention of Lowell and Norton, as assistant editor of Godkin's *Nation* in New York.

Howells later claimed that Fields had selected him above others not primarily for his literary abilities but for the proficiency as a proofreader and "practical printer" that he had gained by assisting his father in the production of various local Ohio newspapers since the age of fifteen. But both the correspondence and Howells's subsequent *Atlantic* career indicate that Fields had guaranteed him a generous measure of editorial responsibility from the beginning, particularly with respect to younger authors, and had intimated to him that if all went right, Howells would eventually become editor-in-chief.

In selecting a probable successor, Fields chose not only a much younger man but also one from far outside the Boston circle. His decision suggests that although he continued to rely heavily on the older generation of Boston contributors to sustain the magazine for the present, he recognized that this generation was thinning, that no comparable younger circle of Boston authors was rising to take its place, and that in the future, the *Atlantic* would have to turn increasingly to younger writers from other regions. When Howells assumed his new duties on his twenty-ninth birthday, March 1, 1866, one of his major responsibilities was to look after "new developments." Fields continued to deal with the older, more established contributors, but Howells was expected to use his literary contacts with New York and the Midwest to broaden the geographic base of the magazine and to cultivate a new generation of *Atlantic* contributors. Among the younger authors whom he encouraged during his assistant editorship were T. B. Aldrich, Sarah Orne Jewett, John DeForest, E. C. Stedman, Bret Harte, and Henry James.

Fields foresaw a time when the *Atlantic* could no longer be sustained by the reputations of its older contributors and would face stiff competition with other magazines for new ones. But these problems, although they began to take shape after the war, were not yet acute during his editorship. In fact, the decade between his assumption of editorial duties in July 1861 and his retirement in January 1871 marked the zenith of the *Atlantic*'s golden day, as it marked the height of New England's "Indian summer." Longfellow, Lowell, Emerson, and Stowe, all substantial contributors to Fields's *Atlantic*, remained among the most respected and read of American authors. The reputations of Holmes and Whittier, greatly augmented by their publications in the *Atlantic* since 1857, were at their full. And there was a great deal of posthumous interest in Fields's additions, Hawthorne and Thoreau. During the sixties all of these were names to conjure with, and their association with the *Atlantic* made it another such—as Fields knew in publicizing his authors and his magazine from California to London. The ascendancy and influence of Boston, Ticknor and Fields, and the *Atlantic* were reflected in a letter from Bayard Taylor to E. C. Stedman, both New York writers: "Rejoice my friend. Boston hath accepted you! . . . in all gravity, this is a good thing, because the 'Atlantic' is accepted by the populace as the representative magazine of American literature and your name there secures you the respect of all the small fry" (31 Oct. 1866, *Unpublished Letters* 94; qtd. in Scholnick, *Stedman* 32). In 1866, the *Nation*, always a stringent cultural critic, also wryly affirmed this ascendancy: "The *Atlantic* easily maintains its supremacy among the monthlies. Indeed too easily" ("Commentary on Magazines," 2 Aug. 1866, 88).

Under Fields's management, the *Atlantic*'s circulation expanded from 32,000 in 1861 to over 50,000 by 1866, the largest readership it was to reach in the nineteenth century (Mott 2: 33, 505). Fields achieved this increase partly through active promotion and an improved system of distribution. He was fully conscious of the large new national market for books and magazines, particularly in the Midwest, created by the rapid increase between 1850 and 1870 in public literacy and in railroad lines. While most publishing, and most literary culture, had before the war been regional, Fields's horizon stretched to the Mississippi and beyond to California. Osgood, as sales representative for Ticknor and Fields, traveled to Detroit and Cincinnati (Charvat, *Profession* 299). Fields also convinced the American News Service in New York to carry the magazine and contracted publishing houses in Philadelphia, Chicago, and London to act as distributors.

Equally important to the expansion of the readership was Fields's managing to preserve the essential elements of Lowell's magazine, including its contributors, its distinctly literary nature, and its liberal humanism, while slightly lightening the editorial mix by reducing the amount of scholarly material and adding some more popular features. A few Boston highbrows looked askance. Norton was disaffected; Charles Francis Adams, Sr., encouraged his son Henry Adams to write substantive scholarship for the *North American* rather than "light literature" for the *Atlantic* (E. Samuels 73). But Fields effected the change unobtrusively, alienating few and adding interest for thousands of men and particularly women with less erudite tastes.

Fields wanted to maintain the *Atlantic*'s cultural stature, which was its primary value to his firm. But he was less willing than Lowell to "defy the public," as Emerson had felt the *Atlantic*'s editor should. Lowell had recognized the need for a balance between education and entertainment. But his personal tastes had led him to resist certain concessions to popularity suggested first by Phillips, then by Fields. Fields's own tastes, though Higginson pronounced them good, were less often at odds with those of middlebrow readers, and accordingly he found less need to resist and instruct his public than Lowell had.

Despite Fields's instinct for the popular, however, and his astuteness at promotion, publicity, and anticipating the future, he was reluctant to tamper with the magazine's essential format. This reluctance led to one decision that probably more than any other limited the *Atlantic*'s long-term growth. In spite of his ambition for a wider circulation and the increasing success of lavishly illustrated *Harper's* and others, he refused to illustrate the *Atlantic*. In 1868, James R. Osgood became Fields's junior partner and soon developed a reputation as "the Boston Bantam" for bold publishing strategies risking considerable capital. Osgood proposed illustration to compete for a circulation the size of *Harper's*. Fields declined. Because of the particular nature of the magazine and its audience, illustration, he felt, would not raise the *Atlantic*'s circulation but rather "would seriously affect its standing as an organ of thought and literature" (to Osgood, 9 Aug. 1869). In this matter, Fields shared the biases of literary high culture. More than any other, this decision, reaffirmed by later publishers, would hinder the *Atlantic* from competing with successive generations of increasingly popular quality illustrated magazines achieving circulations of 200,000 or more. The decision not to illustrate would both preserve the *Atlantic*'s continuity with its own traditions and increasingly relegate it to a small-circulation, highbrow, literary niche.

In other ways, however, Fields's editing anticipated the mass-market future. At a time when most editors of literary periodicals considered advertising undignified, Fields was the first to adopt a section advertising products other than the firm's books. This appeared in February 1860, immediately after the *Atlantic* was purchased by Ticknor and Fields, and signaled the new owners' clear intention of making a significant profit on their venture. Throughout the decade, advertising filled between eight and fifteen pages of each issue, all decently relegated to the end of the magazine. Among the prodigies recommended to *Atlantic* readers were Dr. Poland's White Pine Compound "for Gravel and All Kidney Diseases"; Perry's Moth and Freckle Remover; Peruvian Serum "to Invigorate the Brain"; Pyles Saleratus; Frank Palmer, "Surgeon-Artist" of artificial limbs, doing a brisk wartime business; and the *Phrenological Journal*, featuring diagnostic "portraits" of President Johnson, Queen Victoria, Julius Caesar, and others. About half the section, however, was taken up by announcements of Ticknor and Fields's books. Despite remonstrances from Higginson, among others, that such advertising suggested too close a commercial relationship between the magazine and its publishers, Fields eventually expanded the firm's advertising to form a separate section, the "Atlantic Miscellany," which contained not only announcements but reprints of favorable reviews and promotional literary chatter about the firm's books and famous authors. In this, as in other promotions of the so-called *Atlantic* circle, Fields was one of the first to use the celebrity system successfully to sell books.

Fields developed other schemes to promote and advertise the famous names in his literary stable to full commercial advantage. He was accused, with some justice, of hoarding the best manuscripts by his most eminent contributors, to the detriment of eleven issues a year, in order to produce a spectacular January issue. Abundantly advertised, this issue served as an inducement for old subscribers to renew and as a lure for new subscribers. New subscribers were also offered a full-sized print of the *Atlantic* Olympian of their choice, portraits that graced many New England and midwestern homes. Furthermore, Fields conspicuously publicized on the cover of his January issues the names of major contributors whose writings would appear in the *Atlantic* during the following year. Like Phillips, he ensured that the newspapers were well informed monthly of the identities of *Atlantic* authors. In 1862, he went further and began publishing authors' names in the semiannual indexes which appeared in the June and December issues. In 1870 he abandoned the genteel, amateurs' tradition of anonymity altogether and, except for reviews, printed the authors' names at the end of each article. This was one more sign that, partly because of Fields and the rise of the American magazine, authorship in America was fast becoming increasingly competitive and professionalized.

Fields's moderate lightening of the *Atlantic*'s contents was evident in his editorial selections and his shaping of nonfiction prose. In this, as in his promotions, he foreshadowed at times the mass-market future that the *Atlantic* spent much of the rest of the century resisting. His editorial solicitations constantly emphasized brevity. Fields's *Atlantic* contained more essays than Lowell's had, but their average length was considerably shorter. In both topic and treatment they tended to be less abstract or scholarly and more journalistic, more contemporary, more colored by personality, anecdote, or picturesque description. The older styles of essay, such as those written by Emerson or Holmes, like those of Johnson and Addison a century and more earlier, characteristically used brief observations of contemporary life as a springboard for speculations and pronouncements on immutable truths of morality or human nature. But a new generation of essayists was now arising, supported by the development of the magazines, who were not discursive philosophers but observers and recorders of the contemporary scene. These new writers aimed not to write lasting works on Eternal Truths but to inform readers of the actual conditions of present-day life. They therefore chose topical subjects and wrote in a style that was more direct, concrete, less literary, and more journalistic. They wrote for an audience with a more practical intellectual curiosity about the world around them rather than an audience mainly interested in books and traditional high culture. This was an audience whom Fields hoped to tap for the *Atlantic*.

The best of the new magazine journalists was an English immigrant named James Parton, the husband of Fanny Fern, another popular journalist. Although Parton was in demand by a number of editors, Fields soon worked out an exclusive arrangement guaranteeing him regular *Atlantic* publication at rates up to about twenty dollars per page. The relationship between Fields as editor and Parton as writer, like Parton's articles themselves, previewed a change in magazine journalism that would take place gradually over the next forty years. Lowell, like most editors of his time, was an essentially passive selector of manuscripts, sometimes suggesting slight stylistic changes or deletions after the fact, usually to the author's irritation. With Parton and a few others, Fields, by contrast, began to discuss and negotiate topics and treatments before a piece was written, thereby giving him more control over the contents of his magazine and enabling him to suit it more specifically to his readership.

Actually, the far-sighted Parton taught Fields more about the new magazine journalism than Fields could teach him. Fields's tastes tended to be heavily literary. What the *Atlantic* needed, Parton declared, was fewer ponderous Emersonian essays and more red-blooded reporting on topics of real interest such as racehorses. The *Atlantic* could easily be made much more popular if "a writer named Mark Twain [were] engaged and more articles connected with life than with literature" (qtd. from Annie Fields's journal in Austin 356). Twain did not appear in the *Atlantic* until Howells's editorship, but Parton's articles did broaden the *Atlantic*'s coverage of contemporary American life and balanced Fields's inclination to be too literary.

In selecting topics and approaches, "the grand object of all," Parton maintained, was "to show how things work in America, and who works them." To do this effectively required a "long period of investigation—out-of-doors" (to Fields, 15 Mar. 1866, in Austin 341). Most of the articles Fields and Parton negotiated required this extensive journalistic fieldwork. Responding to a new postwar interest in the expansion westward, Fields commissioned Parton to travel through the Midwest and write on flourishing, raw new cities such as Chicago, Pittsburgh, Cincinnati, and St. Louis. Parton also reported on such contemporary phenomena as Henry Ward Beecher, the sewing machine, Chinese immigrants, the use of tobacco and liquor, and the status of Catholicism and Judaism in America. He proposed and produced investigative reports, inspired by the beginning of the Grant era, on lobbying and the spoils system in the federal government.

Howells later commented that Parton, while not considered by aesthetes a writer of elegant literature, was a "true artist" and "divined American character as few Americans have done" (*Literary Friends* 143). In fact, Parton's work for Fields's *Atlantic* was the prototype of an increasingly important form of reportage that helped to develop Howells's literary realism and later supplemented it in the *Atlantic* and other quality magazines as a description and critique of current American life.

The rise of investigative reportage and first-person accounts of current American conditions was essentially a postwar rather than a wartime phenomenon in the *Atlantic*. Parton, like Howells, did not begin writing for Fields until 1866, and it was not until the end of 1864 that Fields began to publish occasional firsthand reports on the war and later the Reconstruction. The best of these was Higginson's "Leaves from an Officer's Journal," a forceful description of the experiences of the black army regiment that he had commanded in South Carolina. "I wish to record," he wrote, "as truthfully as I may, the beginnings of a momentous experiment... towards remoulding the destinies of two races on this continent" (qtd. in Austin 246). Personal observations of Reconstruction included two papers by John Trowbridge, who was partly staked by Fields to travel to and describe former battlefields, and John DeForest's realistic account of his experience as director of the Freedman's Bureau in Greenville, South Carolina.

First-person reportage on the agonies of war, the appalling conditions of battle, the field hospital, and the prison camp were largely absent from Fields's *Atlantic* by design, although he did publish Theodore Winthrop's account "Life in the Open Air" in 1862. Fields's editorial instinct in treating the war itself was compounded of Victorian desire to avoid the unpleasant, a publisher's sense that good cheer is a more popular commodity than pain, and a patriotic fear of being dispiriting at a time requiring conviction and commitment. Political articles advocated resolute and unflagging prosecution of the war, but the cost to individuals was seldom described. Occasionally Fields allowed the tragic note in fiction or in Harriet Stowe's papers. His preferred tactic, however, was diversion. And one of his favorite diversions was the travel sketch.

If Fields often exercised an active popularizing editorial influence, suggesting topics and approaches, he often used this influence, especially during wartime, to favor the diversions of foreign lands, especially if treated with humor and lightness of tone. In March 1864, he wrote Bayard Taylor: "Touching the other paper I suggested. It struck me you might have laid away for the public (in your brain cells at least) some humorous thoughts as to persons and places that might be worked up for the A.M. What we most need are *short* storyish papers that have fun as an element in them" (Austin 334).

Fields himself enjoyed travel sketches, felt that his readers shared this taste, and encouraged his authors to undertake them. The result of his suggestion to Taylor was a thirteen-part series titled "The Byways of Europe," written and read while the battles of the Wilderness, Spotsylvania, and Petersburg raged and Sherman burned his way through Georgia. It was Fields also who during the nadir of the war in 1862 persuaded the reluctant Hawthorne to delve back into his English journals and to fashion from them the series of sketches which, after their appearance in the *Atlantic*, were published as *Our Old Home*.

The correspondence concerning *Our Old Home* provides insights into the characters of both editor and author. By 1862, Hawthorne was feeling the gathering gloom of his last years and experiencing a mordant dissatisfaction with everything he wrote. He disliked this series in particular and complained to Fields: "I always feel a singular despondency and heaviness of heart in reopening those old journals now" (qtd. in J. Fields 102). Fields responded with his habitual hearty enthusiasm, and Hawthorne agreed to persist, though without faith. "I am sensible," he wrote, "that you mollify me with a good deal of soft soap, but it is skillfully applied and effects all you intend it should" (103). The writing continued to be a torment, and it was clear that Hawthorne endured it only because he felt a financial responsibility to his family and wished to accommodate the persistent Fields. At the end of his labor he felt the same sense of futility and desolation. "Heaven sees fit to visit me with an unshakeable conviction that all this series of articles is good for nothing; but that is none of my business, provided the public and you are of a different opinion" (103).

Without constant pressure from Fields, *Our Old Home* would never have been written. One may condemn him for encouraging Hawthorne to labor so painfully and with so little satisfaction in the minor vein of travel literature. But it is doubtful whether without Fields's urging, Hawthorne would have completed anything in the desultory years after his final return from Europe. Certainly when Fields encouraged him to try fiction again in 1863, the results were even more excruciating for Hawthorne.

Besides travel literature, another form of nonfiction prose reflecting Fields's editorial plan to moderately popularize the *Atlantic* was the "domestic essay." Fields was well aware that approximately half of his readers were women. Accordingly, while he declined Harriet Beecher Stowe's proposal that he officially open a women's department, he was eager to print several long series of discursive essays on domestic relationships and the management of the home. In a series of monthly articles beginning in January 1864 the indefatigable Stowe, under the masculine pseudonym Christopher Crowfield, expounded on the practical and aesthetic aspects of maintaining a house and on the moral and sentimental qualities that made a house a home. The popularity of the series induced both Fields and Stowe to continue it throughout the next two years under the titles "The Chimney Corner" and "The Little Foxes." It also induced the editors of *Harper's* to initiate a domestic department. This imitation suggested that since the *Atlantic* under Fields had taken on a slightly more popular tone, the two magazines were beginning to compete in earnest for a certain number of readers.

Fields's popularization of the *Atlantic* with more reportage, travelogues, and domestic papers and correspondingly less scholarship increased the magazine's scope of interest as well as its appeal. But it did not destroy the *Atlantic*'s reputation as a forum for the presentation of ideas, nor did it change its essential values of liberal Yankee humanism. Senator Charles Sumner chose the *Atlantic* as a platform for defining and defending his nationally influential radical Republican proposal for southern Reconstruction. Charles W. Eliot chose the *Atlantic* for two progressive papers entitled "The New Education," advocating radical changes in college curricula to institute an elective system and replace the old emphasis on classical languages with a new emphasis on professional training, sciences, and mathematics. These papers helped substantially in gaining Eliot election as president of Harvard, where he effected major changes that in turn widely influenced higher education throughout the nation. Louis Agassiz, a friend of Fields, was eager to publish his extensive series entitled "Methods of Study of Natural History" in the *Atlantic*, as Henry James, Sr., was to contribute his four-part investigation of the ethics of marriage. Fields solicited and printed Emerson's Phi Beta Kappa address entitled "American Civilization," his frank and moving essay on Thoreau, and Thoreau's own "Life without Principle." Fields, then, did not make his magazine an intellectual lightweight or close it to intellectually serious work, but he did change the mixture and extend the magazine's range.

One area in which Fields's dual role as publisher and editor did intellectually weaken the magazine and undermine its credibility was in literary criticism and reviews. Even here, however, Fields was more cautious in trying to bend the prestige of the *Atlantic* to commercial use than he had previously been in using reviews. William Charvat, who has documented Fields's earlier commercial exploitation of book reviews, concludes that after 1855 Fields bothered less with this rather risky manipulation and concentrated on more direct promotions of his literary celebrities (*Authorship* 187). Still, while more subtle than formerly, he was never one to miss opportunities.

Fields continued Lowell's precedent of publishing a good many essays on literary subjects. In fact, he accepted more of these than Lowell had, but their nature reflected his own character and interests. Lowell had reserved a place in the *Atlantic* for scholarship, but Fields was inclined to think that scholarly writing belonged in the *North American Review*. Fields's friend Whipple was allowed to do a series on Elizabethan dramatists for the *Atlantic*, but most scholarly treatments of Dante, Shakespeare, Bacon, and their ilk were referred to Norton, who now edited the old *North*. Fields, by contrast, actively solicited often chattily biographical accounts of popular living writers, particularly Ticknor and Fields authors, written by professional magazinists. In several cases, his purpose was frankly promotional. G. W. Curtis's piece on Longfellow opportunely appeared in the magazine only five days before the firm issued Longfellow's *Tales of a Wayside Inn*. After reading the high praise awarded his fellow poet, Whittier asked rather plaintively whether a similar *Atlantic* piece might not be done on his work. Fields obliged him by commissioning a laudatory piece from David Wasson.

In general, the literary reviewing of the period, in magazines as elsewhere, suffered chronically from what one critic characterized as an excess of "laudatory twaddle" and a deficiency of "just and discriminating severity" (qtd. in Mott 3: 233). Fields, unlike Lowell, was not anxious to change this condition. Higginson, who wisely declined the offer to take charge of the *Atlantic* reviewing department, commented to Norton that "the trouble [with *Atlantic* reviews] is that Fields' good nature combines with his interests in making him averse to anything trenchant" (8 Nov. 1864, Norton Collection). Certainly Fields disliked delivering bad news and enjoyed delivering the good. Certainly also, the prevailing ethics of reviewing were lax by present standards. For instance, not only did Fields feel unabashed in asking Longfellow for a "loving notice" of one of the firm's books, but Longfellow felt equal equanimity in requesting a "friendly review" in the *Atlantic* for the work of an acquaintance (Letters, n.d. 1861; 25 Dec. 1864). Nor were these reciprocal favors limited to the Boston circle; Taylor, Aldrich, Stedman, and Stoddard in New York could all be counted on for generally sympathetic reviews of Ticknor and Fields's books and could count on generally kind treatment in the *Atlantic*. Reciprocation reached as far as England, as when Fields requested Osgood to "ask Howells to have one of his warmest notices" for a friend of Dickens and could count on similar solicitude from Dickens and friends for his firm's important books (1 July 1869). Occasionally, Fields would directly censor reviews. John Weiss refused to write further reviews when Fields mutilated one of his by systematically excising the critical passages. More often, Fields followed the prevalent, subtler method of locating a reviewer he knew to be sympathetic, sometimes a friend of the author.

Still, Fields, to his credit, selected as the magazine's major critics men of integrity—Higginson, Lowell, and later Howells—who were not always tractable to his promotional purposes. Higginson exerted a constant pressure on Fields to avoid giving preferential treatment to the firm's books. And in his own reviews not even so august a figure as Emerson was immune from a balanced criticism. While praising Emerson's *Society and Solitude* as "a high water mark" of American literature, he also suggested that the sage's later style was beginning to resemble that of a lecturer whose notes had become scrambled by the wind (July 1870, 120). Howells, who took over the bulk of the reviewing after 1866, was more vulnerable because of his position but managed to balance generalized praise with some trenchant, specific criticism, even of the august, that reflected the development of his standards of literary realism.

Fields's own literary tastes have been criticized as conventionally genteel. He is accused of promoting a sentimental and gently humorous literature—light, sociable, and facile (Green 115–16). His selections of fiction for the *Atlantic*, however, suggest that the accusation is a very partial half-truth. He was not a profound critic, and he had no systematic philosophy of literature. But it is difficult to dismiss as merely conventional the tastes of a man who had from the beginning admired and encouraged Hawthorne and who, as the *Atlantic*'s editor, regularly published very early works of younger realistic writers such as Henry James, Rebecca Harding Davis, John DeForest, and Howells. Fields relied heavily on the magazine's established poets, but in fiction he was clearly open to the new. He published much of the best American writing of the period by both well-known and as yet unknown authors. He also gave significant support to women writers, to local color fiction, and to the earliest work of a new generation of American realists.

It was for a distinguished literary list that the firm of Ticknor and Fields was mainly known, and they had purchased the *Atlantic* largely to augment that reputation for literature. In literature, as elsewhere, Fields's primary editorial tactic was to secure the big names and to publicize liberally their relationship with the magazine. The popular and critical reputations of the major New England poets already closely identified with it were at their zenith, due in no small measure to his own promotions. The *Nation* commented in 1866 that "the four living American poets who fill the highest places are Emerson, Bryant, Longfellow, and Lowell." Whittier, the article suggested, was probably fifth and Holmes sixth (qtd. in Mott 3: 237). Fields solicited and strategically published large numbers of poems by all except Bryant, including twenty-three by Longfellow and forty-one by Whittier. Poems from Fields's *Atlantic*, such as Lowell's second series of "Biglow Papers" and his "Commemorative Ode," Emerson's "Terminus" and "Boston Hymn," Whittier's "Barbara Frietchie," and several by Longfellow, continued to be anthologized well into the next century.

Neither Fields's own tastes nor his admiration for the New England Olympians closed his mind to Whitman. He did reject three war poems submitted as a batch in 1861, claiming that their effectiveness depended on timeliness and that his space for poetry was booked far into the future. But he paid $100 on acceptance for the major poem "Proud Music of the Storm" (Feb. 1869), Whitman's only other submission of the decade (Scholnick, "Whitman" 233).

During Fields's editorship the most prestigious name in American fiction was Nathaniel Hawthorne, and Fields was constantly anxious to make him an *Atlantic* author. When in 1861 Hawthorne outlined to his publisher a possible plot for a new romance based on the legend of a deathless man which Thoreau had told him, Fields excitedly urged him to begin work immediately and to plan on serial publication in the *Atlantic*. Hawthorne, who had never published his fiction serially, was reluctant but consented on the condition that Fields should not "see the first chapter until I have written the final sentence of the story" (J. Fields 96). When Hawthorne attempted to begin, however, he found himself mentally unable to undertake a long work of fiction. Depressed over the war, his own failing health, and the apparent waning of his imaginative powers, he let the idea drop for two years while he labored over the more mechanical task of preparing the *English Notebooks*.

After the *Atlantic* publication of the *Notebooks* in 1862 and 1863, Fields again felt the need for new material by Hawthorne and urged the despondent author to return to the serial romance. Hawthorne doubted his capacities more than ever, but he needed to sustain his income and agreed to renew the attempt. In November 1863 he wrote frankly to Fields: "I want a great deal of money.... If it were not for these troublesome necessities, I doubt whether you would ever see so much as the first chapter of the new Romance" (J. Fields 110). Fields, feeling that Hawthorne might be stimulated by time pressure and eager to include him in the list of contributors for 1864, persuaded the author to let him announce that the new work would commence publication in the January *Atlantic*. Hawthorne acquiesced, although he had scarcely drafted the first chapter, much less "written the final sentence."

Hawthorne missed the November 15 deadline for January but promised "a chapter or two of absurdities for the February issue" (letter, 14 Nov. 1863). The pressures of the announcement and economic need did seem to have some effect, and he completed one installment by early December. On reading the manuscript, Fields must have been shocked by the recognition that the central figure, a superannuated quack physician, Dr. Dolliver, was quite plainly a half-satiric, half-pitying psychological portrait of the author himself. Long sunk in "the sloth of age and the breaking up of intellect," long past any desire to live, the decrepit grandsir Dolliver lay on his bed torpidly gazing at the graveyard outside his window, where he had for decades wished to be buried, and prepared himself to endure the agonies of rising to yet another day.

In the weeks following the arrival of this first chapter, Fields received a series of notes indicating that Hawthorne felt his mental and physical condition deteriorating and that Dr. Dolliver would, in fact, never be resurrected. Finally, at the end of February, the following letter arrived:

Dear Fields,
... I hardly know what to say to the public about this abortive Romance, though I know pretty well what the case will be. I shall never finish it. Yet it is not quite pleasant for an author to announce himself, or to be announced, as finally broken down as to his literary faculty. It is a pity that I let you put this work in your programme for the year, for I had always had a presentiment that it would fail us at the pinch. Say to the public what you think best, and as little as possible; for example... "We are sorry to hear (but know not whether the public will share our grief) that Mr. Hawthorne is out of health and is thereby prevented, for the present, from proceeding with another of his promised (or threatened) Romances, intended for this magazine"; or "Mr. Hawthorne's brain is addled at last, and, much to our satisfaction, he tells us that he cannot possibly go on with the Romance announced on the cover of the January magazine. We consider him finally shelved, and shall take early occasion to bury him under a heavy article, carefully summing up his merits (such as they were) and his demerits, what few of them can be touched upon in our limited space...." I cannot finish it unless a great change comes over me; and if I make too great an effort to do so, it will be my death; not that I should care much for that.... I am not low-spirited, nor fanciful, nor freakish but look what seem to be realities in the face, and am ready to take whatever may come. (J. Fields 115–16)

In March 1864, Hawthorne arranged a trip to Washington for his health in the company of his friend, Fields's partner, William D. Ticknor. In Philadelphia, the apparently healthy Ticknor suffered a violent "bilious attack" and died suddenly. Hawthorne returned pale, shaken, and more depressed than ever. In May, after a continued decline, he set out on another journey with his old friend General Franklin Pierce. Two days later, Fields received a distraught telegram from Pierce in Plymouth, New Hampshire, announcing that Hawthorne had died quietly in his sleep. A few days later, Fields, along with Longfellow, Emerson, Lowell, Holmes, Pierce, and others, bore the body to its burial place in Concord Cemetery. On top of the casket lay a manuscript of the unfinished "Dolliver Romance." It was buried with its author.

More of Hawthorne's work was published posthumously in the *Atlantic* than when he had been alive. The first "Dolliver" fragment appeared in July 1864, prefaced by Holmes's account of his interview with its author shortly before his death. Fields, never one to lose an opportunity to promote subscription renewals, hoarded the second fragment for his next January spectacular (1865). A thirteen-part series from Hawthorne's *Notebooks*, edited by his wife, Sophia, and Fields, began in January 1866. Fields's own reminiscence of Hawthorne, a part of his *Yesterdays with Authors*, appeared in 1871, after his retirement from the editorship. And in 1872, the *Atlantic* published, for the first time, another late, abortive romance, *Septimus Felton*.

Fields had honored, solicited, and promoted Hawthorne as the greatest writer of American fiction. But he adulated Dickens as the greatest living writer in the language. Fields had met the great Boz in England in 1859 and, during the novelist's American lecture tour in the late sixties, became both his American publisher and a personal friend. Fields frequently pressed the novelist to permit publication of his stories in the *Atlantic* simultaneous with their publication in Dickens's own magazine *All the Year Round*. Mainly because of the absence of an international copyright law and the resulting hazards of piracy, he succeeded only once in obtaining fiction, although Dickens contributed several essays. Dickens received $1,000 for the three installments of "George Silverman's Explanation"—a low fee for him, but probably the largest payment, relative to the length of the piece, made during Fields's editorship.

The curmudgeonly Charles Reade was another noted English novelist whose work Fields particularly sought for the *Atlantic*. The serialization of Reade's novel *Griffith Gaunt* in the *Atlantic* between December 1865 and November 1866 was interesting for several reasons. First, its initiation in the December number reflected Fields's willingness to use serials bridging two years as an inducement to subscription renewals. Second, the virulent attacks on the moral probity of the inoffensive *Griffith Gaunt* by the American press, and the absence of such attacks following its simultaneous publication in England, indicated that American literary morality was considerably stiffer than its British counterpart (Mott 2: 509). The subsequent history of English fiction in the *Atlantic* suggests that this difference remained for at least another fifty years.

Fields had earlier planned a similar serial project with Reade but had canceled it at the outbreak of the war and ventured to publish *Griffith Gaunt* only after Appomattox. These decisions reflected not only the difficulty of communications with England between 1861 and 1865 but, more important, the unpopularity of things English with the *Atlantic* audience during that time. Lowell, Holmes, Stowe, and David Wasson, all of whom had had close personal contacts in England, expressed in the *Atlantic* a bitter resentment of the British indifference to the Union cause and often a general repudiation of British culture. Fields was himself an ardent Anglophile, visited England often, and maintained important publishing contacts there. But even he absorbed the general distaste for things English. He did not attempt actively to solicit English manuscripts again until after the war, and even then the number of English pieces in the magazine was never high. As the original publisher's statement had projected, the *Atlantic* continued to rely mainly on American authors, known and unknown.

Particularly notable among Fields's American authors was the high proportion of women. Josephine Donovan notes that "the New England women writers were favored by having [access to a prestigious source of publication] and by having a woman friend as a central publishing power. The local color school could not have existed without the Boston publishing network that surrounded and issued from James T. (1817–1881) and Annie Adams Fields (1834–1915)" (38). Elizabeth Stuart Phelps, whom both Fieldses had substantially supported early in her career, said that Fields "was incapable of that literary snobbishness that undervalues a woman's work because it is a woman's" (Donovan 41). While Fields deserves personal credit, he had two good practical motives for encouraging women writers. First, he understood well, as Howells would after him, that women constituted substantially more than half of the readership for fiction. Second, he was married to a forceful woman who had strong personal and social ties with many women writers and used her influence on their behalf. Annie Adams Fields, herself a minor writer, for more than fifty years from her marriage in 1854 until long after her husband's death in 1881 and past the turn of the century, held Boston's best-known literary salon in her memento-laden drawing rooms on the water side of Charles Street. While sometimes imperious in her later years, she had, like her husband, the gifts of responsiveness, good humor, and a warm sympathy. The depth of her friendships with several women writers indicates that these qualities were genuine, not simply advantageous social behaviors.

Both for Harriet Beecher Stowe and for the younger writer Celia Thaxter, Annie Fields was probably the closest friend of their adult lives. Rebecca Harding Davis, writing for the *Atlantic* at the very beginning of her career, also found in Annie her warmest and most supportive literary friendship. And after James Fields's death in 1881, Annie lived and traveled with Sarah Orne Jewett in a "Boston marriage" for nearly thirty years until Jewett's death in 1909. For these women and others, Annie effectively helped to form a network of personal relationships, to encourage their literary production, and to ensure their publication, generally in the *Atlantic*. She was at least partly responsible for the fact that during the 1860s about one-third of *Atlantic* pieces were written by women, including Stowe, Thaxter, Davis, Louisa May Alcott, Caroline Cheesebro, Rose Terry Cooke, Gail Hamilton, Lucy Larcom, Elizabeth Stuart Phelps, and Zina Pierce.[1]

American literature in Fields's *Atlantic*, much of it by women, ranged broadly from a traditional realism, sometimes admixed with grotesquely melodramatic propaganda during wartime, through the New England local color realism that Lowell had promoted, to a new, largely postwar, antiromantic realism. It reflected the eclectic breadth of Fields's taste. It showed also that while he promoted the magazine's relationship with established writers, both he and Annie Fields were, with some reservations, open to a new generation of writers beginning to develop new modes. Despite the wartime resurgence of idealism, the trend was strongly realistic.

A great deal of the poetry and a smaller but significant portion of the fiction published in the first half of Fields's editorship was directly concerned with the war. The approach and onset of the war unquestionably brought a massive revival of the old literary ethicism, even the bald didacticism that Lowell had ridiculed. As Edmund Wilson has written in his study of the literature of the Civil War: "The minds of nations at war are invariably dominated by myths, which turn the conflict into melodrama and make it possible for each side to feel that it is combatting some form of evil. [The] vision of Judgement was the myth of the North" (91).

The best-known expression of this vision of the war as Armageddon and judgment was Julia Ward Howe's "Battle Hymn of the Republic," for which Fields paid only four dollars, although he did give it the lead place in the *Atlantic* for February 1862. Similar conceptions of the conflict as a holy war in which God enacted His divine will through human history, "sifting out the hearts of men before his Judgement seat," appeared frequently. Holmes's "Choose This Day Which You Will Serve" portrayed the North as Israel, receiving Jehovah's charge to vanquish the barbarous southern tribes of Ammon and Moab who worshiped "the gods of slavery." In Emerson's "Battle Hymn" God sternly warned those who would obstruct emancipation:

> My will fulfilled shall be
> For in daylight or in dark
> My thunderbolt has eyes to see
> His way home to the mark.
>
> (Feb. 1863, 228)

Emerson, however, showed himself characteristically more subtle than most when he suggested in "Voluntaries" that the war was a divine judgment not on the South only but on the North as well for having so long tolerated bondage while professing freedom.

The traditional, inspirational images of heroism were intact. The Union soldiers in Howe's "Battle Hymn," H. H. Brownell's "Abraham Lincoln," and other poems were not only willing instruments of divine justice but also imitations of Christ's sacrificial death. Lowell, among many others, sounded the *dulce et decorum* theme in his elegy "Memorium Positae R G S" on his nephew Robert Gould Shaw, the young leader of the Massachusetts Fifty-fourth, a black regiment slaughtered in a brave but futile attempt to take Fort Wagner:

> But the high soul burns on to light men's feet
> Where death for noble ends makes dying sweet.
>
> (Jan. 1864, 89)

War, according to *Atlantic* poetry and fiction, summoned the highest attributes of those who gave themselves to it. As Emerson wrote in "Voluntaries":

> When Duty whispers low "Thou must"
> The Youth replies "I can."
>
> (Oct. 1863, 505)

Battle made men of boys, gave noble purpose to shallow lives, and provided a furnace for the forging of heroic spirits.

If images of the northern patriot often rose to the sublime, images of the South and the southerner in *Atlantic* literature often descended to the ridiculous. Lydia Maria Childs's prewar story "Loo-Loo" contrasted a morally upright young northerner, appropriately named Alfred Noble, with a swinish southern cotton planter, equally aptly named Mr. Grossman. Grossman was particularly memorable: "The predominance of animal propensities was stamped upon his countenance with more distinctness than is usual with sensualists of twice his age. The oil of a thousand hams seemed oozing through his pimply cheeks; his small grey eyes were set in his head like the eyes of a pig; his mouth had the expression of a satyr" (May 1858, 802).

The southerner in *Atlantic* fiction was quintessentially the anathema of all highminded New Englanders, the sensualist man, devoid of spiritual aspiration and of intellect. He rationalized his pleasures and his privileges by proclaiming himself an aristocrat and ruthlessly enforcing a vicious caste system. Absurdly proud of his bogus lineage ("Pure Higgs," boasts one), he scorned honest work as beneath his station. Manual labor he left to his slaves; commerce he considered appropriate to base-blooded northerners. The only exertions that he felt commensurate with his breeding were dueling in defense of his spurious honor, whipping unoffending slaves, begetting mulatto children from his octoroon mistress, and night-riding with vigilante mobs. (No northerner passed through the southland of *Atlantic* literature without at least the threat of being lynched or tarred and feathered.) The accomplishments of the male portion of this redneck aristocracy were drinking, fighting, and an amazing proficiency in expectoration. The southern woman was portrayed as equally vacuous, and often equally vicious. Normally sedate and saccharine, she could, when angered, galvanize the vigilante rabble with her bloodthirsty screams and was seriously rumored during the war to flaunt jewelry made from the teeth and bones of dead Yankees.[2]

The war did predictably cause some resurgence of literary melodrama, didacticism, and sentimentality. But both during and after the war a more authentic, less tendentious local color realism was the norm. The term "local color" was itself first used in a 1864 *Atlantic* review as praise for George Eliot's *Romola* (McMahon 14, citing "English Authors in Florence," 14 Dec. 1864, 666). Some of this local color writing, particularly that of Rose Terry Cooke, Abbie Morton Diaz, Elizabeth Stuart Phelps, and John Trowbridge, was set in the present and, as in Lowell's time, sometimes critically explored women's relationships and limited options. But especially after the war, *Atlantic* fiction reflected a need to remember and reassess the national past. *Atlantic* writers, despite a prevailing postwar rush of optimism in New England about the national future, seemed conscious that the war marked a sharp break with the settled and traditional life of rural, small-town America. In these remembrances there was sometimes a strong elegiac nostalgia. But unlike in the fiction of the later genteel tradition, the past was not viewed uncritically as a utopian lost golden age.

Certainly there was a strong affection as well as a fascination for the small-town American past of the early nineteenth century, into which many of the *Atlantic* writers of the sixties had been born. Harriet Stowe's "Oldtown Fireside Stories," published serially in 1869, remembered the New England village life of her husband's childhood in Natick, Massachusetts, and often showed a clear affection for its homely characters, its plain piety, and its honest rigors. When T. W. Higginson began a series of sketches and stories set in Newport, where he was living after the war, he significantly rechristened the town "Oldport." He did not primarily write of its energetic, pretentious, newly monied gentry, for whom he felt mainly contempt, but rather wrote nostalgically of those lingering remnants of the quieter past which seemed on the brink of extinction. More than one *Atlantic* story or novel of the period ended, like D. G. Mitchell's *Dr. Johns*, with the alien shriek of the train whistle shattering the quietude of village life, and many *Atlantic* readers were drawn to the unchanging isolation of Celia Thaxter's "Isle of Shoals."

But *Atlantic* local color writing during the sixties, unlike later, was no mere genteel wringing of hands over the intrusion of the rude present on an idealized past. In fact, much of it criticized a recent past that was still a potent influence in many quarters, particularly the effects of orthodox religion. Mitchell's *Dr. Johns*, the longest serial of the period, specifically condemned the esoteric, inhumane Calvinism and the anti-Catholic bigotry of the title character and the repressive, shrewish piety of his spinster sister. These values, Mitchell suggested, destroyed even the closest of human relationships. Holmes, among others, took up similar themes of moral and religious intolerance in his *Elsie Venner* (originally *The Professor's Story*), and in his later *Guardian Angel*, he added to them the accusation of religious hypocrisy. Stowe consciously set out to counteract Holmes's ridicule and condemnation of orthodoxy. But in her earlier *Minister's Wooing* and even in her later, generally affectionate, "Oldtown" stories, a dogmatic, male-oriented Calvinism, a narrow village insularity, and an implacable, joyless Yankee sense of duty impoverish the emotional life and crush sensitive spirits.

Much of the local color writing in Fields's *Atlantic* was, then, realistically critical of the past. But the magazine also contained a new strain in American fiction based more on direct observation of the commonplaces of contemporary life, often self-consciously antiromantic, and written by a new generation of American realists now in their twenties and thirties.

Fields's correspondence with Rebecca Harding indicates both the extent of his willingness to support a potent form of the new realism in fiction and its limits. In 1861, Miss Harding, then living in Wheeling, West Virginia, was encouraged by the *Atlantic*'s reputation for publishing fiction by women and in the more realistic modes to submit her first work anonymously to Fields. "Life in the Iron Mills" was a grim story of working-class life in a midwestern factory town, detailing the brutalization of the immigrant laborers, the cynicism of factory owners, the laissez-faire injustice of the legal and economic systems, and the fatuity of philanthropists.

The writer's style awkwardly combined naturalistic detail with melodrama, and her attitude toward the middle-class reader was a strange blend of apology, accusation, and warning: "This is what I want you to do. I want you to hide your disgust, take no heed of your clean clothes and come right down with me—here into the thickest of the fog, and mud, and foul effluvia. . . . There is a secret down here in this nightmare fog that has lain dumb for centuries. I want to make it a real thing to you" (Apr. 1861, 431).

Perhaps the story reminded Fields of Dickens, although it entirely lacked Dickens's humor and charm. At any rate, he immediately accepted it, sent its unknown author $50, and offered a $100 advance on anything else she might send. Shortly, he received a second manuscript. This story was longer than the first one but was similarly set in a midwestern factory town and provided another picture of "this commonplace, this vulgar American life" among "people whom you see everyday and call 'dregs' sometimes" ("A Story of Today," Oct. 1861, 127). Fields felt the story's power. But the grimness was too unrelieved for his tastes, and he hesitated to subject the magazine's readership, already agonized by a war which was going badly, to fiction that he found disturbing and demoralizing. The story, he suggested in his initial rejection, "assembled the gloom" too depressingly; its pathos was undeniable, but it offered no hope (Austin 370). He asked Annie Fields to write Rebecca Harding, giving encouragement for future work.

Miss Harding responded by asking whether Fields might reconsider if the ending was made more cheerful as she insisted was her original intention, though she was frank in saying that she would retain some of the gloom. Fields agreed, and the first installment of "A Story of Today" ran in the *Atlantic* for October 1861. The ending, published in the last installment six months later, featured a bogus reclamation of the nihilistic hero by the love of the long-suffering heroine, their marriage, and the fortuitous discovery of an oil well which would rescue them from grinding poverty. Still, the rest of the story, including the descriptions of the brutal conditions and effects of factory work and the suffering of the pathetic Lois, was essentially the same, and Miss Harding added a prologue defending her realism. Clearly she had Fields's objections in mind as well as those she expected from other *Atlantic* readers when she wrote:

> I know the glimpses of life it pleases you best to find here: New England idylls delicately tinted; passion veined hearts, cut bare for curious eyes; prophetic utterances, concrete and clear, or some word of pathos or fun from the old friends who have indenizened themselves in everybody's home. You want something, in fact, to lift you out of this crowded, tobacco stained commonplace, to kindle and chafe the glow in you. I want you to dig into this commonplace, this vulgar American life, and see what is in it. Sometimes I think it has a new and awful significance that we do not see. (Oct. 1861, 472).

There were few tobacco-stained commonplaces in the work, early or late, of Henry James, Jr. But with Fields's endorsement, James's form of realism too was to challenge the moral and literary assumptions of the *Atlantic* audience. James's first-published fiction, "The Story of a Year," was the lead piece in Fields's *Atlantic* for March 1865. It was followed by ten other pieces during the next five years. Howells has generally been credited with giving James the exposure afforded by the *Atlantic*, and certainly as assistant editor he consistently supported the publication of James's work. But Fields had accepted the first stories before Howells came to the magazine.

James's early *Atlantic* stories were in many ways radically different from his later novels. But these stories contained in experimental form several of the realistic, antisentimental themes he was to develop. Those who complain that nothing ever happens in a James story would be surprised to find that within the first three pages of "My Friend Bingham," the hero shoots and kills the heroine's child. But even here James seemed to be testing the outer limits of, or even parodying, the conventional complications required for a fictional romance. Some of these early stories, including "Bingham," ended with the conventional marriage, but several others conscientiously avoided the predictable resolution. The pathetic hero of "A Passionate Pilgrim" dies just as the heroine becomes free to marry him. In "The Story of a Year" James's heroine betrays her absent soldier-fiancé in favor of a more polished young fop, while in "An Extraordinary Case" she unexpectedly marries her wounded lover's doctor. In all cases, James seemed to be consciously breaking the form of the standard wartime love story with its conventional morality in which the heroine waits for her hero or nurses him back to marriageable health with the patient self-negation of Griselda and the loyalty of Penelope. Some of these early stories also reflected James's development of "psychological realism," particularly through the observant first-person narrator, tangential to the plot, who provides the "fine central intelligence" through which events are interpreted.

Another of the younger realists whom Fields recognized early and published regularly was John W. DeForest. DeForest, like James and Howells, was interested in subverting or evading the conventional plots and sentiments of contemporary fiction. In one of his stories, "The Lawson Tragedy," he announced to the reader that "lovers are habitually insipid," dismissed the romantic protestations of his courting couple as not worth listening to, and rendered a realistic portrait of marital misery (Apr. 1870, 445).

Fields had initiated the publication of these younger realists himself. But when Howells arrived in 1866, both his influence on editorial decisions and his reviews considerably strengthened the magazine's enthusiasm for realism. Howells's own initial literary efforts had been mainly in poetry. But Fields and the *Atlantic* may have played an important part in shifting his focus to realistic prose over the next few years. Howells wrote to Annie Fields reporting an "improving conversation Mr. Fields and I had on Sunday afternoon concerning a future state and the impossibility of finding men who could write little short lively sketchy things of from six to eight pages in length" (Austin 149). The assistant editor seems to have been persuaded to take on the task himself. In 1867, Howells began to write for the *Atlantic* a number of short prose sketches, generally humorous in tone and drawn more or less directly from life. Such pieces as "Mrs. Johnson," a sketch of his black cook, and particularly "A Day's Pleasure," the narrative of a family outing, directly foreshadowed the realistic observation of contemporary life in his first travelogue novel, *Their Wedding Journey*.

Fields's *Atlantic* was moderately liberal and progressive in its commentary on social, religious, and political issues, as well as in its encouragement of literary realism. Much of this liberalism, especially as it applied to social and political values, was founded on the Emersonian principle of cultural and moral progress that asserted a natural tendency in civilizations and individuals to evolve toward a discovery of ever-larger moral truths and toward a higher state of self-realization. This Emersonian version of moral evolution was a part of Yankee humanism before Spencer articulated his version of "social Darwinism," and Emerson was one of the very few influences Spencer acknowledged. A strong sense of social responsibility, however, derived from the gentry tradition and from liberal religion, prevented the Yankee humanists from generally accepting Spencer's ideas of laissez-faire competition and made most of them value instead moral leadership and social activism.

This liberal belief in social progress was frequently, though not always, reflected in *Atlantic* papers on women's issues as well as those on religion and politics. Several writers suggested that the status of women was an index of social progress. Harriet Beecher Stowe's "Chimney Corner" pieces of November and December 1865 asserted the basic tenets of the nineteenth-century women's rights movement, including the right to vote (no taxation without representation!), expanded property rights, more equitable divorce laws, access to professions, and equal educational opportunity (16, 567, 672; Donovan 51). Higginson remained an activist for women's self-realization, especially in education, dress, and physical fitness, as well as in bringing women into the profession of authorship.

In an extraordinary series in 1868 and 1869 titled "Cooperative Housekeeping," Zina Pierce advocated a radical restructuring of women's lives and domestic relationships. Currently, Pierce asserted, the man is "a cruel and lonely lord," while the woman is "always a subject, generally a servant, too often a psychophant and a slave" (Mar. 1869, 299). The "conventional repressing process" made women into children, while machines were now depriving middle-class women of their last economic functions. Social progress and the well-being of both sexes required that women must earn their own living by organizing among themselves, pooling resources, and taking over all distribution and retailing of goods for domestic consumption through cooperatives. Pierce, who continued to write for Howells, was more radical than most, but most *Atlantic* writers of the sixties saw an expansion of women's rights as a necessary condition for social progress.

The *Atlantic*'s treatment of religion and science gave further evidence of the magazine's liberalism as well as its belief in the Emersonian doctrine of moral and social evolution. During Fields's editorship, the *Atlantic* retained its reputation as a critic of religious orthodoxy. In fact, Stowe refused to publish most of her "Oldtown" stories in the magazine because she wished them to reach an orthodox audience who would not read the *Atlantic*, since it was the organ of the Unitarians, transcendentalists, and other infidels (F. Wilson 532). Criticism of traditional Calvinist-Congregationalist religious doctrine permeated not only the fiction of Holmes, D. G. Mitchell, and others but also the antidogmatic, liberal theological speculations of Cyrus Bartol, David Wasson, and James Freeman Clarke. All three of these ministers, like Fields, were liberal Unitarians, having been strongly influenced by Emersonian transcendentalism with its humanistic rejection of dogma and its emphasis on liberating the divinity within humankind.

Clarke's extensive *Atlantic* series analyzing and comparing the major religions of the world clearly demonstrated the Emersonian idea of moral progress as well as Victorian cultural biases. The world's religions, Clarke reasoned, formed an evolutionary progression toward an increasingly comprehensive understanding of higher truth, each prevented from seeing the whole truth by an ethnic culture institutionalized into religious dogmas. Liberal Protestant Christianity was, of course, the furthest stage of evolution, not rejecting, but containing the partial, ethnic visions of the others and surpassing them in universality because it was "not a creed or a form but a spirit . . . able to meet all the changing wants of an advancing civilization by new developments and adaptations" ("A New Chapter of Christian Evidences," Mar. 1869, 315).

Fields gave more attention to science than his successors did. In 1865, he added "Science" to "Literature, Art, and Politics" in the subtitle of his magazine, probably at the urging of his friend Louis Agassiz. Agassiz, an effective popularizer, contributed an influential and useful series on the scientific method. In "The Silurian Beach" (Apr. 1863), he also defended the idea of an "intelligent Creator" with "a great central plan" against the "purely mechanical" evolutionary theories of Darwin and Asa Gray. Later papers by other writers, however, satirized the bluster of respectable citizens denying their descent from apes and endorsed Darwinism while claiming that it did not necessarily conflict with religious faith. Charles Sprague in "The Darwinian Theory" (Oct. 1866) gave a preview of the synthesis of Darwinism with liberal religion and theories of social progress that would soon be more fully articulated in the *Atlantic* by John Fiske, Howells's major writer on science and one of Spencer's major American apologists. Quick to apply Darwinism to social evolution, Sprague ethnocentrically noted the primitivism of some civilizations compared to the "wonderful advancement" of the Caucasian. He logically prophesied, however, that "the boasted perfectness of this day of ours, perfect because it is our day, will be as primitive to the later denizens of this globe as the barbarity of the cave savages is to modern civilization" (423–24).

Atlantic essays on politics during the war and Reconstruction shared with treatments of religion and science this same central vision of social evolution. In fiction and poetry, this vision had sometimes been cast in traditional religious terms that saw the war as a divine judgment leading to a just and harmonious millennium. In political commentary, under Fields as under Lowell, it was generally cast in terms of an Emersonian moral evolution. American society was painfully progressing by at last squaring itself with the high moral principle of human liberty. While sometimes condemning the North for seventy years of morally corrupting equivocation, many *Atlantic* commentators also saw the war ethnocentrically as a struggle between a morally and culturally advanced North and a backward South. The South, Emerson maintained in his essay "American Civilization" (Apr. 1862), was still essentially feudal, aristocratic, and semibarbaric. Emerson and others decreed that progress both in the South and in the nation as a whole depended on the victory of northern conscience, ideals of freedom, democracy, and intellectual vigor. In the universal nature of things, that victory was inevitable and would of necessity be followed by a new dispensation of peace, prosperity, righteous government, and cultural progress.

Under Lowell the *Atlantic* had strongly, but sporadically, denounced compromise with the "slave power," and when the war broke out, it had urged the rigorous suppression of the rebellion against the Union. Fields himself was far less interested in politics than Lowell had been, but the national cataclysm demanded a response. Throughout most of his editorship he published at least one political article a month, sometimes more, dealing directly with the war and its aftermath. Many of these were written by those who had written for Lowell, and they projected the same aggressive liberalism and the same "politics of moral principle."

During the early years of the war, Lowell continued to be a major political contributor both in his essays and in his second series of "Biglow Papers." His first essay after resigning the editorship, "Self-Possession vs. Prepossession" (Dec. 1861), introduced the characteristic *Atlantic* positions on the war: an insistence on prosecuting the rebellion with a maximum of military rigor and a minimum of political divisiveness, an acerbic condemnation of British and French sympathies with the Confederacy, and an affirmation of the need for rapid emancipation.

T. W. Higginson, an admirer of John Brown, did not wish to wait for legal emancipation. While he enlisted in 1861, and in 1862 took command of the first regiment of freed slaves, the First South Carolina Volunteers, Higginson managed to contribute to the *Atlantic* sympathetic accounts of the slave revolts of Toussaint L'Overture, Denmark Vesey, and Nat Turner. Lowell and Emerson, however, became the magazine's principal spokesmen on emancipation. In "American Civilization," Emerson declared that emancipation had become both a moral and a practical necessity. Its enactment, he said, would provoke a massive desertion of the South by the slaves and thus hasten the internal collapse of the Confederacy. It would also place the Union cause squarely in line with the ineluctable laws of moral progress. "Emancipation is the demand of civilization," he declared. "That is a principle; everything else is an intrigue"; those who fought for the higher principle must inevitably be victorious (Apr. 1862, 509). Lowell's Hosea Biglow made the same point more colloquially when he said that emancipation would have the effect of:

> Rammin scripture in our gun,
> An gettin Nature fer an ally.
>
> ("Latest Views," Feb. 1863, 264)

Emerson jubilantly hailed Lincoln's Emancipation Proclamation of September 1862 as "a step forward in the direction of catholic and universal interests" ("The President's Proclamation," Nov. 1862, 638). But although he sensed that it was only a step in the nation's long moral evolution, he interpreted emancipation as a much more final cleansing of the national soul than history proved it. "It does not promise the redemption of the black race," he wrote; "that lies not with us: but it relieves it of our opposition . . . [and] it relieves our race once and for all of its crime and false position" (640). Lowell's Hosea Biglow was more prophetic when he predicted that the larger problem remained: to change not laws but hearts and minds ("Sunthen in the Pastoral Line," June 1862, 796).

The references to Lincoln in *Atlantic* political essays were generally supportive, as might be expected of a strongly pro-Union periodical during the war. Fields was honored when Lincoln requested in 1863 that a report of a southern refusal to negotiate peace be published in the *Atlantic*. But some essays suggested an ambivalence characteristic of the attitudes of many New England intellectuals toward this awkward, little-known lawyer from the Illinois backwoods, whose pragmatism they sometimes saw as want of moral principle. Lowell had strongly endorsed Lincoln for the presidency in 1860 after admitting his preference for the more radical Seward. But between 1860 and 1862, he continued to chafe over Lincoln's hesitancy to commit himself to emancipation and to prosecute the rebellion rigorously. Hosea Biglow expressed some of Lowell's frustrations when he said:

> Soft-heartedness in times like these
> Shows sof'ness in the upper story.
>
> ("Latest Views" Feb. 1863, 264)

In 1864, the *Atlantic* again supported Lincoln for the presidency, although two articles by C. C. Hazewell clearly suggested that the motive was more political necessity than personal admiration.

The other cause of the Bostonian ambivalence toward Lincoln, an uneasiness over his uncultivated character and manner, was scrupulously omitted from the *Atlantic*, although one senses it in some commentaries. Hawthorne, after a trip to Washington in 1862, wrote an account of his observations, including an essentially sympathetic but somewhat satiric sketch of the gangling, rustic "Uncle Abe," who reminded him of nothing so much as a shrewd country schoolmaster. Fields considered the passage neither "wise or tasteful to print" and asked him to delete it. Hawthorne acquiesced but lamented to his editor: "What a terrible thing it is to try to let off a little bit of truth into this miserable humbug of a world" (Austin 218–19).

The ambivalence of the New England intellectuals toward Lincoln reflected their essential ambivalence toward democracy itself. Most wanted to believe, but could not rid themselves of a deep mistrust of either a man or a political system that worked not on the elevated plane of principle but rather on pragmatic compromise between conflicting, frankly self-interested, political forces. The Emancipation Proclamation and the increasing momentum of the Union victories, however, gradually overcame this New England skepticism toward Lincoln. The assassination transformed even his suspected faults into virtues. He was eulogized by George Bankroft and others as the supreme representative of the democratic will of the American people in his homely birth and character, as well as his moderate policies ("The Place of Abraham Lincoln in History," June 1865). Lowell in his "Ode Recited at the Harvard Commemorative" hailed the nation's "Martyr Chief" as the "new birth of our new soil; the first American" (Sept. 1865, 368).

Had Lincoln lived to administer the postwar Reconstruction, the *Atlantic*'s political commentators would have found themselves again at odds with his policies of moderation. The same righteous sense of moral principle that made the *Atlantic* writers condemn political compromise and advocate early emancipation now made them advocate the political subjugation of the South. The magazine's position on Reconstruction, as on slavery, was essentially radical Republican. In fact, several of its major statements were written by Fields's friend Senator Charles Sumner, one of the leaders of that faction, who considered the magazine a means of influencing important public opinion.

As early as October 1863, Sumner proposed in the *Atlantic* the political foundations for radical reconstruction of the vanquished South. In "Our Domestic Relations," he argued that the rebel states had clearly forfeited their rights either to govern themselves or to participate in the federal government. However, prolonged military governance of these states, under the ultimate control of the executive branch, was both dangerous and unconstitutional. The Constitution clearly indicated that government of the conquered areas should be given over as rapidly as possible to a Congress composed of representatives from states loyal to the Union.

In this article Sumner referred to then senator Andrew Johnson as a patriot, "faithful among the faithless, the Abdiel of the South" (521). Two years later, after Johnson had become president and attempted to moderate the abject subjugation of the South by the radical Republican Congress, Sumner was denouncing him bitterly. Johnson, he raged, was a usurper of congressional authority, a covert successor to Jefferson Davis, who was "preparing to invest belligerent traitors, who for four bloody years have murdered our fellow citizens, with those Equal Rights in the Republic which are denied to friends and allies [the freedmen] so that the former can rule over the latter" ("Clemency and Common Sense," Dec. 1865, 758). By 1866, *Atlantic* commentary on Johnson and his policies of leniency had fallen from righteous moralizing to sheer invective. Johnson's speeches, wrote E. P. Whipple, were "a volcanic outbreak of vulgarity, conceit, bombast, scurrility, ignorance, insolence, brutality and balderdash." "His brain is to be classed with the notable cases of arrested development" ("The President and His Accomplices," Nov. 1866, 635).

Whipple, whose own volcanic outbreaks of bombast lowered both the *Atlantic's* political tone and his own credibility, declared that the question of readmitting the southern states must be viewed "across a great sea of blood" and that clemency would take America "down a step in the zoological scale" ("The President and the Congress," Apr. 1866, 502). The stated motive for *Atlantic* resistance to such readmission, however, was not revenge but protection and provision for the four million former slaves liberated by the war.

"The stern logic of events," Frederick Douglass wrote in the *Atlantic* in 1866, "has determined the interests of the country as identical with and inseparable from those of the negro" ("Reconstruction," Dec. 1866, 765). From the beginning, *Atlantic* writers insisted that the reconstitution of the rebel states should be dependent upon their ratification of the Thirteenth, Fourteenth, and Fifteenth amendments, designed to secure equal rights and enfranchisement for the freedman. Douglass and Sumner warned against allowing Confederate states to institute Black Codes, which were "abhorrent to civilization and dangerous to liberty" (Sumner, "Clemency and Common Sense," Dec. 1865, 760). Douglass, E. E. Hale, Whipple, T. W. Higginson, and others argued forcibly that the only just treatment of the freedmen was to give them confiscated land, full legal equality, and the vote. These steps were not only morally imperative but necessary to make these people "a stable and valuable part of society" (Hale, "How to Use the Victory," June 1864, 767). William Parker, himself a freedman, wrote a narrative of personal experience demonstrating the freedman's fitness for suffrage and determination to protect his rights by force if necessary ("The Freedman's Story," Feb.–Mar. 1866).

"When the freedmen are lost in the mass of freemen," Higginson wrote, "the work [of the war] will be complete" ("Fair Play the Best Policy," May 1865, 623). He added also that the "lingering caste institutions" in the North would have to disappear with southern slavery (630). Both Higginson and Douglass warned that if blacks were denied full rights, economic opportunity, and sufficient means of protecting themselves, the sacrifices of the war would be wasted, and violent social upheavals would be inflicted on generations of Americans—black and white—yet unborn (Douglass, "An Appeal to the Congress for an Impartial Suffrage," Jan. 1867, 117).

Despite the original claim in its credo that the *Atlantic* would be the organ of no political faction, the magazine during the Reconstruction period published articles seriously stating that the Republican party was "the Party of Righteousness" and an agent of the divine will. Conversely, the Democrats were blamed for the war and denounced en masse as potentially traitorous copperheads "doing the Devil's work for the Devil's pay." In the aftermath of Grant's Republican victory in 1868,

Whipple in an article titled "The Moral Significance of the Republican Triumph" rejoiced that "the Lord reigns!" (Jan. 1869, 124).

The vision of the Republican party to which the *Atlantic* was loyal was defined by Henry Wilson, later vice-president during Grant's second term. In "The New Departure of the Republican Party" (Jan. 1871), Wilson emphasized that the party had come into being as an organization of reform, progress, human rights, and moral principle. The slave power had been defeated, but the Republicans must now enforce the civil rights guaranteed by the constitutional amendments. Furthermore, two new threats loomed. The first was the potential tyranny of the money power, especially the railroad interests, which must be controlled by government. The second threat was a vast, uneducated voting populace including, among others, the freedman and the immigrant. The need here was for enculturation and education. To educate the populace, develop their capacities, and prevent increasingly sharp social and economic divisions, Wilson proposed that the party's next major reform be a federal system for universal education. This was a combination of idealism and self-interest that appealed to the educated middle-class *Atlantic* audience. Over the next several decades, the magazine constantly promoted public education, including using it to spread the values of the New England literary culture. *Atlantic* writers also continued to be critical of both unregulated corporate capitalism and the political power of an increasingly culturally diverse populace.

In 1868, then, the magazine was still strongly Republican. It supported Grant for the presidency, although there was a noticeable undercurrent of ambivalence toward the man himself reminiscent of the initial ambivalence toward Lincoln. Questions had to be raised and answered about his moral and intellectual capacities. Distrust was also expressed concerning the immense wealth of Grant's backers, but he was ironically credited with "an unerring faculty for selecting the right men for subordinates" (C. G. Came, "Our New President," Mar. 1869, 383). Significantly, however, in the year of Grant's inauguration, the astute and timely James Parton initiated a series investigating and calling for reform of federal lobbying practices, congressional pork-barreling, and the political spoils system. This advocacy of civil service reform and other forms of "morality in government" was eventually to separate the *Atlantic* from the Republican party and to become a major tenet of *Atlantic* political commentary during the rest of the century.

In the years immediately following Appomattox, the scandals of the Grant administration, the moral bankruptcy of the Republican party, the polarization of corporate capitalism and labor, and the political cynicism of the late nineteenth century were barely on the horizon. Between 1865 and 1870 the *Atlantic* reflected a postwar mood of immense and visionary optimism about the future of the nation. This visionary optimism had been implicit in the northern interpretation of the war. If the conflict had been divine judgment, victory would issue in the millennium. Righteousness had prevailed, and the rewards of righteousness would follow. As Emerson had said in his celebration of emancipation, the national conscience had been cleansed "once and for all"; morality had superseded debasing compromise as the foundation of national policy and law; the national destiny had been squared with the ineluctable laws of moral evolution, and that evolution must inevitably propel it forward into a new dispensation, an expansive new age of economic, geographic, and cultural progress.

The historian George Bankroft participated in this vision of manifest destiny when he prophesied in the *Atlantic* in 1865: "With one wing touching the waters of the Atlantic and the other on the Pacific, [the country] will grow to a greatness of which the past has no parallel; there can be no spot in Europe or in Asia so remote or so secluded as to shut out its influence" ("Abraham Lincoln's Place in History," June 1865, 764). J. K. Medbury, writing about the opening of the West in "Our Pacific Railroads," exulted in the "magnificent commercial certainties" that would result when the unfortunate, obsolescent Indians and Mormons had acquiesced to "the inevitable civilization of the locomotive." "The corollary of the Pacific Railroad," he wrote, "is the transfer of the world's commerce to America, and the substitution of New York for Paris and London as the world's exchange" (Dec. 1867, 715).

Senator Sumner outdistanced all of the visionaries when he predicted in "Prophetic Voices about America" (Sept. 1867) that the whole of the American continent must now inevitably become one great democracy, one "Plural Unit," through the peaceful and voluntary annexation of Mexico and Canada. "The name of the Republic," he expatiated, "will be exalted until every neighbor, yielding to irresistible attraction, will seek new life in becoming a part of the great whole." Nor was his enthusiasm dimmed by his prediction that within this "Plural Unit" individuals would become lost in the "transcendent mass," "each citizen [becoming] little more than an industrious insect" (306).

Most *Atlantic* prophets of the Republic's cultural and spiritual future were enthusiastic about the projected expansion of territory, commerce, population, democratic rights, and national power. But there were dissenting voices and considerable debate over whether the development of culture and values would keep pace with material development. One reactionary commentator, less enthusiastic than Sumner at the prospect of a mass-culture society of "industrious insects," warned that while utilitarian democracy seemed historically inevitable and perhaps even desirable, its price was the loss of individuality and high culture. The independent-minded gentleman was already near extinction, and the future belonged to "the impudent Celt and the black." A leveling democratic materialism ensured that future Americans would be homogenized by conformity, their only ambitions "to make money and be amused" (Sheldon, "The Dead Level," Dec.

1869, 666). This cynical view never dominated the *Atlantic*, but it echoed more frequently after 1880 in reaction to a strong sense of dispossession among the New England cultural elite.

Sometimes from fear of democratic materialism, sometimes from a progressive sense of new American cultural potential, many *Atlantic* writers of this period sounded a call for a renewed emphasis on developing and disseminating an American intellectual and literary culture. Many also spoke for the active leadership of a cultural elite. Emerson was the most sanguine of the *Atlantic*'s cultural prophets. But his insistence on the need for the moral and intellectual guidance of American democracy had become more emphatic than ever. In December 1864, he wrote to Sumner reporting that Holmes, Lowell, and himself unanimously endorsed the establishment of a National Academy of Arts and Sciences. All three agreed, he said, that "we are at an important point of national history and one from which very great expansion of thought and morals and political activity in all kinds will follow." They further agreed, however, that an academy should be established at this crucial point to act as "a constituted jury to which questions of taste and fitness in literature might be carried" and thus help to guide this projected expansion (*Letters* 5: 395–97).

This same combination of spacious optimism about cultural development with a strong precaution about its proper guidance was apparent in Emerson's *Atlantic* essay "Aspects of Culture" (Jan. 1868). Here he enthusiastically projected intellectual, moral, and cultural advances equivalent to those that were territorial and commercial. He insisted, however, that this evolution would come not from "the foolish and sensual millions" but through the leadership of a "cultivated class," an educated and independent-minded minority (91).

T. W. Higginson, perhaps the *Atlantic*'s most frequent cultural commentator, expressed both the hopes and anxieties of the time. In "A Plea for Culture" (Jan. 1867), Higginson shared the fear that America's culture, literature, and values were not keeping pace with its immense material progress. The postwar goal of American life, he complained, "seems a commonplace and debasing [commercial] success"; Americans were wanting in the idealism and moral vision that culture should supply. The responsibility for this failure was two-sided. The public, uneducated and immersed in getting and spending, lacked interest in art, literature, and the intellect. At the same time, he argued in "Americanism in Literature" (Jan. 1870), the nation's traditional cultural leaders were developing a "timid and faithless spirit," a facile antidemocratic cynicism, leading to a disdainful isolation and abdication of their social function and relevance (60).

Higginson expressed optimism that these apparent dichotomies between material progress and cultural stasis, between political democracy and high culture, between the majority and the intellectual elite, could be resolved. Higginson joined

Holmes, D. A. Wasson, and other *Atlantic* writers in reacting against Britain's lack of wartime sympathy with the Union by rejecting British culture and reasserting a more democratic American culture. Refuting Matthew Arnold's criticism of American moral Puritanism, he claimed that America's cultural genius lay specifically in its moral intuition, its rejection of European cynicism, and its faith in a "new impulse in human progress" ("Americanism," 56). Furthermore, he said, he saw new evidence that the split between the democratic majority and the cultural elite was healing and that "the literary class has come more into sympathy with the popular heart." In a Whitmanesque conclusion, he wrote: "I affirm that democratic society, the society of the future, enriches and does not impoverish human life, and gives more, not less material for literary art" (62).

By frankly noting the division between the democratic majority and the cultural elite, Higginson had accurately defined the central problem, both in literature and in politics, that the New England high culture represented by the *Atlantic* would face over at least the next sixty years. Contrary to Higginson's projections, that strain would grow, aggravated by industrialization, immigration, increasing class divisions, and the proliferation of mass culture. A portion of the traditional, largely Anglo-Saxon cultural elite would react against these changes with attitudes ranging from the disengaged aestheticism of Thomas Bailey Aldrich to the mordant antidemocratic cynicism of Henry Adams and the genteel tradition's willful blindness to the present and bland nostalgia for the past. These attitudes would be represented in the *Atlantic*. But most of the magazine's editors—Howells, Scudder, Page, and Perry, like Fields and Higginson—sought, each in his own way, to bridge the gap, to keep the magazine in touch with the democratic life of the nation while preserving something of the old, high-culture Yankee humanism.

Fields, as publisher of a broadly popular and critically respected group of New England authors before the rise of mass culture, had an easier time bridging the culture gap than did his successors. His instinct for accommodating audiences and for commercial promotion, sometimes foreshadowing the techniques of mass culture, helped considerably. Partly for these reasons, the postwar period was generally prosperous for Fields, despite the need to take in some financial sail in the recession of 1867–69. William Ticknor's death in 1864 had left Fields in near-complete control of the publishing house, which continued to thrive and expand under his management. In 1868, Ticknor's son Howard, whom Fields considered "of no account ever," was forced out of the business, ostensibly for being discovered kissing a secretary in a back room (Fields to Longfellow, 31 Oct. 1868; Tryon 330). The remaining Ticknor interest was purchased by Fields and James R. Osgood, his assistant of many years, who now became the junior partner of Fields, Osgood and Company.

In spite of his prosperity, however, these were often difficult years for Fields. He had been in the business for more than three decades and now, at the height of his success, began to show signs of tiring in body and spirit. The lawsuit brought against him in 1866 by Gail Hamilton and Sophia Hawthorne alleging but never proving financial improprieties not only damaged his reputation but personally hurt him. To escape the attendant publicity and unpleasantness, he made an extended trip to England, and at its end found himself reluctant to return home to the treadmill. After this, he began regularly to take the summers off, and in 1869 he again returned to his beloved England, this time for six months. He had hired Howells in 1866 partly with the idea of giving himself some relief from the editorial burden, and Howells had rapidly proven himself both eager and fully able to take over the major responsibility for the *Atlantic*. Increasingly, the assistant editor was given charge of not only the mechanics of editing but also correspondence, the selection of manuscripts, and the composition of issues.

During Fields's six-month trip to Europe in 1869, Howells was left to edit the *Atlantic* himself, with informal advice from the magazine's godparents, Lowell and Holmes. Shortly after Fields's departure an article arrived from Harriet Beecher Stowe in which that quixotic crusader for righteous causes defended the memory of her deceased friend Lady Byron against recent attacks by Byron's last mistress, the Countess Guiccioli. Not only had her dear friend too patiently borne the wrongs of the libertine poet, but those wrongs included "a secret adulterous intrigue with a blood relation, so near in consanguinity that discovery must have been utter ruin and expulsion from civilized society" (qtd. in Austin 293). Howells was in a quandary. Even Fields did not dare to reject the insistent Stowe; the subject of incest, however, was uncomfortably controversial. Lowell cautioned against publication, but Holmes, always eager to shock public piety in the name of truth, advocated acceptance, and Howells acted on his advice. Fields, who was informed after the acceptance, offered no objection and in fact arranged for simultaneous English publication. In August, he wrote to Osgood that Howells's last two issues had been "exceptionally good" and that "Mrs. Stowe's article on Byron in the September number should attract considerable attention, though the main fact in that paper has been for a long time known to certain circles" (7 Aug. 1869).

For once, Fields had misjudged the *Atlantic* audience. "Considerable attention" turned out to be a gross understatement; the article created a furor both in America and in England. Immediately, Howells reported to Fields, there arose "howls of rejection on every side where a critical dog is kept" (24 Aug. 1869, *Life in Letters* 1: 147). Stowe's stated intention had been to justify the maligned Lady Byron and to rescue "the youth of America" from Byron's "brilliant, seductive genius" (qtd. in Austin 293). But the Victorian public was so outraged by the publication of the sordid fact that it was indifferent to the intent. Typically, the issue containing the article sold fast and furiously; then in the aftermath, when public curiosity was satiated and succeeded by righteous indignation, the *Atlantic*'s circulation began to plummet. In 1870 circulation was down to 35,000, a loss of at least 15,000 from its peak in 1865. Other factors, including a milder reaction against Holmes's serial "The Guardian Angel" and particularly the increasing competition from other magazines, contributed to the decline. But unquestionably the Stowe debacle had cost the *Atlantic* many thousands of fastidious readers, whom it never regained. The incident would make future editors, including Howells, more conservative about offending Victorian decorums.

Even before the storm broke, Fields had indicated that he was ready to retire. On 23 July 1869, he wrote to Osgood from Europe, more than half seriously: "If you hear of anybody who would like to buy me out and thus rid me of ever reading a Mss again, let me know. I dread returning to my work. . . . I am tired and would like a respite from labor and eye-strain."

He did return, however, and for more than a year continued, at least nominally, as the *Atlantic*'s editor-in-chief. Throughout 1870, he complained frequently of mental and physical fatigue, and when it appeared that Osgood, with two associates, had both the ambition and the capital to buy him out, he sold his full share in the firm and announced his retirement as both publisher and editor.

On January 2, 1871, Fields, Osgood and Company was to become James R. Osgood and Company, and Howells was officially to succeed Fields as editor of the *Atlantic*. On January 1, a farewell was held in the elegant reception room for authors in the firm's impressive and prosperous-looking new offices at 123 Tremont Street. The occasion was attended by Emerson, Longfellow, Whittier, Holmes, and other members of the old *Atlantic* "circle," one that Fields had helped create both in fiction and in fact. Most of these authors had often chatted with Fields behind the green baize curtain in his modest niche at the Old Corner Bookstore, and some had even bought books from him there long ago when the Old Corner was Ticknor's retail store and Fields was a clerk.

In speeches at the reception, many of Fields's guests acknowledged that his considerable commercial success as a publisher had benefited them personally and had furthered the cause of American literature. Subsequent historians have confirmed that Fields had indeed benefited the profession of authorship in America through his creation of new markets for good writing, as well as new techniques for promotion and distribution. The *Atlantic* had been an important part of this accomplishment. Twenty years before, there had been no prospect of a regular source of publication that would nationally circulate 50,000 copies of virtually anything the major New England authors chose to write, thereby not only developing a larger audience for their books but also paying them liberally and dependably for the privilege of publishing them.

In publicly acknowledging Fields's accomplishments at the farewell reception, some of the guests might have had private reservations. Emerson, who, despite his vatic reputation, was financially astute and fully appreciative of Fields's commercial acuity, might privately have noted to himself a moderate lightening and concession to popular taste in the *Atlantic*. James Parton, for his part, would have claimed that the magazine had improved by trading transcendental Emersonian musings for more direct reportage of American realities. Howells might have been privately resentful at having to fudge some reviews for the protection of Fields's friends and clients. But he could be truthfully grateful to his former employer for giving him generous editorial freedom, maintaining the literary focus of the magazine, and giving encouragement and solid remuneration to several younger, more realistic authors, including Howells himself.

A dispassionate observer would have been bound to conclude that there was considerable truth in the speeches made at the farewell to Fields. Fields had generally united the capacities of a shrewd publisher with those of a sympathetic editor. He had reconciled, not perfectly but to a degree matched by few, the conflicting claims of commerce and of literature. But if that observer could have added omniscience to objectivity, he would have foretold that, partly because of the more competitive publishing market Fields himself had helped to create, both the *Atlantic*'s unchallenged golden day and the *Atlantic* circle assembled for the farewell were passing with the long waning of New England's literary Indian summer.

William Dean Howells during his *Atlantic* editorship, 1871–1881. By permission of the Houghton Library, Harvard University (Howells Collection).

4
William Dean Howells
(1 8 7 1 – 1 8 8 1)

Editorial Realist

Howell's editorship of the *Atlantic*, in a different way from Fields's, was clear evidence that the Boston literary culture which had produced and sustained the magazine in its early years was no monolithic, closed patrician circle. Literary Boston's embrace of Howells showed that it was socially and intellectually open to younger, provincial American writers, especially those from the West. Nor was this support ultimately conditional upon a respectful deference to all of their values.

Howells, for his part, was initially filled with imitative admiration for the *Atlantic* Olympians and was ambitious for their recognition. But he also saw himself, sometimes with defensive pride, partly as a westerner and an outsider, and later as the proponent of a literary creed that would supersede theirs. Howells worked out much of this complex relationship with the established Boston writers through his editorship of the *Atlantic*. He was by nature a pragmatic realist whose instinct was often to accomplish his purpose through tact and compromise. Still, during this period he developed and articulated an independent sense of his own values while continuing to receive strong support from literary Boston.

During his five years as Fields's assistant (1866–70) and later ten as editor-in-chief (1871–81), Howells himself changed from a sentimental, imitative, romantic poet to a major practitioner, theorist, and advocate of realistic fiction. He discovered in realism a means to bridge the gap between literary high culture and the social and economic mainstream of American life. His social and political sympathies became increasingly liberal. Howells also changed the magazine significantly. While the *Atlantic*'s circulation dropped sharply during his time, largely because of competition from New York illustrated monthlies, he made the magazine more fully national and democratic in content and authorship. He introduced into it a younger generation of American writers, mainly from beyond New England, and used his editorship to guide and support their careers. He added the section "Contributors' Club" to stimulate writing by new authors, and he greatly increased the volume of literary criticism, making the *Atlantic* both the leading exponent of literary realism and the most authoritative source of reviews in the country. Finally, although literary debate absorbed too much of his editorial attention, he published fiction and sociological reportage that gave the magazine fuller sympathies with a broader range of contemporary American life.

Howells's first contact with literary Boston in 1860 reflects the extraordinarily generous, if paternalistic, encouragement given to this unknown, self-educated, twenty-three-year-old newspaper reporter from Ohio by Lowell, Fields, Hawthorne, and Holmes. It reflects also Howells's literary ambition and tenacity of purpose. Significantly, Howells had begun the journey to write a book on "the principal manufacturing industries in the United States" for his Columbus, Ohio, publisher, but after being ejected from an iron foundry as a suspected industrial spy and enduring a desultory visit to a shoe factory, he dropped the project to pursue his real passion, literature. (Not until well into his *Atlantic* editorship was he able to see the connection between literature and reportage on contemporary economic conditions.) Thereafter, he turned the trip into a literary pilgrimage. But Howells did not go to the literary Mecca of America in 1860 just to worship. Characteristically, he had a more practical ambition in mind: to find himself a job that would deliver him from journalism to literature, and from the literary fringes of the West to the literary hub of the East.

Determined but with considerable misgiving, the young Ohioan first braved Lowell, still the *Atlantic*'s editor at the time, who, anxious to encourage a promising young "western" writer, had accepted seven of his early poems. Lowell, feeling the young aspirant's sincere admiration, received him warmly, praised his poems, and after long conversation invited him to dinner that evening at the Parker House. Almost certainly that conversation included inquiries concerning an assistantship on the *Atlantic*. When Howells arrived at the small upper room of the Parker House, he discovered that Lowell had also invited Holmes, always influential in *Atlantic* affairs, and Fields, who had within the year become the magazine's publisher. "Lowell and Holmes," Howells wrote to his father, "both seemed to take me by the hand, and the Autocrat, about the time coffee came in, began to talk about the apostolic succession" (*Life in Letters* 1: 29).

A few days later, over a breakfast of blueberry cakes in Fields's dining room, Howells asked the publisher directly whether he would take on an assistant to Lowell. Fields replied that the job was filled by Howard Ticknor. But the young aspirant from the provinces was characteristically persistent. On returning to Columbus by way of New York, which disgusted him with its pose of cynicism and its bohemian literary pretensions, he wrote Fields with ambitious confidence,

"'Better fifty years of Boston than a cycle of New York,' if one may so dilapidate 'Locksley Hall.' The truth is, there is no place quite so good as Boston—God bless it! and I look forward to living there some day—being possibly the linchpin in the hub" (M. Howells 1: 30).

Five years later, after serving as consul in Venice, Howells had just begun working for E. L. Godkin on the *Nation* in New York when he again met Fields at a literary gathering in Bayard Taylor's apartments. Fields was now in search of an assistant. Lowell, who with Norton had helped Howells get the job at the *Nation*, had recently written proposing Howells for the place: "I hope you will do whatever you can, for Howells is sure to be somebody if he lives" (M. Howells 1: 97). After an interview, Fields wrote a letter offering Howells the position. Howells's job with the *Nation* was an enviable one for a twenty-eight-year-old. But his admiration for literary Boston, the heady memory of his reception there, his sense that it offered a writer more opportunities, respect, and security than New York, and his ambition to be the linchpin in the hub were undiminished.

Howells was too much of a pragmatist, however, to let his enthusiasm show in negotiations. His response to Fields's offer reflects his self-confidence, his disciplined ambition, and his instinct for tact and compromise. "The question," he wrote, "is whether I can be of sufficient use to justify you in offering me something better than I now have in the way of place and pay." In his initial draft of the letter, he added: "My ambition would be to hold on the *Atlantic* the position of editor, subject, of course, to your advice and instruction" (unsent letter to Fields, 14 Jan. 1866). But feeling the hubris of this assertion coming from a largely unknown, twenty-eight-year-old Ohio journalist with few publications to his credit, he decided against sending the first draft and wrote more tactfully: "I should be glad to have you write saying whether you could pay me the salary named [$55 per week] and stating more explicitly the duties you wish me to perform" (14 Jan. 1866, qtd. in Austin 144). After negotiations, Fields raised his salary offer from $40 to $50 a week and specified the duties as sifting unsolicited manuscripts, corresponding with contributors, proofreading, and writing four or five pages of book reviews per month, any additional contributions to receive independent payment (M. Howells 1: 105). Howells began these tasks at the *Atlantic* on 1 March 1866, his twenty-ninth birthday.

During his fifteen years on the *Atlantic*, from 1866 to 1881, Howells's relationships with literary Boston, including Lowell, Fields, and the *Atlantic*'s major original contributors, were more complex and ambiguous on his side than on theirs. Most of them were paternalistically generous and supportive. But despite his acceptances and success, Howells from the beginning felt somewhat defensively different from them, and as he clarified his own values and direction, his sense of difference increased.

In Howells's early Boston years, Emerson was "gentle but cold," forgot his name, and had to be introduced anew every time they met. But by far the majority, particularly those closest to the magazine, such as Fields and Lowell, and those purportedly most patrician, like Holmes and Norton, gave the young Howells not only a rapid social and intellectual acceptance but also, in several cases, sustained personal friendship and support. Some may have unconsciously savored the chance to give support and encouragement to a young man from the West who so clearly honored their values and reflected the national and democratic influence of their culture. But they seemed mainly motivated by personal liking and disinterested generosity toward a personable and apparently talented young writer. Howells later recalled that "the intellectual life there was a complete democracy and I do not believe that since the capitalist era began there was ever a community in which money counted for less.... A mind cultivated in some sort was essential and after that came civil manners" (qtd. in Green 72).

Both Fields and his wife, Annie, felt immediately responsible for introducing the Howellses to literary Boston. As Howells's biographer, Cady, describes it: "The genial, glamorous, wealthy Fieldses with their marvelous collection of literary souvenirs, their boundless prestige and savoir faire, their famous breakfasts, and celebrity packed 'evenings' could introduce the Howellses into every compartment ... of Boston's literary-social life.... they saw that everybody met him and his wife" (*Road to Realism* 130). Howells's kindly "chief" also invited the Howellses for festive family occasions, including Christmas Eve, at which the stout Howells played Santa Claus.

Long before becoming Fields's assistant, Howells had already begun a long and warm friendship with Charles Eliot Norton, who as editor of the *North American Review* had published some of Howells's essays on Italian literature. Norton not only located a house for the Howellses to buy on Sacramento Street in Cambridge but arranged the loan and endorsed the mortgage as well. Mrs. Norton arranged credit at the local market that the cosmopolitan members of the Dante Club dubbed the Mercato Tom Brewero (Howells to C. E. Norton, 25 May 1866 in *Selected Letters* 1: 253–54). When Howells settled in Cambridge in May 1866, Norton and Lowell both ensured him a place at the Wednesday meetings of the Dante Club at Longfellow's house, during which the poet read his most recent Italian translation, followed by dinner and discussion among the members, including Holmes, Henry James, Sr., Thomas Appleton, and Richard Henry Dana.

Lowell's treatment of the young westerner, particularly in the late sixties, reflected an affection that was nearly paternal, or at least avuncular (Cady, *Road to Realism* 144; Lynn 123). Soon after his arrival, Howells resumed his place as Lowell's protégé begun in 1860. Lowell had Howells to dinner weekly, frequently called on him to go on long rambles filled with heady discussions of literature, gave him shrewd advice on his professional career, and introduced him to all distinguished literary visitors to Cambridge. Howells's long relationship with Lowell, like his attitude toward the Yankee humanism for which Lowell stood, was complex and ambiguous, especially on Howells's side. Howells much later recalled a consciousness of seniority and authority in Lowell's friendship. But he added that Lowell's "nature was so noble and his reason so tolerant that whenever . . . I found it well to come to open rebellion, as I more than once did, he admitted my right of insurrection, and never resented the outbreak" (*Literary Friends* 213).

During Howells's assistant editorship, Cambridge also offered an extraordinary group of younger intellectuals with whom Howells soon became closely acquainted and who would exert a strong influence on his own development and on his conduct of the *Atlantic*. In the late sixties, Howells became a charter member of The Club, a circle including Henry and William James, Henry and Brooks Adams, John Fiske, Thomas Sergeant Perry, and Oliver Wendell Holmes, Jr. Henry James had recently discarded law for literature, and Howells later recalled, "We seem to have been presently always together, and always talking of methods of fiction whether we walked the streets by day or night, or we sat together reading our stuff to each other; his stuff . . . we both hoped might make itself into matter for the *Atlantic Monthly*" (M. Howells 1: 397).

Howells's post as assistant editor of the *Atlantic* from 1866 to 1870 kept him in close contact with the various spheres of intellectual Boston. In numerous ways, from humble proofreading to critical reviewing and evaluating manuscripts, it also put him in a position to pass judgments on their work. This seat of judgment was often uncomfortable when it required criticism of older, established writers. But it provided the young Ohioan a chance to confer the *Atlantic*'s prestige on the native-born, younger writers of Boston, as well as on fellow outlanders. It also engaged Howells in an intellectual dialogue that helped him define his own set of values different from either generation of intellectual Boston. Much of Howells's growth during this formative period in his career was a direct result of his *Atlantic* job and is recorded in his contributions to the magazine.

Howells was by nature pragmatic, a realist who believed that progress is often made through compromise rather than grand moral gestures of defiance. While his extraordinary talent for friendship reveals that he was not an egotist, he was immensely ambitious and unwilling to jeopardize his career. Through his father, an Ohio newspaper editor, and through his own experience as a reporter, he knew well the demands that audiences and publishers place on writers and editors. Finally, despite the rapid recognition and generous support he received from intellectual Boston, he could not have had the security that Lowell had as a native Brahmin, or that Fields had as the magazine's publisher. Particularly in his dealing with the *Atlantic*'s established writers, he was acutely conscious, more so than they, that he was both younger and a westerner. The result of all these motives was a tendency, strongest during his assistantship, waning but still present during his editorship, self-consciously to exaggerate conflict and to defuse real or imagined conflict with publishers, writers, or readers by being conciliatory within the confines of his own sense of integrity. He would not transgress his own fairly strict sense of integrity, but he often sacrificed his ego. This allowed him as a young newcomer to intellectual Boston to accomplish what he might not have otherwise, and it did not prevent him from developing his own values.

Even in his early relationship with the genial and supportive Fields, Howells oddly combined ambitious confidence, anxious insecurity, and pragmatic determination to defuse potential conflict through humility. After suppressing his unrealistically confident initial impulse to claim the job of editor-in-chief, Howells adopted the unrealistically modest view that Fields was hiring him primarily for his printing and proofreading skills rather than for his literary judgment. Howells claimed that though he felt some humiliation at this low estimate of his worth, he "digested (this course of humble pie) perfectly" (*Literary Friends* 112). Fields may well have valued Howells's proofreading abilities, but it is not credible that he chose the assistant on whom he would rely to attract new authors, to evaluate manuscripts, to write virtually all reviews, to contribute his own writings, and to be first in line to succeed him as editor, mainly for his ability to read proof. Howells's interpretation of Fields's motives reflects a considerable exaggeration and readiness to detect a slight, resulting from the insecurities of an ambitious young midwesterner within the Boston literary establishment. Eleven years later, a similar sense of insecurity about his place in intellectual Boston would lead him to exaggerate wildly Boston's umbrage over Mark Twain's Whittier dinner speech, in which Twain portrayed Emerson, Holmes, and Longfellow as seedy confidence men. Characteristically, Howells counseled Twain to defuse the conflict by unnecessary abject apologies to the Olympians. In both instances, and others, Howells in his insecurity ate more humble pie than Boston required of him.

To suggest that Howells sometimes exaggerated conflicts, slights to his authority, or the need to be tactful, especially in dealing with established figures, is not to imply that some members of literary Boston did not have egos that required careful handling. Reading proofs, which was a part of Howells's job, had particular potential for creating friction. Howells recalled that the *Atlantic*'s linguistic standards were "almost fearfully scrupulous and perfect" (*Literary Friends* 138). Howells took his job with the red pencil seriously and was inclined to edit heavily. While some senior authors were prepared to accept correction from a junior editor graciously, others were not. He recalled Harriet Stowe's patience and gratitude for the assistant editor's help in unsnarling her syntax. But he also recalled considerable anxiety at pointing out errors in Latin quotations to the imperious Sumner, who was arrogant about his own learning and who once commented to Howells that he had never met an educated man from the West. And there seemed no painless way of telling the Sage of Concord that he had committed an error of subject-verb agreement (*Literary Friends*, 137, 139).

Reviewing, one of Howells's major responsibilities as assistant editor, also offered its share of anxiety, slices of humble pie, and opportunities for conflict with his "chief" and literary elders. But it offered, too, important opportunities to define his own literary values and to lend critical support to deserving new writers. Howells was responsible for supervising reviews from 1866 on, writing most of them between 1866 and 1871 himself and many thereafter. His conduct of the *Atlantic*'s reviewing department as assistant editor reflects his ability to balance (not without tension) pragmatic compromise, on the one hand, and, on the other, aesthetic integrity and support for his evolving ideas of literary realism. As René Wellek notes, "Howells's theory of the novel crystallized in the early years of his editorship" largely as a result of his exposure to large quantities of Russian, German, and French, as well as American, fiction (207).

To Fields, reviewing had been largely a genteel way of promoting the firm's books. For Howells, even more than for Lowell, reviewing and literary criticism constituted one major way in which he and the *Atlantic* could stimulate the writing and reading of genuinely good literature, educate public taste, and help to develop intellectual and literary standards in a nation largely devoid of such standards. As Fields's assistant, and even later, Howells was pragmatically sensitive to the interests of his publisher. Yet unquestionably, he changed reviewing and literary criticism in the *Atlantic* from an occasional exercise in impressionistic comment, biographical anecdote, and promotion to a major intellectual forum for the discussion of literature and aesthetics, influential among writers and intellectuals if not a large public.

Among the compromises Howells had to make were either writing himself, or arranging for others to write, generally sympathetic though not uncritical reviews of many of his publisher's books. On one occasion he admitted to Higginson, who continued to write some *Atlantic* reviews: "You needn't be told that sometimes we have to speak of books not worth mentioning" (24 Dec. 1869, *Selected Letters* 1: 384). If Howells could not find anything to praise in the book himself, he attempted to farm it out to someone he believed would treat it favorably; if he could not find a sympathetic reviewer, he left the book unscathed. Again, he writes frankly to Higginson: "Nevertheless (let me guiltily own) I asked *you* to write of Mrs. Hunt because I knew you were her friend, and I wanted a more cordial review of her book than I knew how to get otherwise. So base are sometimes the motives of editors" (16 Feb. 1872, *Selected Letters* 1: 391). But his motive in selecting reviewers was not always so base; he did not want to limit the *Atlantic*'s judgment solely to his own: "I try to make the *Atlantic* a place where a man's merit, if I feel it, should be recognized and I am willing that any competent critic who feels the merit of an author when I don't should recognize it there" (to Higginson, 18 Oct. 1873, *Selected Letters* 2: 36).

Writing his own reviews was another job requiring tact and sometimes compromise. As a primary reviewer for the *Atlantic*, Howells was often put in the precarious situation of having to elucidate and pass judgment on the works of revered authors who were also valued properties of Ticknor and Fields. Often, Howells could praise with candor, but when he could not, he sought some compromise with his conscience. In the early years, his insecurity, self-deprecation, and pragmatism sometimes prevailed, probably not without some resentment at the humble pie he was eating to preserve established reputations and a slight blush at his own complicity, all reflected in a letter to Norton: "I have been writing a notice of [Emerson's] 'May Day' in which I leave what I think its defects to the justice that rules the world. This is a slow method, but a safe one—for the critic. With Jean Ingelow, I have not dealt so patiently. I could understand her absurdities and I treated them according to knowledge. But it is a very different thing with a poet so many heads above one as Emerson" (31 July 1867, *Selected Letters* 1: 281–82).

As Howells became surer of himself and his aesthetic values, he still felt the need to compromise but was more often frankly critical. In some reviews, one can read Howells's anxiety in the contrast between a catalog of defects and a rather bland laudatory summary. While writing on Longfellow's *New England Tragedies*, he complained to his sister Aurelia that he found it "pretty hard work to get at praiseworthy points" (22 Nov. 1868, *Selected Letters* 1: 307). In the review, he wrote candidly that the "background was lacking in the local presentation of fact," the characters were "vague and generalized," the plot overburdened by moralizing, and "nearly every person . . . has a private pulpit from which he preaches." Still, he concluded incongruously, the work contained some "genuine tragic feeling" (Jan. 1869, 132–34). Howells was not above equivocation, but clearly he was beginning to develop the tenets of his realism and publicly apply them with some frankness even to the works of his Olympian friends and protectors.

Despite some compromises, Howells defined and advocated literary realism in his reviews with increasing incisiveness and clarity. He created, even during his assistantship, a progressive reviewing department in the *Atlantic* that kept readers current on publications in philosophy, science, art, politics, and history but which focused on fiction. He greatly increased the frequency and volume of reviews. While Fields typically devoted only four or five pages at the end of each issue to comment on books, Howells eventually increased this to twelve to fourteen pages per issue. While Fields's criticism of fiction in the mid-sixties had amounted mainly to a few biographical reminiscences and about five reviews per year, by 1870 the magazine annually carried thirty-two reviews or articles on fiction, most written by Howells, and by 1880, at the end of his editorship, this number had increased to seventy-one.

Eventually, this great expansion of literary criticism almost certainly had a negative effect on *Atlantic* circulation. But it did help to formulate and support the new literary realism at a crucial point in its early development, and it maintained the magazine's authority in literary matters. Howells himself felt a sense of accomplishment in his revamping of the reviewing department. "The *Nation*," he wrote to his sister Annie, "has good notices, but on the whole I think the *Atlantic*'s the best in the country" (3 Feb. 1873, *Selected Letters* 1: 12). The tough-minded editor of the *Nation*, Godkin, not given to condoning Bostonian self-congratulation, agreed and commented in both 1868 and 1870 on the incisiveness of the *Atlantic* reviews, adding the left-handed compliment that they were "the most profitable part of the magazine" (qtd. in Cady, *Road to Realism* 133).

During Howells's assistant editorship, he first gave evidence that in his literary judgments and his own writing, he would quickly absorb and exceed the moderate realist sympathies that had guided Lowell and Fields's *Atlantic* selections. When he began in 1866, he was a sentimental poet and travel writer with no clear sense of his own literary direction. The evolution of his commitment to realism is imprinted on the pages of the *Atlantic* in his reviews, his own writing, and his editorial decisions of the late sixties and early seventies. This commitment shaped his judgments as editor-in-chief after 1871. As early as 1866, in comments reminiscent of Lowell's, he praised a "strict fidelity to place and character" in preference to "ariel romance which cannot light in any place known to the gazeteer," and he regretted "a shyness among American novelists... in regard to dates, names, and localities" (review of *Story of Kensett* by Bayard Taylor, June 1866, 777).

In this same vein, he soon began giving strong support to the rise of local color writing in such works as Edward Eggleston's *Hoosier Schoolmaster*, Harriet Stowe's *Oldtown Fireside Stories*, and John DeForest's *Kate Beaumont*, all of which he praised as "very faithful studies of American life" of the recent past (Mar. 1872, 364). But Howells went further in pressing for literature that directly observed the commonplace life of the present. In one 1870 review, he advised young writers to portray what they observed around them exactly as it was. In another he commented "that the finest poetry is not ashamed of the plainest fact; that the lives of men and women, if they can be honestly studied, can, without surprising incident or advantageous circumstance, be made... interesting in literature... [and] that telling a thing is enough and explaining it too much" (reviews of *Vagabond Adventures* by Ralph Keeler, Dec. 1870, 760; *Arne, the Happy Boy* and *The Fisher Maiden* by Bjørnstjerne Bjørnson, Apr. 1870, 512). In these reviews and others, including his criticism of the Olympians, the essential tenets of Howells's realism were gradually defined: his insistence on an accurate portrayal of familiar, contemporary life; his sense that meaning is created by the careful selection and expression of particular, concrete observations, not by flights of imagination or exposition; and his dislike for intrusive narrators, didactic moralizing, emotional manipulation, and the sentimental morality of romantic gesture.

Howells's realism was a progressive extension of the *Atlantic*'s aesthetic and philosophical traditions, not a break with them. Howells later wrote: "I could not claim there was anything original in my passion for the common, for the familiar and the low.... Lowell had the same passion for it in the intervals of his 'toryism of the nerves' and nobody could have tasted its raciness with a keener gusto than my chief [Fields]. But perhaps it was my sense not only of the quaint, the comic, but of the ever-poetic in the common that made it dear to me" ("Recollections" 600).

These principles of realism informed much of Howells's editorial advice during his *Atlantic* assistantship. One of his major tasks as assistant editor was to review unsolicited manuscripts, correspond with younger authors, and scout new talent. Remembering his own recent aspirations and becoming increasingly committed to the development of American realism, he was generous with advice and encouragement to unknowns. Lowell had advised Howells, then an aspiring poet, that he must "sweat the Heine out of you as men do mercury," and Howells in turn counseled young poets to avoid imitation and observe life directly (qtd. in Lynn 79). Poetry, he wrote one poet, must come directly from personal experience, not through literature (to Don Wyman, 16 Feb. 1867, *Selected Letters* 1: 275). To another, he was more explicit in advocating poetic realism, responding enthusiastically: "That ballad seemed to me extremely good because it took a theme of this common, modern, actual life of ours and treated it with warm poetic feeling and perfect artistic self-restraint" (to Will Carleton, 21 Apr. 1871, *Selected Letters* 1: 368).

Perhaps the most important support he gave to young fellow realists during his assistantship was his advocacy of his friend and aesthetic fencing partner Henry James. Beginning in 1864, Fields had published two or three James stories, but he had grown concerned about the pessimism of James's tone and his realist's refusal of neat resolutions satisfactory to the reader. In 1867, Fields sent Howells a copy of James's story "Poor Richard" for his opinion and advice on publishing it. Howells's response was emphatic: "Yes, and all the stories you can get from the writer" (Howells, "Henry James" 25). Howells recognized from the beginning that while James's writing was of the first quality, his aesthetic creed would cause him difficulties with editors and audiences. He wrote to Norton, "I cannot doubt that James has every element of success in fiction. But I suspect that he must in a very great degree create his audience. In the meantime, I rather despise existing readers" (10 Aug. 1867, *Selected Letters* 1: 283). Howells knew that James Fields in some sense represented that existing audience. Fields's qualms about James became something of a joke between the younger men. Howells wrote James, " 'What we want,' says Mr. Fields with perfect truth, 'is short, cheerful stories.' And our experience of you is quite in that way of fiction" (2 Jan. 1870, *Selected Letters* 1: 352). Howells continued to support James at this formative point in his career by being his advocate at the *Atlantic*.

In addition to his reviews and editorial decisions, Howells's own fiction published in the *Atlantic* during his years as Fields's assistant reflected the rapidly evolving commitment to realism that he would exercise after 1870 in his editorship. His first *Atlantic* contributions, in the early sixties, had been romantic and sentimental poems. While in Venice he had written a travel book titled *Venetian Sketches*. Beginning in 1867, motivated partly by Fields's request for "short, lively, sketchy things of from six to eight pages" and thinking perhaps of an audience west of the Appalachians, he had conceived the idea of writing something like travel sketches of commonplace scenes, ordinary people, or commonplace events in Cambridge and Boston. The subjects of these "Suburban Sketches" were realistic, drawn from direct observations of ordinary life—a street musician, a black cook, a day's excursion to the beach—although the narrative perspective was distant and amused, like a tourist's appreciating quaint local color, rather than fully empathetic.

Howells accurately sensed that these sketches were something original in American literature and set a fundamentally new direction for his work. "I persuaded myself," he wrote to James in 1870, "(too fondly perhaps) that they're a new kind of study of our life, and I have an impression that they're to lead me to some higher sort of performance" (2 Jan. 1870 *Selected Letters 1852–1872*, 352). Pursuing this new lead, the direct observation of contemporary middle-class life, Howells's realism developed rapidly in the early seventies. Immediately after completion of the *Sketches*, he set to work on *Their Wedding Journey*, "a geographically expanded version of *Suburban Sketches*" that "carries on the efforts of the earlier book to assess the resources of American life from the point of view of a would-be realist" (Lynn 208).

Howells's first real novel, *A Chance Acquaintance*, written just after he became editor-in-chief in 1871 and serialized in the *Atlantic* in 1873, provides at least a partial summary of his growth to that point and a preview of his direction over the following decades. The novel manifests his advocacy of an explicitly American realism, his ambivalence toward Boston, his identification with the small-town "outsider" or westerner, and his attraction to democratic egalitarianism. The heroine, Kitty Ellison, is the first of Howells's admirable "American girls." Raised among what Howells calls "people of culture" in Kansas and Erie Creek, New York, she is intelligent, well read, lively minded, democratic, trusting, open to experience and humanity, independent, and self-reliant. On vacation in Quebec, she encounters an effete, snobbish Europeanized young Bostonian named Miles Arbuton who is closed to human experience by a false sense of social and cultural superiority. Arbuton, who mouths the arguments against American culture articulated by both Henry James and T. S. Perry, represents Howells's early perception of a change in Boston culture that became compounded in the following decades, namely, a shift from the expansive, socially engaged, liberal idealism that had lasted through the fifties and early sixties and had produced both a new national literature and political change, to an excessively refined, Europeanized, genteel culture increasingly alienated from American realities.

William Dean Howells 1871–1881

As *A Chance Acquaintance* was appearing in the *Atlantic* and Howells was receiving congratulations from the literary Boston he had satirized, including some who claimed to be Arbuton's original, Howells wrote to his father: "It sets me forever outside the rank of mere culturists, followers of an elegant literature, and proves that I have sympathy with the true spirit of Democracy. Sometimes I've doubted whether I had, but when I came to look the matter over in this story, I doubted no longer" (20 Apr. 1873, *Selected Letters* 2: 7).

In this letter, Howells bravely overstated the firmness of his developing democratic convictions, as he admitted he had overstated the antidemocratic cultural narrowness among some members of Boston's younger generation in the "mere culturist" Miles Arbuton. But clearly both the novel and the letter were evidence that Howells was committed to a literature dealing with current American society; that he wished for a literary culture engaged in contemporary national life, as Boston's had earlier been, rather than merely in aesthetics; and that he was gradually developing more liberal literary and political values at a time when Boston seemed to be growing more conservative. Howells's "democracy" at this time, however, was largely limited to pointing out that what he called people of culture (similar to the "cultivated classes" which Emerson had charged with transmitting culture to the nation) were not necessarily people of "social distinction" and that many of them lived west of the Berkshires. Most of intellectual Boston showed they had mastered these facts in their reception and support of Howells himself and others.

Despite continued tensions between Howells and intellectual Boston during his decade as editor from 1871 to March 1881, he still found Boston culture not only generally congenial but also exhilarating, and Boston continued to heap its praises on him. He was invited by Harvard's new president, Charles Eliot, to deliver a series of lectures on Italian literature. In 1872, he celebrated his growing financial success, founded on an editorial salary of $5,000 and increasing royalties from his works, by building a large, comfortable house on Concord Street in Cambridge. There he edited the *Atlantic* from his elegant chestnut-paneled library with its monogrammed mantel, traveling only once a week to his small Park Street office. Later, to avoid being overwhelmed by the social life generated by his editorship and literary recognition, he gave up his new house to rent a larger one in outlying Belmont. In 1874, he was elected to the select, intellectual Saturday Club, sponsored by the elder Henry James. Soon thereafter, he was elected the first president of a new literary society formed by younger Bostonians, the Tavern Club, and became a charter member of the St. Botolph's Club.

In 1876 and again in 1880, he found himself having influential political connections through the presidencies first of Rutherford Hayes, a close cousin of his wife's for whom Howells wrote a campaign biography, and then James Garfield, an early Ohio neighbor and friend of the Howells family. Through Hayes he secured ambassadorships to Spain and later to the Court of Saint James for Lowell. Howells must have savored the complex satisfaction of reciprocating Boston's generosity, repaying an uncomfortable indebtedness, and being finally in a position of influence, bestowing favors on his former mentors rather than receiving from them.

Although his political consciousness began to evolve during the decade, literature was still his passion. And during the seventies, there was still no more active center for literary debate than Boston, and no more stimulating or influential literary position in the country than the editorship of the *Atlantic Monthly*, despite some ominous signs for the future of both the intellectual life of the city and the fortunes of the magazine.

During the sixties, Fields, confident in Howells's abilities, had given him increasing responsibility, including the power to accept manuscripts and make up issues, in consultation with Lowell and Holmes, while Fields was on his extended stays in England. Thus, when Howells assumed the editorship of the *Atlantic* in July 1871, he had already had experience in trying to balance the influences of intellectual Boston (old and new), his own developing values as an American realist and a democrat, and his sense of obligation to the "people of culture" beyond the pales of New England whom he wanted to read and write for the magazine. As editor-in-chief, however, he now had to deal more directly with another set of influences: the magazine's publishers, circulation, and financing. Major changes in the magazine's publishers and persistent circulation problems throughout the decade of his editorship created additional pressures to which Howells had to be sensitive.

When Fields retired from the *Atlantic* editorship in July 1871, he retired from publishing altogether, selling all of his business assets to his junior partner, James Osgood. Osgood was a genial, sanguine bon vivant who established a reputation for treating authors generously. Many younger authors, including Howells, Twain, Aldrich, and Harte, regarded "the Boston bantam" as a personal friend and drinking companion. But in his business practices, he was prone to excessive optimism, a lavishness close to prodigality, overextension of credit, and overexpansion. Osgood supported Howells and the *Atlantic* with a very generous hand from 1871 to 1873. But losses in the Great Boston Fire of 1872 and the financial panic of 1873 forced him to sell off many of his assets to the firm of Hurd and Houghton. Among these assets was the *Atlantic*, sold for $20,000. While Howells privately regretted the change, Henry Oscar Houghton, his new publisher, assured him that there would be no change in support for the magazine or in his editorial independence. Although Houghton was restrained, Howells was conscious of subtle, largely financial pressures from his new publisher.

Henry Oscar Houghton, whose firms published the *Atlantic* from 1873 to 1908. By permission of the Boston Athenaeum.

Though the partnerships and name of the house underwent several changes—from Hurd and Houghton (1874–77), to Houghton, Osgood Co. (1878–79) and then Houghton, Mifflin Co. (1880 to present)—Henry Oscar Houghton, until his death in 1895, was to be the dominant partner in the house that published the *Atlantic*. Ellen Ballou argues persuasively that Houghton was Howells's main prototype for *Silas Lapham* (274–75). Like Lapham, he had grown up in a large, poor family in northern Vermont. He was "a man of simple, homely loyalties . . . but clear, bold, straightforward, singleminded and persevering" (Ballou 274). A Yankee Republican and Methodist, Houghton held strong political and religious convictions. Apparently he did not force these convictions on his employees and had a strong sense of fairness. Business judgment, as well as scruples about intruding his private views, inclined him to avoid political partisanship and religious controversy in editorial matters, both of which had provided much of the vitality of the early *Atlantic*. He had become involved in publishing through printing rather than, like Fields, through bookselling and had little pretension to literary judgment, for which he claimed to rely entirely on his editors. In business he was conservative, shrewd, scrupulous, and far-sighted, the polar opposite of Osgood's excessively sanguine, somewhat careless liberality.

Houghton believed that the *Atlantic* could not only attract new writers and bring prestige to the house but also create an audience and provide advance advertising for its books. Having a long view, he therefore recognized that the magazine's success could not be measured simply in terms of the revenue generated from subscriptions. But true to his conservative business practices, he expected the magazine at least to avoid running deficits. In the depression years following 1873, this expectation rapidly became problematic, causing both Houghton and his editor to be conscious of cost and of a need to experiment with ways of raising circulation that had not prevailed in the flush times under Fields and Osgood.

Since Stowe's Byron scandal in 1869, the magazine had continued to lose circulation alarmingly. From a high of 50,000 in 1869, it had plummeted to 35,000 in 1870, fallen again sharply to under 21,000 by 1874, and then, frustratingly for Howells, stagnated at about 17,000 before declining again in 1880–81 to a nadir of around 12,000 (Mott 2: 505; Ballou 210–13; Mitchell). Dr. Holmes's novel *The Guardian Angel* (1867), again bedeviled by sectarian religious factions, had renewed charges of atheism against the magazine from some quarters and alienated some readers. Stowe's article on Byron unquestionably accounted for the loss of many thousands. Certainly the waning of production among the magazine's aging established writers, and possibly also the fading after the war of its chief political cause, were factors in the decline. The severe economic depression that struck in 1873 and which lingered for most of the decade was another source of lost subscriptions beyond Howells's and Houghton's control.

By far the most direct and lasting cause of the *Atlantic*'s decline was competition from the New York illustrated magazines, particularly the thriving *Harper's* and the new *Scribner's*. *Scribner's* had been founded in 1870 and was edited through the decade by Howells's literary antagonist, the sentimental poet and novelist Dr. Josiah Gilbert Holland, best known to the public as Timothy Titcomb, a nationally popular writer and lecturer on moral topics. Despite the depression, *Harper's* topped and the new *Scribner's* neared 100,000 circulation in 1874, while the *Atlantic* was losing ground for the fifth consecutive year (Mott 3: 6).

William Dean Howells 1871–1881

A brief comparison between Howells's *Atlantic* and Holland's new *Scribner's* (later renamed the *Century*), which circulated more than five times as many copies, suggests that *Scribner's*, like *Harper's*, was a magazine of an increasingly prosperous and growing middle class, while the *Atlantic* was the magazine of a narrower, more liberally educated, intellectual elite which had begun a long decline in influence.[1] The *Atlantic*, besides lacking *Scribner's* lavish illustrations, was committed more narrowly to literary high culture, had little except fiction that appealed to nonintellectual interests, and featured fewer special departments appealing to diverse audiences.

The heavily literary emphasis of Howells's *Atlantic* diminished its breadth. The one exception to this literary emphasis was Howells's increasing but irregular coverage of political and economic issues. In both magazines, however, these topics accounted for only about 5 percent of total space. The *Atlantic*'s articles were superior for incisiveness and range of views, partly because Holland wrote most of *Scribner's* political material himself, and he was timid about political debate. Fiction, with an emphasis on the serial novel, constituted about 34 percent of Howells's *Atlantic*, while *Scribner's* carried between 15 and 25 percent. *Scribner's* would increasingly compete with the *Atlantic* for some good writers, especially after Howellsian realism gained wider acceptance and Richard Watson Gilder succeeded Holland in 1881. But much of its fiction was of the sentimental and didactic type that had earned Holland's own writings immense circulation, critical sneers, and wide popular affection. A considerably higher degree of realism was the norm in Howells's magazine. Much of *Scribner's* poetry, with titles such as "Boozy Little Bat," was sentimental, light, or humorous "magazine" verse, often illustrated, that would have raised snorts of contempt among many *Atlantic* subscribers. Howells also published about twice as much literary criticism as Holland, a good deal of it concerned with the aesthetics of the realistic novel, a topic that understandably consumed him but was of limited interest to most potential readers.

While *Scribner's* contained less literature, and especially literary criticism, it contained greater diversity of subject matter and tone designed to attract a variety of readers. A regular department, "Home and Society," aimed specifically at women, discussed such practical topics as principles of roasting and the use of chestnut flour, as well as fashion and social etiquette. A section titled "The World's Work" addressed the presumably male fascination with invention and engineering, describing with excellent technical illustrations such mechanisms as the audiophone, electric signals, fruit presses, and bridges. A final section titled "Bric-a-Brac" contained light verse, jokes, and cartoons, providing something accessible for the young and the tired. Illustrations by artists like Frederic Remington, Joseph Pennell, Timothy Cole, and Charles Dana Gibson were abundant and of consistently high quality, giving *Scribner's* a deserved reputation as the best illustrated magazine of the nineteenth century.

The pious Dr. Holland was also determined to make his magazine "as true to evangelical Christianity as the *Atlantic* has always been to Unitarianism and paganism" (Holland to C. Scribner, 26 July 1869, qtd. in John 24). To this end, he insisted that "no man shall write a poem, or a story, or a review, or a disquisition who does not recognize Jesus Christ as the center and sum of our civilization" and that each issue should contain "at least one contribution of direct spiritual significance" (John 24). With these features, as well as articles on travel, adventure, history, biography, art, science, and contemporary manners, *Scribner's* was calculated to appeal to a range of audiences, including the male professional, but focusing especially on that combination of orthodox middle-class women and the ministry that Ann Douglas has proven to have had such a potent effect on Victorian American culture.

The new *Scribner's*, then, was a morally earnest, high-quality, and quite successful effort to provide cultural education for the upwardly mobile middle class, and particularly its women. It contained enough middlebrow, middle-class popular culture to provide its audience entertainment and pleasure, and enough highbrow material to make them feel they were being culturally improved. By contrast, Howells's *Atlantic*, as the decade wore on, reflected the intentions of its publisher and editor to stay the course of high literary and intellectual culture, to accept a niche between the scholarly magazines like the old *North American Review* and the popular quality illustrated magazines like *Scribner's*, rather than trying to compete with the latter by imitating them. Houghton and Howells founded their decisions on cultural conviction, on continuity with the magazine's past, and on the business judgment that the *Atlantic*'s greatest value to the house was its literary distinction and that direct competition by imitation would fail.

Cultural and financial considerations combined also in Houghton's decision not to attempt to compete by illustrating the *Atlantic*. Beginning in the 1870s, technical developments rapidly increased the quality of printed illustrations. This ushered in the great era of the illustrated magazine. The spectacular success of *Scribner's/Century* during the seventies and eighties owed a great deal to the quality and quantity of its illustrations, typically as many as seventy-five in 160 pages. Fulkerson, the astute magazine business manager in Howells's novel *Hazard of New Fortunes*, comments that a man would have to be mad to try to start a magazine in the latter part of the nineteenth century without generous provision for illustrating it. Fulkerson's comment probably came from Howells's frustrating experience in trying unsuccessfully to maintain *Atlantic* circulation without illustrations. Apparently Houghton chose not to compete in illustration for two reasons. First, he judged that many of the *Atlantic*'s loyal readers shared the high-culture bias against illustration and would simply be alienated by any attempt to make the *Atlantic* look like what Henry James, Jr., called "the New York picture books." Second, Houghton's financial conservatism prevented him from risking the very substantial outlay of capital necessary to produce first-rate illustration, particularly on a publication that he felt, of its nature, would never be broadly popular.

Despite Houghton's conservative avoidance of direct competition, competition was inevitable, in which the *Atlantic* was at a disadvantage. Unquestionably, *Scribner's*, like *Harper's*, not only drew a large number of potential subscribers from the *Atlantic* but with them drew also advertising and authors. Advertising revenues based on circulation fell at the *Atlantic* and rose at its competitors. By the mid-seventies, Houghton was irritably refusing public disclosure of the *Atlantic's* dwindling circulation, with the consequence that the magazine could charge only 75¢ per line, compared with $1.75 for *Scribner's* and $2.00 for *Harper's* (Mott 3: 11).

Furthermore, the success of the New York quality, illustrated magazines initiated in the early seventies a much more competitive and fluid market for good writing, especially fiction. In this market, the *Atlantic*, with its lower circulation and smaller revenues, found it difficult to compete for popular authors. The market was further heated up by the increasing interest by *Harper's* in American fiction and by the development during the seventies of an increasingly broad public taste for moderate forms of realism, a taste which Howells and the *Atlantic* had promoted. Also, while Fields's celebrity circle of *Atlantic* writers aged and faded through the seventies, increasing competition eroded the old restraints of trade courtesy and displaced them with a much freer bidding market for literary wares. This was particularly true among the younger generation of writers, Howells's contemporaries, who considered themselves free agents, but it made inroads on old loyalties even among the venerable reputations of the older generation.

Fields and later Osgood had carefully nurtured their reputations for liberality to writers and in fact, with little competition, had paid at least as well as any other magazine publisher—and very often better. The most notorious instance of Osgood's liberality was the 1871 contract with Bret Harte, then at the early peak of his vogue, to produce for the *Atlantic* and Osgood's illustrated *Every Saturday* at least one piece per month for a year, for a total remuneration of $10,000, with all work to be accepted sight unseen. The stories and poems resulting were mostly of disappointing quality, and Howells, a personal friend, had to nag the feckless Harte persistently to get them. But Houghton, with his conservative business principles, was less given to prodigal enthusiasms. When Harte, who the year before had received $300 for two poems from Osgood, asked $200 for one poem, Houghton offered $125. Harte placed the poem elsewhere with a sneer at Houghton's "Yankee cheapening" of his work but soon sent Howells another story. This time, Houghton's frugal offer touched off an explosion:

September 8/74

My dear Howells, (he wrote in protest),
When I tell you that, since my arrival East, I have never received so small an offer for any story as that made to me by Mr. Houghton; that the lowest offer from any magazine

or newspaper was $150 *more* than his, and that before sending it to you I had already refused $450 for the *ms* that I might make it the basis of terms with the *Atlantic*, you can readily imagine that I was considerably exasperated. . . .

    I do not question Mr. Houghton's right to appraise my work by its value to his magazine, but before soliciting exclusive contributions from a popular author it seems to me he ought to have informed himself of the prices they are in the habit of receiving. . . . I do wish you lived out of a literary atmosphere which seems to exclude any vision of a broader literary world beyond—its methods, profits, and emoluments. . . . A horrible thought strikes me that perhaps Mr. Houghton believes that it is worth $300 to me to appear in the *Atlantic*. The *Times* paid me $600 for "The Roses of Tuolumne," $500 for "John Oakhurst." Scribner paid me $1000 for "Fiddletown"—16 pp. long and $500 for "Monte Flat Pastoral"; 7 pp. (Ballou 207)

Even discounting for Harte's vanity, his letter suggests changes in the literary marketplace that substantially benefited professional authorship but would for a long time put the *Atlantic* at a disadvantage in competing for writers and in fact prevent it from publishing some popular authors. The increase in the number of publishing options created especially by the rise of the New York illustrated periodicals was rapidly generating much more competition between publishers. It eroded older author loyalties, the drawing power of the *Atlantic*'s prestige, and the "courtesy of the trade" that had inhibited editors from too openly enticing writers from other magazines. Instance after instance shows that among the new generation of authors in the seventies, including Aldrich, Harte, Howells, James, and Twain, the "man of letters" had become, in Howells's phrase, "a man of business." As Susan Coultrap-McQuin has shown in *Doing Literary Business*, a number of American women writers like Helen Hunt Jackson became equally adept at playing the market. These authors, some of whom supported an ample style of life on their literary earnings, were independent agents who knew how to negotiate book and magazine publication astutely and who encouraged competition for their work. Howells himself illustrated this truth when immediately after resigning his *Atlantic* editorship in 1881, he sent his next novel to *Scribner's*. When Emily Dickinson asked Howells's old antagonist Josiah Holland how he had lured the *Atlantic*'s former editor, Holland's reply was simple: "Money did it" (qtd. in John 58).

    Thus, in the new publishing competition that began in the 1870s, the *Atlantic* lost not only several authors but finally the works of its former editor. As Ellen Ballou notes, although Houghton promised Howells editorial independence, in the new literary marketplace of the seventies, the pay scale he established "performed an editorial, selective function," since he was unwilling in many cases to compete with the New York illustrated magazines having much higher circulation and advertising revenues (207).

    As editor-in-chief of the *Atlantic*, then, Howells was subject to several distinct, sometimes conflicting, influences. First, there was the influence of the magazine's traditions of Yankee humanism and its older circle of writers. Howells was in essential sympathy with many of the magazine's traditions: its conviction that America needed cultural and literary leadership, its emphasis on discovering and encouraging American authors, its attempt to create literary standards distinguishing serious literature from the sentimental and formulaic, its belief in a socially engaged literature, and its liberal Republican politics. The Olympians had been generous to him, and he felt both affection and a burden of gratitude toward most of them. But he also sometimes experienced a young writer's resentment at the apparently invulnerable established reputations of authors and aesthetic creeds which he considered outmoded and was trying to supersede.

Second, there was the influence of the younger generation of intellectual Boston whom he had parodied in *A Chance Acquaintance* as cultural snobs, although many of them were personal friends and allies in forging a more realistic literature. Third, there were his own evolving literary and political values. Beginning by imitating the Romantic poets, he had by the early seventies already evolved far toward becoming a realistic novelist of ordinary American life. Furthermore, he clearly felt a cultural mission to nurture the new realism by cultivating it among writers, critics, and readers. And he had begun to identify this realism, this openness to commonplace experience, with a political liberalism sympathetic to the average American. The final influences were the magazine's balance sheet and publisher. Although Houghton was a man of "long purse and longer patience," Howells was constantly aware of the need to reverse the disastrous plunge in circulation and of his limited resources in competing with his New York rivals.

The strategies by which Howells tried during his decade as editor-in-chief to harmonize these influences and to solve the problem of the balance sheet involved a cautious attempt to keep the magazine's original readership and yet to expand it, especially among women and in the West. To do this he sought to retain and promote identification of the older New England writers with the magazine while actively cultivating a new generation of writers representing all sections of the nation. He felt that he could draw new writers and new readers by publishing more realistic fiction, though he faced some problem in educating his audience and had to be cautious that his realism did not seriously offend moral and aesthetic sensibilities. He also experimented with the magazine's format, most effectively in creating a new section of short, informal pieces called the "Contributors' Club," intended to attract a greater variety of readers and writers. To pursue his commitment to realism, retain literary leadership, and provide a comprehensive overview of current books, he greatly expanded reviews and literary criticism. Beyond these strategies, in the end, were Howells's instinct for good writing and his personal commitment to support new writers. There were occasional compromises, but these should not obscure his accomplishment. No periodical in the country between 1871 and 1880, and perhaps none since, published better literature or criticism, and none supported literary realism as vigorously and consistently as Howells's *Atlantic*.

Howells was encouraged by his publishers to address the problem of falling circulation by continuing Fields's strategy of actively soliciting contributions from the old New England circle and promoting their identification with the magazine. If the production of most was declining, their national reputations had, if anything, ascended. Fields had taught both Howells and Osgood the subscription-renewal value of a January extravaganza featuring works by famous names and a prospectus promising more during the year. Emblematically, one of Howells's first missions as editor-in-chief was to accompany his new publisher Osgood on a visit to Oliver Wendell Holmes to persuade the somewhat reluctant autocrat to produce a new series, "The Poet at the Breakfast Table," which they hoped would buoy the fortunes of the *Atlantic* as the "Autocrat" series had. Howells's first January issue contained not only Holmes's "Poet" but also a major poem by Longfellow and the first installment of Hawthorne's posthumous *Septimus Felton*, in addition to works by younger authors including James, Fiske, Thaxter, Harte, and Howells himself. When Houghton became the publisher in 1874, he strongly supported the policy of promoting continued identification of the old circle with the magazine, initiating a series of well-publicized dinners, ostensibly in honor of Whittier (1877), Holmes (1879), and Stowe (1882), partly for this purpose. With the encouragement of his publishers and the aid of his personally friendly relationships with most of them, Howells continued to secure a good deal of material from the older writers, mainly from Holmes, Longfellow, and Whittier, each of whom contributed about thirty pieces during Howells's ten years as editor-in-chief.

Howells maintained even later that the quality of work by the *Atlantic*'s old guard during the seventies was comparable to the quality of their writings in the fifties and sixties. Inevitably, however, Howells found the work uneven, especially with Whittier and Longfellow. During Howells's assistantship, Fields had negotiated with established writers, but now Howells was faced with making editorial judgments on his elders' work. His insecurity as a younger outsider, his anxiety to defuse conflict, and his sensitivity to his publisher's interests made him deferential. Howells later recalled having rejected a poem by Whittier, begging the poet for something else, and then later regretting the rejection. Although Whittier showed no displeasure and continued to send poems regularly, Howells concluded with the blend of respect and subtle irony characteristic of his attitudes toward the old guard. "Never again did I venture to pass upon what contributors of his quality sent me. I took it and printed it, and praised the gods; and even now I think that with such men it was not my duty to play the censor in the periodical which they had made what it was. They had set it in authority over American literature, and it was not for me to put myself in authority over them. Their fame was in their own keeping, and it was not my part to guard it against them" (*Literary Friends* 136–37).

Despite the continued celebrity of the Olympians, Fields had foreseen and Howells had known by 1866 that the *Atlantic* could not be carried by the New England writers who had filled its early numbers—even if one wished it, and Howells did not. Hawthorne and Thoreau were dead; Emerson's mind had, in Perry Miller's phrase, begun its retreat into the oversoul; Lowell was occupied with the *North American* and after 1877 with his ambassadorships. Although Holmes was still intellectually vital and Howells judged his work as good as before, it seemed to have lost its popular appeal, to be already a little outmoded. The "Poet" failed to have the salutary effect of the "Autocrat" on circulation. But while the production of most older contributors flagged, it must have seemed to Howells that as they sent less of their own work, they submitted more of the infernal effusions of nieces, nephews, in-laws, cousins, casual acquaintances, and dying friends, all of whom coveted publication in the *Atlantic* as a mark of cultural benediction. Longfellow was a particular cornucopia of unwanted third-person manuscripts. At least he made no protests of their merits, unlike Holmes, who was irritated at Howells's rejection of his brother-in-law's series on historic Salem.

Worse yet, at least for the magazine's publishers, even some steadfast early contributors were beginning to find other sources of publication. The relationship between Howells and T. W. Higginson had always been strained by the latter's sense that the Ohioan, fifteen years his junior, was an ambitious interloper at the *Atlantic*. With Higginson, unlike with the older writers, Howells was not disposed to accommodation but was inclined to hold his ground defensively. Even after Howells became editor-in-chief, Higginson sometimes routed submissions through Fields or Osgood, to the editor's considerable irritation. When, in September 1871, Howells halfheartedly accepted a contribution from Higginson with the comment that he liked it "well enough," Higginson's pride was touched and he replied:

> I would not on any account have you print anything of mine which you only thought "well enough," so I have arranged for it elsewhere—with a regret which you can hardly understand, as you have not, like me, written for but one literary magazine for thirteen years and felt identified with it. . . . I shall . . . in future count on a merely business relationship with the Atlantic and try to make the additional feeling of freedom (as to writing elsewhere) atone to me for the lost esprit de corps. (30 Sept. 1871)

Higginson wrote for the New York magazines during the mid-seventies, at least once publicly forecasting Howells's "surrender" of his editorship and sniping at "the lowering of the literary standard of the [*Atlantic*] (to meet a supposed popular demand) which has been so conspicuous under Mr. Howells" (*Women's Journal*, 14 Feb. 1874, qtd. in W. Howells, *Selected Letters* 2: 54n). In 1875, Howells suppressed a highly critical review by Horace Scudder of Higginson's most recent book because of "a purely personal reluctance to wound the feelings of a very spiteful enemy" (to Scudder, 10 Mar. 1875). Although Higginson contributed again to the *Atlantic* after a conciliatory visit from Howells in 1877, the allegiance was broken, and he also continued publishing elsewhere.

Higginson was an exception in Howells's treatment of the magazine's old guard, probably because he was more personally challenging, younger, and more expendable to the magazine than the others. Most of them Howells treated solicitously, and they in turn still felt an allegiance to the *Atlantic*, not only as a convenient source of publication, but as a way of reaching an appreciative, "cultivated" audience and as an intellectual enterprise with which they were personally associated. But there were defections even among the inner circle. The major cause was not Howells's ill treatment but, as with younger authors, the lure of New York's money. Emblematic of these defections was Longfellow's sale of his 1875 Bowdoin anniversary poem, "Morituri Salutamus," to *Harper's*. The price, which he set himself, was $1,000, probably double what the *Atlantic* would have offered, and the deal was brokered by an agent who knew that literary values had appreciated steeply in the last decade: the *Atlantic*'s former editor and publisher James T. Fields, now publishing occasional pieces of his own in *Harper's* and *Scribner's* (Ballou 243).

Fields and Howells, Osgood and Houghton all knew that, while they must try to hold the allegiance of the magazine's established writers, they would have to work harder to discover and secure the allegiances of writers new to the magazine. While the *Atlantic*'s initial prospectus and early years had strongly emphasized American writing, English fiction continued to dominate many American magazines (Mott 3: 249). Although his partiality for English literature had been tempered by the war, Fields, like the Harpers and other editors, had been lured by England after 1865 as a source for expanding the magazine's fictional repertoire. But he had hired Howells partly to scout new American prospects. In 1869, Howells had written boldly to his chief, then in England: "I don't think it pays at all to take English stuff unless it's first chop," adding that most of the English material Fields had been accepting was decidedly not "first chop" (24 Aug. 1869, *Selected Letters* 1: 335). Howells's lack of interest in and often active distaste for English writing was reflected in its general absence from the magazine during his tenure, an absence particularly conspicuous after Fields's Anglophilia. Howells, like the magazine's founders, saw the *Atlantic* as explicitly representing American literature, but he knew clearly that to do this, it would have to look well beyond New England—as indeed it had in publishing his poems in 1860.

The geographic diversity of younger writers published and encouraged by Howells, many of them at formative points in their careers, is striking, although strains were still noticeable in the magazine's relationship with the South and with some New Yorkers. A later *Atlantic* editor, Bliss Perry, proclaimed that Howells "transformed a 'Bostonian' magazine into an American magazine," built up subscriptions and contributions across the nation, and "rendered Beacon Hill opinion of the *Atlantic*... negligible" (*Gladly Teach* 174). Howells himself later claimed with both truth and humility that the *Atlantic* had been hospitable to geographic diversity from the start but that only in his time had a large proportion of good material come from beyond New England ("Recollections" 599–600). At the least, Howells should be credited with nurturing writers from across the nation and recognizing the claims of a fully national audience.

Western and midwestern writers were particularly strongly represented in Howells's *Atlantic*, several of them among his closest friends and protégés. A few came to the *Atlantic* riding a wave of popular national recognition, such as Harte, with whom Osgood and Howells had secured the exclusive contract for 1871; John Hay, whose *Pike County Ballads* had created a stir; and Howells's closest friend and literary conspirator, Twain. For most, however, including W. H. Bishop from Milwaukee, Constance Fenimore Woolson from Cleveland, Mr. and Mrs. J. J. Piatt, Howells's early friends from Columbus, Charles Warren Stoddard from California, Maurice Thompson of Indiana, and H. H. Boyesen, who had emigrated from Norway to Ohio, Howells was among the earliest to recognize their talent and the most patiently persistent in encouraging it.

The relationship between the *Atlantic* and the South had always been strained at best, and because the *Atlantic* pursued Reconstruction issues much more forcibly than did either *Harper's* or *Scribner's*, the mutual suspicion continued to be stronger. The southern poet and editor Paul Hayne praised *Scribner's* in 1871 for its "high moral conservative tone" and deemed it free enough from sectionalism to "be safely patronized by the public of the South" (*Augusta* [Ga.] *Constitutionalist*, 12 Dec. 1871, qtd. in Woodress 139). But although southerners sent little, and Howells rejected some they did send, he did publish several of Hayne's poems beginning in 1873. Hayne, though he found Howells's tastes "crochety" and finally became exasperated with his rejections, credited him with opening the *Atlantic* to the South after the war (Woodress 145). In 1874, Howells ran an autobiographical series by a Confederate officer named George Eggleston that caused some stir among Boston readers, and in 1877 he encouraged a young southerner named Belton Townsend to write a series of realistic descriptions of postwar South Carolina, to which he gave prominent place in the *Atlantic*. In 1878, he responded enthusiastically to a vivid story of local color set in the Cumberland mountains of Tennessee called "The Dancin Party at Harrison Cove," and thus began the publishing career of its twenty-three-year-old author, Charles Egbert Craddock, who, on presenting himself at the *Atlantic* offices several years later, turned out to be Mary Noailles Murfree.

New Yorkers had always defensively felt excluded or overshadowed in the *Atlan-*

tic. An embittered R. H. Stoddard wrote Howells that "if the 'old duffers' of New England were dead (as they soon will be), I should expect some recognition from their readers. As it is, I don't" (n.d.). Stoddard's cynicism prevented him from submitting much, but Howells did regularly publish work by the New Yorkers Bayard Taylor and E. C. Stedman, with whom he had developed friendships during his brief stint at the *Nation*. About Walt Whitman, Howells was clearly ambivalent. Whitman's Americanness he liked, but not the poet's means for expressing it. Whitman, Howells had written Stedman in 1867, always "performs... on a steam calliope" (*Life in Letters* 119). Whitman submitted no poetry during Howells's editorship but in 1877 did receive a vigorous defense in the magazine against his critics ("Contributors' Club," Dec. 1877, 449–51; also see Scholnick, "Whitman"). Howells also published four poems by a young New York society woman, yet unknown to literary circles, named Edith Jones, later Edith Wharton. Howells himself felt prouder, however, of having "discovered" the work of Philander Deming, an upstate New York writer whose local color realism in *Adirondack Sketches* particularly delighted him.

While the proportion of New England writing in Howells's *Atlantic* declined steeply, it was still well represented. But even among the New England writers, there was more diversity—regional, generational, aesthetic, and social—than before. Certainly the inner circle of young Cambridge intellectuals who had formed "The Club" constituted a strong influence. Henry James was a staple in Howells's *Atlantic*, second in frequency perhaps only to Howells himself, serving both as art critic and major contributor of serial fiction. The cosmopolitan T. S. Perry, whom Howells considered the best-read man he had met, wrote over ninety reviews during the decade. Howells solicited a large number of contributions on religion and science from his Cambridge neighbor John Fiske.

But Howells's *Atlantic* also represented contributors from circles in the environs of Boston other than the "jeunesse dorée" of Cambridge. One was Ralph Keeler, an Ohio-born journalist and one-time minstrel show performer, for whom Howells secured a job reading *Atlantic* proofs and whom he later eulogized in the magazine. Others included Thomas Bailey Aldrich, editor of another Houghton magazine, *Every Saturday*, who would succeed Howells at the *Atlantic*; Sylvester Baxter, a Boston journalist; and the Irish-American poet and editor Thomas Boyle O'Reilly. North of Boston was represented by frequent contributions from Sarah Orne Jewett and Celia Thaxter, while south of Boston, John DeForest and C. D. Warner in Connecticut, and Silas Weir Mitchell of Philadelphia counted Howells among their earliest and strongest encouragers.

Howells's record as *Atlantic* editor for not only discovering but also supporting and patiently nurturing talented younger writers from all sections of the country is by any measure excellent, certainly better in fiction and probably better overall than that of any other *Atlantic* editor. His record is so good, in fact, that to make him credible one feels obliged to note that he was neither the benign, plaster patron saint of writers praised by his contemporaries nor the complaisant, bland, paternalistic "Dean" ridiculed by "the lost generation." He made mistakes in judgment, as when he declined Cable's early story "Bibi" for being "unmitigatingly distressful" and thus lost Cable to *Scribner's* (Turner 52, 54). Harriet Preston Waters and the more balanced Horace Scudder later accused him of being blinded to work in other modes by his dogmatic defense of realism. The partial truth of their charge is reflected in his rejection of several stories by Sarah Orne Jewett, including "The White Heron," for their romanticism. He generally avoided confrontations with his literary elders but became embroiled in several personal feuds with his contemporaries or juniors. Edgar Fawcett, the satirist of New York society, wrote Aldrich complaining of atrocious treatment: "I believe Howells to be a very clever man in more ways than one and ... some day you will get a cat-like dig from him that will produce an unpleasant awakening to the truth. I think him to be a man of small literary parts, great industry, and a towering ambition.... [H]e has no intention that anyone save himself shall win anything positive in the way of reputation from the *Atlantic*" (n.d., Aldrich Papers). Fawcett was the cat, and his accusations are mainly the pique of a frequently rejected contributor. But Howells's distaste for Whitman and his run-ins with Higginson, the unfortunate Lathrop, and others show that he could occasionally be blind, unfair, or insensitive.

If Howells was no bland dispenser of universal good will, his literary judgment, sincerity of purpose, and usual personal generosity were extraordinary. Howells's biographer, Kenneth Lynn, is clearly accurate in saying that "in American literary history, Howells is rivaled only by Pound for his sure identification of the literary geniuses of his generation, and for his doughty critical battles in their behalf" (154). As a writer himself and as editor of the *Atlantic*, Howells was at the center of the new American realist movement and in contact with virtually all of its major and many of its lesser practitioners. His passionate immersion in the development of a new form of American literature, his pragmatic ability to compromise, his breadth of social experience, and his vigorous, intelligent good nature led him to friendships with an astonishing diversity among them—the span symbolically indicated by his close relationships with both Twain and James. But trying to secure their allegiance to the *Atlantic*, especially after they had achieved reputation enough to earn New York fees, was often a source of frustration.

Certainly Howells's personal and editorial treatment of Henry James bears out Lynn's claim for his sure recognition and steadfast support of literary genius. Probably Howells's most significant effect on James came during his assistant editorship, but he published James as frequently as he could throughout his editorship, and the relationship remained important to both lifelong. On Howells's seventy-fifth birthday, James wrote:

> You held out your open editorial hand to me at the time I began to write—and I allude especially to the summer of 1866—with a frankness and sweetness of hospitality that was really the making of me, the making of confidence that required help and sympathy.... [Y]ou wrote to me, and confessed yourself struck with me—I have never forgotten the beautiful thrill of that. You published me at once—and paid me, above all, with a dazzling promptitude.... [Y]ou talked to me and listened to me. ("Open Letter" 558–59)

Howells's confidence and support were unswerving, but he also perceptively recognized early that James would have difficulty creating an audience, largely because James, like Howells, was experimenting with ways of intentionally subverting the expectations created by the romantic novels of writers such as Augusta Jane Evans and Mrs. E. D. E. N. Southworth and the sentimental pieties of Sylvanus Cobb and Josiah Holland. Howells, despite his circulation problems, was willing— in fact anxious—to expose the *Atlantic* audience to James at every opportunity, even agreeing to try to publish a piece by James each month. During Howells's tenure he published fourteen reviews of both art and literature by James, seventeen short stories and travel pieces, two novellas, *Watch and Ward* and *The Europeans*, and three major serial novels, *Roderick Hudson* (1875), *The American* (1876–77), and *The Portrait of a Lady* (1880–81).

While he generally tended to edit heavily, Howells recognized James's craftsmanship and, although he loved to talk aesthetics with James, was generally restrained in giving advice on manuscripts. It was Henry's brother William, and not Howells, who, on seeing proofs of *The American*, already proofed by Howells, found some phrases, probably unconscious sexual symbolisms, "so shocking as to make the 'reader's flesh creep' " and who asked Howells, with Henry's permission, to remove them (18 Dec. 1876, James, *Letters* 2: 84). Howells's only significant intervention during the fifteen years of his editorial relation with James was to express the hope that Newman, the sympathetic protagonist of *The American*, would be allowed to marry Claire de Cintre, despite the opposition of her cynical and ruthless family. James refused, claiming that this would be "throwing a rather vulgar sop to readers who don't really know the world and who don't measure the merit of a novel by its correspondence to the same" (30 Mar. 1877, *Letters* 2: 105).

Howells's suggestion was particularly odd because he himself had insisted, for reasons of realism, against strong pressure from readers and friends, on "an evaporated marriage" between a culturally incompatible hero and heroine at the end of *A Chance Acquaintance*. The incident demonstrates that Howells during this period was conscious of trying to create an audience both for James and for himself and was at times willing to make considerable concessions to his novel-reading audience in return for their willingness to read realistic fiction. As Michael Anesko has abundantly demonstrated, James was perfectly capable of making similar concessions in what he called his potboilers. Soon after this controversy, he promised Howells that his next work would fit into 100 *Atlantic* pages, have a happy ending, and contain "a distinct matrimony" (James to Elizabeth Boott, 30 Oct. 1878, *Letters* 2: 189). The result was *The Europeans*, which had, in fact, three marriages at the end. When James later adapted *The American* to the stage, he took Howells's advice and ended it with matrimony. Neither writer nor editor, however, suggested compromise in James's last serial of the decade, *Portrait of a Lady*, which, like the novel Howells had begun at the time, *A Modern Instance*, took the bolder step of looking realistically at the agonies of a bad marriage.

During the seventies, James developed rapidly not only as a novelist but also as an astute business agent for his own works. To his credit, Dr. Holland of *Scribner's* was ready by 1873 to try James's more popular stories, as were the Church brothers at New York's lively but short-lived version of the *Atlantic*, the *Galaxy*. In December, Howells wrote: "I hope you won't send any of your stories to *Scribners*. We have, of course, no claim on you, but we have hitherto been able to print all the stories you have sent, and so it shall be hereafter. *Scribners* is trying to lure away all our contributors with the siren song of Dr. Holland and my professional pride is touched" (5 Dec. 1873, *Letters* 2: 39). James, now thirty, living in Europe, and embarrassed by his financial dependence on his family, replied: "I *can't* really get on without extracting tribute from that source. . . . [N]ow I need more strings to my bow, more irons always on the fire. But I heartily promise you that the *Atlantic* shall have the best things I do" (9 Jan. 1874, *Letters* 1: 424).

The *Atlantic* did have the best things James wrote because of Howells's constant scrambling during the decade to keep James identified with his magazine, although the "small potboilers," as he called them, mainly went elsewhere. James needed to run more than one work at a time in American magazines. But he also understood the value to him of competition and kept several editors, including Howells, aware of what he had sent elsewhere and what he had been offered. As a result, his payment from the *Atlantic* increased from $100 per installment for *Roderick Hudson* in 1875, to $250 per installment for *Portrait of a Lady* in 1880, sight unseen and with the author retaining rights to publish simultaneously in a British journal. But because of what Howells called James's "buxom muse," his installments generally ran twenty-five pages or more, making the page rate only $10, about average for the *Atlantic* at this time and only half of what Mark Twain received.

Unlike James, for whom Howells was clearly trying, patiently and with some compromises, to create a sympathetic audience, Twain already had a large popular audience before he began publishing in the *Atlantic*. In fact, publishing Twain was another Howells-Houghton strategy for trying to boost the magazine's dwindling circulation. Fields had never followed up Parton's suggestion in 1868 to boost *Atlantic* circulation by hiring Twain, but by 1874 Houghton, with his earthier tastes, had developed an enthusiasm for Twain's works and an idea that they would help the magazine. In the meantime, Howells had developed a close friendship with Twain that began in 1869 when Twain stopped by the *Atlantic* offices to thank in person the unknown reviewer who had given *Innocents Abroad* an enthusiastic notice in the magazine. By 1874, Howells was actively soliciting material from Twain and was authorized by Houghton to offer twenty dollars per page, twice the normal rate and more than the magazine offered virtually any other writer at the time. During the decade, Howells took almost everything Twain sent him. He declined only one piece he thought would strain his readers' religious tolerance and *The Adventures of Tom Sawyer*, which he judged to be a boy's book for which Houghton would not meet Twain's price of $6,500, a price Twain claimed *Scribner's* had just offered Bret Harte. From 1874 to 1881, Howells published twelve short pieces by Twain, as well as *Old Times on the Mississippi*, which ran in 1875 in seven installments. Despite Twain's popularity, however, Howells concluded that his work had not increased the subscription lists an iota, largely because it was pirated from advance copies given to the newspapers and, in the case of *Old Times*, by Canadian publishers in the absence of an international copyright law (*Literary Friends* 324–25).

Though he received higher fees from other magazines, Twain continued to submit short pieces to the *Atlantic*. One reason was certainly his genuine friendship with Howells and his gratitude for Howells's critical support. A second reason was that the *Atlantic* offered him a context that encouraged him to go beyond surface humor and a different audience from which he still coveted recognition.

Twain's 1877 Whittier dinner speech showed that he was even more ambivalent than Howells in his attitude toward the Boston literary establishment. He wanted its recognition, but wanted also to distinguish himself from it as distinctly western. Houghton, trying to publicize the *Atlantic*'s continuity with its past and reaffirm authors' identification with it in the face of increasing competition, had assembled at the Brunswick Hotel in Boston fifty-eight writers associated with the *Atlantic* nominally to celebrate Whittier's seventieth birthday and to honor Emerson, Holmes, and Longfellow. Howells had proposed Twain as a major speaker. Twain, addressing the guests of honor, spun a tale of a miner who is bilked by three seedy, inebriated, poetry-spouting con men named Emerson, Holmes, and Longfellow. Several newspaper accounts reported the next day that Twain's speech had been received with good humor. But Twain, later making his description of the event itself into a tall tale, recalled "the famous faces before him 'turned to a sort of black frost'" and Howells in the same vein described "a silence, weighing many tons to the square inch" that turned the entire dinner into a "cruel catastrophe" (Lynn 169–75). Twain, following Howells's counsel, made a humiliating and unnecessary apology that could only have fueled his sense of resentment.

Certainly the Olympians were not used to being "roasted" and certainly Twain's humor had an aggressive edge. But Twain and Howells's exaggeration of Boston's umbrage and their own humiliation also reflected both a continuing insecurity and a continuing desire to see themselves as distinctly western and democratic while constructing Boston as stiff and self-important. As Kenneth Lynn suggests, the episode reflected also the ambivalence of Twain and Howells between wanting recognition and approval by Boston (while reserving the right to satirize it) and feeling twinges of self-contempt for seeking its approval (169). This same ambivalence and irony are reflected in Howells's recollections of publishing Twain in the *Atlantic* in which the editor seems both to acknowledge his own sense of a cultural legitimacy conferred by the magazine and simultaneously to ridicule it, sharing a private joke with Twain. "I myself," he recalled, "felt that we were throwing in the highest recognition of his writing as literature, along with a sum we could ill afford; but the late Mr. Houghton . . . had always believed that Mark Twain was literature" ("Recollections" 601).

The real issue, as both Howells and Twain knew, was not cultural snobbery but rather the problem, crucial in Twain's development as a writer, of whether he was to be and to be recognized solely as another funny man, or as a funny man with a profound knowledge of human nature, an extraordinary ability at realistic recreation of experience, and a capacity to combine laughter with disturbing moral questions. Twain was aware that writing for the *Atlantic* helped him to be, and to become recognized as, the latter, as he acknowledged in a comment to Howells while writing *Old Times*. "The *Atlantic* audience," Twain wrote, "is the only audience that I sit down before with perfect serenity (for the simple reason that it don't require a 'humorist' to paint himself stripèd and stand on his head every fifteen minutes)" (8 Dec. 1874, *Twain-Howells Letters* 34).

Howells's *Atlantic* reviews of Twain's works focused squarely on this same insistence that the author was not only a first-rate humorist but also a writer with trenchant observations about humanity meriting serious reflection. Before meeting Twain, Howells had written in reviewing *Innocents Abroad*: "There is an amount of pure human nature in the book that seldom gets into literature. . . . This book ought to secure him something better than the uncertain standing of a popular favorite. It is no business of ours to fix his rank among the humorists California has given us; but we think he is, in an entirely different way from all the others, quite worthy of the company of the best" (Dec. 1869, 765–66). In reviewing *A Tramp Abroad* at the end of his editorship, as in intervening reviews of Twain's works, Howells sounded the same themes: "There is no danger [readers] will not laugh over it . . . but there is a possibility they may not think enough over it. . . . In this delightful work by a man of most original and characteristic genius, the 'average American' will find much to enlighten as well as to amuse him" (May 1880, 688).

Howells's generous and perceptive reviews in the *Atlantic*, which Twain called "the recognized critical Court of Last Resort in this country," and his offers of regular access to the magazine in the seventies helped to establish Twain's credibility as a major literary figure (*Twain-Howells Letters* 26). Howells's editorial advice to Twain, however, has often been criticized as genteel emasculation. It is true that Howells did at times compromise the realism of Twain's language. But as Howells's biographer Kenneth Lynn demonstrates, to insist on these incidents to the exclusion of Howells's generative advice badly distorts the truth (Lynn 157–58).

One notorious incident involved *Old Times*. On receiving the first installment, Howells proclaimed it so realistic that "it almost made the water in our ice pitcher muddy as I read it," and added "I don't think I shall meddle much with it" (23 Nov. 1874, *Twain-Howells Letters* 32). On receiving the second, he wrote, "This installment is capital. I've just been reading it aloud to Mrs. Howells . . . and she has enjoyed it every word—but the profane words. These she thinks could be better taken for granted; and, in fact, I think the sagacious reader could infer them" (11 Dec. 1874, *Twain-Howells Letters* 35). Twain's reply, typed completely in capitals, dramatized the fallout: "MRS. CLEMENS RECEIVED THE MAIL THIS MORNING, & THE NEXT MINUTE SHE LIT INTO THE STUDY WITH DANGER IN HER EYE & THIS DEMAND ON HER TONGUE: WHERE IS THE PROFANITY MRS. HOWELLS SPEAKS OF?" (14 Dec. 1874, *Twain-Howells Letters* 36–37). The result was that several instances of "hell" and "damn" were excised from the manuscript, to the detriment of the dialogue, and critics ever since have accused Howells of sacrificing Twain's realism, and his own, to a Puritanical feminine gentility.

Twain later had his good-humored revenge, flooding Howells with obscene and blasphemous bogus submissions. Howells also agreed with good nature to append the following note from Twain to an expurgated story: "When the proofs of this article came to me, I noticed that the *Atlantic* had condemned the words which occupied the place where is now a vacancy. . . . Let the blank remain a blank; and let it suggest to the reader that he has sustained a precious loss which can never be made good to him" ("Some Rambling Notes," Jan. 1878, 19). The critics have been less good-humored. Those evaluating Howells's record, while acknowledging the compromise of realism with the tastes of a genteel readership, should also acknowledge his other editorial suggestions to Twain. Looking no further than *Old Times*, we must remember that it was Howells's constant solicitation of Twain, and specifically his request for an *Atlantic* serial for 1875, that initiated the project. Howells greeted Twain's proposed subject with enthusiasm, accepting it sight unseen, and gave sound advice during the writing. After reading early installments, for instance, Howells suggested considerably cutting the night watchman's story, which Twain acknowledged to be "lame and artificial," and advised him to "stick to actual fact and character in the thing, and give things in *detail*. . . . Don't be afraid of rests or pieces of dead color. I fancied a short hurried and anxious air in the first" (3 Dec. 1874, *Twain-Howells Letters* 33). Lynn's analysis shows that this advice considerably enriched not only subsequent installments of *Old Times* but later *Huckleberry Finn* (Lynn 159). Finally, Howells's suggestions for realistic detail and expansion of the narrative to other memories led Twain to generate much more material than he had planned. As a result, he curtailed the magazine serial and determined to bring out a subscription book of twice the length that became *Life on the Mississippi*. Twain, in fact, found Howells's suggestions on *Old Times* so astute and productive that he continued regularly to submit manuscripts not intended for the *Atlantic* for Howells's advice.

As Howells's editorial handling of Twain suggests, editing includes two related functions: the critical, including prescriptive revision of style or content of a manuscript, and the generative, often taking the form of more general suggestions on how to develop a work. As an editor who was also a prolific writer, Howells was often inclined to participate heavily in both, though the degree of each depended entirely on the writer he was working with. With Twain and James, his critical editing of manuscripts was light, but with some younger writers it was not, especially those who like Harriet Preston and Hawthorne's son-in-law George Parsons Lathrop wrote reviews for the *Atlantic*. Some, like H. H. Boyesen and Sarah Orne Jewett, sought, appreciated, and learned considerably from Howells's blue pencil. Others, such as Bret Harte, Preston, and Lathrop, felt it limiting and insulting. Lathrop, who had been hired as Howells's asssistant in 1875, wrote with wounded dignity:

> I think you can hardly realize how trying it is to find my contributions so often interfered with....
>
> You certainly are aware that I acknowledge considerable debts to you for your encouragement and kindly treatment on all occasions.... [B]ut considering the subject without any heat at all ... it seems to me very plain that it is not wise or profitable for either of us that I should occasionally be sat upon.... You have been so long in the editor's chair that perhaps you do not see as plainly as I how important it is for a new writer like myself to devise his own mode of addressing the public.... I am sure that I do not make a mistake in concluding that you have not always respect enough for individuality. (4 July 1877)

Howells's irritable and unfair response was to accept Lathrop's letter as a resignation of his position. But Lathrop's assessment accurately pointed up Howells's tendency to overedit for stylistic uniformity, particularly the contributions of junior staff members. Still, the great majority of Howells's editorial relationships, like those with Twain and James, emphasized not authoritarian, prescriptive editing but rather the collegial support and suggestions that made him a major generative force for a generation of young realists including H. H. Boyesen, John DeForest, and Sarah Orne Jewett.

Boyesen was a young college teacher, miserably displaced in a small Swedenborgian college in Ohio, when he accidentally met in a Harvard library the ballad collector Professor Francis Child, who invited him to dinner with Howells. On hearing Boyesen read his Norse idyll *Gunnar*, Howells was immediately appreciative and invited the impoverished author to a prolonged stay at his house. Howells later recalled that "for a fortnight after I think we parted only to dream of the literature which we poured out upon each other in every waking moment" (*Literary Friends* 256). Boyesen later maintained that "it was this incident which had the most decisive influence upon my life, as it was probably the cause of my remaining in this country. . . . It changed the face of the United States to me and launched me fairly upon my career as a man of letters" (Glasrud 24–25, quoting *Book Buyer* 3: 343). Thereafter, Boyesen spent several summers in Cambridge, partly in a detailed review and revision of the *Gunnar* manuscript with Howells. During the seventies, Howells ran in the *Atlantic* not only *Gunnar* but a quantity of reviews, poems, and stories by the young Norwegian. Partly as a result of his discussions with Howells, Boyesen turned toward writing realistic novels, for which he acknowledged Howells and Turgenev as his major influences (Glasrud 212).

In 1868, Howells wrote an enthusiastic review of a Civil War novel titled *Miss Ravenel's Conversion* by John W. DeForest. He particularly praised the writer's realism in contrast with the false sentimentality of most war novels: "These people of Mr. DeForest's are so unlike characters in novels as to be like people in life. . . . Mr. DeForest is the first to treat the war really and artistically." Undismayed by the salty soldiers' language that had caused *Harper's* to cancel magazine publication, he noted approvingly that "all the talk is free and natural" (July 1867, 120–21). Howells much later recalled: "*Miss Ravenel's Conversion* was one of the best American novels that I had known, and was of an advanced realism before realism was known by name. I had a passion for that book, and for all the books of that author; and if I have not been able to make the public care for them as much as I did, it has not been for want of trying" (*Literary Passions* 223).

Howells's editorial record attests to his efforts. Soon after writing the review, Howells wrote DeForest soliciting material. DeForest, though writing mainly for *Harper's*, sent several sketches of the Reconstruction South. Howells printed these and asked for something longer. "Mr. Howells," DeForest later recollected, "wrote to me for a novel. . . . I wrote the first chapters of 'Kate Beaumont' and sent it to him without the first idea how it was coming out. When I read the first four chapters in the *Atlantic* I could not believe that it was my own work. . . . I said to myself: 'What is Howells doing here, putting in his ideas on top of mine?' . . . The book when finished sold very well, and is, I think, about the best thing I ever did" (qtd. in Oviatt 856). Here again, Howells's generative influence is clear, as is his record of publishing during the decade nineteen stories and articles and three novels by DeForest. In addition, the *Atlantic*, at Howells's instigation, ran the only comprehensive review of DeForest's work published during his lifetime, Clarence Gordon's article "Mr. DeForest's Novels" (Nov. 1873).

In his "Recollections of an *Atlantic* Editorship," Howells overestimated that women may have contributed up to half of the articles published during his editorship (598–99). For all contributions, about 20 percent would have been more accurate, but in fiction and poetry the proportion rose to about a third, somewhat lower than in the days of his predecessors. In 1879, he waxed optimistic about the state of American literature in a letter to Lowell: "We are in a fair way to have a pretty school of really native American fiction. There are three or four younger fellows than myself writing, and there are several extremely clever . . . young women" (22 June 1879, *Selected Letters* 2: 231). In the same year, Howells joined T. W. Higginson in lobbying for the inclusion of women in the National Institute of Arts and Letters. Among the women whom Howells published and substantively encouraged while at the *Atlantic* were Rose Terry Cooke, Sarah Orne Jewett, Fanny Kemble, Louise Chandler Moulton, Mary Murfree, Elizabeth Phelps, Sarah Bryan Piatt, Harriet Spofford, Celia Thaxter, Constance Woolson, and Lillie Chase Wyman.

In 1869 Howells received a story titled "Mr. Bruce" from a young woman in Berwick, Maine, who signed herself Alice Eliot. He liked the quiet but precise observation of Maine life in the story and wrote back suggesting considerable revision but forgot to sign the letter. The story came back revised, with expressions of the author's gratitude for his suggestions, addressed to "the editor with the fine handwriting." Miss Eliot, who turned out to be the twenty-year-old Sarah Orne Jewett, submitted several more sketches over the next two years which Howells declined in a kindly, encouraging way, cautioning her against overindulging in the pleasures of autobiography. On receiving in 1872 a sketch containing realistic but undramatized observations of small-town life titled "The Shore House," he responded that he thought she had found her medium in exactly this kind of realism, but encouraged further development of both plot and character with the suggestion that "the characters were good enough . . . to say a good deal more of them" (qtd. in S. O. Jewett to Horace Scudder, 13 July 1873, in *Jewett Letters* 29).

Here and in his advice over the following years, in which he accepted seven more story/sketches of small-town Maine, Howells taught Jewett lessons he was still learning in his own work about turning direct, realistic observation into fictional narrative and character study. It was Howells, too, who in 1877 urged Miss Jewett to collect her small-town stories into her first book, *Deephaven*. He gave her abundant suggestions for editing it and, in an *Atlantic* review, praised the author's subtle delight "in the very tint and form of reality" and "delicious fidelity in description and dialogue" (June 1877, 759).

Howells's editorial relationships with James, Twain, Boyesen, DeForest, Jewett, and others less known demonstrate the generative quality of his editing. His influence was particularly strong in fiction, but there were instances in nonfiction too. Howells suggested that his Cambridge friend John Fiske write up ideas developed in their conversations on religion. The resulting essays were published in the

Atlantic and collected into a book titled *Myths and Myth-Makers* and dedicated to "My Dear Friend William Dean Howells in Remembrance of Pleasant Autumn Evenings Spent among Werewolves and Trolls and Nixies." It helped substantially to establish Fiske's career as a popularizer of current intellectual movements (Lynn 243). When the actress Fanny Kemble sent a poem, Howells rejected it but asked for and received her autobiography. When Longfellow forwarded a drearily sentimental poem by a woman living in the Canadian north woods, Howells wrote asking her for realistic descriptions of a woman's life on the Canadian frontier. Similarly, when a young southern literary aspirant named Belton Townsend sent some imitative verse, Howells, perhaps remembering his own conversion, asked him instead for sketches which directly observed and recorded the social and economic conditions of South Carolina during Reconstruction. Howells featured the resulting descriptions in the magazine in 1877, and the subsequent book was dedicated to him (Howells, *Selected Letters* 2: 84 and 171). In most of these instances, as in his handling of fiction, the guiding principle behind Howells's suggestions was his concept of realism, inducing authors to look with new eyes at their own everyday life, reflect on its meaning, and record what they saw, heard, and thought simply and directly, avoiding literary formulas and embellishments.

Howells's passion for the realism of direct observation was also instrumental in developing a genre of nonfiction reportage on social conditions that became increasingly important in the *Atlantic*. Howells's own earliest *Atlantic* contributions during his assistantship had been nonfiction sketches of Boston or Cambridge street scenes. The broadening of his social sympathies can be read in the contrast between these entertaining pieces of cultural tourism and a grim piece of reportage he contributed in 1881 in which he records his observations and reactions to a Boston police court. In describing the case of an alcoholic and a prostitute accused of rolling a customer, he expresses both empathy with the accused and angry frustration at the inability of the social system to reclaim these damaged lives ("Police Report," Jan. 1882). This piece, among others such as *A Hazard of New Fortunes* which it anticipates, demonstrates the growth of Howells's realism during his fifteen years at the *Atlantic* and gives the lie to the too often repeated platitude about Howells's vision being limited to "the smiling aspects of life."

Howells encouraged others to do similar social reporting, particularly on urban and industrial conditions. One notable example was Lillie Chase Wyman, who wrote first-person observations of conditions in the textile mills at Fall River. Howells began publishing these in 1877 and encouraged Wyman to develop them into fiction, which she did over the next decade. When her stories were collected in 1886 in a book titled *Poverty Grass*, he wrote a review praising "its absolute and unswerving realism" in dealing with current social problems. It is, he said, "simple, grim, true to misery, toil, pain, vulgarity, savagery and . . . surely not a book for those who would like fiction to make out that life is a pretty play . . . and would have all sorrows end well that their sensibilities may be tickled and pampered" (*Editor's Study* 65).

Another important instance of Howells's encouragement of social reportage was his contracting with the Reverend J. B. Harrison to write a series describing from observation the economic and social effects of industrialism titled "Studies of a New England Mill Town." In his *Atlantic* review of the resulting book, Howells praised Harrison's "unsparing reality" and "humane temper." He further asserted that "those interested in the growth of a literature which shall embody our national life must have felt that here was a man with the artist's eye for seeing as perhaps no other American has seen our condition" ("A New Observer," June 1880, 848). Harrison, like Wyman, later used his observations as the basis for realistic fiction. Thus, in his own writing and his encouragement of others, Howells developed a genre of nonfiction reportage on social conditions which he hoped would influence literature and which foreshadowed the work of later writers such as Jacob Riis, Lincoln Steffens, Upton Sinclair, and Stephen Crane. In fact, largely because of later genteel resistance to this sociological strain in literature, nonfiction reportage, rather than literary fiction, became the major source of information about the damaging effects of industrial capitalism for *Atlantic* readers and many other middle-class Americans.

Howells deserves very considerable credit for his generative suggestions and editorial selections advocating direct observation of ordinary life under a broader range of social conditions. But he stands accused by modern critics of a reductive censorship, a capitulation to the tastes of fastidious and genteel readers in his editing, as in his own fiction, that compromised the very realism he claimed to advocate. By modern standards, he is certainly guilty, and in some respects he was more conservative in this than Lowell or Fields. But those who judge his record should understand both his motives and the context in which he worked. While he was personally squeamish, especially concerning sex, and sometimes timid about offending the *Atlantic* audience, especially concerning religion, he was highly conscious of the need to build a new readership, particularly among women and among readers beyond New England, not just to shore up the *Atlantic*'s dwindling circulation, but more specifically for realism and for the authors who practiced it in its early years. His editorial record shows that he was both willing to expose audiences to constant doses of realism in order to build a readership and willing to make strategic compromises with those audiences to avoid alienating them.

In part because of his midwestern Swedenborgian background, Howells was particularly reticent about sexual themes. In "The Theater Year in Boston" (May 1867), he condemned the "lascivious dancing and singing that expressed only a depraved cockneyism" and predicted prematurely that "no novelty now remains that is not forbidden by statute" (643). This influence he blamed on the moral decadence of Europe, particularly the French, and though instrumental in arranging *Atlantic* reviews for French and German literature, he clearly felt that American realism should avoid the direct treatment of sex that characterized French realism and naturalism. In rejecting a poem by T. B. Aldrich, he amusedly objected to "the continued pectoral imagery," citing three references to the heroine's bosom and concluding, "My dear friend, is it not time to expose some other portion of her person?" (10 Feb. 1875). In a more somber mood, he rejected a manuscript submitted through Norton with the comment that although it was "bright and shapely," "I no longer wish to be put in pain about a woman's virtue, or to ask that suffering from others. It's odious" (to Norton, 16 Apr. 1878, *Selected Letters* 2: 197).

Certainly his sensitivity to his publisher's concern about low circulation added at times to his own inhibitions. He had learned practical lessons in caution from witnessing the wholesale cancellations following *Atlantic* publication of Charles Reade's novel of bigamy, *Griffith Gaunt* (1867); Holmes's *Guardian Angel* (1867), with its lecherous, hypocritical minister; and most disastrously, Harriet Stowe's exposure of Byron's incest (1869) (Cady, *Road to Realism* 133). This sensitivity to circulation, and probably direct instructions from the religiously orthodox Houghton, also made him, despite his own increasing agnosticism, timid about offending religious sensibilities. This sensitivity was heightened by a lingering public association of the *Atlantic* with religious skepticism reflected in Dr. Holland's comment on its "paganism," which contrasted with the orthodoxy of *Harper's* and *Scribner's*. In declining a satire on sectarianism by Twain, Howells tried to use humor to cover embarrassment at his timidity: "The *Atlantic* as regards matters of religion is just in that good God, good Devil position when a little fable like yours wouldn't leave it a single Presbyterian, Baptist, Unitarian, Episcopal, Methodist or Millerite paying subscriber—all the deadheads would stick to it and abuse it in the denominational newspapers. Send your fable to some truly pious concern like *Scribner's* or *Harper's*" (8 Sept. 1874, *Selected Letters* 2: 69).

In avoiding sexual and religious issues, Howells was, however, motivated by more than personal squeamishness and the desire to avoid further circulation loss. He was also quite consciously attempting to expand the readership not only for the magazine but also for American literary culture, and particularly for realistic fiction, especially among two overlapping groups likely to be conservative on issues of sex and religion: women, particularly younger women, and educated but not culturally sophisticated middle-class Americans, particularly those from west of the Appalachians. Lowell had edited largely for intellectually sophisticated, literary New Englanders. Fields had tried to carry the New England literary culture to a broader audience by incorporating more popular fiction. But Howells was more conscious than either of his predecessors of the existence and tastes of large numbers of educated Americans west of the Appalachians like those among whom he had grown up, and especially of "the American girl," whose psychology he was exploring in his fiction.

Howells's consciousness of editing for actual or potential midwestern readers is clearly reflected in his advice to William H. Bishop, one of the many young midwestern writers he encouraged. Interestingly, he chose Bishop, recently transplanted to New York from Wisconsin, rather than a native New Yorker, to write for the *Atlantic* a monthly article on current aesthetic trends in the city. Instead of suggesting that Bishop write for a Boston or New York audience, Howells counseled: "Imagine yourself still a cultivated and amiable inhabitant of Milwaukee. Imagine yourself also the New York friend of your Milwaukee self. Such accounts of New York matters as you would write your Milwaukee self are probably what I should want for the magazine" (11 Sept. 1877, *Selected Letters* 2: 153). Howells not only encouraged contributions from across the nation but also consciously edited for a national rather than a New England audience.

Both Howells's and Houghton's intention to aim the *Atlantic* at a fully national audience, and particularly to increase midwestern and western readership, was reflected also in the range of newspapers in which they chose to advertise the *Atlantic*. Approximately forty newspapers were targeted, including the *Alta California*, *Chicago Tribune*, *Chicago Union*, *Cincinnati Gazette*, *Cleveland Herald*, *Harrisburg Patriot*, *Louisville Courier Journal*, *Milwaukee Sentinel*, *Missouri Republican*, *Richmond Inquirer*, *St. Louis Democrat*, and *Toledo Blade*. Significantly, advertisements for Howells's *Atlantic* also appeared not only in the Unitarian *Universalist* but also in the *Christian Union*, the *Church Journal*, and even in the *National Baptist* and the *Missionary Herald* (Advertising Journal: 1875–77, Harvard).

The text of newspaper advertisements for Howells's *Atlantic* showed a conscious attempt to broaden and redefine the magazine's audience not just geographically but socially as well. The *Atlantic*, read one ad, "has not aimed to secure popularity by sensational articles, or by superficial treatment of subjects in which the people are interested. On the other hand, it has not sought merely to reach persons of the highest cultivation, but rather . . . it has endeavored to command the attention and reward the careful reading of all American citizens." The implication was that while the *Atlantic* was above prostituting itself for the mob, it wanted to shed its genteel, New England high culture image and appeal to a broader, educated middle-class. Clearly Howells was trying to cast a wider net for readers, geographically, socially, and culturally, than his predecessors had. He wanted not only urban, New England "culturists" like the effete Miles Arbuton and Bromfield Corey of his novels to read it but, more important, unpretentious, intelligent middle-class Americans like his heroines Kitty Ellison and Penelope Lapham.

Howells's consciousness of editing for "the American girl," of whom he often wrote, is reflected in his response to Brander Matthews requesting revision of an article on current French drama. "I am," Howells admitted, "somewhat anxious for 'the cheek of the young person' who might be pained by the equivocalities necessarily touched upon. She reads the *Atlantic* a great deal and must be tenderly regarded" (25 Aug. 1880, *Selected Letters* 2: 197).

In this letter Howells was clearly capitulating to the "virginibus maxim" of printing nothing that would bring blushes to the cheek of the jeune fille, the Iron Maiden who Boyesen later complained was crushing American literature in her embrace. But the critic of Howells's editorial record must also acknowledge that he is one of the first American editors and authors representing literary high culture to take the intellect and reading habits of young American women, or even of educated midwesterners, wholly seriously. He is one of the first editors with sufficient respect for the intellect and tastes of these audiences to believe that they would be interested in New York aesthetic movements or French theater, or that they could learn to prefer a realistic fiction with its analysis of contemporary life, its moral complexities, and its subtle studies of character, to a sentimental fiction with its melodramatic plot, unreal passions, and formulaic morality of self-sacrifice.

As Larzer Ziff shows, Howells rejected the European cultural model, in which the freedom to discuss sexual matters frankly was purchased at the price of the rigorous exclusion of young women from adult intellectual discourse (42–43). His intellectual respect for "the American girl" and his desire to include her in this discourse are clear in his novelistic portraits of such perceptive and well-read young women as Kitty Ellison, Lydia Blood, and Penelope Lapham, and they are also clear in his editing. Howells, like Lowell, Emerson, Higginson, Fields, and others involved in establishing the *Atlantic*, had faith that first-rate literature and a serious consideration of ideas could be further democratized and carried to a broader audience than they currently reached. In his choice of audiences, then, as in his choice to write about the commonplace lives of apparently ordinary Americans, Howells was attempting to bridge the culture gap that Higginson had defined between the cultural elite and the democratic majority—or at least the middle-class majority.

The problem Howells faced with audiences was clearest in fiction. He knew that the majority of the novel-reading public were women, most of them habituated to the formulas of sentimental and romantic literature which he, James, DeForest, Twain, and others were consciously trying to break. He knew, as he had noted about James, that the audience for realism would have to be actively created. He reiterated this point frequently in his criticism, as when he commented in reviewing DeForest's *Kate Beaumont* that the nation was "not so much lacking in an American novelist as in a public to recognize him" (Mar. 1872, 365).

Howells's editorial strategy for creating that audience was threefold. First, he exposed his readers as frequently as possible to the work of writers such as DeForest, James, Jewett, Twain, and himself, recognizing that there would be resistance to this work but patiently believing that intelligent audiences, including the American girl who figured prominently in much of this literature, would ultimately be weaned away from sentimental, formulaic fiction. Second, he supported these writers and explained their work to the reading public through extensive reviews and literary criticism. Third, he made strategic compromises with the audiences' tastes: avoiding explicitly sexual themes, cutting a few uses of "hell" and "damn," and allowing an occasional marriage. In his relationships with audiences, then, as in his relationships with literary Boston, Howells showed himself a pragmatist who was willing to compromise to bring new readers to the literature he believed in and bridge the gap between elitism and democracy.

Many of the motives visible in Howells's editorial decisions during his decade as editor—the advocacy of literary realism, the pressure to expand circulation, the creation of opportunities for new writers, the attempt to appeal to a broader audience—are visible also in changes he initiated in the *Atlantic*'s format. In 1872, with the support of Osgood, who was eager to experiment in hopes of raising circulation, he created a series of departments in which regular commentators were to analyze current interests in each field: science by John Fiske, music by W. F. Apthorpe, politics by Arthur George Sedgwick, and recent literature by Thomas Sergeant Perry. Houghton, though a strong Republican, generally disapproved of unsigned political editorials, probably on the assumption that they alienated some potential subscribers, and instigated an education department in place of that on politics. Over the next five years, all of the departments gradually lapsed, although the magazine continued signed articles by various writers on these topics. Another brief and apparently unsuccessful experiment was the publication in 1876–77 of original musical scores with poetic lyrics by Taylor, Stedman, Thaxter, Whittier, and others. This innovation was probably aimed particularly at the young women Howells hoped were beginning to read the *Atlantic* in greater numbers.

The most substantial and lasting changes Howells made in the *Atlantic*'s form, however, were a tremendous increase in the quantity of reviewing and literary criticism and the institution in 1877 of a section called the "Contributors' Club," in which he published brief, informal, anonymous commentary on subjects of the author's choice. During his editorship, Howells literally doubled the very substantive increases he had made in the volume of reviewing and literary criticism during his assistantship. Major new works in all fields were reviewed, but the emphasis was squarely on fiction. By the end of his editorship in 1881, Howells was printing fully seventy reviews and articles on fiction per year. This amounted to almost 300 pages annually and constituted about 18 percent of the *Atlantic*'s space, compared with 5 percent at *Harper's* and 10 percent at *Scribner's* (John 43).

Howells himself continued to write from five to fifteen reviews a year, but he also assembled a reviewing staff that generally shared his enthusiasm for realism. The most prolific and influential of these was Thomas Sergeant Perry, perhaps the most widely read of the jeunesse dorée of Cambridge. Between 1871 and 1881, Perry wrote thirty articles of literary criticism and 397 reviews for Howells's *Atlantic*, including notices of all major French and German fiction as well as some Scandinavian and Russian. He shared Howells's basic critical premise that "literature should fairly represent life rather than advocate morality or excite the feelings unduly" (Harlow 67). Perry, who enjoyed writing "coruscating notices" of sentimental novels, was a strong advocate of James, Flaubert, and Hardy but drew a line at Zola and the naturalists (Perry to Howells, 28 July 1880). The adulation for Turgenev which he and Howells shared led the latter to joke that the subheading of the *Atlantic* should be changed to read "Devoted to Literature, Art, and Turgenev." Other major reviewers during the decade included Harriet Preston Waters, G. P. Lathrop, and Horace Elisha Scudder, the last two also generally contributing to the advocacy of realism.

In October 1876, Howells invited Mark Twain to "spit your spite at somebody or something" in a style written "as if it were a passage from a private letter" for publication in a new *Atlantic* department to start in January 1877 called the Contributors' Club (M. Howells 1: 228). Writing to E. C. Stedman in New York, he solicited "desultory memoranda of an aesthetic nature . . . intended to provoke comment and question." "I expect," he added, "to interest cultivated people everywhere [in contributing]. . . . If you know any bright women who are disposed to write in the Club, invite them for me" (12 Dec. 1876, qtd. in Eppard and Montiero xix). From the beginning, the response to this section by both writers and readers was enthusiastic. In its first year, Howells had enough submissions from a wide variety of pens to publish 150 pieces, and the *Boston Evening Transcript* noted that the Club "bids fair to become—to a certain class of readers, at least—the most interesting [part] of the magazine" (19 Dec. 1879, 6). Thereafter, the Club continued to achieve the two primary purposes for which Howells had founded it: first, to provide less formal, briefer, and often briskly controversial material to make the magazine attractive to a broader audience; second, to provide an opportunity for little-known writers to establish contact with the *Atlantic* and perhaps begin a career in print.

Despite Howells's conscious attempts to restore circulation, his *Atlantic* was intensely literary. During his editorship, he was mainly absorbed in developing new literary forms, writers, and audiences. Even the "Contributors' Club" during his tenure was filled with the discussions of young writers about dialogue, characterization, technique, and ethics in the latest works of American, British, and Continental novelists. Politics and current affairs were clearly secondary. The department on politics provided regular comment between 1872 and 1874, but after that, coverage was erratic, as it had been under Fields. Current affairs generally constituted only 4 or 5 percent of Howells's *Atlantic*, about the same as *Harper's* and *Scribner's*, although there was some increase reflecting Howells's response to the labor unrest of 1877. Despite the small space these articles were allowed, Mitchell concludes that "the *Atlantic* early recognized and discussed" social issues that "had to wait years for an intelligent hearing from the country as a whole" (236).

Articles on politics and social issues advocated quite a wide range of views, but three major themes emerge. First, although Houghton discouraged explicit editorials on political issues, the magazine's norm was clearly reform Republican. Second, however, a number of articles later in the decade seemed to reflect Howells's own ambivalent but developing antiestablishment, democratic sympathies, which he associated with his commitment to realism and had announced in his letter to his father about *A Chance Acquaintance*. Finally, coverage of political and economic issues in Howells's *Atlantic* reflected a waning of the expansive visionary optimism expressed after the war by men such as Emerson, Bancroft, and Sumner. These writers had envisioned a great and inevitable surge of both material and cultural development in a nation at last squared with the universal laws of progress and following the leadership of the "educated classes." Only a few *Atlantic* commentators of the seventies sounded the notes of cynicism and lamentation that were to resound later. But many viewed with anxiety, even alarm, what they perceived as a widening three-way split between the "educated classes," an increasingly militant labor force, and the aggressive new corporate capitalists.

Howells's own background was strongly antislavery Republican. His campaign biography of Lincoln had won him the Venetian consulate. In 1876, at the suggestion of Houghton, another strong Republican, he also wrote a campaign biography of Rutherford Hayes, his wife's cousin, and was rewarded with the president's personal friendship and an influence which he used to win both Harte and Lowell diplomatic appointments. Garfield had been a neighbor in Ohio and remained a friend of the family. Given these ties, the *Atlantic*'s Republicanism during Howells's decade as editor seems surprisingly lukewarm. Clearly the Republican party was no longer "the party of righteousness" but rather the lesser of two evils. The Democratic party, comprising "the ignorant masses and old rebels," was not an option. The magazine initially endorsed Charles Francis Adams in 1872 as a reform Republican alternative to the corruption of Grant's regime. But after Adams failed to be nominated, the *Atlantic* supported Grant because "we know the worst [of him]" and "his relations are now, we believe, all comfortably provided for" (Sedgwick, "Politics," July 1872, 128). Hayes and Garfield were endorsed, but rather late and with surprisingly little fanfare, given Howells's personal connections with them. This was probably again due to Houghton's nonpartisan policy. The *Atlantic* was not as cautiously neutral as *Scribner's*, but Howells's attempt at balance was reflected not only in a more critical treatment of the Republican party but also in a series of paired articles he arranged taking opposite sides on the key issues of hard money/soft money, free trade/protectionism, and public support for parochial schools.

Political and economic commentary in the *Atlantic* reflected the fact that the seventies were a period of severe political strain, caused by severe depression following 1873, massive immigration, the rise of corporate monopolies, and scandals exposing rampant corruption in both parties. *Atlantic* commentators displayed a new and anxious consciousness of divisions between a laboring class increasingly foreign-born, aggressive, and urbanized; an expanding, entrepreneurial middle class, at the top of which the recently wealthy industrialists formed a new socioeconomic elite; and the so-called educated or cultivated classes, with their traditions of social responsibility and high culture. The *Atlantic*'s position was consistently that of the third group, viewing the other two alternatively with critical alarm and with sympathetic attempts to find common ground.

Several *Atlantic* political commentators, especially the conservative A. G. Sedgwick, noted that the political influence of the educated gentry had been displaced by "large gangs of ignorant foreigners superintended by a few skilled agents, employed ... by capitalists at a distance" ("Politics," Aug. 1873, 252–56).[2] Sedgwick, Goldwyn Smith, R. R. Bowker, and others called for a reassertion of the sense of social responsibility among the "educated classes" in the cause of political reform to counteract the power of the ward bosses and monopolists and reintroduce moral principle into government. Others, like the minister and sociologist J. B. Harrison, who wrote a series of articles in 1879 on the dangers of a large, poor, discontented working class, asserted the need for the cultivated classes to take the lead in humanitarian and cultural, rather than explicitly political, reforms, to improve nutrition, economy, recreation, taste, and, most important, education.

Attitudes toward labor covered a broad range, from alarm to sympathy to advocacy. Several conservative articles expressed anxiety about a perceived decline in the quality of the democratic electorate and a simultaneous rise in labor's aggressiveness and expectations. Charles Dudley Warner in "Aspects of American Life" (Jan. 1879) expressed little patience with the discontent of the working classes fueled by the false American dogmas of equality and materialism. Some writers saw education as a necessary means not to create economic mobility but, first, to reconcile the working class to their situation by demonstrating that life could be rich in values even while materially modest and, second, to protect property rights by explaining how the capitalist system benefited both capital and labor, despite its inevitable economic cycles. One unsigned article, "Sincere Demagoguery" (Oct. 1879), advocated establishing a workingman's magazine for this purpose, a project which Houghton was contemplating at the time.

Howells's *Atlantic* also, however, showed signs of the broader democratic sympathies toward which the editor himself was evolving. As noted, Howells encouraged reportage that would give middle-class readers direct observation of social problems. His *Atlantic* contained several descriptive accounts of working-class life—"Workingmen's Wives" (Jan. 1879), for example—which were highly sympathetic, though only occasionally written from the laborer's point of view. Articles such as Emma Brown's "Children's Labor" (Dec. 1880) and Octave Thanet's "Indoor Pauper" (June and Aug. 1881) graphically described miserable and abusive conditions and called for reform. Some of these articles advocated humanitarian assistance rather than political or economic change, but several advocated more fundamental solutions. In "A Workingman's Word on Overproduction" (Apr. 1879), Frank Richards, a machinist, described the working family's suffering from low wages and unemployment and advocated wage increases to fuel consumption and thus production. Alfred Mason in "The Abolition of Poverty" (May 1879) declared, "We have heard too much of the gospel of laissez-faire—that political gospel that makes the policeman the sole representative of government." Mason advocated governmental enforcement of universal education, stringent building codes, and land distribution to farmers. Beyond this, the poor must empower themselves, he said, by forming first distributive, then productive cooperatives to become themselves owners of the means of production (602).

Attitudes toward capitalists and the rise of large corporations, like those toward labor, ranged widely. Many articles assumed an overlap, or at least a common interest, between the "cultivated classes" and the economic elite; property and culture, they suggested, were twin bases of civilization. Most readers of the *Atlantic* had, after all, at least a modest stake in property rights, and many of the new capitalists, as a sympathetic lead article entitled "The Career of a Capitalist" (Feb. 1879) made clear, advocated unhesitating "acceptance of the responsibility of propagating knowledge and true culture" as the only defense against anarchy and class antagonism. Thus several commentators, including A. G. Sedgwick and Brooks Adams, expounded the gospel of economic laissez-faire and social Darwinism coupled with cultural colonization of the working class.

Alan Trachtenberg in *The Incorporation of America* has seen a complicity of interests between the new corporate elite and the cultural elite, between a rapacious industrial capitalism and a refined idealism, as the essential dynamic in late-nineteenth-century Victorian American culture. *Atlantic* voices such as those of Sedgwick and Adams support this argument. But these voices never represented a consensus in the *Atlantic* and were vigorously opposed by many. Clear differences between the "cultivated classes," for whom most *Atlantic* writers spoke, and the economic elite were reflected in a strong current of mistrust for corporate capitalism (a mistrust Howells shared) and some calls for government curtailment of its abuses.

In a 1873 letter to his father claiming "sympathy with the true spirit of Democracy," Howells had hoped that the current farmer's revolt against railroad price fixing would "lead to some sort of communism and society which is the only thing that can save them from becoming mere peasants" (20 Apr. 1873, *Selected Letters* 2: 7). In support of this hope, Howells published articles in 1873 by Charles Seymour and W. M. Grosvenor sympathetic to the farmers and exposing the railroad monopolies. George Julian's article "Our Land Policy" (Mar. 1879) roundly condemned "the wholesale prostitution of the people's heritage" by a government policy "subservient to the interests of the monopolists" and advocated "the multiplication of small homesteads upon which the man who holds the plough is owner of the soil" (331 and 335). In 1876, the *Atlantic* ran several articles by Charles Francis Adams, later president of the Union Pacific Railroad, detailing scandalous financial and safety abuses by the railroads. And shortly before resigning, Howells accepted an article which was one of the opening shots of progressive muckraking: Henry Demarest Lloyd's "Story of a Great Monopoly," a well-documented exposé of the conspiracy between the railroads and Standard Oil, calling for government regulation of monopolies. Howells knew that the article had already been rejected as too explosive by the *North American Review*, which had a smaller, less diverse audience than the *Atlantic*, but he took the risk. The March 1881 issue, in which the article was printed, sold out seven editions and brewed a great controversy about corporate abuse and government regulation that foreshadowed the debates of the following decades.

Before the issue containing Lloyd's article appeared, Howells had resigned his editorship, effective February 1881. The immediate cause was another in the long series of confrontations between his publishers Houghton and Osgood. In 1878 Houghton had forced Osgood to merge his foundering firm with Houghton's, but by 1880 the two temperamentally opposite partners were embroiled in an angry dissolution of the partnership. Houghton was to take the *Atlantic*, but there was hot dispute about who was to get Howells's books, which had begun to be valuable properties. In January 1881 Howells wrote both publishers, "I cannot suffer myself to be made your battle ground" (M. Howells 1: 294). Shortly thereafter, he decided to resign the editorship.

As early as 1873, he had written his father: "If I only were sure of enough without editing! But I couldn't risk it yet awhile" (16 Mar. 1873, *Selected Letters* 2: 19). By 1880, his books had begun to sell well, and the risk of freeing himself from an editorial harness that had become burdensome in order to devote himself full-time to writing was easier to take. The relationship with Houghton was respectful on both sides but somewhat strained by Houghton's discontent over the low circulation and by his related failure to increase Howells's salary. A salary of $5,000 had seemed generous enough when Osgood had first set the amount in 1871, but to be getting the same from Houghton ten years later, despite increased contributions of his own writing to the magazine, irritated Howells (to W. C. Howells, 13 Feb. 1881, *Selected Letters* 2: 275). After his resignation, Osgood offered him $5,000 a year for one novel, leaving him free to write and publish other work for additional fees.

A frozen salary and the judgment that he could now sustain his family solely by writing were major motives for Howells's resignation, but a letter to Scudder, himself later to take up the editorial burden, reflects a third motive: "I have grown terribly, inexorably tired of editing. I think my nerves have given way under the fifteen years of fret and substantial unsuccess. . . . The praise the magazine got ceased to give me pleasure, the blame galled me worse than ever. Then to see a good thing go unwelcomed or sniffed at!—The chance came to light soft, and I jumped" (8 Feb. 1881, *Selected Letters* 2: 274–75).

In terms of the *Atlantic*'s circulation, Howells's sensitivity about "substantial unsuccess" was understandable. During his fifteen years there, he had experienced the relentless, steady decline of the subscription lists, despite all his efforts, from 50,000 to a meager 12,000. The chief reason was competition from the popular New York illustrated monthlies, which continued to boom. But publishing and editorial decisions had contributed substantially. The Stowe debacle had proved that editors would pay a heavy price for transgressing certain taboos. More important, first Fields, then Houghton, had underestimated the impact of illustration and its future in the development of periodicals. They, and Howells too, had decided against a radical leavening of the magazine's intellectual contents in favor of the pure printed word and a continued strong editorial emphasis on high literary culture. Howells's own enthusiasm for literature, reflected in the fact that well over half of his *Atlantic* was either fiction or criticism, had somewhat limited his development of other aspects of the magazine. He had built an admirable reviewing department, authoritative among authors and intellectuals, but with limited appeal to the general reader. As a result, despite Howells's explicit efforts to edit for the "cultivated westerner," Houghton on a trip to Chicago, Milwaukee, and other midwestern cities heard complaints that the *Atlantic* was too scholarly, too bookish, and too short on articles about contemporary life and issues (Ballou 264).

At a time when quality periodical circulations, advertising revenues, and authors' fees were regularly setting new records, the *Atlantic* had already entered a syndrome in which all of these related factors declined together. Falling circulation led to falling advertising fees, both of which led to relatively low authors' payments and an inability to afford highly popular writers—which in turn kept circulation low. The *Atlantic* had begun the seventies paying Harte extravagantly, but a decade later it could no longer compete for Harte, Twain, and finally Howells himself, either as editor or as novelist. The considerably less popular James was the only major novelist left. By the late seventies, the older generation of New England writers who had established the magazine's reputation were producing little, and even some of their work was going to New York.

This inability to compete with the illustrated monthlies for writers who commanded large audiences was to make the *Atlantic* more inclined during the eighties and nineties to embrace a purely high-culture niche and become content to address the few. Making a virtue of necessity, it would represent itself as standing for old-fashioned intellectual and aesthetic standards above commercial compromise. The reputation, if not necessarily the reality, of this stand would particularly appeal to the magazine's next editor, Thomas Bailey Aldrich. Aldrich, one of the "mere culturists" from whom Howells had distinguished himself, would not be interested in trying, like Howells, to synthesize high culture and American democracy.

Howells, especially as a young man establishing his career, was too literary to be a first-rate editor, even of the *Atlantic*. Later at *Harper's* he wrote the "Editor's Study," a department of literary comment, but was not responsible for soliciting and balancing the magazine's contents. His one later experience as editor-in-chief for John Brisben Walker's fashionable *Cosmopolitan*, a disastrous mismatch, was quickly terminated by mutual agreement. But in literature, Howells's editorial accomplishments at the *Atlantic* were admirable. Howells's *Atlantic* was unquestionably a progressive literary force and "a good thing," even though it was, to his frustration, largely "unwelcomed or sniffed at" by the upwardly mobile, middle-class readers who were buying the illustrated magazines.

Howells's pragmatism in literary matters had made him a highly effective synthesizer. Despite his periodic sense of tension, he had made himself and the magazine an effective link between New England culture and the West, between the older generation of American writers and the new. He had drawn freely on the lessons, the support, and the prestige that the older New Englanders had freely given him. He both extended their tradition of liberal Yankee humanism and evolved beyond them, opening the magazine to new writers, readers, and literary modes. Most important, he had developed and used the magazine to promote a literature that aimed to synthesize high culture with a broader spectrum of American life. Richard Brodhead reminds us that both post–Civil War regionalism and American realism were products of the "high culture of letters" (474). Howells was an essential force behind this evolution of high culture into American literary realism. His *Atlantic* represented its earliest development and one of its high points.

Howells's specific accomplishments during his fifteen years at the *Atlantic* include his own growth from sentimental poet to realistic novelist, his support for democratization of subject and style in fiction, his development of nonfiction reportage on social conditions, his patient cultivation of an initially small but growing national audience for realism that included both highbrow and middlebrow readers, and his initiation of discussion among writers and critics about a realistic aesthetic. Perhaps his most important editorial achievement, however, was his support in the form of generative literary counsel, responsive sympathy, frequent publication, and authoritative critical praise for younger regional and realistic writers across the country. Those who received this support at a crucial formative time in their early careers included Boyesen, DeForest, Harte, James, Jewett, Murfree, Twain, and many others. Howells's accomplishments during his fifteen years at the *Atlantic* had an indelible influence on the development of American literature arguably equal to that of any other editor of an American periodical.

Thomas Bailey Aldrich, editor of the *Atlantic*, 1881–1890. By permission of the Boston Athenaeum.

5
Thomas Bailey Aldrich
(1 8 8 1 – 1 8 9 0)

Editorial Aesthete

History has not been kind to Thomas Bailey Aldrich. When remembered at all, he has been identified as a writer of delicately shaped and trivial verse, author of a few entertaining stories, an indolent and inefficient editor, and an amusing but somewhat languorous, shallow, and supercilious human being. The only one of his poems now read is his infamous diatribe against immigration, "Unguarded Gates," habitually cited to demonstrate the ethnic bigotry of the "genteel tradition." Aldrich himself has often been excoriated as an archetype of that tradition.[1]

Most late-twentieth-century observers of Aldrich's editorial record would reaffirm the judgment of history that quickly discredited his restrictive aesthetic values and antidemocratic social conservatism. But the fair-minded observer is bound to acknowledge a degree of competent professionalism in Aldrich's editing, his self-disciplined patience with fractious contributors, his genuine wit, and his editorial resistance to the commercial forces that in the 1880s were beginning to marginalize traditional high culture and promote mass culture.

Partly due to Aldrich's editorial professionalism, his *Atlantic* was never reduced to the narrow dimensions of his own values. But it did reflect a moderate shift away from the optimistic liberalism that had characterized the magazine's first twenty-three years and toward a more insular cultural and aesthetic conservatism and a disengagement from politics. The founders had helped to create and publicize a moderately liberal literary and intellectual culture, actively supporting a range of literary production and engaged in contemporary national life, including political and social issues. Howells had made the *Atlantic* even more literary but had built on its tradition by developing a realism that fused literature and contemporary social life and by trying to democratize both the subject matter and the audience for serious literature. Aldrich believed in a more disengaged and less democratic literary culture. Under Aldrich there was a further narrowing of the magazine's focus to the more purely belletristic, an increased separation between the life of the mind and the political life of the nation, and a growing resistance to aesthetic and social change.

This moderate shift toward social disengagement and conservatism was due in part to Aldrich's own values. It was due also to the publisher Houghton's acceptance of the *Atlantic*'s market niche as an unillustrated, largely literary magazine intended to appeal to a well-educated readership. Perhaps more than anything else, however, it was due to a growing alarm shared by Aldrich and many who wrote for or read his magazine about the pace and direction of contemporary change, including increasing class conflict, political corruption, and pressures to democratize literature. Aldrich and others felt an uneasy sense, like that expressed by Matthew Arnold at this time, that traditional high culture was becoming the heritage of an ever-smaller minority, that the minority espousing it continued to lose influence in an industrialized world, and that their culture, instead of setting standards, increasingly evoked indifference, hostility, or ridicule.

The years of Aldrich's editorship, 1881–90, like several following decades, saw sharply accelerating rates of industrialization, urbanization, and immigration. The eighties witnessed the height of the careers of Jay Gould, Andrew Carnegie, and John D. Rockefeller; the unfettered heyday of the Standard Oil trust and virtual monopolies in steel, telegraphy, railroads, and other industries; record levels of immigration ranging from 334,000 to 789,000 per year; the rise of the Knights of Labor and the American Federation of Labor; and several violent labor-capital confrontations, including the Haymarket bombing during the Chicago strikes and subsequent execution of several of the accused anarchists.

It was increasingly clear that the relatively homogeneous, small-town, socially stable America in which Aldrich himself, as well as most of his writers and readers, had grown up was receding with their own childhoods, replaced by a world that often seemed hostile to their culture and sense of values. The result was a considerable anxiety and loss of confidence on the part of those who referred to themselves as the cultivated classes. In Boston, the confident, liberal-minded, socially committed cultural leaders of the generation that had founded the *Atlantic* were dying off or, like Lowell and Norton, were experiencing a hardening of the political arteries in old age. The younger generation, represented in different ways by Henry James, Henry Adams, and Aldrich himself, were, as Howells had observed, far less certain of their ability to influence the development of American culture and politics and less committed to doing so. During the eighties and nineties many became increasingly alienated from American cultural and political life and cynical about its direction. Even those who did not capitulate to reaction or cynicism felt with Matthew Arnold that traditional culture was threatened with obsolescence by the materialism and intellectual impoverishment of all classes and required defense. Both Aldrich and his *Atlantic* reflected these anxieties.

Although Howells had made the *Atlantic* fully national in its writers and readership, the intellectual culture specific to Boston still influenced the magazine and its editor. Changes in that culture were becoming increasingly clear in the 1880s to the New Englanders themselves. Even the *North American Review* noted in September 1881 that the liberal New England movement in thought, religion, and literature was "at the point of pause" (276). First, the generation that had produced the New England renaissance and founded the *Atlantic* was receding into the Indian summer twilight. Fields died in 1881, Emerson and Longfellow in 1882, Whipple in 1886, with Lowell, Whittier, Parkman, Holmes, and Stowe following in the early 1890s. But as the substantive productivity of these writers slipped further into the past, promotion of their reputations continued to grow. Their fast-waning intellectual energy was being replaced by a new cottage industry in intellectual Boston dedicated to preserving their memories. This memorializing the recent past, compounding the growing nostalgia for a simpler America, gave a retrospective cast to Boston culture of the end of the century.

Second, not only were the best of the younger generation of intellectual Boston less committed to a democratic culture, but they were also much more cosmopolitan, even Europeanized, and as a result Boston generated less intellectual energy by regional cohesion now than previously. While it had been the dominant intellectual center twenty years before, it was now one of several, though still a potent one. New York now held precedence as a publishing center, a position it would strengthen over the following decades.

Finally, by the eighties, Boston literary and intellectual culture had traveled far toward the end of the continuum that stretched from the Concord ideal of high thinking and plain living to the gilded age opulence of Isabella Stewart Gardner's Italian palace. Not only Whittier and Emerson but even Lowell in his *Atlantic* years, if invited to one of "Mrs. Jack's" eight-course dinners, would have been appalled not only at the opulence but even more at the extent to which "culture" had been turned into material objects for the delectation of the few. Aldrich and Henry James, who did attend such dinners, would have found this all entirely natural. In fact, they were delighted that the plutocrats seemed eager to become patrons of the arts and consistently suggested that wealth and privilege were necessary to the support and appreciation of high culture.[2]

Several social and economic forces, then, caused Aldrich's *Atlantic*, like other gilded age periodicals, to veer toward aesthetic, cultural, and social conservatism. But even during Aldrich's editorship, the *Atlantic* was by no means merely reactionary, retrospective, or monolithically opposed to social and aesthetic change. In part because of the magazine's tradition of intellectual openness, in part because of the lingering influence of Howells and the presence of Horace Elisha Scudder (who was to succeed Aldrich), and in part because of Aldrich's own professional sense of what would make an interesting magazine, the *Atlantic*'s norm was moderate in both politics and aesthetics, and latitude was given for the expression of a broad range of opinion. Despite Aldrich's personal aesthetics, namely, a light and decorous classicism disengaged from social issues, the magazine continued to support Howellsian realism, while expressing distaste for the rising wave of popular and naturalistic fiction. Aldrich's *Atlantic* also provided the major source of American publication for the innovative fiction of Henry James at a time when James was failing to find support in more popular markets. On the social front, it was alarmed by unlimited immigration and the radical advocates of unionism and socialism. But it broke with a Republican party that it felt had been coopted by plutocrats and corrupt politicians, and it contained some graphic documentation of social ills as well as calls for both economic and political reform.

Aldrich was fond of saying, "Though I am not genuine Boston, I am Boston plated" (Greenslet, *Aldrich* 78). In fact, he was, like Fields and Howells, another relatively poor, largely self-educated young man from a small-town, middle-class family. Like them, he was drawn to Boston because it was the best of the very few places where a person who loved literature could make a living in publishing. Born in 1836, Aldrich, like Fields, spent most of his boyhood in Portsmouth, New Hampshire, an experience he drew on heavily in writing his novel *The Story of a Bad Boy*. Aldrich's fond recollections of childhood in the stable, homogeneous society of small-town prewar America with clear traditional values constituted a part of his later conservatism.

Aldrich's father, an unsuccessful merchant, had relocated the family for several years in New Orleans, an experience to which Aldrich later attributed his love of exoticism. The father's death and the consequent decline of the family's fortunes prevented Aldrich from going to Harvard as planned and sent him instead, for a year, into his stepfather's countinghouse in New York. Achieving brief national fame with "The Ballad of Babie Bell," a lachrymose poem on the death of an infant, written while he was supposed to be tending accounts, Aldrich quit clerking for literary journalism. He was first a reviewer, reporter on New York society, and assistant editor for Nathaniel Willis's *Evening Mirror* and *Home Journal*, and later an assistant editor of the *Illustrated News* and the bohemian *Saturday Press*. With bohemian journalists such as "Weeping Willie" Winter and Henry Clapp, whose jejune cynicism had disgusted Howells, Aldrich occasionally visited Pfaff's beer hall, the literary salon of bohemia. In the midst of one beery literary discussion, a satirically genial Walt Whitman, who had recently read Aldrich's first book of poetry, *The Bells*, told him: "Yes, Tom, I like your little tinkles. I like them very well" (C. Samuels 37, quoting Winter 64). Aldrich, however, preferred the more aesthetically high-toned salon that met regularly at the house of Richard and

Elizabeth Stoddard, a group including Bayard Taylor, Edmund C. Stedman, and Edwin Booth, who shared his reverence for the noble vocation of poetry and remained among his closest friends.

In late 1865, a few months before Howells arrived, Aldrich moved from New York to Boston at the invitation of Fields and Osgood to edit a new periodical of their firm. The magazine, an eclectic weekly titled *Every Saturday*, was composed mainly of free European reprints and attempted unsuccessfully to compete with the immensely successful *Harper's*. Houghton bought *Every Saturday* with the *Atlantic* from Osgood in 1873, and in 1874 he put the ailing weekly to rest. Freed from editorial labor, Aldrich in the next six years produced three novels serialized in Howells's *Atlantic*, two books of poetry, and a book of short stories, the title story of which, "Marjorie Daw," was by far the most popular piece of literature published in the magazine during Howells's tenure.

When Howells resigned in February 1881, Houghton passed over applications for the job from the perennially wishful Francis Underwood, in whose brain the *Atlantic* idea had seeded itself twenty-five years before, and from George P. Lathrop, the assistant whom Howells had fired. Horace Scudder, a literary adviser and trade editor with Houghton since 1864 and later Aldrich's successor, also confessed to some disappointment at being passed over in Houghton's deliberations. Without knowing Aldrich well, Houghton settled on him because he had both ten years of editorial experience, first in New York, later in Boston, and a national reputation that placed him among the most highly regarded writers in the country. Houghton's judgment on this last score was confirmed by a poll taken by the *Critic*, a magazine of commentary on literature, ranking the greatest living authors. Aldrich was designated seventh, after most of the surviving members of the old *Atlantic* circle, but well ahead of James (thirteenth), Clemens (fourteenth), and Whitman (twentieth) (*Critic*, 10 Apr. 1884, 169).

When he took over the *Atlantic* editorship on March 1, 1881, Aldrich was a youthful-looking forty-four, a year older than Howells. Physically he was short, 5'7", slighter than the stout Howells, with quick gray eyes, pomaded brown hair parted in the center, and a full mustache coming to carefully waxed points which according to a contemporary "seemed to accentuate with a certain justness and chic the quips and cranks that issue[d] from beneath" (Bishop 61). His appearance, his fastidious tastes, his wit, his European travel, and the style of his social life earned him a reputation as an elegant litterateur. Although he became Henry James's most loyal American editor during the eighties (and was several years older than James), the catty novelist thought of him as "plump, youthful and opulent," a "gilded youth, who edits periodicals from Brown's Hotel" (to Alice James, 19 May 1879, *Letters* 2: 235 and Ballou 354).

When he had first come to Boston, Aldrich had enthusiastically written to Bayard Taylor in New York:

Thomas Bailey Aldrich   1 8 8 1 – 1 8 9 0

> There is a finer intellectual atmosphere here than in our city.... The people of Boston are full-blooded *readers*, appreciative, trained. The humblest man of letters has a position here which he doesn't have in New York. To be known as an able writer is to have the choicest society opened to you. Just as an officer in the Navy (providing he is a gentleman) is the social equal of anybody—so a knight of the quill here is supposed necessarily to be a gentleman. In New York—he's a Bohemian! outside of his personal friends he has no standing.... The luckiest day of my professional life was when I came to Boston to stay. My studies and associations are fitting me for higher ends than I ever before cared to struggle for. (26 Mar. 1866, Greenslet, *Aldrich* 81–82).

Aldrich's letter, affirming Howells's observations about the social openness of literary Boston, reflects his self-consciousness about social standing as well as his perception that, in Boston, literary ability was a ready means to social standing.

Aldrich's professional position, his gregarious nature, and Fields's genial social stewardship soon gained Aldrich social standing. Fields, who took pains to treat his two young editors equally, introduced Aldrich and Howells together to Boston literary society in the late sixties. But this social standing did not produce for Aldrich the personal friendships within the intellectual community that it had for Howells. While Howells had met with real affection among many of the Olympians, Aldrich's relationships were respectful on his side and somewhat blandly hospitable on theirs. Aldrich rented Lowell's house, Elmwood, for two years during Lowell's ambassadorship and was on respectfully friendly terms with its master, but Lowell took none of the personal interest in him that he had taken in Howells. Aldrich particularly admired Longfellow, to whose example he attributed his own dedication to poetry. Longfellow, unfailingly kind, visited his new house and composed "The Hanging of the Cranes" in anticipation of the birth of Aldrich's children. But several of the more judgmental among the old school, such as Norton, shared James's opinion that Aldrich was an affectedly elegant intellectual lightweight. Early in Aldrich's career, Holmes had responded to a presentation copy of Aldrich's latest book with a generous but frank letter warning him against becoming a verbal voluptuary and "making nosegays when you should write poems" (n.d., Greenslet, *Aldrich* 64). Holmes, who like Lowell had taken a particular interest in Howells, was impersonally genial and supportive throughout Aldrich's editorship but privately thought him "a stick of sugar candy" (Tryon 291). The difference between the receptions of Howells and Aldrich among the intellectual old guard suggests the truth of Howells's recollection that while socially polite and often generous in giving literary aspirants their time, they were inclined to screen their personal acquaintances severely, not on the basis of family or money, but rather on moral and intellectual quality. Howells's midwestern earnestness they approved, but Aldrich's air of dandyish aestheticism they did not.

By the time of Aldrich's *Atlantic* editorship in 1881, however, both Boston intellectual society and Aldrich's style of life showed marked signs of gilded age change. There was now more fashionable company to be had. The Olympians were seldom met in person, but their literary ghosts lived on in the pictures and gossipy reminiscences in the drawing room of James Fields's widow, Annie Fields, the "salon of pet names" where Aldrich and his wife, Lilian, became "Duke" and "Duchess" (Ballou 379). They lived on also as mementos enshrined in ornate autograph letter books kept by Aldrich himself at his two richly furnished residences— a country home at Ponkapog, south of Boston, and a town house at 59 Mount Vernon Street on Beacon Hill. Some time before accepting the *Atlantic* editorship, Aldrich had apparently become independently wealthy through a moderate inheritance. Though he chose to work, his financial comfort was reflected in his social life and use of his leisure. He was devoted to his family, which now included twin boys, and spent a good deal of time with them at Ponkapog. But in town, he enjoyed an active social life. His delight in conversation and society in small groups made him eminently "clubable," and he listed among his clubs the St. Botolph's and Tavern clubs in Boston, the Players in New York, and honorary membership in the Seville in London. Through eight-course dinners at Mrs. Jack Gardner's Italian Palace or the Somerset Club, he displayed the puckish wit that made him a favored guest. He enjoyed cruising the northeast coast with socially prominent friends in his yacht the *Bethulia*, which his biographer, Ferris Greenslet, characterizes without detectable irony as "probably the only steam yacht of its size ever owned by a poet of his rank" (*Under the Bridge* 109). Literary ability more than ever conferred social standing in Boston, and Aldrich enjoyed that standing.

Another pleasure of the gilded age that Aldrich enjoyed during his editorship was travel. His initial salary at the *Atlantic* was $4,000, which was $1,000 less than Howells had received during the previous decade (Ballou 357). To Aldrich, who had other income, salary was less important than leisure, and a reduced salary allowed him to take three- to four-month vacations every summer after 1881. In most of these years Aldrich and his wife left for Europe in June and returned in late September, visiting England, France, Germany, and more exotic regions such as the Balkans and Russia. Henry James, whom Aldrich visited in London and Paris, and who seems to have developed a particular contempt for him, described Aldrich the tourist as "the great little T. B. Aldrich," cloaked in a "queer, impenetrable atmosphere of travel, luxury, and purchase" (James, qtd. in Ballou 354). As James suggested, one purpose of Aldrich's travel was collecting, and his residence at 59 Mount Vernon Street soon became "a treasure-house of choice books, literary relics, autographs, and objects of art" (Greenslet, *Aldrich* 151).

Not only the art collected in travel but also Aldrich's attitude toward books reflected the value he placed on aesthetic taste and the material artifacts of high culture. He ordered all of his own books bound in scarlet morocco leather, flat-backed and gilt topped with edges trimmed. He collected and mounted his letters from the famous in leather-bound autograph books with gold lettering. And he lamented bitterly to Houghton when a volume of his poems, which he hoped to be the "most artistic little book ever printed in America," was, to his fastidious eye, poorly produced (n.d. 1883).

The further Aldrich became immersed in the world of refinement, wealth, taste, and privilege, the more constricted his sympathies with those outside it became. In fact, his sympathies often seemed appallingly circumscribed by class and race. During his editorship, Howells had grown increasingly empathetic with the social and economic outsider in America, but during the eighties Aldrich grew progressively more bigoted and misanthropic toward those outside the pale of his own social circle. After the death of his setter, Trip, for whom he had a deep sentimental attachment, he wrote to George Woodberry, less than half joking: "The dear little fellow. He had better manners and more intelligence than half the persons you meet 'on the platform of a West-End car.' *He* wasn't constantly getting drunk and falling out of the windows of tenement houses, like Mrs. O'Flararty; *he* wasn't forever stabbing somebody in North Street. Why should he be dead, and these other creatures exhausting the ozone?" (14 May 1892, in Greenslet, *Aldrich* 169). Aldrich's only political association was a lifetime membership in the Immigration Restriction League.

Even within the circles of class and race that increasingly circumscribed his sympathies, Aldrich's affections and friendships, including those with authors, were neither as broad nor generally as deep as Howells's, though perhaps the comparison is unfair because Howells's relationships were so extraordinary in range and impact. But Aldrich was not without witnesses to testify to amiable qualities. Mark Twain, with whom Aldrich maintained a long friendship, was as admiring as James was caustic, perhaps because Aldrich felt more at ease with him. Twain, whose authority should be good, declared that "Aldrich was always brilliant, he couldn't help it. . . . [W]hen he speaks, the diamonds flash." Twain once asserted chauvinistically to French reporters that Aldrich had more of what is miscalled "French wit" than Talleyrand (qtd. in Greenslet, *Aldrich* 160). Aldrich may have disparaged Mrs. O'Flararty, but the poet, editor, and Irish patriot John Boyle O'Reilly was a good friend and drinking companion. After "*Atlantic* dinners" and other formal occasions in the seventies and eighties, Aldrich, Twain, Howells, O'Reilly, Osgood, and others of the younger generation would rent quarters to drink, "tell lies and have an improving time" (Twain to Howells, Dec. 1874, *Twain-Howells Letters* 1: 51–54). Following the *Atlantic* celebration for Harriet Stowe in 1882, Twain described "a mid-night dinner in Boston . . . where we gathered around the board of the Summerset Club; Osgood full, Boyle O'Reilly, full, Fairchild responsively loaded, and Aldrich and myself possessing the floor and properly fortified" (4 Nov. 1882, *Twain-Howells Letters* 1: 419). Howells too recalled "the heat lightning shimmer" of Aldrich's wit (M. Howells 1: 199).

Twain and many others would have agreed with the *Critic*'s description of

Aldrich as "a social genius [who] understands the arts of good-fellowship" (Rideing 310). Aldrich's life was generally successful and comfortable, and this gave him a reserve of good humor and high spirits that counteracted a tendency to sentimentality in his work, as well as making him an enlivening social presence and, for some, a supportive friend. His biographer describes his life in the eighties while he edited the *Atlantic* as "a placid, sun-kissed lake rather than a flowing river," replete with an affectionate family life, high recognition as a poet and editor, leisure to read and travel, material comfort, and an active social life (Greenslet, *Aldrich* 151). From this pleasant abundance came both a sense of privilege that severely limited Aldrich and a buoyancy of spirit with which he often entertained and inspired those whom he loved. His long, close friendship with the melancholy Edwin Booth and his good-natured, generous encouragement of the saturnine George Edward Woodberry attest to the sympathy and support that dour natures found in him, as Twain, Howells, and many others attest to the lively amusement he gave.

Despite his friendships with Twain and Howells, Aldrich did not share their commitment to a more democratic literary culture. Later critics have overstated the genteel preciosity of Aldrich's literary aesthetic. They do not mention Howells's praise of his early novel *The Story of a Bad Boy* for its realistic fidelity to boyhood, nor do they mention that it initiated the vogue of more realistic novels about childhood in prewar America that eventually included *Huckleberry Finn*. They do not remind us that Aldrich was in his day a popular professional writer, one of the first masters of the surprise ending, considerably more popular and widely read as a poet, for instance, than Whitman, or as a writer of fiction than James (*Critic*, 10 Apr. 1884, 169).

Still, Aldrich did not share the fundamental desire of the *Atlantic*'s previous editors, Lowell, Fields, and Howells, each in his own way, to make literary culture more engaged in contemporary American life and more accessible to new and larger audiences. In fact, he was probably as close as America came in the eighties to a resident aesthete. He believed that the purpose of literature was aesthetic pleasure, not social comment or moral enlightenment. He liked to think of himself as a "knight of the quill," a phrase suggesting not only the writer's social status as a gentleman but also his dedication to the high and courtly calling of literature. As a knight of the quill, he professed a strong allegiance to the literature of the past, to traditional literary forms, to the purity of literary language, to the sacrifice of popularity to literary integrity, and to the ideal of conscious literary craftsmanship. Although he could, and did, write some popular works himself, he felt that his official mission as editor was to defend the high bastions of literature, not to engage in the crass business of building circulation. For all his aestheticism, he knew literary markets relatively well, but he was quite content with simply preserving the *Atlantic*'s dwindling high-culture market niche.

Aldrich's aestheticism, his buoyancy of spirit, his nostalgia for the American past, the narrowness of his sympathies, his sociability, his love of leisure, and his financial independence all had a significant impact on his editorial selections and his editorial methods. But the impact of his character on the magazine was moderated by a strong sense of disciplined professionalism developed at the various editorial jobs he had held since he was twenty. This professionalism was often at odds with his temperament and suffered occasional lapses that eventually angered Houghton. But on the whole it resulted in a more restrained and businesslike editorial correspondence and, importantly, a greater breadth in the contents of the magazine than would have occurred if Aldrich had given his personality full scope.

Both Aldrich's professionalism and his personality were reflected in his editorial work habits. Howells, like Lowell, had done much of his editorial work in the comfort of his study at home, coming in to the office as seldom as possible and reserving as much time as possible for his own writing. But according to Howells, when Aldrich was not on his extended vacations, he spent "six hours every day at the office where I used to put in a scant afternoon once a week" (Howells to John Hay, M. Howells 1: 312). Aldrich chose as his office a small, isolated back room in Houghton Mifflin's building at 4 Park Street, overlooking the Old Granary Burying Ground, in which, he told visitors with satisfaction, "lay those who would never submit any more manuscript." Within this small space he enjoyed the comforts of home: an open fire, his pipe, shelves of elegantly bound volumes, and the companionship of his setter, Trip (Greenslet, *Aldrich* 142). His assistant, Susan Francis, recalled that his amusing conversation frequently distracted those with a more businesslike focus on their duties and that "he was happily so circumstanced as to regard work and the various complications attending it, with a cheerful detachment not possible to the ordinary toiler" (qtd. in Greenslet, *Aldrich* 145). His correspondence does not, however, reflect flippancy or inattention but a habitual discipline, a courteous candor, and a general concern for detail. It lacks Lowell's wit and energy as well as his carelessness, Fields's cajoling heartiness and good nature, and Howells's humor and warm encouragement; but it usually has a more direct, professional tone than the correspondence of his predecessors.

Aldrich did actively solicit manuscripts, if not broadly, sometimes in surprising quarters. He also orchestrated the reviewing, which constituted the magazine's major editorial contents during this time, although, in major contrast to Howells, he wrote no reviews himself. But the main focus of his editorial energy was stylistic and aesthetic. Howells had been a powerful, generative force, encouraging new authors, generously supporting their work by reviews and publication, and constantly promoting the debate over realism; only secondly was he an authoritative wielder of the blue pencil and, when he felt it necessary, arbiter of taste. But Aldrich's heart was in the prescriptive rather than the generative editorial function. He tended to concentrate on manuscripts more than on contributors; he felt more responsibility to the purity of the language and elevation of aesthetic taste than to writers or even ideologies. Aldrich's conservative zeal in matters of literary style and form was closely related to his social conservatism. Both reflected a reverence for tradition, a class-conscious resistance to popular taste, and a defensive reaction against perceived adulteration.

Aldrich's laudatory biographer Greenslet concluded that "with all his contributors, both known and unknown, he was something of a martinet" (*Aldrich* 148). Certainly he took a strict construction of the doctrine of editorial sovereignty, as in fact did Lowell, Howells, and most contemporary editors. This doctrine he would regularly recite to authors offended by what they considered his excessive liberties. To Richard Grant White, who threatened to stop writing for the *Atlantic* when Aldrich cut a piece, he wrote with courteous directness:

> You are wrong, Dear Mr. White, in assuming that I have no responsibility because an article is signed. I am responsible for every word that appears in the *Atlantic*. Especially in respect to verse and fiction—being myself a humble writer of fiction and verse—I am supposed to admire what I seem warmly to endorse by printing. I know of no editor who does not reserve the right to strike out a phrase or passage if it seems to him objectionable, or if the exigencies of the make-up require it. Mr. Howells exercised this right to its fullest extent. Mr. Alden of *Harper's* magazine cancelled half a page of a paper of mine. (8 Feb. 1884)

To George Mifflin, junior partner of the house, he stoutly maintained that " an editor must necessarily reserve the right to correct inaccurate dates, to revise faultily constructed sentences, and to leave out anything that seems to him in bad taste or not in accordance with the tone of the magazine" (17 Aug. 1887).

Aldrich was not unusual among contemporary editors in his claims of editorial prerogative. As he noted, Henry Mills Alden at *Harper's Monthly* cut freely, while Richard Watson Gilder, the new editor of what had been *Scribner's* but was now renamed the *Century*, made wholesale excisions from *Huckleberry Finn* and deleted reference to the poor dynamiting the houses of the rich in Howells's *Silas Lapham*. Nor was Aldrich more narrow than most contemporary editors in his sense of decorum. Gilder's guidelines were "no vulgar slang; no explicit references to . . . the generative processes; no disrespectful treatment of Christianity; no unhappy endings for any work of fiction" (Gilder to G. W. Cable, 1 Feb. 1882, qtd. in Tomsich 122).

In both fiction and religion, Aldrich's *Atlantic* can reasonably claim modestly greater liberality than Gilder's *Century*. On issues of propriety, Aldrich was not personally as prudish as Gilder or Howells and occasionally was inclined to take more risk, although the general standards were roughly similar. He was the first to publish the romantic stories of Amalie Rives, "the audacious Virginia girl" who was scolded for writing "with a low-necked pen" (*Current Literature*, July 1888, 3, qtd. in Mott 4: 123). But Aldrich, whom Howells had scolded for breast fixation, excised from a story with a medieval setting not only passages describing the heroine, breast exposed, suckling her child but even references to "wenches and hussies." He prohibited R. G. White from referring to "a nose like a perforated pimple" and gave one poet fits trying to replace the "distasteful" phrase "graveyard smell." Miss Susan Francis, who assisted Aldrich as she had Fields and Howells, performed the most extensive hatchet job of the decade, exacting the revenge of the grim virgin on portions of Thomas Hardy's *Two on a Tower* that came in during one of Aldrich's long excursions. Presumably, however, Gilder never would have published the novel at all, since it involved its heroine in a confusing series of liaisons of dubious legitimacy—and it failed to provide a happy ending. Even expurgated, the novel caused a flap among *Atlantic* readers, but this did not prevent Aldrich from trying unsuccessfully to solicit another Hardy novel. Aldrich was willing to take some risk if he felt aesthetic quality was high, as when he published some mildly fleshly and adulterous sentiments in verse by Edward Rowland Sill.

But if Aldrich's sense of moral purity was slightly on the liberal side of the genteel norm, his determination to preserve aesthetic purity, the purity of language and literary style, was extreme. From the beginning the *Atlantic* had been intended to set a high standard of literary style to act as a model for American literary production. This standard had clearly recognized the claims of dialect in literature and admired American directness over European elegance. But it also insisted on scholarly accuracy, grammatical correctness, and a reasonably elevated tone and usage in formal writing. Howells had noted an almost "frightful rigor" in proofreading applied not only by the editors but by the professional proofreaders at the press, and most sternly by the iron hand of Susan Francis. But even Francis, although she did much of the actual work, could not outdo Aldrich, whose commitment to traditional formal usage, scholarly accuracy, grace and clarity in prose, and the conventions of poetic form made him a more draconian linguistic conservative than any of his predecessors.

Aldrich was accused by contemporaries, as well as later critics, of linguistic preciosity. "He is," one contemporary wrote, "so squeamish concerning words that in pondering them he is in danger not infrequently of neglecting the thought that they express. He is a passionate worshipper of the daintiest dainty English" ("Writers Who Lack College Training," *Critic*, 11 Dec. 1886, 297). John Jay Chapman fulminated against "these Aldriches who think style is the *means* of saying things well! ... 'Use beauty-wash' they cry—patent Italian sonnet-varnish—the only thing that has stood the test of time" (qtd. in Ballou 356). But a closer look at Aldrich's editing supports Bliss Perry's judgment that in prose his standard was not elaborate elegance but rather a formal type of "clear, competent, and workmanlike writing" (*Park Street Papers* 162). Strunk and White would have endorsed most of his efforts to say more in fewer words, cut redundancy, replace arcane or inexact words, and unscramble inversions. On these and on all points of formal grammar and usage, he and his staff were merciless.

Aldrich was also "bristling with philological prejudices" such as his odium for compound words, elisions, and even such well-established usages as "people" instead of "persons" (*Critic*, 11 Dec. 1886, 297). In dealing with poetry, his linguistic Toryism and passion for the conventions were even more extreme. He loathed all of the dialect poetry becoming popular at the time as a degradation of the art. He held a mortal prejudice against the Shakespearean form of the sonnet, was unsparing in counting metrical cadences, and was so exacting about rhyme that he disallowed matches like "tender" and "splendor," "quarrel" and "moral," or "garden" and "pardon" (J. T. Trowbridge to Aldrich, 14 Oct. 1881). In all this linguistic fastidiousness and adherence to tradition, his aesthetic values mirrored his conservative social values. He worked to maintain a literary style above what he considered debased popular usage and forms and felt a rather pessimistic anxiety about defending waning linguistic and literary traditions against the threatening tide of vulgar mass culture.

The Procrustean rigor with which Aldrich and his assistants exercised editorial prerogative and went about enforcing his idea of "*Atlantic* style" was accepted by many established authors with surprising equanimity. Most magazine writers at the time acknowledged broad editorial rights. Lowell invited Aldrich to "cut out what you will," and E. R. Sill, a seasoned contributor, maintained that "nothing except poetry has any rights which a competent editor is bound to respect" (Lowell to Aldrich, 17 Dec. 1886; Sill to Aldrich, 18 Nov. 1882, in Parker 194). The British novelist Margaret Oliphant welcomed "a bold hand" in whatever revisions Aldrich wished to make (8 Oct. 1886). Many even felt gratitude for Aldrich's lessons in stylistic grace and clarity. Sarah Orne Jewett told him that "seeing how carefully you do your work is always one of my best lessons"; the irascible T. W. Higginson thanked him for his "frank criticism"; Sill wished Aldrich had "nothing to do but criticize my manuscripts" (Jewett to Aldrich, n.d., in Matthiessen 93; Higginson to Aldrich, 9 June 1881; Sill to Aldrich, 16 Nov. 1886). Some writers, however, were offended. Phillip Hammerton finally refused to correct proofs so overwritten with red and blue markings, Lucy Larcom was reduced to fatigued discouragement, and even the buoyant Helen Hunt Jackson lamented "proofs blue enough to give an author his death of the blues" (Hammerton to Aldrich, 14 July 1887; Larcom to Aldrich, 14 Aug. 1881; Jackson to Aldrich, 19 Apr. 1881).

In editing for style, Aldrich's sense of professional duty reinforced his aesthetic conservatism, and the two combined to make him a trying taskmaster. But contributors too could be trying, and in handling these, Aldrich usually showed a courteous professionalism that kept his satiric temperament in check. Many deserved less respect than he showed. Among the perennial plagues were contributors who sought the intercession of third parties. The southern approach emphasized elaborate politeness, flattery, and family status but was nonetheless a hard sell: "Dear Sirs, Allow me the pleasure of introducing and recommending to you one of our literary ladies belonging to one of our best and oldest families, who desires to contribute to your valuable periodical. . . . I trust you will be able to avail yourself of her offer and make it equally beneficial. I am, yours very truely, Gustave Toutant Beauregard" (to Houghton Mifflin, 8 Feb. 1886). Northern "friends of the magazine," often called on to intercede, were franker but still asked Aldrich's indulgent attention to material they knew was fifth-rate. Henry James ingenuously lamented being asked to be "Godfather" to the "incubations of incompetent mondaines" but assured Aldrich that he himself discouraged the worst: "It was only two days ago that I headed off F. F. Palgrasi. He isn't a mondaine—save by breadth of bottom—but he is almost as incompetent (to write the readable) as if he were" (12 Nov. 1887).

Other types of presumption by contributors consumed Aldrich's time and tried his patience, but his professional manner was calm and fair, whatever his private thoughts. Christopher Cranch's complaint that his poem had been held an entire week without response elicited a kind note. When R. G. White, New York socialite, father of Sanford White, and prolific magazinist, pestered Aldrich for a comprehensive review of his work, Aldrich generously contracted a reviewer. When White insisted that it be done instead by E. P. Whipple, Aldrich, at considerable trouble, engaged Whipple to do it. When the resulting piece proved flattering but mediocre and digressive, White bitterly blamed Aldrich for printing it. But Aldrich's response, as throughout this irritating affair, was consistently frank, polite, and equitable (letters of R. G. White and Aldrich, Oct. 1882).

In 1886, Aldrich encouragingly accepted a story from a young woman named Amelie Rives of Castle Hill, Virginia, requesting, however, that she delete certain passages as too torrid. This brought down upon him several months' worth of ten-page letters begging, "Please, please do not think that I am voluntarily vulgar or coarse. You know I have . . . spent nearly all my life in an old Virginia homestead among my books, horses, dogs, and flowers." Among these virginal protestations, he received an invitation to visit the old plantation. Miss Rives gushed, "Oh! I think I want to wait on you a little and fetch things for you, and learn to do things you like, and to earn your approval and the right to your friendship" (1 Jan. 1886, in Tuttle 648).

Aldrich made polite excuses but was soon embroiled in another problem. Miss Rives asked and he reluctantly granted genteel anonymity for her work in the *Atlantic*. But on finding that she had published poems over her name in the *Century*, he justifiably felt a little ill used. Miss Rives responded to his polite but formal inquiry by swearing to him that an enemy had forged the letter requesting anonymity and scolded him for believing her capable of conduct so false and unladylike. Aldrich placidly accepted her preposterous explanation, and she responded with tearful gratitude for his understanding. Thereafter, though she dedicated her first book of stories to him, he showed decreased interest in her fiction, which showed the same sentimentality and improbability as her correspondence (Tuttle 633–60).

Aldrich sometimes lamented that part of the editor's job was to make as many as a hundred enemies a month in the persons of rejected contributors. One rejected contributor turned out to be a swashbuckling lunatic who hounded Aldrich relentlessly. The aggrieved aspirant had submitted an article titled "Shakespeare's Viola" to the *Atlantic*, which he later characterized as "an effete, barren periodical" that he had "sought to infuse . . . with new life" (J. F. Morton to Aldrich, 26 July 1886). On receiving the editor's regrets, perhaps mentioning that R. G. White had already supplied the magazine with ample Shakespearean material, the contributor retorted that the editor was "an audacious and impudent *liar* and deserve[d] to be horsewhipped" and that the *Atlantic* hypocritically accepted manuscripts only from "the swarm of half-starved literary paupers to whose support you are obliged to contribute" (J. F. Morton to Aldrich, 19 July 1886). The exchange of letters continued, Aldrich apparently maintaining with polite professionalism, though not full frankness, that the article had been fairly considered, the truculent scholar asserting, "My robust nature abhors your contemptible duplicity. I can neither express nor yet wholly restrain my justly aroused indignation" (J. F. Morton to Aldrich, 26 July 1886). Aldrich liked to recall that the exchange ended when "the gentleman with the robust nature was politely invited to call at No. 4 Park Street on any day that week . . . , but . . . failed to materialize" (Greenslet, *Aldrich* 150).

The issue raised by the "robust nature," if not his manner of raising it, was a serious one: who had access to Aldrich's *Atlantic*? Aldrich did rely heavily on certain authors such as White, Fiske, Sill, Scudder, Edith Thomas, G. E. Woodberry, and Harriet Waters Preston, the latter three of whom might well have described themselves as "half-starved literary paupers." Also, as noted, Aldrich's literary and social views were frankly narrower than those of previous editors. But the accusation that the *Atlantic* was a closed club was not accurate for several reasons. First, while Aldrich was an editorial autocrat concerning style, his sense of professionalism and of effective magazine editing made him, in the words of Susan Francis, "very fair-minded towards articles treating of subjects which did not appeal to his personal tastes, if the writers thereof were clear-headed and had a reasonable amount of literary skill" (qtd. in Greenslet, *Aldrich* 144). Second, again despite Aldrich's editorial autocracy, others inevitably influenced the *Atlantic*'s contents. Most of those who had written for Howells continued for Aldrich. Aldrich also inherited from Howells a year's worth of commitments, including at least three serial novels, even after he had returned to their authors a half bushel of manuscripts that Howells had inherited eleven years before. Not only the shadow of his predecessor, Howells, but the daily presence of his eventual successor, Horace Scudder, gave Aldrich's magazine more diversity. Scudder, the trusted chief literary adviser to Houghton Mifflin, annually acted as interim editor for the three summer months of Aldrich's absence, with power to solicit and to accept manuscripts (Aldrich to Scudder, 25 Aug. 1882). The indefatigable Scudder, who was more sympathetic to Howellsian realism than Aldrich was, also wrote the great majority of reviews of American fiction during Aldrich's editorship.

Thus, Aldrich's sense of editorial professionalism and the influence of Howells and Scudder, as well as the *Atlantic*'s traditions of intellectual tolerance and literary realism, added diversity to the magazine in the eighties. They significantly modified Aldrich's personal narrowness of taste and the conservative reaction among many intellectuals against social unrest and incipient literary naturalism. The norms and range of fiction, literary criticism, and social commentary in Aldrich's *Atlantic* will be examined later. His editorial correspondence, however, shows that he sometimes actively solicited work from writers with views different from his own. Among Aldrich's literary solicitations were not only Bret Harte, Joel Chandler Harris, Arthur Sherburne Hardy, and Francis Marion Crawford but also the utopian socialist Edward Bellamy and, despite his qualms about realism, Henry James, Thomas Hardy, and John DeForest. Despite his social conservatism and indifference to politics, he frequently solicited papers from such reform liberals as E. L. Godkin, editor of the *Nation*, and the soldier, statesman, and author Carl Schurz. In the wake of the Haymarket bombing of May 1886, Aldrich invited Terence Powderly, leader of the Knights of Labor, denounced by the *Century* as a fraud, to state freely labor's position.

Aldrich's correspondence suggests not only that he often solicited work differing from his personal views but also that he generally accepted work on its merits rather than because of who wrote or sponsored it, including his employer. He was quite capable of rejecting papers by the likes of Norton, Higginson, or Harvard's president Charles Eliot. While he delegated reading most unsolicited manuscripts to his first reader, Susan Francis, he nevertheless was entirely capable of publishing the work of unknowns if he liked it. When a story called "The Goophered Grapevine" by an unknown writer from Cleveland named Charles Chesnutt came to him by way of the sludge pile of unsolicited submissions, he printed it and welcomed more. The story, soon followed by two others, "Po Sandy" and "Dave's Neckliss," was the first that Chesnutt published in a national periodical and marked the beginning of a twenty-year association between the *Atlantic* and one of the first black American writers of fiction.

Aldrich demonstrated further professional integrity in rigorously refusing to allow the interests of his publisher to influence his editorial decisions, although he was not above being influenced by his personal relationships. Unlike Fields and unlike Howells when assistant editor; he did not balk at publishing authors, reviews, or some other kinds of material not cordially received by members of the firm. When G. E. Woodberry was embroiled in a financial controversy with the house, Aldrich continued to accept his submissions, noting with the chivalrous pride of a knight of the quill above business considerations: "I have no connection with the office downstairs. I shall edit the *Atlantic* so long as I occupy this chair" (to Woodberry, 21 Oct. 1884). Houghton generally restrained himself from interfering in editorial decisions and sometimes pointedly told authors he would not try to influence Aldrich's judgment. For instance, when Elizabeth Stuart Phelps tried to evade Aldrich and appeal directly to Houghton, the publisher told her that decisions governing the magazine were made by the editor (to Elizabeth Stuart Phelps, Nov. 1882). But Houghton was certainly conscious of wanting to treat certain "friends of the house" with respect and sometimes acted as a conduit for submissions. Aldrich did not hesitate to turn these down when they did not suit him (Greenslet, *Aldrich* 151). He was to find later that while Houghton had restrained himself well to avoid editorial interference, he was sometimes choleric at what he considered tactless handling of important authors.

Aldrich practiced a strict separation between the business and editorial functions with respect to payments as well as selection of contents. As with Lowell and Howells, determining the rate of payment was the prerogative of the business office, in this case primarily Houghton and his assistant, Francis Jackson Garrison. Aldrich was authorized to accept manuscripts at the standard fee, between six and ten dollars per page, or at a fee previously given a specific author. If an author asked for more, the issue was referred to the business office. With very few exceptions, Aldrich seems to have remained even more neutral than his predecessors in setting the price. Correspondence with authors about payments came directly from the business office, not the editorial office.

The rapid escalation of the market for well-written prose, especially fiction, spurred by the sharp increases in circulation of the quality magazines in the seventies continued in the eighties. The former *Scribner's*, which had broken from its publishing house and was now the *Century Illustrated Monthly Magazine*, passed the 200,000 mark. But Aldrich also had to compete for popular authors with *Harper's*, *Lippincott's*, and a new *Scribner's Magazine* founded by that publishing house in 1887. Most portentously, the new syndicators such as Charles Dana of the *New York Sun* and S. S. McClure were beginning to tap mass markets that in the next decade would revolutionize magazine journalism. *Atlantic* circulation, however, remained well below 20,000 during the decade, bottoming out in 1886 at only a little over 10,000 (Ballou 365).

Houghton, continuing to be squeezed between low circulation and rising prices, characteristically declined extravagance and thus had to forgo some popular fiction writers, especially if their books were published by another house. His tactic was to begin at a relatively low base of between $6 and $10 for a page slightly smaller than a page of the *Century*, which by the late eighties was paying an average of about $20 for nonfiction and sometimes several times that for fiction (Ballou 375–76; Perry, *Gladly Teach* 180; John 149). Nonfiction received a lower rate than fiction because, as Aldrich explained to one economist, it was of less importance to the magazine (to J. Laurence Laughlin, 24 Feb. 1886). John Burroughs had to argue his way at the *Atlantic* from $5 to $8, though he received $20 from the *Century* (Burroughs to Aldrich, 29 Nov. 1882; John 149). The business office balked at $8 a page to Woodberry for reviews, and Norton declined to review because other journals paid much more. At these rates, average writers publishing only in the *Atlantic* would have had to contribute five to ten pages of acceptable material each month, a virtual impossibility, to maintain parity with the modest salaries of compositors and proofreaders at Houghton's Riverside Press, where the magazine was published.[3] Obviously Houghton and Aldrich could not expect the exclusivity and identification of authors with the magazine that Fields had used so effectively.

Despite his low average scale, Houghton could fill most of his magazine with what Aldrich considered good material at $10 or less per page. But a combination of reputation and assertiveness could raise the author's stakes considerably. Howells, always astute at business, got $15 per page, money down on acceptance, before shifting to the more lucrative *Century* and finally an exclusive contract with *Harper's*. James continued to receive his former rate of about $15 per page for serials, while Charles Dudley Warner regularly received $20.

Houghton was willing to pay to keep the remaining Olympians identified with the magazine, but even for them he would not directly compete with New York. Holmes, characteristically trying to shore up Boston's waning claims, wrote to Lowell on the latter's return from his ambassadorship:

> [Houghton] does not wish to bid against other publishers; but to use his own language, it would not be money that would stand in the way of your writing for the *Atlantic*. How much he or others would pay you I do not know, but I do know that Mr. Houghton has treated me very liberally, that he is an exact man of business, that he takes pride in the *Atlantic* which I suppose in a literary point of view is recognized as the first of the monthlies, and that he is very anxious to see you again in the pages of the old magazine you launched so long ago. . . . Other things being equal, you might perhaps prefer to publish in Boston, and add to the prestige of the city and the University. (7 Oct. 1885, Morse 1: 221–22)

Lowell responded by assuring Aldrich, "I have entered into no engagement with the Heathen, nor have I forgotten my old relation with the *Atlantic*" (10 Oct. 1885). He did continue to send some poems to the *Atlantic*, but with him, as with his friend Norton, the mammon he scorned sometimes outweighed cultural and provincial allegiance. When Lowell insisted he must have $250 for a poem because he could get more in New York, Houghton refused the competition, letting it and several subsequent poems go with regret. Others who threatened to go elsewhere, such as Annie Fields, G. P. Lathrop, and Rose Hawthorne Lathrop, were allowed to go with less regret.

Wage discrimination against women was standard labor practice at the time. At the Riverside Press, for instance, wage records were categorized by sex, and women compositors and proofreaders routinely received little more than half the wage men received, often even for the same job. Salaries for male compositors, for instance, ranged from $30 to $60 and averaged about $48 per month, while those for female compositors ran from $18 to $32 and averaged only about $25 (H. O. Houghton and Co. Payroll Books: 1880–83). The *Atlantic*'s business office, however, perhaps recalling the accusations brought against James Fields by Gail Hamilton and Sophia Hawthorne, and certainly aware that a good portion of the magazine's readers were women, did not noticeably discriminate against women authors if they were equally valued by the editor with male authors and were at least moderately assertive, as most were. If the *Atlantic* was typical, this difference between an accepted, structural discrimination in business and the lack of at least overt discrimination in the profession of authorship, particularly in fiction, would have made writing relatively economically attractive to women.

Houghton's scale was comparatively low, and all authors had to assert themselves to receive more than the average or to raise their fees. Some women professed a genteel embarrassment to be thought grasping, but most asserted their claims nevertheless and received comparable treatment with men. Jewett reflected a genuine discomfort when she wrote to Aldrich: "I hate all this business part of my work and have had such hot and cold fits about big prices and little prices that I am going to let my ink bottle dry up and all my Esterbrook pens get rusty.... I should like Mr. Houghton to know how many times I have been paid $200 for short stories—then he could not think that I was the heartless mercenary I now appear" (Friday afternoon, n.d.). Despite her squeamishness about money, she successfully raised her rate to about $13 a page during the decade, approximately what James received and more than John Burroughs, R. G. White, or Francis Marion Crawford. Other women were less diffident. Jewett's companion Annie Fields was contemptuously caustic when Houghton refused to meet her demands, and Helen Hunt Jackson asked Aldrich to return an accepted manuscript because she could get $75 more for it elsewhere and needed a new rug (Ballou 377–78; Jackson to Aldrich, 10 Apr. 1884; and Tuttle 98). Generally the women who were professional writers were as assertive as the men, though more apologetic about their assertions, and they received comparable payment. The popular Helen Hunt Jackson was the highest-paid contributor of the decade at a rate of $20 to $28 a page (Ballou 377).

Other magazines, particularly the *Century*, made even the top rates at the *Atlan-*

tic look paltry. Aldrich himself sent most of his work to the New York magazines during his editorship because, he claimed, he did not want his writers to be able to say that the editor had displaced them in his own periodical (Aldrich to E. C. Stedman, fall 1881, in Greenslet, *Aldrich* 146). This decision, however, could have been justified on entirely mercenary grounds. *Harper's* paid Aldrich $500 apiece for two poems and offered $500 apiece for articles on Russian travel, while the *Century* offered him $75 a page for stories (Frank Scott to Aldrich, 10 Jan. 1891). Both *Harper's* and the *Century* paid up to a top rate of $100 a page for some stories during the decade (*Critic*, 2 July 1887, 5). This differential between what the large-circulation monthlies would pay and the $5 to $20 Houghton could or would pay virtually excluded the *Atlantic* from publishing with any frequency popular authors like Howells, who wrote for *Harper's*, Twain, whose *Huckleberry Finn* was excerpted in the *Century*, and even Aldrich after his departure as editor.

Aldrich could do little to modify the disparity between what he and his competitors could offer. To his credit, he did try to ensure that if the payment was modest, at least it would not be years in coming. Company policy was payment on publication, not on acceptance. Howells, always an effective entrepreneur and one of the few allowed to break the policy, only half joked of "Mr. Houghton's loathing for a man who wants his money down" (to Aldrich, Aug. 1881). To ensure the shortest possible lag between acceptance and payment, Aldrich, unlike his predecessors, deliberately kept his backlog of accepted manuscripts small. During one of his extended absences, he reminded his replacement Scudder: "As we do not pay on acceptance, it is impracticable to fill that chest with rich mss" (3 Aug. 1889). His tendency to live editorially from hand to mouth has generally been ascribed to his indolence, but one main motive was fairness to authors.

Despite often major differences in pay scale, many authors continued to submit to the *Atlantic* work, and often their best work, that would have earned them substantially more elsewhere. Bret Harte had sneered at the idea of literary prestige compensating for low pay, but Helen Jackson, who could and did publish widely, wrote, "I am always glad to have papers in the *Atlantic* at less rates of pay than I get elsewhere, because I consider the having them read by the *Atlantic* audience part of the pay" (to Aldrich, 16 Oct. 1882). Perhaps she would have been more candid to add that, even for popular writers, the more different magazine audiences they were exposed to, the better the prospects for their book sales, and *Atlantic* readers had always been enthusiastic book buyers. Constance Woolson spoke for many less-known writers, especially the substantial number from the Midwest, when she wrote to Aldrich, "I have never outgrown the reverential respect with which I used to read [the *Atlantic*] when I lived in Ohio. And those of my sketches which have come out in its pages since then have always had the air to me of having been presented at court" (30 June n.y.). Another midwesterner, E. R. Sill, touching a chord that echoes through the magazine's history from Emerson to the present, considered the *Atlantic* audience "the illuminati," from whom ideas would "work down" into popular thought and practice (to Aldrich, 3 Oct. 1882). Joachim Miller was "anxious to have [his poem] uttered by what Europe reckons the mouthpiece of the most civilized center of our Republic because I think it will have a better chance of doing some good there" (to Aldrich, May 1881). Holmes and Lowell, who no longer relied heavily on authors' payments for livelihood, as well as Whittier and Sarah Orne Jewett, who did, contributed partly out of loyalty to the magazine and to New England culture but also, as Holmes had suggested, because the *Atlantic* really was still recognized as publishing more consistently good literature than any other periodical, despite its inability to compete for some of the most popular authors.

If we suspect Holmes's or Sill's judgments of chauvinism, we find them supported by contemporary commentaries on magazines in both the *Critic* and the *Nation*. Despite suggestions that the *Atlantic* was a bit heavy and old-fashioned, these commentaries continued to find it, on balance, more intellectually challenging, more aesthetically sophisticated, and of higher literary quality than the other monthlies. The *Critic* found the *Atlantic*, by contrast with the others, "appallingly full of information" and somewhat daunting in its determination to educate rather than primarily to entertain (*Critic*, 1 Nov. 1884, 209). The *Nation* noted that in contrast to *Harper's*, "the current *Atlantic* . . . still flies the flag of belles lettres, and will, we dare say, till the tattered ensign goes down with the ship or is safely stored in some museum library. There is nothing in the issue which has not in its kind the special quality of excellence which appeals to taste, apart from a mere curiosity or vacuity of mind to which the day's literature is mainly addressed" (*Nation*, 25 Feb. 1886, 171).

These comments strike a tone that characterizes attitudes toward the magazine for the next thirty years: respect and admiration for *Atlantic* intellectual standards, taste, and literary quality mingled with satiric suggestions that the venerable maga had changed little with the times and was out of touch with contemporary life. They also suggest both the strengths and faults of Aldrich's *Atlantic*. It assumed an intellectually serious reader and was not to be browsed from mere "vacuity of mind." This seriousness was emblemized by a cover featuring not the elegant illustrations of the New York monthlies but a plain listing of the table of contents. It continued to assume also a liberally educated readership as evidenced not only by untranslated passages of French and Latin but also by many papers on the canonical works of Western culture, including a series on Latin authors. In fact, the number of such papers had increased since the days of Fields and Howells.

Far more than the other monthlies, the *Atlantic* reflected a commitment similar to that which Matthew Arnold was pursuing during the 1880s, namely, to keep alive traditional humanistic, literary culture rather than allowing it to be lost in the gilded age frenzy of getting and spending or embalmed in academic scholarship. It had serious educational designs on its reader and still aspired to speak, as Lowell had intended, to those "such as give tone to public opinion in literary matters" (Lowell to Fields, St. Headache, 1860). But it had also become distinctly a publication for a cultural minority of well-educated readers interested in the liberal arts, and primarily in literature. It was more the literary equivalent of Godkin's relentlessly highbrow *Nation*, which now had a roughly similar circulation of 10,000, than a competitor with the middlebrow *Century*, which had 200,000. It had disappointed the sanguine hopes of Lowell, Fields, and Howells to reach more types of readers. Aldrich himself, as a knight of the quill, seemed much more interested in preserving stylistic purity and a high literary tone than in gaining circulation. Both Aldrich and his publishers thought of it as "the leading literary magazine in America," which should avoid authors and works of "too light culture" (G. Mifflin to H. O. Houghton, 26 May 1884).

The content of Aldrich's *Atlantic* was, like Howells's, mainly literary but achieved somewhat more breadth later in the decade. Aldrich actually increased fiction to about 40 percent of the magazine's contents, compared with about 34 percent during Howells's tenure, but eventually he decreased the proportion of literary criticism from 17 percent, inherited from Howells, to about 10 percent. This decrease in literary criticism was healthy, though most of the slack was taken up by history and biography rather than current affairs. Discussions of science, instead of coming to grips with the dynamo of technology that was transforming the economic life of Americans, most often focused on those most belletristic creatures the birds and butterflies. Commentary on social issues, politics, and international affairs was irregular and consisted of signed articles rather than a monthly editorial department.

There were clear continuities of attitude and values. In literature, a moderate realism was still the norm, and on social and cultural issues there was still clear belief in the concept of progress through the leadership of an educated elite. But the liberal faith in American educability and the post–Civil War confidence in the spread of high culture was giving way to apprehensions about change, even prophecies among some writers that instead of converting the nation, their culture might itself become a relic. This sense of threat, which Aldrich shared, gave a more conservative and retrospective tone to some *Atlantic* voices.

Matthew Arnold visited the United States in 1883 and 1886 and probably met Aldrich while under Norton and Lowell's care in Cambridge. Arnold felt that in both England and America canonical, humanistic high culture, "the best that has been thought and said," was distinctly and imminently threatened. Many *Atlantic* writers at this time would have agreed with Arnold that traditional humanism was being subverted by the "barbarism" of the upper classes, which in America he associated with the newly monied elite, the "philistinism" of the dominant middle classes abetted by science and the utilitarian spirit, and the "brutalization" of the working classes. If Arnold had browsed American monthlies, he would have found less middle-brow philistinism and more traditional humanistic culture in the *Atlantic* than elsewhere. Like his friend Norton, he would have found some essays insufficiently sophisticated. But certainly he would have found many papers on historical and literary subjects intended for the lay reader that, as he feared, would forty years later be consigned to academic treatment in scholarly journals, and one hundred years later would be banished even from the academy and become references unrecognizable to most college-educated Americans. He would have found essays on Cicero, Marcus Aurelius, and St. Augustine; William Rufus, Sir Thomas More, and Samuel Johnson; Dante, Savonarola, and Tommasso Salvini; Mme De Stael, Mazarin, and Mendelssohn. Arnold would have found also an attention to the canonical texts of Western literature whose influence he felt threatened, in papers titled "Closing Scenes of the Iliad," "A Difficulty in Hamlet," or "The Hyppolytos of Euripides." "Where else," the *Nation* asked rhetorically, "would one find without surprise a study of a play by Euripides simply for its own sake?" (3 Mar. 1887, 188).

If he read Aldrich's *Atlantic*, Arnold might have wondered, with the unswervingly highbrow Norton, whether this was the best America could do in a literary periodical. But he would have noted with grudging approval that it maintained more contact with canonical humanistic and literary culture than the middlebrow monthlies. Probably, like another of his consultants on America, Henry James, Jr., he would have found Aldrich himself a literary and intellectual lightweight. But he would also have conceded that both the fiction and the literary reviews in Aldrich's magazine often championed values he felt were endangered by philistinism, including the work of James himself. As the *Nation* noted on several occasions, the *Atlantic*, despite lapses, had less tolerance than others for the literature of light entertainment, sentimentality, or pious moralizing, and a correspondingly greater scope for intellectual challenge, subtlety, and aesthetic quality (25 Feb. 1886, 171, and 29 Nov. 1888, 436).

In *Atlantic* prose fiction and literary criticism during Aldrich's editorship, the issue of aesthetic quality superseded the debate between realism and romanticism. Realism continued to be the dominant mode, but the fiction favored by the *Atlantic* was often the subtle, aesthetically refined, and socially restricted realism of James and Jewett. And while Howells in the eighties increasingly emphasized the ethical and democratic implications of his realism, Aldrich, and to a degree even Scudder, increasingly emphasized the claims of a disengaged, purely literary aesthetic. Furthermore, *Atlantic* criticism raised aesthetic questions that suggested clear limits to realism, and a few plaintive voices even called for the return of romance. In the magazine's poetry, what Aldrich perceived as a popular, vernacular realism was frankly discouraged in favor of more traditional, even classical verse.

Thomas Bailey Aldrich   1881–1890

Aldrich did not control the *Atlantic* nearly as autocratically as he would have liked, but his own aesthetic creed had a distinct influence, clearest in poetry, but visible elsewhere. To Aldrich, the aim of literature, particularly poetry but prose as well, was pleasurable aesthetic experience, not moral action. He privately disliked the ethicism of the older New England writers, and he rejected Helen Hunt Jackson's novel *Ramona*, which she hoped would be the *Uncle Tom's Cabin* of Native Americans, for its overt social protest. Aesthetic pleasure, Aldrich felt, came from contemplating not commonplace reality but life's highest possibilities, especially ideal beauty, delicate emotions, or refined states of feeling. In subject matter, he preferred the explicitly beautiful in image, thought, or feeling to the "god of the dull Commonplace" ("At the Funeral of a Minor Poet," *Poems* 298). The muse, he said, should wear a rose, not a cabbage leaf.

Aldrich's defense of aestheticism clearly reflected the concern of representatives of high literary culture during the eighties with resisting the inroads of popular journalism and lowbrow print culture (Brodhead 476). He loathed naturalism in fiction and populist poetry, the folksy dialect verse of poets like Joaquin Miller and particularly James W. Riley, who was then widely read in the *Century*. In a letter to George Woodberry, he parodied what he contemptuously called "those natural, human poems that go to the heart of the common people."

> When the moonlight shines on the pumpkin vines
> And our winter's coal is in,
> I love to sit by the fireside's flit
> And swig my Old Tom Gin
> My Daddy's gin,
> My Mammy's gin,
> My horny-handed, whole-souled gin,
> When the moon on the lake is beaming!
>
> (Sunday morning, n.d., Harvard)

Aldrich's contempt for Riley's verse was partly class based, but it was also aimed at a commercially calculated sentimentality that was becoming immensely successful in mass culture and turning verse into a mass-produced commodity. Aldrich and the other nabobs of high culture could do nothing to prevent this trend, and by the turn of the century Riley was America's most beloved poet with an income of around $23,000 a year (Charvat, *Profession* 106).

Aldrich's literary aesthetics resisted not only commercial sentimentality but also personal revelation. They required the writer to exercise self-restraint and impersonality. Aldrich considered Whitman a morbid egotist who would be remembered by posterity as a freak, like a bizarre biological specimen preserved in alcohol. In rejecting a self-revelatory sonnet from a new aspirant, he asked: "Why should we print in a magazine those intimate revelations which we wouldn't dream of confiding to the bosom of an utter stranger at an evening party?" (to unknown contributor, 26 Apr. 1887). In his own poetry, the result of this restraint was a light tone, an ironic touch, sometimes witty, sometimes stoic, usually avoiding the self-indulgently melancholy or dispirited. He lectured the habitually lugubrious Louise Chandler Moulton: "Can you not let me have one that does not blot out everything beyond the grave as well as this side of it?" and later, "It is so much easier to be depressing than it is to be inspiring and entertaining. . . . Literature ought to warm the heart and not chill it. I always regret it when I write sad verses" (n.d. and 25 Apr. 1889, Library of Congress, quoted in Tuttle 394–95). Aldrich thus avoided the sentimentality, most memorably parodied by Twain's "Ode to Stephen Dowling Botts," that plagued much popular poetry of the period. But it made him prefer either a light, sociable, cavalier literature, containing sentiments and reflections that presumably could be confided at an evening party, or a literature affirming high ideals and noble values. Both have made him seem shallow to modern tastes raised on the poets of personal pain from Eliot to Plath.

Another conviction that put Aldrich entirely beyond the pale of modern taste was his belief in strict adherence to conventions of form. A genuine artist, he insisted, could achieve any desirable effect within traditional structures. He never received submissions from Emily Dickinson, but an article he published anonymously in the *Atlantic* in 1892 indicates that he certainly would have rejected them. Dickinson's critics had exaggerated, he wrote, when they claimed that she would have been a fifth-rate poet if she had learned her trade. She would have been second-rate. According to Aldrich, Dickinson's poems show "intermittent flashes of imagination," but their rhymes are "impossible," their significance too "involved," and the "incoherence and shapelessness of the greater part of her verse are fatal" ("In Re Emily Dickinson," Jan. 1892, 143–44).

Aldrich, then, dismissed the two great poets of the period, Whitman and Dickinson, and resisted the force that would create modern poetry: experimentation with greater latitude in subject, tone, language, and form. But if he failed to anticipate twentieth-century tastes and paid the price of being almost instantly forgotten, he was virtually the only American editor to risk publishing long poems, he resisted the period's sentimental excesses, and he encouraged several interesting minor poets, particularly E. R. Sill, Edith Thomas, and George Woodberry, who are today, like Aldrich himself, contemptuously dismissed unread. Nor was Aldrich guilty of hubris about the strength or longevity of the type of poetry he advocated. In fact, his attitude toward what he might have called high poetry reflects more general doubts about high culture in the eighties and nineties: that it was increasingly vitiated and perhaps doomed by the rising tides of popular taste. On assuming the editorship in 1881, he wrote to his close friend E. C. Stedman: "I find it devilish hard to get good poems for the Mag. Our old singers have pretty much lost their voices and our new singers are so few. My ear has not caught any new note since 1860." Later he lamented, "I am slowly making up my mind to publish none but incontestably fine poems in the *Atlantic*—which means only about four poems per year.... If you could see the piles of bosh sent to this office you'd be sick at heart" (1881 and 1887, both qtd. in Greenslet, *Aldrich* 146). Aldrich, like Stedman, was conscious of living in what they themselves termed the twilight of traditional poetry.

As editor, Aldrich did what he could to sustain traditional aesthetics in poetry. He himself read all poetry submitted and during the decade published poems by 120 aspirants in verse, most previously unpublished, of whom 40 were women (Greenslet, *Aldrich* 143, and Tuttle 299). While this record exonerates him from charges of catering to a coterie, he did publish, in addition to the regular contributions of Whittier and Holmes and occasional contributions by Lowell, over twenty poems apiece by his two poetic "discoveries," E. R. Sill and Edith Thomas.

Sill and Thomas were both interesting examples of a type of contributor and reader who seemed powerfully drawn to the *Atlantic* throughout its history. Both were ardent admirers of canonical high culture but were trapped by a stoic sense of family duty in small, shabby, uncongenial midwestern towns. Both anticipated later American novelists in seeing these towns as bastions of philistinism, and both seemed like characters out of *Winesburg, Ohio*. Edith Thomas, living with an aging mother in Geneva, Ohio, was driven by cultural starvation. Helen Hunt Jackson, who engineered Miss Thomas's introduction to Aldrich, described to him the desperation and determination of the twenty-six-year-old poet who appeared one day in her New York living room: "A gaunt-cheeked, hollow-eyed, tall, shy girl in a waterproof cloak, with a big scrap book under her arm;—a tremendous hunger in her face—and the strangest mixture I ever saw of indomitable self-reliance, and appealing for sympathy.... It makes me laugh and shudder both to recount how I half snubbed and patronized her.... I believe I advised her to try and interest herself in enlightening the Geneva children" (19 Aug. 1881).

Jackson, astonished at the power of some passages in the scrapbook, encouraged Edith Thomas, as she had encouraged the equally isolated but more diffident Emily Dickinson, to publish. Fortunately for Miss Thomas, her Emersonian nature poetry was more classical in form and less psychologically tormented than Dickinson's and quickly attracted the attention of Aldrich and one or two other editors, who published and encouraged her. Edith Thomas later thanked Aldrich for his advice and support as "Godfather" to her first book: "You can scarcely understand how great a favor you conferred unless you understand how poor I am in council and councillors (living as I do, rather remote, unfriended, melancholy, slow)" (21 Sept. 1884).

Edward Roland Sill, a former professor of classics, rhetoric, and English literature at Berkeley, felt like "a fish in a sandbank" in Cuyahoga Falls, Ohio, where he had dutifully gone with his wife to care for her father (Ferguson 191). In the *Atlantic* tradition of cultural evangelism, Sill spent part of his time developing a circulating library "to see how long it would take books and periodicals . . . to bring ["a crude little town with a fine generation of raw material growing up in it"] up to some sort of hopeful civilization" (Ferguson 182). For his own intellectual life, he relied on writing for the *Atlantic*, contributing a steady stream of poems and "Contributors' Club" pieces, as well as essays defending, like Arnold, a broad, classics-based liberal education for both men and women against the inroads of science, vocationalism, and the elective system.

Sill's life in his "horrid little village" was outwardly one of stoic renunciation and duty (Ferguson 191). But like a tormented character from *Winesburg*, he could not entirely suppress a more impulsive side of his personality, which found a voice in his poetry. Psychically compelled to compose a large body of work that he refused to publish over his own name, Sill begged Aldrich to allow him to use a pseudonym. The July 1885 *Atlantic* carried the poem "Tempted" by "Andrew Hedbrook" (69):

> Yes, I know what you say,
> Since it cannot be soul to soul,
> Be it flesh to flesh, as it may;
> But is earth the whole?
> . . . .
> Which were the nobler goal,
> To snatch at the moment's bliss
> Or to swear I will keep my soul
> Clean for her kiss?

In submitting this poem, Sill expressed a problem that must have accounted for the pale ideality of much American Victorian poetry before the advent of modern moral tolerance and the vogue of the "poetic persona": How could the poet publicly express socially unacceptable private emotions, without fearing personal condemnation and scandal?

> But my dear Mr. Aldrich—Don't you see the difficulty in the way of my printing such poems as that "Tempted" over my own name—I a staid citizen, the husband of one wife . . . , the model for ingenuous youth, the sometime professor of coeducated young men and maidens, and all that. I tell you there is no comfort for a man the minute he begins to write anything that is *intimate* or that sounds (whether it is or not) like the voice of any personal feeling or experience beyond the humdrum—no comfort but behind the mask. Print me over a nom de goosequill . . . and I will send you some remarkable poems. I cannot be sure what they will be most remarkable for—they may make your hair stand on end and set your teeth on edge by their "sincerity," but at any rate I would like to try the experiment. (10 Apr. 1885, qtd. in Parker 246–47)

Aldrich warned Sill against excessive self-revelation; Sill protested that he too despised "the howling dervishes of song" and the "indecent exposures of the small poets and poetesses" (8 Oct. 1885 and 18 Apr. 1885, qtd. in Parker 248). But impressed by the aesthetic value of Sill's poetry, Aldrich did accept "Tempted" with its modestly fleshly and adulterous speculations, and did allow Sill to publish his poetry in the *Atlantic* henceforth under the pseudonym "Andrew Hedbrook." While it is hard to imagine Hedbrook's poetry making the hair stand up on anyone's head, the pseudonym did permit the exploration of emotions alien to the stoic, scholarly public persona of E. R. Sill. Publication of Hedbrook's poetry also demonstrated that Aldrich's *Atlantic* was somewhat less terminally genteel than its reputation.

Aldrich deserves further credit for being willing to publish longer serious works of poetry. In this, as in other decisions, he placed his commitment to his aesthetic ideal above the interests of his publisher, who, as Howells had found, silently frowned on long poems. One example was Aldrich's decision not only to accept the young George Edward Woodberry's nine-page visionary, patriotic "Ode to My Country," apparently rejected by *Harper's*, but to give it the lead position in July 1887. In a self-congratulatory note to Woodberry, Aldrich rejoiced: "Alden [*Harper's* editor] is now gnashing his few remaining teeth and completing his baldness because he didn't have the foresight and nerve to print nine pages of Ode. Well, when new poets are to be born, I am glad to be the (Atlantic) Monthly nurse" (July 1887).

The *Nation* summarized the norm for magazine poetry during the period by noting: "There is no excuse for the marked difference to be observed in the magazines between the quality of what they are willing to publish as prose and of what they admit provided it is rhymed. Excellence in poetry is now hardly to be looked for, while on the other hand the high grade of our journeyman prose is often remarked upon." The *Nation's* critic, however, acknowledged that "the *Atlantic* has held to a better standard than the other magazines . . . partly no doubt because of its strong traditions" (8 Dec. 1887, 461). Aldrich himself acknowledged the mediocrity of most magazine verse, including much in the *Atlantic*. He supported some minor but not uninteresting talents and opposed the commercially motivated, smug, versified cuteness of the age. But he is very appropriately blamed for enforcing traditional aesthetic standards that perpetuated mediocrity and retarded poetic experiment and revival.

In fiction and literary criticism, Aldrich did not make the magazine an organ of a particular ideology, unlike Howells, whose "Easy Chair" column at *Harper's* now became the rallying point of realism. As Aldrich himself noted, the editorial shadow of Howells fell strongly on the *Atlantic*, and in both fiction and criticism a moderate realism was the dominant mode (Aldrich to Woodberry, 15 Nov. 1885). But there were occasional apologists too for romantic idealism, and while Howells in New York was forging a more democratic and engaged realism, the *Atlantic* seemed to defend a more conservative aestheticism. But despite aesthetic limitations and some self-serving blunting of criticism, Aldrich and his reviewers strongly supported some of the best American writers of the time, particularly

James and Jewett, and challenged the commercial middlebrow literature of light entertainment that reflected the developing mass culture.

Aldrich wrote almost no reviews himself. The industrious Horace Scudder wrote most criticism of American fiction, George Woodberry covered biography and some poetry, and Harriet Waters Preston wrote on English, French, Italian, and classical literature. Higginson, G. P. Lathrop, and Henry Cabot Lodge supplemented occasionally. Aldrich sometimes exerted his influence where he could, but his purpose was to protect personal and editorial relationships rather than to advance either an ideology or Houghton Mifflin's book trade.

Aldrich exercised particularly close control over the impoverished, sardonic Woodberry, who had returned from a miserable Siberian cultural exile at the University of Nebraska partly on the promise of reviewing work. Though sometimes extensive consultations were necessary before or after the writing, Aldrich could often suggest the right tone to Woodberry when he allocated the book: "a happy page" on Henry James, freedom to "rap the knuckles" of Julian Hawthorne, or high praise for E. C. Stedman's *Poets of America* (30 Jan. 1884; 17 Oct. 1885). Woodberry's assurance of his compliance on the Stedman review reflected his cynicism: "I will come up if you summon me, but I don't think you need be so timorous before my fire-eating phantom, and you may as well send Stedman down. I won't eat him raw ... and in serving the dish I will lay aside all thought of sauce piquante. He shall slip down in oil like a new oyster, then shall be only big eyes of admiration and a gulp.... I am not unsusceptible to the flowing flatteries he has poured on me. No, I will not bite the hand that pats me" (20 Oct. 1885).

A second letter, written after the review, reflected a sense of shame and a desire to disclaim intellectual responsibility for work he admitted lacked integrity: "I have done the best I could, but at what sacrifice of humorous reflection.... You may cut and slash as you will, but you will see that I have shied off a good deal. There is every reason why my authorship should not be known, except to [Stedman] if necessary.... I wonder if you would like a page and a half of namby pamby on Gosse's extraordinary volume?" (31 Oct. 1885).

Reviewing in general during Aldrich's time still produced much namby-pamby homogenized by the small world of personal relationships between writers, editors, and reviewers in Boston and New York. This world, though restricted, reached as far as London, from which the British poet Austin Dobson wrote to thank Aldrich for an "admirable notice" and mentioned that he "had an idea, too, of paying you in kind" (11 May 1882). Though Houghton was too circumspect to apply direct pressure and Aldrich too proud to obey direct orders, the old networks of mutual financial benefit also still exerted an influence. In 1882, George Cary Eggleston, literary editor for the *New York Evening Post*, wrote thanking Azariah Smith, Houghton's director of advertising, for his friendship and support (probably in helping Eggleston maintain his position through a change of ownership) and promising that "I shall probably have occasion for a long time to come to commend to a goodly company of readers the notable books in all departments of literature which the Riverside Press is sure to produce" (Smith to Houghton, Oct. 1882).

While Aldrich was undoubtedly conscious of a web of personal and financial reciprocity and did sometimes manipulate his less independent reviewers, there is no evidence that he did so overtly for business considerations. *Atlantic* criticism in fact included considerable honest debate over the aesthetic and ethical issues of realism and a serious attempt, which Arnold would have appreciated, to discriminate between the meretricious and the genuine.

Both the *Atlantic*'s essential sympathy with realism and the most obvious limits of that sympathy were reflected in a review of a new edition of Whitman's *Leaves of Grass*. If Whitman's critics, wrote G. P. Lathrop,

> can see nothing in this book except indecency and bombastic truisms, the inference must be that their sensibilities are not delicate enough to recognize the fresh, strong, healthy presentations of common things in a way that revivifies them, the generous aspiration, the fine sympathy with man and nature, the buoyant belief in immortality, which are no less characteristic of the author than his mistaken boldness in displaying the carnal side of existence and his particularity in describing disease or loathsome decay. (Jan. 1882, 124)

Horace Scudder, the *Atlantic*'s primary reviewer of American fiction and Aldrich's successor as editor, also showed support for realism, but a realism aimed at providing nondidactic moral insight rather than simply reflecting existing conditions. Scudder insisted that while the novel should accurately observe contemporary life, genuine literary art has "a penetrating power, interprets life" by selecting significant detail rather than being "a perishable photograph" ("Illinois Life in Fiction," Feb. 1889, 274).

Scudder's reviews of Howells's novels define his own critical ideology. Howells's early work, he said perceptively, showed a "thorough kindliness" and "quick sympathy" but used too small a canvas, painted often in too fine strokes, and ignored powerful characters and subjects in its concern with the commonplace.[4] Through the decade, however, he approvingly traced Howells's growth from a humorous observer of contemporary American manners toward a "larger and profounder art" grounded in a nondidactic treatment of fundamental moral issues in *A Modern Instance* (1882), *Silas Lapham* (1884), and particularly *A Hazard of New Fortunes* (1890). In these three novels dealing respectively with the ethics of divorce, capitalism, and class conflict, Scudder noted "an equilibrium of ethical and artistic powers which gives the greatest momentum to art" (Nov. 1882, 710; Apr. 1890, 563–66). Particularly moved by *Hazard*, Howells's most profound questioning of capitalism, which alienated many reviewers, Scudder praised the writer's avoidance of preaching while presenting characters like the hard-bitten millionaire, Dryfoos, and the German socialist, Lindau, who "throb with a life which is in contact with great currents of thought and passion." He admired also Howells's presentation of the dilemma of the American liberal Basil March, "who sees the injustice in which he bears an unwilling part, is opening his eyes gradually to the inconsistencies of modern civilization, yet is painfully aware of his own helplessness and knows enough only to do the nearest duty" (Apr. 1890, 566).

Scudder, then, promoted a morally and socially engaged realism, as long as it avoided overt didacticism, excessive introspection, and, of course, sexual content. This represented the *Atlantic* norm during the eighties and nineties, as in the seventies. But the magazine also gave the reactionary opponents of realism their say, and these voices of genteel idealism were to grow shriller and more numerous as Howells's middle-class realism gave way to a grittier, more skeptical naturalism and modernism over the next thirty years. Charles Dudley Warner in "Modern Fiction" (Apr. 1883) lamented the pessimism and morbid psychological introspection of some realism and hoped for a resurgence of inspiring literary idealism. In an interesting reversal of the old moralistic critiques of realism, Agnes Repplier, a sharp-minded, Jesuit-educated young essayist and literary Tory from Philadelphia, scolded what she called "fiction in the pulpit" and particularly Howells for depriving readers of aesthetic pleasure by forcing them to swallow the pill of his social morality. Repplier revealed the class bias that underlay her aesthetics when she complained that "the present stand of realism . . . is but one more phase of the intrusion of ethics upon art—the assumption that I cannot have a sincere regard for the welfare of my washerwoman because I do not care for her company either in a book or out of it" ("Fiction in the Pulpit," Oct. 1889, 535). This class antagonism rationalized as aesthetic quality fueled much later opposition to realism and naturalism.

The banner of aesthetic quality was used not only to avoid the company of fictional washerwomen but also to attack the middlebrow vulgarity of the wealthy. In aesthetic as well as in political commentary, *Atlantic* writers criticized the influence of both the working class and the new economic elite. At Aldrich's suggestion, Woodberry ripped into the gilded age equivalent of the coffee table book for its vapid and sentimental text and frequently meretricious debasement of art. The broader circulation of art, Woodberry argued, was an important means of public education. But the process should not cheapen the art itself. He condemned one representative example as "a holiday book for the center table of the uneducated rich . . . symptomatic of the increase of negligent and ignorant work in books pretentiously fine" ("Review of *The Artist's Year*," Dec. 1882, 849). The *Atlantic*'s highbrow aesthetic standards were often used to attack what Godkin called "chromo-civilization," the thin cultural gilding of the gilded age.

Atlantic fiction of the eighties reflects essentially the aesthetic attitudes expressed in the magazine's criticism. In fiction, as in literary criticism, regionalism and the realism of Howells and James are dominant. But a new literary romanticism is resurgent, disengaged from contemporary social issues, indifferent to character analysis, but emphasizing a strong plot and exotic or historical setting. Especially in these romances, there were bids for broad popularity. But Aldrich could have claimed with some justice that aesthetic quality was the overriding consideration, and his record clearly shows that he was willing to go further than other editors to support intellectually and aesthetically subtle writers such as James and Jewett.

The predominance of realism and regionalism, as well as the admixture of romanticism, can be seen in the eighteen serial novels published between 1881 and 1890. This was the heyday of the serials, and Aldrich ran generally two and sometimes three at a time, often giving them the lead place. Most of the novels that Aldrich published were written by authors who had written for Howells. Among the relatively realistic novels of contemporary life were four by James (*The Portrait of a Lady, The Princess Casamassima, The Tragic Muse,* and *The Aspern Papers*); two novels with feminist themes by the relatively popular Elizabeth Stuart Phelps; two apiece by G. P. Lathop, the assistant Howells had fired, and W. H. Bishop, the young midwestern author he had befriended; and one, *Dr. Breen's Practice,* by Howells himself. Regionalism was represented by three novels from Charles Egbert Craddock, including her first and best, *The Prophet of the Great Smokey Mountains,* and Sarah Orne Jewett's *Marsh Island.*

Aldrich deserves credit for continuing to cultivate and publish these writers. In some cases, such as James's *Tragic Muse* and Craddock's *Prophet,* his solicitation seems to have instigated the work or significantly changed its form. But works he solicited from writers new to the *Atlantic* were relatively modest, and he failed to secure any major new writers for the magazine or the house. Work by writers new to the *Atlantic* included two by Margaret Oliphant, a mediocre British novelist; a disappointing contribution by Thomas Hardy, *Two on a Tower;* and works by two young American romantic novelists, Arthur Hardy and Francis Marion Crawford. Both Crawford and Arthur Hardy gained sudden popular success during the eighties, mainly with historical romances. But Aldrich failed to secure the loyalty of either. He rejected *But Yet a Woman,* a first novel by Arthur Hardy, then an unknown mathematics professor at Dartmouth, only to have it become immensely popular and its author the object of a bidding war between publishers. With Crawford, Houghton had established an early friendly relationship that led to two early serial romances, but Aldrich's rejection of *Zoroaster*—and probably better offers elsewhere—seemed to sour Crawford and led to a break after 1886 with both the magazine and the firm (Ballou 369–70). The romanticists Francis Crawford and Arthur Hardy, like the realists Twain and Howells, demonstrated that the *Atlantic* could not regularly afford the most popular novelists.

If market competition put the most popular novelists increasingly beyond Aldrich's reach, the magazine's highbrow aesthetic stance and its small but literary audience did allow him to cultivate and support several aesthetically demanding authors who had limited popular appeal. The *Atlantic*'s payment rates and the competitive fiction market made exclusive contracts such as Howells had with *Harper's* impossible. But James, Jewett, and a few others found Aldrich more consistently anxious to publish them, Scudder more sympathetic in reviewing them, and the *Atlantic* audience more responsive in reading them than editors, reviewers, and readers of other American magazines. The *Atlantic* continued as the major source of magazine publication for both James and Jewett during the decade. Aldrich published more novels by Henry James (four) and more stories by Sarah Orne Jewett (twenty, and one novel) than by any other authors; works by James appeared in 65 out of the 110 issues Aldrich edited.

Modernist critics have always emphasized the repressive aspects of the genteel tradition of which Aldrich and his *Atlantic* are often cited as representatives. But they have consistently failed to acknowledge, or have actively denied, its support for high-culture literary and intellectual productions that would not have been supported or permitted to develop by the mass market. Aldrich's editorial treatment of Henry James is a case in point. John Tomsich has claimed that the cultural leaders of the genteel tradition, prominently including Aldrich, repudiated James as "too depressing" and were "always insensitive to the greatest American artist of their day" (189). Despite James's acid disdain for Aldrich, Aldrich's editorial solicitations and Scudder's highly sympathetic *Atlantic* reviews of James's work flatly contradict this conclusion.[5]

Howells had foreseen and tried to ameliorate James's problem in gaining a readership. By the early eighties, partly because of Howells's persistent support and the popular success of *Daisy Miller* in 1878, James seemed to be developing a broader audience and more financial bargaining power, particularly with the large-circulation New York illustrated magazines. During Howells's time he had placed occasional potboilers in the New York "picture books," as he derisively called them, but now he planned a full-scale assault on their larger and more remunerative market.

Aldrich frequently and actively solicited James throughout the decade but at first met with little success in securing fiction because of James's larger aspirations. James offered and Aldrich accepted quite a few critical essays on major European writers, but he seemed to have other plans for his fiction, and what Aldrich did get came at a stiff price. In 1882, Aldrich gloated to Houghton that "after a great deal of diplomacy and Old Port, combined with several attacks on Henry James in his bathtub, I have secured the dramatization of 'Daisy Miller' for the *Atlantic*. I think it is a great card" (Sept. 1882). The great card, for which Houghton risked the unparalleled price of $1,000, proved a losing gamble and established a long-standing and seldom-broken *Atlantic* policy of not publishing dramatic literature. But despite the Daisy Miller disappointment, Aldrich continued regular solicitations of James.

For 1883 and 1884 Aldrich secured a series of French travel sketches and critical essays, and finally James agreed tentatively to a twelve-month serial for 1885. In discussing terms, however, James noted that he currently had two stories and a novel, *The Bostonians*, scheduled for publication at the *Century*, and several more stories at Charles Dana's *Sun*, for all of which he had received very handsome prices and could expect a readership over 200,000. "I mention it," James wrote, "simply to denote that by July 1885, I expect to be in the enjoyment of a popularity which will require me to ask $500 a number for the successive installments of the Princess Casamassima" (13 Feb. 1884).

James was never again to enjoy this degree of confidence in his ability to win popularity and command its financial rewards. When Houghton balked at the price, James backed down to his former *Atlantic* rate of $15 a page, or about $300 to $375 per installment. In the event, the total he received for the *Princess* was nearly what he had originally asked, because, as with all of James's productions, it far outran the contracted length. But neither the *Princess* nor *The Bostonians* (printed in the *Century*) proved popular with most reviewers and readers. Of *The Bostonians*, which Leon Edel rates as the best novel of the decade, the *Century*'s R. W. Gilder told James frankly that "they had never published anything that appeared so little to interest their readers" (James to Edmund Gosse, 25 Aug. 1915, in *Letters* 4: 778). In a largely admiring *Atlantic* review of *The Bostonians*, Scudder had exclaimed, "One stands in amazement before the delicacy of workmanship" (June 1886, 852). But the *Critic* typified much critical as well as popular response to the two novels when it complained that *The Princess Casamassima* was a tedious tale that could appeal only to "the lover of... emotions analytically examined, of hairs radiantly split, of spectroscopic ratings capable of dividing a ray of light into 32,000 lines to the square inch, or of intellectual engines describing 50,000 sensations to the twenty pages" (29 Jan. 1887, 51–52).

The indifference or actual hostility with which these two novels were generally received profoundly and bitterly discouraged James and eventually led him temporarily to give up writing novels and turn, with painful lack of success, to the theater in hopes of raising his income and recognition during the decade after 1886. In early 1888, he wrote to Howells: "I am still staggering a good deal under the mysterious and (to me) inexplicable injury wrought—apparently—upon my situation by my last two novels, the *Bostonians* and the *Princess* from which I expected so much and derived so little. They have reduced the desire, and the demand, for my productions to zero" (2 Jan. 1888, *Letters* 3: 209).

James's despondency had made him exaggerate. The *Century* and other large-circulation magazines with generous payments had lost interest, at least in his major work. But Aldrich, whom James held in personal contempt, and Houghton, whom he had called shabby for his financial tightness, continued to consider James a very major contributor whose difficult fiction was important to the *Atlantic*, highly valued by its small audience, and likely to last. When James wrote to Howells in early 1888, Aldrich had already accepted and paid for a novella, *The Aspern Papers*, which commenced publication in March 1888. More important, by that time Aldrich was already laying siege to him for a full-length serial novel for 1889. James's response suggests that in his discouragement, he had not planned on writing another full-length novel but was persuaded to do so specifically by Aldrich's solicitation:

> I succumb to your arguments and will undertake to manage a serial for the full twelve-month of 1889. It shall be of seventeen or eighteen pages—with the option of rising au besoin to twenty—and shall be paid for at the same rate as *The Princess*—ie. $15 per page. . . . To compass this end (I mean the end of giving you a longer rather than a shorter serial) I shall probably run two stories (ie. two subjects I have had in my head) together, interweaving their threads. But equally probably the thing will bear the name I gave you: "The Tragic Muse." (3 Mar. 1888, *Letters* 3: 223)

The central theme of *The Tragic Muse*, reflecting James's own frustration in developing a readership, was the paradoxical conflict between the public world and the integrity of the artist, and the ultimate impossibility of reconciling the two. In integrating his two plot concepts around this theme to meet Aldrich's request for a full-length serial, James had worse than usual problems corseting his buxom muse. Some installments ran well over twenty pages, and the novel ran not twelve installments as contracted but seventeen. Aldrich, while concerned at the constant requirement to curtail other material, was indulgent.

In reviewing the novel for the *Atlantic*, Scudder countered the widespread criticism of James's verbal abundance by asserting that it was the "lavishness of true art, not the prodigality of a spendthrift in words." He concluded that "we can only advise students of literature and art who wish to see how a fine thing may be presented with a technique which . . . proves to be the facile instrument of a master workman who is thinking of the soul of his art, to read *The Tragic Muse*" (Sept. 1890, 419–22). Clearly Aldrich's *Atlantic*, representing a relatively small cultural minority, honored the aesthetic and intellectual quality of James and had continued major support for the most important novelist of his time when others had withdrawn. Unfortunately, when the magazine later took on ambitions for a larger circulation and broader audience, *Atlantic* editors would not always continue to besiege James in his bathtub and ply him with Old Port.

The *Atlantic*'s sustained support for James, like its insistent attention to canonical Western literature and history, Aldrich's defense of dying poetic traditions, the magazine's dwindling circulation, and comments on its old-fashioned quality, indicate not only that many of its values represented a distinctly minority culture but also that it was defensively conscious of its minority status. This consciousness was especially acute in comment on politics during the eighties. These commentaries contained two major patterns. The first was an increased alienation from a political process many felt had been corrupted by an uneducated majority misled by venal politicians of both parties. The second prominent pattern was a continuing anxiety over the conflict between labor and capital, which seemed to destroy the vision of an organic, cooperative, principled society that had long been the ideal of the cultural elite.[6]

The increased political alienation of those who wrote and read the *Atlantic* was evident both in the paucity of political coverage and in the withdrawal of the magazine's traditional support from the Republican party. As a young suitor, Aldrich had been rejected by a spirited ward of Wendell Phillips for his languorous indifference to the great cause of abolition. Except for brief explosions over the dangers of unionism and unlimited immigration, he retained an aesthete's indifference to politics throughout his life. But the fact that in the election year of 1888 the magazine gave more coverage to "The Home Life of the Redstart" than to the presidential contest indicated more than Aldrich's indifference. It indicated that the magazine lacked both conviction and a party.

While ties with the Republican party had been substantially weakening since the corruption of Grant's first administration, the real break came in 1884, the year that the mugwump reform Republicans bolted the party to endorse the Democrat Cleveland. In September 1884, Herbert Tuttle's article "The Despotism of Party" denounced party politics as "a political system in which . . . the voice of demagogues and blatherskites has equal weight with that of honest men who can think and reason, who have convictions, and who are unselfishly devoted to the interests of the republic" (383). Clearly this was the voice of a cultural elite descended from the Federalists that felt itself dispossessed of its political privileges by ward bosses and plutocrats who controlled both parties. The writer concluded that "any event which shakes the doctrine of indefeasible allegiance to party, any revolt which emphasizes the citizen's right of independent judgment, even though it may involve the downfall of a party whose annals are resplendent with great deeds, is an inestimable gain to the cause of good government" (384). The writer could not bring himself to recommend explicitly voting for the Democrat, Cleveland, but he said it in all but words.

If the Republican party was no longer the party of righteousness, or even of enlightened good government, independence from the party system and civil service reform were the only hope. Civil service reform seemed particularly promising as a way to remove government from control by the spoils system of party politics, in which the best qualified no longer seemed to have a role, and to restore it to a meritocracy of the educated. The *Atlantic*, like *Harper's Weekly* and the

Century, warmly endorsed the concept of a professional governmental bureaucracy selected through a public contest of merit which anyone could enter but which would favor educational attainment and intellectual capacity.

Atlantic commentary continued to distribute blame for the corruption of the political process, for rising class conflict, and for the destruction of social and cultural values fairly evenly between labor and capital. Many writers agreed with Arnold that the working classes were ignorant and brutalized, while the plutocrats were the new barbarians. After the Haymarket bombing of 1886, G. F. Parsons attacked labor as irrational, ignorant, and violent, but he excoriated wealthy capitalists as cannibals whose splendid mansions were as surely built on plunder and destruction as if they had been hung with shrunken heads instead of paintings ("The Labor Question," July 1886, 97–113 and "The Growth of Materialism," Aug. 1887, 163). Aldrich also published a scathing attack by Henry Demarest Lloyd on "the orgy of fiduciary harlotry" perpetrated by the financier Jay Gould with the complicity of Tammany politicians. In the article, Lloyd again anticipated both muckraking and the progressive era by denouncing laissez-faire as the cynical rationalization of the rapacious and by advocating extensive government regulation of transportation, health, education, housing, and other areas.

Several *Atlantic* articles criticized unionism as monopolistic, demagogic, and destructive of social order. But Aldrich did solicit Terence Powderley, president of the Knights of Labor, for a defense of unionism, which Powderley failed to produce. He also published several graphic descriptions by Lillie Wyman, whom Howells had encouraged, of the physically and psychologically destructive effects of industrialism on workers in the Rhode Island mills. Wyman not only argued for government regulation but defended labor unionism as the moral equivalent of the recent struggle for political union and against slavery in the Civil War.[7]

Atlantic political commentary during the eighties, then, reflected frustration at the political impotence of the "educated classes" and criticism of the destructive social effects of both labor and capital. Henry Houghton, though a rock-ribbed Republican, discouraged unsigned political editorials, yet he seems to have allowed his editor to publish a reasonable range of opinion in signed papers. But if Houghton did not believe in directly interfering with editorial prerogatives, he was nevertheless growing increasingly dissatisfied with Aldrich. The problem was not what Aldrich published. What bothered Houghton was Aldrich's casual habit of dropping the job for three or four months of globetrotting each summer. (Scudder, who had to pick up the slack, must have shared that disapproval.) Houghton also periodically exploded over what he perceived as Aldrich's lack of editorial tact in dealing with authors important to the house.

Houghton himself had developed a friendly relationship with the young novelist Francis Marion Crawford at the beginning of his career and persuaded him to publish with the firm. Crawford's original relationship with Aldrich, whose aesthetic values he largely shared, was very cordial and produced a twelve-month serial, "A Roman Singer." But when Crawford submitted a second novel, *Zoroaster*, in 1885, Aldrich refused it, asking for a work with a contemporary Turkish setting instead. Declined for the *Atlantic*, *Zoroaster* went to Macmillan instead of Houghton Mifflin. Although Aldrich eventually received his Turkish serial, "Paul Patoff," Crawford had in the meantime made other publishing contacts and become much in demand. It was the last thing either the magazine or the house got from him.

Houghton, angered by what he perceived as Aldrich's loss of an increasingly popular writer, considered replacing him as early as 1886 with Horace Scudder, long the firm's literary adviser and trade editor, in whom he had full confidence. Apparently Scudder refused at this point either to displace Aldrich or to "act as a committee to confer with [him] about the improvement of the editing" (Ballou 379). He continued as before to pick up Aldrich's job during summers, including soliciting manuscripts. In 1889, Scudder solicited, among others, Woodrow Wilson, then a young graduate student at Johns Hopkins, who acknowledged Scudder as his "literary godfather," and Charles Eliot, president of Harvard. When their papers arrived, however, Aldrich rejected them without checking with Scudder and breezily delegated the refusal letters to Susan Francis. Wilson made no protest, but the formidable Eliot was quick to transmit his anger to Houghton, who, in turn, went into a "towering rage" (Ballou 372). In December 1889, Aldrich submitted, then withdrew, his resignation, leaving Houghton "at his wit's end to know how to dispose of [him]" (Ballou 379). The loyal Scudder, however, solved his problem. When Aldrich announced his intention to again spend the summer abroad, Scudder finally refused to take up the burden, and in June 1890 Aldrich was forced to resign.

Aldrich, who did not have to worry much about the stoppage of a salary, felt both liberation and resentment. "What a blessed relief it is," he wrote Stedman, "not to make a hundred bitter enemies per month by declining MSS" (19 Nov. 1890). From the exotic solace of Constantinople, he wrote Woodberry: "Christian, having thrown off his burden and quitted 'the shop' forever, is walking in the streets of the City Beautiful. He unwinds the turban of care from his brow and sits down by the fountains of delight. If he thinks of the unctuousness of the spacious Houghton or the corrugated wisdom of the multifarious Scudder, he longs not for them" (22 July 1890).

But even in Constantinople, his aesthetic calm was broken by irritating newspaper accounts of Scudder's succession suggesting, accurately enough, that Scudder had already edited and influenced the *Atlantic*. Aldrich again wrote Woodberry, this time asserting that "neither Mr. Scudder nor anyone else was associated with me in shaping the course of the *Atlantic Monthly*" and asking Woodberry to "drop a line somewhat to that effect among the literary notices of the *Nation*" (28

July 1890). Woodberry complied, and the *Nation* carried a notice stating that Aldrich had been the sole source of "the excellence of the *Atlantic* during the past decade" (28 Aug. 1890, 170).

While his denial of Scudder's assistance was neither just nor generous, Aldrich was a better editor than he has sometimes been given credit for. Despite his four-month vacations and errors of tact, he was not habitually indolent or flippant but methodical in his office work and professionally frank with most contributors. He was pedantic and narrowly conservative in issues of literary style and form, but he knew that in matters of substance, to make an interesting magazine he would have to publish a considerably broader range of both aesthetic and social opinion than was represented by his own narrow values. He actively solicited some manuscripts, including a great many from Henry James, who despised him as a fatuous, indulged creature of mediocre intellect but who received the *Atlantic*'s support after other magazines had largely abandoned him. The number of new writers Aldrich published, including Sill, Thomas, Woodberry, Repplier, and Chesnutt, indicates that while he was not a generous developer and promoter of new talent like Howells, he continued to make the *Atlantic* accessible to unknowns. Partly motivated by a combined social and aesthetic snobbery, he resisted both popular taste and the commercial benefit of his publisher while generally attempting to promote traditional high literary culture.

But Aldrich was clearly not the sole shaper of his magazine. Fields and Howells had developed relationships with Aldrich's most important contributors, while Scudder's reviews of American fiction dominated the magazine's critical stance. Nor did Aldrich have a lasting influence on the *Atlantic*'s character. Despite strong prejudices, he lacked both a strong character and the passion of a cultural mission. Unlike both his predecessor Howells and his successor Scudder, he had no coherent vision of what the *Atlantic* should be or what he could accomplish through it. He lacked the sense of literary mission in Howells's commitment to a progressive realism and Scudder's zeal for the education of America through the propagation of a literature of high values. Aldrich's instincts were to conserve what he felt was a waning literary culture against the barbarous popular culture of the majority. Too often he tried to do this through narrow prescriptions of language and poetic form and through a retreat from broader social, political, and cultural engagement into a refined aestheticism. Unlike his predecessors and his successor, he made little attempt to integrate or engage good literature and traditional high culture into contemporary American life.

Horace Elisha Scudder, editor-in-chief for Houghton Mifflin and editor of the *Atlantic*, 1890–1898. By permission of the Houghton Library, Harvard University (Portrait file).

6
Horace Elisha Scudder
(1 8 9 0 – 1 8 9 8)

Missionary of Yankee Culture

Horace Elisha Scudder was by temperament almost Aldrich's opposite. While the slight, erect, youthful-looking Aldrich was known for his aestheticism, his aversion to prolonged work, and his quick, sometimes wounding wit, the roundish, stooped, balding, bushy-bearded Scudder was an incarnation of Victorian earnestness, dedication to work, patient kindness, and moral idealism. If Aldrich's character and values were grounded essentially in aesthetics, Scudder's were grounded in religion. One form of Scudder's religion was a humane, nondogmatic, but firm and sustaining Congregationalism. He attended church regularly, read and annotated his New Testament daily in the original Greek, wrote a commemorative biography of a missionary brother who died young in India, and was an early admirer of the Christian socialism of F. D. Maurice, later personified for him in his beloved niece, Vida Scudder. Scudder's second religion was Western literary culture, particularly the works of those older New England writers whom he had felt privileged to know from afar. This culture and these works, he believed, were a deep source of moral and spiritual as well as intellectual values and a potent force for good in American society. To the preservation, development, and propagation of this humanistic culture, he committed his energies with the patient zeal, the self-effacement, and sometimes the cultural myopia of a missionary.

Although his official term as editor was briefer, Scudder had a far more powerful influence on the *Atlantic* than Aldrich did. He had been employed by Houghton since 1863 in increasingly responsible positions, was editor-in-chief of Houghton Mifflin's trade division from 1886 until his death in 1902, and had far more credibility and influence with the magazine's publishers than Aldrich had. He also wrote more for the magazine, mainly in literary criticism, than anyone else before or since and worked far more systematically at shaping the magazine's contents and policies. His instincts and values were also more consonant with the magazine's traditions than Aldrich's. He had none of the belligerent reactionism with which Aldrich often responded to aesthetic and political change. Nor was Scudder infected with the antidemocratic cynicism that Aldrich shared with many Boston intellectuals of the nineties. He shared none of the despair of Charles Eliot Norton, Henry Adams, and Barrett Wendell, even of the expatriate Henry James, that traditional Western high culture and its Brahminical Yankee advocates were doomed to irrelevance in an American wasteland of commercial, democratic mass culture. Rather, Scudder carried on the sanguine faith of the magazine's earlier editors and writers that traditional intellectual and literary culture, especially that which had spread from New England over the past fifty years, could still profoundly influence American values, and that to do so it must remain in close contact with the society of which it was part, not alienated and distant.

Scudder, who was Lowell's official biographer, general editor of the standard editions of several Olympians, the anthologizer of all, and the major promoter of their classroom use, thus shared with the *Atlantic*'s early conductors several convictions that shaped the magazine during his editorship. First, he was motivated by a strong sense of cultural mission. Although he was much more pragmatic than Aldrich about the commercial context in which he worked, he instinctively defined for himself the magazine's purpose in terms of education rather than entertainment or commercial success. Circulation, improving slightly under Scudder, remained a distinctly secondary consideration. Second, like Lowell and Emerson, he felt that intellectual culture and its proponents should be broadly engaged in contemporary American life. Therefore, he moderately but noticeably increased the *Atlantic*'s commentary on political, economic, and social issues, and particularly on education, about which he sometimes wrote himself.

Despite a wish to engage the magazine more often in contemporary life, however, Scudder still considered the magazine's distinctive heart and soul what he would have called "high, pure literature," not journalism. Scudder, whose training and professional life consisted mainly of editing and writing books, still thought of the *Atlantic* ideally as Emerson had imagined it: a monthly book containing serious reflective writing and literature of permanent worth. When Scudder in 1895 hired Walter Hines Page, trained in the intensely competitive new magazine journalism current in New York, as his assistant and presumed successor, his own mid-nineteenth-century high-culture ideal came in conflict with Page's twentieth-century progressive instinct that a magazine should be essentially a journalistic commentary on contemporary issues with a life span of thirty days.

As his hiring and management of Page demonstrated, Scudder was not blind to developments in publishing and culture that were becoming new realities as the twentieth century approached. But both he and his *Atlantic*, while not reactionary, were fundamentally embodiments of the magazine's nineteenth-century traditions. They were retrospective rather than progressive. They attempted, against a rising tide of mass culture, to sustain an elite humanistic culture into an alien age and under sharply changed circumstances. Their essential function and instinct were to preserve and propagate what had been accomplished rather than to experiment with creating new thought or forms. Scudder sought to continue the application of moral principle to politics that had produced the abolitionism of Lowell and Emerson, to respect the tradition of rational inquiry that motivated Holmes's criticisms of religious orthodoxy and Higginson's advocacy of higher education for women, and generally to support the literary realism developed by Howells. But while the progressive elements in American culture had absorbed these gains and continued beyond them, Scudder and the *Atlantic* had largely stopped evolving and turned their attention to preserving. They sometimes expressed misgivings that religious skepticism and the new literary naturalism had already gone too far toward denying a moral order and progress in the world. In their high-minded, conservative idealism they were deeply committed to the old liberal Emersonian convictions about the power of the individual will, the existence of a fundamental moral order in the universe, and the ethical evolution of civilizations.

It was significant that while Lowell had been thirty-eight when he assumed the editorship, Fields forty-four, Howells thirty-four, and Aldrich forty-four, Scudder, who had always had health problems, was fifty-two when he started, beginning later than any editor before or since. He possessed the virtues and faults often characteristic of an admirable man in late middle age and passed many of them on to the magazine. He retained a deep commitment to his basic ideals and values, which had been formed in the sixties and seventies when he had been moderately progressive. He added to them an experienced realism, a pragmatic patience, and a prodigious capacity for work. But while he had sustained his old idealism to an unusual degree, he was not as attuned or as adaptable to the future as a younger man would have been, and he was restrained by a habitual late-middle-aged caution and skepticism about change. He partly foresaw the future but could not and would not willingly embrace it. Scudder himself barely survived the nineteenth century. His *Atlantic* was to undergo some difficult transitions, partly at the hands of the much younger Page, before fully entering a more progressive phase in the twentieth.

Horace Scudder, unlike his *Atlantic* predecessors Fields, Howells, and Aldrich, was born in Boston.[1] His family, however, were no Brahmins in the popular sense of a social elite with intellectual pretensions. Scudder was born in 1838, the seventh child of a modestly successful Boston hardware merchant and his wife, both devout and charitable Congregationalists who refused to hang curtains in their house because many around them could not afford blankets. The family possessed, however, an element of the humbler Brahminism defined by Holmes: an old Puritan line likely to produce ministers or educators infused with New England conscience, a mission to serve, and a respect for learning. Two brothers, including the missionary, David, went into the ministry, which Scudder himself briefly considered, while another, Samuel, became a notable entomologist, author of major works on American butterflies, and a founder of the Boston Museum of Science.

After graduating with Henry Adams from Roxbury Latin School, Scudder attended Williams College, where he edited the literary *Quarterly* and developed a lifelong friendship with another literary aspirant, Henry Mills Alden, later for full fifty years editor of *Harper's Monthly*. Scudder, like Aldrich, briefly sought his literary fortunes in New York in the 1860s before coming to Boston. His passion was fiction, but he also wrote literary criticism, including an article on Blake for C. E. Norton's *North American Review*. From the dream of writing fiction, he later wrote, "I awoke to find myself at the desk of a literary workman" (Scudder to Alden, 1887, qtd. in Allen 553). In New York, he lived by such modest literary work as tutoring, writing a manual on the rules of croquet, and finally producing a briefly popular series of children's books. The children's books led to a job editing a magazine for children and a lifelong interest in children's literature and the educational values of fiction.

Scudder moved from New York to Boston in 1863, three years before Aldrich and Howells, and for the same reason: to edit a Boston periodical. He was to develop the *Riverside Magazine for Young People*, a venture of Hurd and Houghton Company. Operating on the belief that children disliked the prevalent patronizing, self-consciously "juvenile" fiction that preached to them but that they would respond to imaginative literature of a high order, Scudder published in the *Riverside* the first stories of Sarah Orne Jewett and Frank Stockton among others, becoming the earliest literary mentor to both. He sought out also the stories of Hans Christian Andersen, with whom he corresponded extensively.

Scudder's *Riverside*, characterized by F. L. Mott as "brilliant but unsuccessful," was swallowed by Dr. Holland's *Scribner's* in 1870 (Mott 3: 176). Scudder, however, continued his lifelong association with the publishing combinations of Henry Oscar Houghton. In 1872, he was taken in as a partner, but his aspirations were literary, not financial, and in 1875 he resigned his partnership to devote more time to writing. By 1878, he was back at his desk as a "literary workman" full-time and in the early eighties became Houghton Mifflin's chief literary adviser and head of the trade department.

In addition to his editorship of the *Atlantic*, Scudder personally had a pervasive influence on the literature published by one of the nation's most prestigious publishers during the last quarter of the nineteenth century. This influence came partly through the confidence of Henry Oscar Houghton in Scudder's combination of integrity, pragmatism, literary judgment, and loyalty to the house. On the one hand, Scudder understood that in a capitalist society most literature must ultimately pay for its own publication, and he declined thousands of manuscripts for which he did not feel there was a reasonable audience. On the other hand, he saw the publication of meretricious but popular literature not only as morally and aesthetically damaging but ultimately as bad business practice, at least for Houghton Mifflin. Offered a slick and empty novel by the popular Frank Stockton which Houghton's advertising men told him they could sell well simply on the author's name, Scudder declined "with a sigh" because "we should have a name only and not a thing, and in the long run such a policy would react upon us" (Scudder to Houghton, 7 Mar. 1893). In 1901, still chief literary adviser, Scudder wrote to then *Atlantic* editor Bliss Perry, "The firm is at times very commercial, at others disposed to take the larger view, and it is our business, I mean distinctly yours and mine, to take every occasion to reinforce them in this latter mind" (27 July 1901).

As Scudder's editorial record with Henry James and Sarah Jewett shows, he sometimes made his compromises with the commercial context in which he chose to work. But for nearly thirty years, he spoke effectively both in Houghton Mifflin's trade publications and on the *Atlantic* for the larger view, the view that not every work need be measured by its immediate popularity, that publishing trash eventually destroys a reputation for quality, that genuine quality will eventually be recognized and rewarded—not always, but often enough to merit some financial risk in supporting it. Unfortunately, the performance of his *Atlantic* at least suggests that the more tangible rewards for publishing material of high intellectual quality do not come as frequently as he liked to believe.

When Howells had suddenly resigned from the *Atlantic* in 1881 and Houghton had instinctively turned to Aldrich on the strength of his literary reputation, Scudder had felt a twinge of disappointment. But he was not an egotist but, rather, saw himself as a part of a larger cooperative enterprise. He had worked in a habitually friendly spirit with Aldrich, patiently agreeing summer after summer to add the burden of editing the *Atlantic* for three months to his already heavy workload while Aldrich tripped about Europe collecting choice bric-a-brac. Aldrich, who was an egotist of the first water, privately conferred on him the epithet "the kindly Scudder," with the mildly patronizing attitude that egotists sometimes use for those they perceive as pliant, dim, and ineffectual. Scudder was accommodating but generally understood when he was being used. By spring of 1890, Houghton was desperate to dispose of Aldrich. Scudder had previously refused to be Houghton's emissary to discuss the improvement of the editing and now "declined to be used as a stick with which to beat Aldrich" (Scudder's diary, 21 May 1890). He also refused, however, to continue acting as Aldrich's unpaid summer substitute. In mid-June, Aldrich submitted his resignation and stormed off to nurse his bruised ego among the exotic scenes and antique merchants of the Levant. Scudder recorded the aftermath and his reactions in his diary entry for 17 June 1890. His language reflects his realism in assessing Houghton, his own talents, the *Atlantic*'s financial condition, and his sense of religious mission in assuming the editorship:

> Yesterday Mr. Houghton told me that Aldrich had resigned the editorship of the *Atlantic*, and proceeded to speak of me in connection with the work. I said, smilingly, you have not asked me to take the place. "No," he said, "some things we don't ask. I believe I never asked Mrs. Houghton to marry me." I think it not unlikely, for his habit of mind is so ineradicably indirect that I can easily think of him talking an hour to Miss Manning, and at the end of it, her finding herself engaged to him. I must take him as he is, although his isness [*sic*] is rather trying at times. . . .
>
> All this is of minor importance. I am more stirred by the fact that I am now invested, permanently, with the editorship. . . . I have known of the dissatisfaction of the firm for a long while, and I am taking the magazine when it is running down financially. . . . My aim is to keep the magazine at the front of American literature, but I will not boast as the one who puts his armor off. . . . I do not think I am likely to make lucky hits, but I can strengthen the magazine all along the line, and my heart beats quicker at the thought of serving God in this cause of high, pure literature.

Scudder's religious conviction in his cultural mission apparently blinded him to the burden he was taking on. Rather than exchanging his full-time job as editor-in-chief of general publications for Aldrich's supposedly full-time job as *Atlantic* editor, he simply added the editorship to his responsibilities for books, as he had during the summers, but now with full control and recognition as well as an increase in salary from $5,000 to $6,000. This made him the highest-paid salaried employee of the firm, including several Houghtons. (Before the promotion, he had shared this distinction with Houghton's head of advertising, Azariah Smith.) True, $6,000 was considerably less than the $10,000 his close friend Alden received solely for editing *Harper's* or Gilder for editing the *Century*. But the *Atlantic* was losing a few thousand a year, while the New York monthlies were still making considerable profits. And if he looked at such comparisons, which he probably didn't, $6,000 would have seemed generous beside the $1,075 paid the only woman on the staff, the long-laboring Susan Francis, who had anonymously assisted *Atlantic* editors since Fields but was still paid at the rate for editorial recruits (Houghton Mifflin Co. "Private Journal": 1887–1896).

Houghton had justified combining the editorship of general trade books with the *Atlantic* editorship by pointing out that the *Atlantic* should function as a means of developing new authors and manuscripts for the house but that with separate editors, as under Aldrich, the coordination had been poor at best. Clearly, Houghton also sought to cut the *Atlantic*'s losses by $3,000 annually, the difference between the $4,000 paid Aldrich and the $1,000 added to Scudder's salary. The pragmatic Scudder accepted both types of logic but did not yet understand the cost to himself.

Moved by a zealous spirit, Scudder threw himself into solicitation of manuscripts and plans for the reinvigoration of the *Atlantic*. A later successor, Ellery Sedgwick, claimed with a patronizing inaccuracy intended to promote his own stature as an aggressive editor that the kindly "old gentleman" asserted with mild pride that he had "*never* invited a contribution to the *Atlantic*" (Sedgwick 154 and Ballou 436–37). The truth was that Scudder had solicited widely while substituting for Aldrich, and now during his first week as official editor he not only wrote the *Atlantic*'s "inner circle," informing them of the editorial change and soliciting manuscripts but also pored over the *Atlantic Index*, Houghton Mifflin's Catalog, and Griswald's *Directory* of American writers for ideas and soon fired off letters to several dozen authors. In the months that followed, he recorded, "Almost every day I think of some new writer or some new article I want and so open correspondence" (Diary, 17 Nov. 1890). The classicist G. H. Palmer, typical of others, found Scudder so tenacious in soliciting that he wrote with mixed protest and gratitude: "You are like that gadfly to which Socrates in the Apology compares himself, continually stinging the beastly Athenian people and preventing them from falling into sloth and incapacity" (2 Aug. 1891).

Nor did Scudder simply solicit randomly. At the end of his first year, he wrote Houghton: "My experience confirms me in my belief that successful editing of the magazine demands a vigilance and closeness of superintendence to be had only by being constantly at the center of things. . . . [T]he editor [must] study the field and . . . have a distinct policy which should be discovered in the papers he solicits rather than in the volunteer ones which he accepts" (Scudder to Houghton, 10 Aug. 1891). Sedgwick's bogus claims to the contrary, Scudder not only solicited more actively but also formulated and enacted a more consciously articulated editorial policy than did any of his predecessors.

Though retiring by nature, subject since childhood to mysterious periods of deafness, and very fond of solitude and a close family circle, Scudder also made a conscientious effort to keep himself near the center of things in the intellectual and publishing worlds. He periodically visited New York, Philadelphia, and Washington and delivered occasional lectures in Ohio, Kansas, or California. He regularly skimmed New York and Boston newspapers; American weeklies including the *Forum*, *Publishers Weekly*, *Critic*, and *Nation*; several English weeklies; and the American monthlies. He also read regularly a surprisingly large number of contemporary books. Many were manuscripts submitted to Houghton Mifflin, but most were books submitted to the *Atlantic* for review. Incredibly, in view of his other obligations, Scudder himself read and wrote brief critical comments on most of the thirty to forty books reviewed monthly in the magazine's "Comment on New Books" section, including not only fiction and poetry but also works of reference, law, history, biography, travel, art, education, religion, scholarship, and politics.

Scudder's reading was much broader, less confined to literature, than that of his predecessors, and his *Atlantic* was correspondingly broader, less heavily literary. But like his predecessors and unlike most of his successors, his exposure to the world was still primarily filtered through books rather than coming through direct contact with the movers and shakers of current affairs. Consequently, his *Atlantic*, while broader in scope than that of his forerunners, remained more bookish than the magazine produced by the *Atlantic*'s twentieth-century editors.

The monthly reading and reviewing Scudder did for "Comment on New Books" would, in itself, have been exhausting full-time work for many. But it was a fraction of his responsibilities at Houghton Mifflin in the early nineties. To compound the excessive workload, Scudder had a temperament that not only made him compulsively conscientious about performing his duties but often mired him in detail. As editor of the trade list and administrative head of the trade department, he was responsible for presenting and discussing all potentially publishable book manuscripts at the weekly Tuesday afternoon "powwow," at which the partners and chiefs of departments met to make final publishing decisions. True, unsolicited book manuscripts from the sludge pile as well as *Atlantic* submissions could be screened by his assistants, Susan Francis and the young Herbert Gibbs. But Scudder insisted on at least briefly "scrutinizing everything which I have the responsibility for declining or accepting" (to Page, 8 Apr. 1898). Nor was his trade book editing limited any more than his *Atlantic* editing to passing judgment on submitted manuscripts. It required active strategic planning and pursuit of authors, including recruiting and guiding writers and editors for Houghton Mifflin's prestigious American Commonwealths and Riverside Literature series.

Scudder considered his work on manuscripts far from over even after he had evaluated them. Frequently he would write extensive comments, sometimes five to ten pages, analyzing problems or detailing suggestions and inviting resubmission. His comments were invariably friendly but frank and were as often directed at professional writers as at novices. Accepting a serial novel by Paul Leichester Ford, he wrote that it gave him genuine pleasure, but he requested extensive revisions of a plot that at several points "challenges credulity" (13 Oct. 1896). He recommended that Canadian novelist Gilbert Parker review a manuscript to eliminate transparent artifice and asked Kate Douglas Wiggin to rewrite the end of a novel he found flat and conventional (to Parker and Wiggin, n.d.). While generally direct and explicit in his commentary, he was not dogmatic but was usually willing to negotiate issues with authors. To one young poet, he wrote six pages of comment on a single poem. Scudder then published the poem when the poet wrote back a letter of sixteen pages changing little but justifying his wordings (to Edward White, 2 Mar. 1891).

Less-established writers particularly were, or often said they were, grateful for Scudder's "exhaustive analysis," "cordial... interest and kindly criticism" (Fannie Murfree to Scudder, 25 Sept. 1885; Elizabeth Wallace to Scudder, 3 Apr. 1894). But if the relationship lasted, particularly with male authors, a note of irritation often crept in and sometimes outright revolt. John Jay Chapman, that strange and protean reincarnation of Emersonian individualism, early on thanked Scudder, whom he called his patron, for his "wise and admirable correction" (17 Sept. 1890) but later rebelled at suggested cuts:

> Many thanks for my manuscript returned O Procrustes. I do now let loose my opinion—hold it no longer. The introduction is too long for a short praise, too short for a long praise, too condensed for a general praise and too general for a condensed praise—and being as it is, you do not like it.
> Enough! O Gate Keeper. But know this—I will not change a hair of his head—not for the sake of getting him baptized by the pope with all the Cardinals of culture for sponsors.... yours, Pantagruel. (28 Aug. 1895)

In addition to reviewing a multitude of books monthly, shaping editorial policy for both the *Atlantic* and general publications, actively soliciting manuscripts for both, evaluating those manuscripts, sometimes commenting extensively and negotiating revisions, actually editing some trade books, including "scholarly" editing of literary texts, attending "powwows," and performing other administrative duties, the conscientious Scudder often took on himself jobs more appropriately delegated to his assistants. Although Susan Francis had a hawk's eye for error in language or fact, Scudder generally insisted on inserting himself in the multi-layered proofreading process. While an admirer of "good strong stuff in forcible Saxon English," Scudder, unlike his successor Page, disliked the modern tendency toward journalistic staccato (Ballou 119). He spent considerable time giving manuscripts the famed "Scudder polish."

Not only Scudder's strong sense of professional responsibility but also his generosity caused him to take on tasks he could have delegated or avoided. He took the time and effort to treat everyone, regardless of status, with respect and a frank kindness. Like Howells, he was particularly generous to younger writers, though because he was in his late fifties, his relationships with them were avuncular rather than peer relationships. From the very beginnings of their careers, he gave influential advice on literary issues and publishing strategies to Sarah Orne Jewett, Josephine Preston Peabody, and Woodrow Wilson, in addition to lobbying for publication of their works and providing them with useful contacts. Similarly, he provided important advice and support for both Mark Howe, whom he hired as an assistant, and Ellery Sedgwick, a later *Atlantic* editor, in the earliest stages of their careers in publishing.

Even in delivering rejections, Scudder generously spent more time than most editors. While the dreaded form rejection was used liberally for unsolicited manuscripts, and Scudder was professionally disciplined not to agonize over most decisions, he often wrote letters frankly explaining the source of his objection. He was patient too in dealing with the disgruntled. A letter to a rejected contributor who angrily accused him of personal animosity reflects the combination of sympathy and rectitude, frankness and patient respect, with which he characteristically treated everyone, even cranks, often at the expense of considerable time and effort:

> My Dear Friend, for so I must call you if I believe, as I do, that you meant every word of your letter. You wrote to bring me to a knowledge of myself and that certainly is a friendly act.
>
> Nonetheless, you are wholly and absolutely wrong in all your inferences. It is perfectly true that I have declined manuscripts you offered to the *Atlantic* and that I have advised Messrs Houghton Mifflin Company against publishing your book manuscript; but I have done this just as I have made numberless such decisions and recommendations upon the best judgment I could reach. I am not at all confident of being right in my literary judgments at all times; but when it comes to a question of motive, you must allow me to say that I know more about my motives than you do, to judge from your letter, since you accuse me of personal hostility to you. . . .
>
> I return your letter. I should be sorry to keep it.
>
> Yours very truly,
Horace Scudder

(To W. G. Dick, 9 Oct. 1894)

Scudder was also generous in his willingness to take on the burdens of both friendship and civic responsibility. When Howells suffered a breakdown in 1881, Scudder read all of his proofs. When Howells's daughter Winny died in 1890, he turned to Scudder, of all his Boston friends, to buy the burial plot and make arrangements for the interment. When the widows of Bayard Taylor and later Asa Gray sought help with the immense task of compiling their husband's "life and letters," the sympathetic and capable Scudder, lamenting only to himself, allowed these tasks to be added to his load. During his editorship, he also served as a trustee of Williams and Wellesley colleges, an overseer at Harvard, and a member of the Church Library Association and the Massachusetts School Board.

Scudder had an immense energy for work, nearly equal to the quantity of work that his job and his temperament thrust upon him. The ultimate source of this energy was his conviction of the moral and cultural usefulness of the work. His approach to his work was highly disciplined and methodical. "As a literary workman," T. W. Higginson wrote, "his nicety of method and regularity of life went beyond those of any man I have known" ("Scudder" 23–24). Scudder was so methodical that he not only kept a daily diary but noted in it the dates when he changed from summer to winter underwear. Six days a week during most of the year, he typically rose at 5:00 or 6:00 A.M., read Greek, breakfasted, wrote three or four pages (usually reviews), took an early train from near his home in Cambridge to the firm's offices at 4 Park Street in Boston, met with contributors and cranks, wrote correspondence, often lunched on fruit at the office, read manuscripts, walked home at 5:00 P.M. over Harvard bridge, talking business with Houghton, read Horace with his daughter Sylvia, dined, attended a lecture or read for future reviews, and finally recorded the day in his diary before retiring. From June to September, he usually spent Friday through Monday at his house in Chocorua, New Hampshire, or as neighbors to the Houghton clan at Little Boars Head on the New Hampshire coast, commuting to town for Tuesday through Thursday. In his summer quarters, he took no prolonged break from work but kept up a reasonably tight schedule, though relaxing to the point of working only a half-day on Saturdays.

With this discipline and capacity for work, Scudder was initially confident he could establish a system for dispatching each day's business as it arose, thus preserving time to plan, solicit widely, and shape policy proactively rather than being merely reactive. After two weeks as joint book and magazine editor, he buoyantly noted, "I am more than ever assured that under the present arrangement I can get through my work without worry" (Diary, 9 July 1890). He continued to be very efficient in evaluating manuscripts. Decisions on both articles and books were often made in one to four weeks, a stunning rapidity by today's standards. But within two months of adding the *Atlantic* to his other work, he was sounding a lament that he was to echo for the rest of his editorship. "I seem," he worried in his diary, "to be buried in various work and to be drawn in a dozen directions. If it were not for the faithful Gibbs, I should be discouraged" (29 July 1890). Often, he was discouraged. The everlasting books to be reviewed accumulated distressingly in the bin behind his desk; book manuscripts with publication deadlines demanded long hours of editing; unsolicited *Atlantic* manuscripts littered the closet; few writers he solicited could meet his requests; even those who assented required constant pressure to perform. He tossed much of the night, planning next year's *Atlantic* program; his *Atlantic* prospectus for 1891 looked unspeakably dreary compared to what he had hoped for; his important first January issue seemed to him "dreadfully dull," and despite almost daily solicitations he lacked enough good copy for the February number (Diary, Sept.–Dec. 1890).

Scudder began to lose sleep; then in March 1891 he was suddenly struck almost entirely deaf. One eardrum was diseased from twenty-five years ago; now the second was punctured. Finding his situation "funny but alarming," he kept up his work routine using an old ear trumpet and asking coworkers to write him notes (Diary, 11 Mar. 1891). Gradually his hearing returned, but in early May, on a trip to New York, his face began to swell mysteriously. Badly disfigured and in severe pain, he was ordered to bed. He was beginning to recuperate when he was hit ten days later by pneumonia. After two months of utter prostration, Scudder chafed to resume work. Forbidden by his doctors to go to the office and urged to take three months of total rest, he nevertheless had large packages of materials sent out almost daily and worked during a very slow six-months' recovery at home. Early in 1892, he had a milder but still incapacitating relapse and thereafter periodically suffered bouts of illness, deafness, and headaches.

After this series of illnesses, which must have been at least partly a physiological reaction to the pressures of his work, Scudder felt far less confident that he could do a first-rate job on both the magazine and the books by himself with the largely mechanical assistance of Susan Francis and Herbert Gibbs. His illness had also given him a dramatic sense of his mortality; he realized with a new urgency that work was not the sum of life and began thinking concretely of a European sabbatical. During a subsequent illness, he wrote to Houghton:

> I need a full assistant, a man of brains, character, and experience, who could at a pinch take my place if necessary. I cannot much longer stand the strain under which I am now working. Work ceases to be pleasure when one not only leaves the bigger half undone, but does what he does under such pressure that he does not do it well. Still, I am so desirous of making no mistake that I would rather stagger along til I can feel confident that I am shifting my load upon a competent shoulder. (7 Mar. 1893)

Scudder was destined to do a lot of staggering. Susan Francis, although experienced in the modest role of reader and a cut above the lamented legion of "half-equipped maidens wanting literary work," was never seriously considered in the largely male world of publishing (Scudder diary, 10 Apr. 1897). Herbert Gibbs was methodical and loyal but limited. Both were thought capable lieutenants but lacking the scope and force to make final decisions or be prospective successors. Houghton recommended Francis H. Allen, a young science editor with the firm, but Scudder felt he lacked the "creative ability and the aggressive qualities required of an *Atlantic* editor." Among those considered were Gamaliel Bradford, Jr., Charles T. Copeland, Royal Cortissoz, Edwin Emerson, Paul Reynolds, Edmund C. Stedman, and William Roscoe Thayer. In 1893, however, Scudder got his longtime first choice, Mark Antony DeWolfe Howe, a twenty-nine-year-old well steeped in the tradition of Yankee humanism and possessed of literary fluency, despite a chronic stutter. Howe relinquished the job Scudder had steered him to as assistant on the *Youth's Companion* and turned down an offer from *Harper's* to assist Scudder on the *Atlantic*. After winning Houghton's approval (though in the interview the old man had apparently fallen asleep during a prolonged stutter), Howe began work in July 1893. Scudder was relieved; he found Howe diligent, approved his literary taste, and worked compatibly with him. Within nine months, however, Howe's eyesight began to fail. By fall 1894 he was working only sporadically, and by March 1895 he was obliged to resign. The poet Bliss Carman was hired as a temporary assistant, but Scudder again felt overwhelmed, with no prospect of relief from his burden, and was again in the market for a capable assistant and prospective successor (Ballou 403–4).

Through the frustrations of his overwork, his prolonged illnesses, and the long search for a qualified assistant, Scudder was producing each month a magazine that was the product of more conscious editorial shaping than the *Atlantic* of his forerunners. Scudder considered the key to his editorial policy a balancing of the magazine's contents. The *Atlantic*'s "singular advantage," Scudder wrote to Houghton, in addition to its traditions, was that rather than being limited to one function, it combined the elements of a "review" of current affairs, "a popular miscellany" containing essays and fiction, and a "critical journal" of comment on literature. "The educated man," he continued, "has two sides to him, one appealed to by discussion and criticism, and the other by creative literature. Every number of the *Atlantic* should have in good balance literature par eminence and the literature which is occupied with topics," including both political and cultural subjects (10 Aug. 1891). Scudder, moderate in everything, made no radical changes in either the balance of the magazine's contents or its ideology. He was later justly criticized by editorial successors such as Walter Hines Page and Ellery Sedgwick for placing too much emphasis on literature and particularly on the cultural past at a time when progressive magazine journalism was focusing increasingly on the political and social issues of the present. Unlike Aldrich, however, he did seek to connect the magazine more with contemporary American life, through both increased emphasis on current affairs and a broader sympathy with contemporary literature.

Certainly Scudder considered the Arnoldian preservation of canonical high culture an important part of his mission, and he gave it almost as much weight in the magazine as Aldrich had. Most notably, Scudder used the *Atlantic* to preserve and propagate the literature of its founders. Lowell died in 1891, Whittier in 1892, Holmes in 1894, and Stowe in 1896. Scudder had somewhat distantly known them all and edited their works, the lucrative copyrights for which still resided with Houghton Mifflin Company. His sincere respect for their work and conviction about its cultural value combined with corporate self-interest to produce eulogies and attempts to establish these writers as the foundation of an American canon, particularly within the educational curriculum. In addition, several series of reminiscences by survivors, such as T. W. Higginson's *Cheerful Yesterdays*, the buoyant E. E. Hale's *New England Boyhood*, and Rose Hawthorne Lathrop's memories of her father, continued the elegiac theme and Indian summer aura discernible in Aldrich's *Atlantic*.

Scudder was also sympathetic to the attempts of the New Humanists and others to preserve and restore to life a more distant cultural past. He published articles by

Basil Gildersleeve, W. P. Trent, Irving Babbit, and P. E. More criticizing the modern tendencies to treat old texts as academic-historical documents rather than sources of moral value and to displace humanistic with scientific knowledge. In support of the humanistic position, Scudder became one of the last editors of an American general periodical to publish essays like those of Henry D. Sedgwick on Montaigne and Macaulay, or J. J. Chapman on Dante, or Harriet Preston Water's series on the Roman orators and the Renaissance humanists, or the philosopher Josiah Royce on Hegel and Schopenhauer.

Scudder also published a great many articles on traditional Eastern culture. As Jackson Lears has shown, these too represented an attempt to discover value in the past and were motivated by a similar alienation from what was perceived as the soulless, homogeneous, valueless, materialistic mass culture of the American present. These articles included P. E. More on Indian sacred texts and a series by Percival Lowell on Japan. The most notable, however, were several series by the odd, misshapen, brilliant Lafcadio Hearn. Hearn had relocated permanently to Japan in 1890, planning to support himself partly by writing for *Harper's*, but some discontent magnified by paranoia had led him to sever the connection, cursing editor Alden in a series of obscene letters. For the next decade, Scudder and the *Atlantic* audience delighted in Hearn's accounts of a society that valued tradition, reflection, mysticism, and aesthetic beauty and therefore seemed the antithesis of the modern, scientific, materialistic, industrial culture in which they lived.

The canonization of the Olympians, the New Humanists' claims for the old texts, and Hearn's portraits of semifeudal Japan all reflected a cultural conservatism, a looking to the past for values and a resistance to the present. They reflected too an editorial emphasis on literature and cultural history at the expense of contemporary social and political issues. Scudder, however, genuinely tried to achieve an editorial and ideological balance.

While the magazine's founders clearly meant it to be a platform for political and social commentary, this commentary had become erratic under a succession of editors primarily absorbed in literary careers and issues. Furthermore, as Santayana observed, by 1890 American intellectual life had become increasingly split between a progressive masculine pragmatism in business and politics and a retrospective, feminized idealism in culture. Scudder tried to bridge this gap with the general purpose of bringing more idealism, more moral principle, to politics and, at times, as an admirer of Howells, bringing more consideration of social issues to literature. While acting as Aldrich's interim, Scudder had solicited articles to increase and strengthen political commentary and, on succession, in his own right gave it high priority. "Politics, as you know, is the last item in the comprehensive title of the magazine," he wrote to Wendell Garrison, "but I may almost say that since I had my hand in the magazine, it has been the first consideration in my mind." He intended to run at least one or two papers per month on topics with "direct bearing on the public life of the country" (30 June 1891).

In his editorial treatment of political and social issues, Scudder partly looked back toward the literary culture of the mid-nineteenth century and partly anticipated the revitalization of the magazine by twentieth-century progressive journalism typified by his successors Page and Sedgwick. As a disciple of the nineteenth-century literary culture, which conferred moral value on the study of history as well as literature, Scudder published numerous studies of recent political history under the assumptions that the lapse of time aids rational analysis and that historical parallels afford moral insight into the present. Often these historical studies dealt only indirectly with contemporary issues. Scudder's excessive emphasis on them left *Atlantic* readers more knowledgeable about the politics of the Lincoln administration than about the terrible financial panic of 1893, the subsequent depression, and the rapid rise of populism.

Scudder believed, as he wrote in soliciting a study of Lincoln from Carl Schurz, "that one of the best aids we can give to the formation of judgment of public affairs is in the just and generous study of our public men" (7 July 1891). Virtually all the studies of this sort that Scudder commissioned, however, were historical, because he also believed that in discussing influential figures "a preliminary funeral is of great service" (Scudder to T. Roosevelt, 30 June 1890). Partly because of genteel high-mindedness and partly because of his publisher's fear of lawsuit, he was reticent to allow strong criticism of living individuals. In rejecting Jane Addams's excoriation of Pullman during the strike of 1896, Scudder noted the need for both caution and fairness. "Even capitalists," he objected, "are persons" (to Mrs. H. M. Wilmarth, 18 Apr. 1896, in Ballou 441–42). But apparently Tammany politicians were not, and Scudder did allow an exception to the funeral rule, over Treasurer James Murray Kay's objection, for H. C. Merwin's direct attack on Tammany boss Richard Crocker.

"Apart from the strictly historical phase of politics," Scudder wrote Houghton, "I want to make the *Atlantic* strong in the treatment of public affairs of immediate, pressing importance" (10 Aug. 1891). While continuing to emphasize history and culture, he made good on this proposal more regularly than any of his predecessors, soliciting papers on election prospects, the political parties, political corruption, civil service reform, immigration law, direct election of the president, national forests, governmental structure, and various foreign policy issues written by Charles Eliot, John Fiske, Wendell Garrison, E. L. Godkin, Albert Bushnell Hart, George Kennan, H. C. Merwin, Theodore Roosevelt, and Woodrow Wilson (Ballou 440–41). Furthermore, although printing the magazine required about five weeks, Scudder periodically responded directly to specific current events. During the Venezuelan border crisis of 1896, he wrote to Charles Francis Adams: "I feel very desirous of using the present occasion for inculcating some doctrine. The education of the public mind must go on unceasingly and it is the function of the serious press . . . to give opportunity for trained publicists to press home clear judgments. In seasons like the present, the public is most impressionable and the time to use your die is when the wax is hot" (14 Jan. 1896).

Scudder felt, as he wrote Theodore Roosevelt, that the *Atlantic* should not simply invite political analysis but also, at times, inculcate "doctrine" and "take its stand unmistakably on all the great public questions" both through carefully solicited signed papers and through unsigned political editorials (30 June 1890). His own high-minded idealism, as well as Houghton's insistence that the magazine not appear partisan or invite suit, caused the editor to be cautious about polemics. Still, early in his editorship he began to invite informed, nonpartisan opinion from those he trusted and to plan short editorials (Scudder to Houghton, 10 Aug. 1891).

Scudder heartily agreed with Lowell and the magazine's other founders that the keynote of its political stance should be a vigorous, nonpartisan application of moral principle. In many ways, the political idealism of Scudder's *Atlantic* also derived directly from Emerson and Thoreau's belief that majorities, particularly when formed through political parties, were not an infallible measure of justice or wisdom. The *Atlantic*, he wrote to Roosevelt, "must give forth no uncertain sound on the right side. There always is a right side and there are, after all, few questions of importance which cannot be discussed independently of party lines" (30 June 1890).

For Scudder, the dictates of principle were more complex than in Lowell's abolitionist days, but nonpartisanship was easier. As a Cleveland mugwump and civil service advocate, he believed not only that there was no "party of righteousness" but that the parties themselves were major sources of corruption. Nonpartisanship thereby became a matter of principle as well as of business caution, and virtually all of the editorials Scudder published criticized the influence of party politics. Roosevelt blasted the party spoils system and advocated civil service reform. There were exposés on gerrymandering, influence peddling, and Tammany. Scudder himself wrote an editorial entitled "The League as a Political Instrument" (Feb. 1892), denouncing the self-serving party machines while advocating voter independence and the formation of cause-related leagues such as the civil service league. He also conceived a clever editorial to expose the hypocrisy of both parties by measuring their 1892 platforms against their past performance and persuaded Edward Shepard, a prominent Democrat, to write it ("The Two Programmes of 1892," Nov. 1892, 688–98).

Unfortunately, Houghton was both more cautious and considerably more Republican than Scudder. His discovery that Scudder had asked a Democrat to write an election editorial marked the end of the editor's plan for unsigned political papers (Ballou 441). Scudder, however, continued to solicit, though less regularly, signed articles on current issues, sometimes with a strong polemical element.

Despite Scudder's efforts, his editorial policy in politics, circumscribed by Houghton's constraints as well as his own idealism and inclination to prefer history over current issues, seemed cautious when compared with the forceful partisanship of the *Atlantic*'s early editorials or the overt polemical journalism of his successor, Page. Still, the magazine's political voice was more distinct, its political coverage more consistent, and the range of opinion broader than under Aldrich. Aldrich would have approved J. H. Denison's reactionary plea in "The Survival of the American Type" (Jan. 1895) for Anglo-Saxon Americans, like virtuous Romans of the Republic, to reassert civic energy and political leadership in order to resist foreign anarchism and the socialist totalitarianism of Debs before these forces extinguished them. In contrast, Scudder's interest in Christian socialism led him to print an extended series of eight essays by J. M. Ludlow (Jan. 1895–Nov. 1896) advocating cooperative production, distribution, and profit sharing by labor. And Howells praised Scudder's courage in publishing Walter Crane's "Why Socialism Appeals to Artists" (Jan. 1892), adding that he believed neither *Harper's* Alden nor Gilder at the *Century* would have run it (qtd. in Ballou 437).

Scudder solicited occasional articles on a range of social issues, including immigration, the status of ethnic groups, labor and living conditions of factory workers, and enlightened institutions for vagabond children. Probably the most prominent social issue in Scudder's *Atlantic*, however, was education. Education, especially public education, was a major interest of Scudder's, and his editorial treatment of it reflects his sense of cultural mission. He was also aware that the *Atlantic* had particularly appealed to teachers and the professoriat in the past. Working to develop this appeal, he ran regular articles of interest to educators and encouraged Houghton Mifflin's advertising staff to target advertisements for the magazine directly at teachers.

Scudder's *Atlantic* regularly asserted the crucial importance of public elementary and secondary schools as the primary source of individual development and economic well-being, as well as ethical development and acculturation. To improve these institutions it proposed a litany eerily familiar a century later: higher professional status and pay for teachers, merit pay, the depoliticizing of school boards, and more content, less methodology in teacher training.[2]

In Scudder's treatment of education, as in Lowell's treatment of politics and Howells's of literature, the *Atlantic* again sought to reconcile a hierarchical and hegemonic view of culture with democratic individualism. This attempt was made explicit in a fascinating early editorial project of Scudder's. Scudder engaged the national commissioner of education, William T. Harris, to write a controversial paper entitled "The Education of the Negro," which was published in June 1892 with responding comments by prominent educators from North and South. Harris's paper was a classical attempt to fuse Darwinian and Spencerian evolution with the Emersonian development of self and Christian ethics. According to Harris, Darwin and Spencer demonstrate that all nature evolves toward individuality, intelligence, and will—in short, toward the Emersonian development of mind and soul in individuals and toward democracy in social organization. Christian altruism is both a product of these developments and a means to furthering them. "Thus religion . . . is confirmed by the scientific, political, and social movements of our age and all agree . . . that the lowest must be lifted up by the highest—lifted up into self-activity and full development of individuality" (722). Therefore, the nation has a moral and social obligation to assist the American black to develop "the sense of personal responsibility, moral dignity, and self-respect which belong to the conscious ideal of the white race" (724). Harris concludes by advocating national funding for the intellectual, moral, economic, and political development of black students as independent, educated individuals (735). The paper focused mainly on black education, but the federal program it proposed was to be universal. Scudder, demonstrating his belief that cultural hierarchies do not follow racial lines, had asked Harris, as Page would later ask Booker Washington, to extend the discussion to demonstrate that its essential principles applied to both black and white (20 Nov. 1890).

Scudder's own writings on education also reflected the attempt to fuse a frank cultural hegemony with the full development of the democratic individual. Public education, Scudder sensed, was an essential medium for his own cultural mission, and he wrote several *Atlantic* articles advocating the uses of "high" literature, and particularly American high literature, in the schools as an important means of developing American values.[3] In fact, Scudder's influence for twenty-five years as Houghton Mifflin's major literary adviser, as well as his writing, editing, anthologizing, school board work, and nationwide speeches to teachers, had a profound influence in making the New England writers a staple of the schoolroom and more generally integrating substantial American literary texts into the educational curriculum. According to Scudder,

> The introduction of a high order of literature into the common schools . . . has begun and if it can be carried forward will have more effect upon authorship in America than all other causes combined. It has not been possible hitherto because there has been no native literature at the service of the schools. Now, the accumulation of a body of prose and poetry with its origin in national life, has become a substantial foundation on which the love of literature may be built. . . . [U]nless I misread the times, these books are to have a profound influence in the education of Americans. They are to constitute the humane letters of the common school and it is impossible to measure the power which they will exert in enlarging and lifting the mental life of the people. ("Authorship in America," June 1883, 817)

Certainly Scudder's campaign to enlarge and lift the mental life of the people was motivated in part by Houghton Mifflin's copyrights to many of the "classic" American authors. Authors, he admitted (and he should have included publishers and editors), have their feet in the clay of the need to make a living. But he also believed sincerely in the power of literature to develop both the citizen and the individual self. While foreign literature was sometimes "antagonistic to our institutions," American literature was sympathetic with more democratic values (qtd. in Ballou 261). Although he candidly sought to enshrine the New England writers, he believed that creating a nation of enthusiastic readers of literature would open up immense opportunities for a great variety of new authors. "There will always be more room and welcome for authors in America," he noted, "because these have been made permanent guests" ("Authorship" 817).

Scudder's educational proposals were clearly progressive for the time in both curricular content and methods of presentation. For elementary students, he advocated banishing the stilted, infantile reading exercises and the "trivial, prosaic, or supersentimental verses found in abundance in the primer," substituting vivid myth and fable, as well as poetry by Blake, Wordsworth, Longfellow, and Whittier. He would substitute Hawthorne, Bryant, Lowell, and Emerson for the patronizing, moralistic, made-for-the-young literature of the secondary classroom. This literature would best develop the full individual not taught as a lesson or tendentiously analyzed but enjoyed and responded to imaginatively.

Scudder considered American literature as central to the mission of his magazine as it was to the mission of American education. While he worked to improve the *Atlantic*'s coverage of social issues, with modest results in politics and substantial results in education, he instinctively thought of literature as the magazine's core. Defending literary criticism to Page, who contemptuously dismissed it as "mere talkee-talkee," Scudder claimed that the *Atlantic*, as "the leading literary magazine should maintain the standard . . . and set the pace" in evaluating and supporting literary quality (11 Oct. 1897). Unquestionably, during the nineties the pace was set by Howells at *Harper's* and the younger writers whom he encouraged, such as Hamlin Garland and Stephen Crane. The *Atlantic* was resistant to the deterministic naturalism toward which many younger writers inclined. Nor did it go as far in its support of James as it should have, though it went further than any other American magazine.

Scudder's *Atlantic*, unlike that of Lowell, Fields, and Howells, clearly no longer led the evolution of American literature. But it could reasonably claim to maintain a high standard of quality, although this also was sometimes compromised by commercial and aesthetic timidity. It still published and critically supported both Howellsian realism and a high quality of local color regionalism by writers such as Sarah Orne Jewett, Mary E. Wilkins, Mary N. Murfree, and Kate Chopin. An examination of the facts reveals that Scudder and his reviewers were not mere "defenders of ideality" but recognized and actively supported much of the best realistic fiction of the period while defending the place of ethics in literature and the value of literature in nonrealistic modes. In literary taste, as in temperament and editorial philosophy, Scudder was an enlightened and moderate man of the nineteenth century who could not take the next step into the twentieth.

Scudder earnestly believed in the value both to authors and readers of fair and discriminating literary criticism, and like his friend Howells, he committed a disproportionate amount of his time, resources, and editorial space to it. A typical number of Scudder's *Atlantic* contained ten to fifteen pages of reviews, approximately 10 percent of the magazine. Like Howells, Scudder wrote many of the major reviews of American fiction himself, as he had during Aldrich's editorship. He also wrote most of the monthly four to seven small-print pages of the "Comment on Books," which briefly reviewed thirty to forty books each month.

Despite Scudder's position as Houghton Mifflin's trusted editor-in-chief, reviews in his *Atlantic* were less influenced by either business or personal considerations than notices under any of his predecessors. Houghton, in fact, took Scudder to task for his frank criticism of the firm's books, but Scudder simply reassured himself, "Surely in every case I spoke the truth" (Diary, 30 Dec. 1890). When both Lafcadio Hearn and Percival Lowell objected strenuously to *Atlantic* criticism of their essays on Japan, which had been serialized in the magazine and published by Houghton Mifflin, Scudder could truthfully reply: "I was disposed, as I always am, not to interfere with the reviewer" (to Lafcadio Hearn, 31 July 1895). If Houghton and some authors were irritated, at least the junior partner, George Mifflin, took pride in hearing that the *Atlantic* had a reputation for being impartially critical.

Aside from attempting scrupulous fairness in his own reviews, Scudder greatly expanded Aldrich's coterie of reviewers, mainly Woodberry and H. P. Waters, to include Sophia Kirk on French literature, Countess Lida Krockow on German, and Frederick Jackson Turner on history. When Norman Hapgood, a young proponent of urban realism, asked for reviewing work, Scudder declined, commenting, "You may be incredulous, but we have to avoid too inconsistent a literary tone in the magazine" (19 Sept. 1894). But he solicited reviews from a range of exceptional younger writers, including George Santayana on philosophy, Charles T. Copeland and Charles Minor Thompson on fiction, William Vaughn Moody and Mark Howe on poetry ("the slaughter of the innocents"), and Woodrow Wilson on politics. Nor did he steer books toward sympathetic reviewers as consistently as his predecessors had done. "Tis always a toss-up," he wrote Wilson, "whether you will get a friend or an enemy to review the book. On the whole, I rather trust a conscientious enemy when it is a matter of politics" (1 Feb. 1891).

Among Scudder's literary reviewers there was a definable consensus, close to the moderate, middle-class realism articulated by Howells in the seventies, supported by Scudder himself in the eighties, and now embodied in the forty-two full-length reviews he wrote as editor. Typified by his enthusiastic 1890 reviews of Howells's

Hazard of New Fortunes and James's *Tragic Muse*, Scudder advocated an ethical but nondidactic realism that dramatized a large, vivid, morally significant segment of contemporary social life. He disliked Zolaesque determinism for both its moral cynicism and its crude ugliness. He also criticized "microscopic fiction" that focused on excessive detail, or "photographic" realism that merely recorded surfaces without aesthetic selection or ethical interpretation. On the other hand he ridiculed the exotic improbabilities and fatuous moral formulas of popular romance.

Responding to the glowing review of *Hazard*, Howells wrote, "I expect you yet to join me in defiling the tomb of Scott and plucking all the fathers of romance by the beard" (27 Mar. 1890). But Scudder was too attached to traditional culture to relish plucking beards. In literature as in politics, he opposed the monopoly of party faction. First-rate literature, he maintained, could be and had been written in many modes, a fact that the realists seemed to deny. As Howells and his younger disciples asserted an increasingly gritty and dogmatic realism during the nineties, Scudder and his reviewers began raising questions and speaking for literary pluralism. In reviewing the realist manifestos in Howells's *Criticism and Fiction* and particularly Garland's *Crumbling Idols*, they explicitly agreed with the basic doctrines of realism set forth but regretted what they felt were an aggressively polemical tone and an arrogantly easy dismissal of all literature—past, present, and future—not reflecting the dogmas of realism. No *Atlantic* reviewer publicly accused Howells of a deficiency of traditional literary culture, though Henry James had privately. The younger realists, however, were accused of being arrogantly ignorant of the full Western literary tradition and therefore unable to see their work as one useful mode, but neither the only one of value nor the end of literary evolution.[4]

Atlantic reviews of fiction during the nineties were essentially sympathetic to several forms of literary realism. This sympathy, however, was often qualified by a defense of literature in more traditional modes and resistance to the edging of realism toward deterministic naturalism. Among the older generation of realists, Twain was hailed as "the Lincoln of our literature," the best type of the American. In "Mark Twain as an Interpreter of the American Character" (Apr. 1897), Charles Minor Thompson affirmed that the great "virtues of common sense and manliness" which Twain taught were far more important than refinement. But he regretted Twain's anti-intellectual antagonism to traditional culture. Scudder had previously called James the master workman of the novel and now pronounced him also "the consummate artist in miniature story telling in this generation" who had "an intimate ... [and] inexhaustible vein of criticism of life" ("A Few Story Tellers Old and New," Nov. 1893, 695–96). Still, he worried that James was becoming too absorbed in minute psychological dissection.

As in previous *Atlantic* criticism, Whitman was given substantial but qualified praise. On Whitman's death in 1892, Scudder wrote that his poetry contained "a tremendous energy in the throbbing lines" and was "best precisely in those passages which celebrate man in his most sensuous organism." But Scudder characteristically concluded that this poetry of sensuality and vibrant egotism, despite its wonderful energy, was of a lesser stature in the universal moral order than poetry celebrating the "profounder law" of restraint and self-forgetfulness ("Walt Whitman," June 1892, 831–35). W. C. Merwin regretted that Whitman's lack of aesthetic discipline made his work extremely uneven but praised him as "the only author ... who has perceived what democracy really means and who has appreciated the beauty and heroism which are found in the daily lives of the common people" ("Millet and Walt Whitman," May 1897, 719). For both Scudder and Merwin, traditional aesthetic principles limited but did not prevent an appreciation of Whitman's emotional power and democratic realism.

Hamlin Garland accused the New York and Boston literary establishments of being a killing frost that withered the best and freshest writing of the younger realists in the nineties (Brooks, *Indian Summer* 505). Literary history has generally accepted his judgment, but *Atlantic* criticism, for its part, does not bear him out. Scudder often had younger reviewers covering the younger writers, and they were generally sympathetic, though not uncritical. Scudder encouraged Charles M. Thompson to do a full article on Garland, a very unusual tribute for a young writer. Thompson mildly ridiculed Garland for an overconfident arrogance in dismissing the entire literary past as worthless and for "manifest deficiencies in his knowledge and taste," but called him "the freshest figure in contemporary literature," one who possessed "courage, persistence, ability," and a "strong grip ... upon the realities of certain phases of American life" ("Hamlin Garland," Dec. 1895, 840–44). The *Atlantic* reviewer of Garland's *Prairie Songs* quipped that they, like much turn-of-the-century literature, seemed to promote melancholia as "the national disease of the future," but praised them as genuine, vivid, and impressive and implied their clear superiority to the fraudulent, undergraduate bohemianism of Carman and Hovey ("Major and Minor Bards," Mar. 1895, 411–12). Similarly, in reviewing Garland's prose, Charles Copeland regretted that he seemed "married to Russian despair and French realism" but emphasized that Garland's naturalistic vision of human beings trapped and brutalized by their environment captured a grim truth and was "a crude force that will have to be reckoned with in our literature" ("The Short Story," Feb. 1892, 266). While the *Atlantic* did not promote Garland with as little qualification as Howells at *Harper's*, its reception of his work was no blighting frost. From the evidence of the *Atlantic*, Garland's well-publicized claim of literary persecution seems as self-dramatizing and distorted as Whitman's.

Charles Copeland's praise in superlatives of Hardy's great work of naturalism, *Tess of the D'Urbervilles*, demonstrated that the magazine's reviewing criteria were not circumscribed either by a narrow literary ideology or by genteel prudery. Copeland judged *Tess* a masterpiece of genuine tragedy and called emphatically for restoration of the controversial chapter about Tess with her dying child, bowdlerized from the American edition ("Recent American and English Fiction," May 1892, 697).

Further evidence that Scudder's *Atlantic* was essentially sympathetic to realism abounded. Scudder praised Mary E. Wilkins, as well as Sarah Orne Jewett, for combining close scientific observation with the "anterior vision" of "the mind behind the eye," which interprets what is accurately observed ("The New England Story," June 1891, 850). He further praised Jewett for examining immigrant Irish as well as Yankee lives. He also praised Kate Chopin, whose first book of short stories, *Bayou Folk*, he had accepted for publication, calling her a "genuine and delightful addition" to American literature. At times, he observed prophetically, she "strikes a passionate note ... which ... impress[es] one as characteristic of power awaiting opportunity" ("Recent Fiction," Apr. 1894, 559). Even the crusty Norton, who by the nineties was famous for lamenting the terminal decline of virtually everything, wrote extravagant praise of Kipling's manifesto of poetic realism, *Barrack Room Ballads*. Acknowledging that "the realists of yesterday and to-day are the legitimate offspring of the romanticists and idealists of the mid-century," he praised Kipling for having "the same imaginative sympathy with all varieties of life, the same sense of the moral significance of life even in its crudest, coarsest ... aspects" ("The Poetry of Rudyard Kipling," Jan. 1897, 112).

Scudder's selection of fiction followed the general pattern of the *Atlantic*'s literary criticism but was sometimes narrowed by his anxieties about cost, morality, and popularity. The core was an ethical, middle-class, frequently regional realism, written with increasing frequency by women. But romance and the historical novel, now coming back into vogue, were represented, as was the relatively unpopular Jamesian psychological character study. Scudder found this literary pluralism a healthy "emancipation from the tyranny of fashion and prevailing schools" ("A Few Story Tellers Old and New," Nov. 1893, 695). Fiction composed about a third of Scudder's *Atlantic*, as it had for his predecessors. Typically, he ran one serial and two stories in a number. Scudder's selections lacked the brilliance of risk and innovation but included works still read today and a few more that deserve to be.

With two important exceptions, Scudder's serials were not a distinguished lot, a situation caused as much by economics as by editorial timidity. Particularly in his early years, Scudder solicited widely for serial novels, as for other work, but was often frustrated by authors' commitments to other publishers, most of whom paid higher rates. Twain was politely evasive; Scudder knew he had a novel in the works, but Twain knew he could get double the money elsewhere. Howells was tied by an exclusive contract to Harper Brothers, who paid $10,000 per year for rights to his entire literary production and $3,000 for his monthly "Editor's Study" column (Ballou 302; Lynn 283). Scudder sounded out Mary E. Wilkins, but she too was under contract with Alden and Howells at *Harper's*. Bellamy was busy founding the Nationalist party to embody the socialist utopianism of his *Looking Backward* (1888). Scudder spent two days at Northampton at Cable's request consulting with the author on his novel *John March, Southerner*. Although Cable's usual publisher, Gilder of the *Century*, had rejected it for its "innate disagreeableness," Scudder hoped to serialize it, but he lost it to *Scribner's* (John 164). Scudder actively tried, then, to publish the mainstream realism of Howells, Twain, Wilkins, and Cable but was unable to meet the competition.

Hard-pressed to find a serial for 1891, Scudder had turned to Frank Stockton, whose earliest work he had accepted and encouraged while editing the *Riverside Magazine*. Stockton's popularity had soared since, but fame, while not impairing his wit, seemed sometimes to have made his work thinner and more formulaic. Stockton demanded $5,000 for his serial, "The House of Martha," and Houghton reluctantly agreed to pay it, asking that the price not be disclosed, since it was about twenty-one dollars a page, beyond the *Atlantic*'s top rate. Scudder privately worried whether the serial was worth it. When Stockton's next offering came in, Scudder found it downright "flat, stale, and unprofitable" and declined not only to serialize it but to publish it at all, even though he and MacGregor Jenkins, the firm's new promotion man, knew that with Stockton's name and a "catching title" it would sell (Scudder to Houghton, 7 Mar. 1893).

While he refused to publish fiction he felt was empty, though briefly profitable, Scudder could not afford to ignore the issue of popularity. Mifflin and other company executives were convinced that James's *Tragic Muse*, which had dragged on through seventeen installments and sold only 897 copies during its first year in book form, had hurt the magazine (Ballou 448). Scudder, slowly gaining readers but still losing money, had to consult current taste. And current taste during the nineties, partly in reaction against insurgent naturalism and other literature seen as morbid, had brought historical romance back into vogue, epitomized by *Quo Vadis*, which the *Atlantic* had ridiculed for the impossible virtue of its Christians. Scudder deprecated the lightness of the genre but appreciated the re-creation of history and the vigorous plots, when they did not defy credibility.

Scudder also had difficulty competing for the most popular authors of romance. Marion Crawford, alienated by Aldrich's seemingly arbitrary rejection of *Zoroaster*, had formed a connection with the Macmillan Company, whose penthouse he now used during the New York social season. But needing considerable money to finance his life as an international society figure and his palatial Roman establishment, he offered Scudder American serial rights to one of his facile and entertaining romances, to run simultaneous with British serialization. Scudder ran Crawford's *Don Orsino*, but Houghton Mifflin lost the book rights to Macmillan; since the publishers did not like to serialize books published by other houses, Scudder got no further serials from Crawford.

Scudder did, however, serialize Mary Hartwood Catherwood's historical novels of early French settlements in Illinois, Paul Leichester Ford's *Story of an Untold Love*, and a Revolutionary War romance by a young Canadian novelist Gilbert Parker. Parker had clearly identified a market niche that would grow during the decade among readers in genteel revolt against naturalism. His serial, he promised, would present "a strong, wholesome, delightful loving braggart and soldier who had the love of two women and did honorably by both. . . . The story will be a kind of protest against . . . morbid matter" (to Scudder, 2 June n.y.). Scudder was certainly aware, and Page would be more aware, that such fiction, with its romantic treatment of love and war, lack of disturbing controversy, and swashbuckling action, could appeal not only to the traditional novel-reading constituency of women but also to men, who were beginning to read fiction again under the influence of strenuously masculine authors such as Robert Louis Stevenson and Kipling.

In selecting fiction, Scudder was concerned with, and sometimes constrained by, not only budget and audience appeal but also his own ethics. Scudder disliked didacticism in fiction as much as Howells had, and he praised Howells for balancing his ethical and aesthetic lenses. He also felt that readers had grown more aesthetically sophisticated: "Whereas once we demanded a clean completion of the whole business, now we have discovered an artistic satisfaction in an ending which was in effect a last statement of the dominant motif of the work" (Diary, 25 Feb. 1891). Still, aesthetic sophistication did not excuse moral equivocation, either for his public or for himself.

In rejecting a novel dealing with "the relations between married men and married women," he wrote the author: "So sensitive has the better class of the public become [to the issue of adultery] that, with or without reason, both publishers and authors are held to a pretty strict account as regards the tendency of the fiction produced. Very fine distinctions are not made, but the question insistently put requires a categorical answer. Does or does not this book tell for restraint, conformity to a recognized social order, an unselfish sense of honor and high principle?" (to Mme von Teuffel, 12 Nov. 1895).

Scudder here was talking from both commercially motivated timidity and personal moral conviction. His distinctions were finer than the public's, as his praise for James, Howells, and others indicated, but the "high, pure literature" he wished to serve was unequivocally an ethical force. It reflected a world of meaningful moral choice, where those who chose the right might well not win prosperity or happiness but at least they would gain self-respect, the reader's approbation, and some sense of squaring themselves with the moral universe. Scudder rejected an essay for teaching a "skepticism which doubts the reality of a good purpose in the Universe" (Lillie Wyman to Scudder, 15 Aug. 1890). Similarly, he rejected fiction that embodied naturalistic determinism with its "hard, grinding fate" or the nihilism of writers such as Ambrose Bierce. Such fiction not only was aesthetically distasteful to him but, more important, denied the possibility of moral action and its consequences.

Conversely, some of the fiction Scudder published had clear ethical designs on the reader, though he consistently urged writers to eliminate didacticism. Margaret Deland, an intelligent woman who did not overestimate her modest literary gifts, had begun her career writing verses for Prang's Christmas cards. She achieved popular success in 1888 when Houghton accepted her mildly controversial indictment of Presbyterian dogma, *John Ward, Preacher*, despite Scudder's report that it contained "towering absurdity in the main theme" (Ballou 366). In submitting a serial novel, *Phillip and His Wife*, she noted to Scudder that she had "tried to avoid being didactic," but "the object of the book has been to say that absolute divorce is not justifiable," and although she had finished the draft, she still had several "points" to make in the revision (30 June 1894). Kate Douglas Wiggin, later author of *Rebecca of Sunnybrook Farm*, wrote: "I want everything about 'Mistress Mary's Garden' to make for virtue, but with a light touch. . . . I flatter myself I haven't the tract style, but I am awfully moral" (14 Oct. 1895). Elizabeth Stuart Phelps, whose novel *A Singular Life* Scudder accepted with reservations about the unrealistic unworldliness of its hero, wrote:

> I'm afraid you are not "swept away" by the story. You know, people expect a more or less religious story from me. Still, I thought there was "world" enough in it to carry the unsanctified reader. . . . If this should be my last book, I should not be sorry to end with Emmanuel Bayard [the hero]. I hope I am a better woman myself for the year spent in his company; and I cannot but venture to hope that some of my readers may be able to say as much.—I have just read "Tess" for the first time—a nightmare, a horror. And Trilby! Must an author touch pitch to be read now-a-days? Then I'll go unread, or dig potatoes for a living! (to Scudder, Sept. 1894)

Scudder winced a bit and asked these women to revise some of the didacticism and lapses of realism in their novels, as he asked P. L. Ford and Gilbert Parker to revise the improbabilities of their romantic plots. But he published them because he believed that literature should affirm a moral order and because that affirmation was commercially safe and attractive to his audience. The genteel requirement that literature should create a moral model found a haven in Scudder's *Atlantic*, despite his contention that a writer's ethical and aesthetic glasses must be focused together.

Scudder himself knew that most of his serials were second- or third-rate, limited as he was by both economic and ethical constraints. In fact, Scudder had begun to question the serial form. Short stories, he accurately predicted, would increasingly become the most popular form with magazine readers—often the shorter the better. "Their concentration of effect," he wrote Alice French, "is what readers are coming to like. A race of modern readers like ours educated upon . . . the scraps into which newspapers are degenerating is particularly caught with stories to be taken down with a gulp" (4 Aug. 1890, qtd. in Ballou 444). Paradoxically, however, he noted that while magazine readers seemed impatient with serials, book buyers consistently preferred novels to collections of short stories. In 1893, Scudder had accepted Kate Chopin's first book of short stories, *Bayou Folk*, and published several more of her stories in the *Atlantic* over the following years. But in 1897, when Chopin broached a second book of stories, Scudder noted that the slow sales of *Bayou Folk* did not encourage another collection. "Have you never felt moved to write a downright novel?" he asked. "The chance of success in such a case is much greater than with a collection of stories" (20 Jan. 1897). Whether or not this publishing advice influenced the writing of *The Awakening*, Scudder could hardly have foreseen or approved the "downright novel" Chopin did write in the following year.

Scudder continued serials, but he experimented too with reducing their length and loosening their narrative structure. He encouraged several novelists, including James, to write two- to six-number stories rather than full serials. Other authors such as Mary E. Wilkins and Sarah Orne Jewett, whose essential medium was the short story, he encouraged to string several stories together on a slender narrative thread that might suit both magazine and book audiences (Scudder to Mary E. Wilkins, 10 July 1891).

Scudder's thirty-year editorial relationship with Jewett reflects both his long and generous support for her form of subtle realism and his susceptibility to the increasing pressures of change in the literary marketplace during the 1890s, particularly the commercial resurgence of historical romance. "Of Miss Jewett's numerous relationships with editors," Richard Cary observes, "this was the longest and most fruitful" (Jewett, *Jewett Letters* 17).[5]

As editor of the *Riverside Magazine*, Scudder had accepted Sarah Orne Jewett's first story in 1869, just before Howells had accepted the twenty-year-old's first *Atlantic* piece. During the next twenty years, Scudder served as her frequent correspondent, literary adviser, and publishing advocate. He praised her highly to Dr. Holland when *Scribner's* took over the *Riverside*. She found in him an honest and unpatronizing source of literary and publishing advice. "The truth is," she wrote him, "I wish to talk with you about my writing. . . . I do know several literary people quite well, but whenever they read anything of mine, they look down from their pinnacles in a benignant way and think it very well done 'for her,' as the country people say" (13 July 1873, *Letters* 28). For two decades, Scudder accepted and edited all of her books, giving her extensive and useful suggestions for revising and particularly for developing.

By Scudder's editorship in 1890, however, Miss Jewett was no longer a young provincial aspirant but a literary personage in her own right. She was full-time companion to Annie Fields and a central member of the Charles Street salon, where literary reputations were brokered and Aldrich was the Duke to Annie Fields's queen. The patient, good-willed Scudder had managed to offend both of these literary potentates—Mrs. Fields by not valuing her work at the same rate as Miss Jewett's, and Aldrich by refusing to carry his job for yet another summer. Hearing that Scudder had replaced Aldrich as editor, Miss Jewett showed that she could be as patronizing toward her former adviser as others had been to her. "Mr. Scudder," she wrote to Aldrich, "is industrious and conscientious, but he cannot do what you have done for heaven hasn't sent the gift, and so we must not expect the performance" (23 July 1890). Aldrich had exercised his own gift in the Middle East by inventing Scudder jokes for the amusement of Mrs. Fields, Miss Jewett, and other salon habitués on his return. "Why is Horace Scudder greater than Moses?" ran an Aldrich riddle. Generations of Bostonians knew the answer: "Moses dried up the Red Sea once only; Scudder dries up the *Atlantic* monthly." Miss Jewett caught the spirit. "What a strange world this is," she would say, zigzagging her hand like a fish, "full of scudders and things" (Ballou 436–37).

Scudder solicited work from both Aldrich and Miss Jewett during his first week in office, but the response was a chilly silence. Three years later, thinking that the palpable animosity from Charles Street might have abated, he wrote Miss Jewett that she was, of course, always welcome in the *Atlantic*, and "I am at your door with a spoken invitation" (23 Jan. 1893). After considerable coaxing, she offered a story at the steep price of thirty-five dollars per thousand words, almost twice what she had received three years before, noting also that henceforth she would again send stories to the *Atlantic* but would publish in several magazines (Ballou 445). Scudder's reply reflects both his tactful frankness and good will:

> It is a disappointment to us that the *Atlantic* should no longer, as once, have practically the exclusive publication of your stories, but it is not difficult to see why this is no longer possible. The illustrated magazines . . . are like buyers in an auction room bidding hard against each other, and I for one am heartily glad that authors are thus in a position to command higher prices. The *Atlantic* is in a sense out of this keen competition. It has its own field and proposes to cultivate it carefully. As the representative, in purpose at any rate, of the most stable and pure American literature, it can ill afford to dispense with stories from you; it has no disposition to part company with an honored contributor. We shall pay your prices as laid down in your letter; the only difference will be that we must content ourselves with less frequent publication. This is our loss, for you can have no difficulty in placing your stories. (27 Sept. 1893)

During the nineties, Jewett did contribute to all four major quality magazines, but Scudder received the greater share and generally the best, and Houghton Mifflin continued to publish her books.

In the fall of 1895, Scudder, discontented with the quality of the magazine's recent serials and suspecting that perhaps the popularity of the long serial novel form was on the wane, planned to experiment with several short serials of three or four numbers in place of a twelve-month serial for 1896. He had earlier solicited Jewett for a single-number story for his showpiece January issue. Now, with this plan in mind, he asked, "Does your mind ever run to a three or four part story?" (25 Sept. 1895). Jewett, in response to Scudder's first request, had recently begun a story tentatively titled "The Last of the Captains," focused on the character of Captain Littlepage. But on receiving Scudder's request for a short serial, she apparently reconceived the story to focus not on the captain and his ghost story but instead on the more realistic narrative framework of a city woman taking lodging at Dunnett Landing with an earthy, self-sufficient herb woman named Almira Todd. In submitting the story in October, she promised to try to develop it into a series. Scudder responded enthusiastically: "I am very glad that you mean to work in the same vein. I do not see why you have not in the locality and in your herb woman excellent [threads] for hanging your tale" (21 Oct. 1895). Jewett continued to develop the autumnal world of Dunnett Landing and the character of her strong and generous "great-soul," Almira Todd, to weave the four installments that together composed *The Country of the Pointed Firs*, which ran in the *Atlantic* in 1896. Scudder's request for a brief serial comprising connected short stories had directly influenced the form of Jewett's best work.

Unfortunately, Scudder also contributed to the production of one of Jewett's poorest works and the misuse of her talent at its high point. By the end of the decade, the historical romance was enjoying mass-market popularity and providing an alternative for those genteel readers and publishers who found contemporary urban naturalism distasteful or depressing. In 1899, George Mifflin, now the firm's senior partner after the death of Henry Houghton in 1895, was jubilant at the phenomenal success of Mary Johnston's historical romance of colonial America, *To Have and to Hold*, and was irrepressibly enthusiastic about trying to repeat the performance. Scudder, at Mifflin's urging, suggested to Miss Jewett that she too make her bid for the larger audience and try her hand at a form completely alien to her experience and her skill. Jewett was tempted but initially declined, writing that "I am now pretty sure that it would not be wise for poor me to undertake such a piece of work ... and I have a great reluctance before the thought of turning aside into a new road" (Jewett, *Letters* 92). Scudder did not push further, but Charles Dudley Warner, championing romance against the defamations of the naturalists, did. So did Mifflin, who requested a conference with Miss Jewett to discuss her next work (Mifflin to Jewett, 26 Jan. 1899). The result was *The Tory Lover*, serialized in the *Atlantic* in 1901, a story that Jewett's biographer Richard Cary dismisses as a "polite and pallid" attempt "to suit the public appetite for flamboyant intrigue" (152). After reading *The Tory Lover*, Henry James wrote Jewett as tactfully as he could that he felt the historical novel "a fatally cheap genre" and begged her to "go back to the dear Country of the Pointed Firs" (Cary, *Jewett* 152). Clearly Scudder had done her a disservice in urging the project. Both his advice, prevalent among editors at the time, and her capitulation, in which she was joined by legions, reflected the increasing inroads that middlebrow commercial literature was making into high literary culture by the turn of the century.

Commercial pressures and the desire to accommodate a more popular audience also clearly influenced Scudder's editorial treatment of Henry James. His editorial relationship with James proved to be as thorny as that with Miss Jewett. As with Jewett, Scudder reached an accommodation with James that initiated at least one important work and influenced its form. But the *Atlantic*'s support for James, while still substantive, was unfortunately limited. The problems between Scudder and James were caused not by social malice or author's fees but by the escalating conflict between public taste and James's increasingly subtle and esoteric art. These tensions also reflected a waning of public taste for the serialization of novels.

In his reviews, Scudder had recognized James as a master craftsman of the highest order both in the novel and the short story. Scudder sometimes regretted the elaborate psychological "vivisection" that increasingly filled James's work and the corresponding loss of surface event, but he had no doubt that James represented the "permanent element" in American literature which the magazine should strongly support. He knew very well, however, that, with the exception of *Portrait of a Lady*, James's books with Houghton Mifflin had sold poorly. He knew too that both Howells and Aldrich had agonized unsuccessfully to contain James's "buxom muse," who had burgeoned beyond all constraints, and that George Mifflin had considered the record seventeen installments of *The Tragic Muse* so many millstones around the magazine's neck and was opposed to further major engagements with James (Ballou 626 n. 20). Scudder also was beginning to suspect that the serial novel in general was becoming less popular with magazine readers.

In 1890, with the *Muse* just finishing its marathon run, Scudder determined not to solicit a serial novel from James for 1891 but to request four short stories instead. "The new editor of the *Atlantic*," he assured the novelist, "values your work highly," and he sent as evidence his appreciative review of the *Muse* (20 Aug. 1890). James had been so deeply depressed by the indifference of editors, the public, and even reviewers to his work over the last five years that he had nearly determined to give up the novel form. Scudder's review, he wrote, "really brought tears to my eyes—giving me a luxurious sense of being understood, perceived, felt." To Scudder's proposal he replied, "I embrace it with enthusiasm.... I will do the very best I can for you; I appreciate the friendly quality of your hospitality" (Aug. 30, 1890).

Scudder's response to the first story James submitted quickly terminated James's "luxurious sense of being understood" at last by an American editor. In a lament echoed by thousands of James's later readers, Scudder complained that "The Pupil" lacked "vivid surface" incident. "I do not need to tell you how much I admire your best work," Scudder wrote. "The *Atlantic* has been hospitable and its doors are wide open to you now.... [But] frankly my reluctant judgment insists upon regarding the story as lacking in interest, in precision, and in effectiveness.... I hate to write all this, but I should hate myself still more if I didn't" (30 Oct. 1890).

James was stunned. He had not received a rejection from the *Atlantic* for twenty-five years, and although he was irritated by the rate of pay, he had considered it a safe haven. "I am very sorry to learn we have made such a bad start," he wrote. "I sent off the 'Pupil' with a quite serene conviction that I had done a distinctly happy thing." The rejection, James said, made him "nervous and insecure" about the other works he had intended to write on demand for Scudder (10 Nov. 1890).

Hearing nothing from James for several months, Scudder now began to feel nervous himself. "Why this death-like silence?" he wrote (19 Feb. 1891). James's response suggested both that the rejection had continued to rankle and that he had a very different idea than Scudder of an editor's rights.

> Your letter demands a frank answer. My "deathly silence" has been the result of the fact that ... I quite failed to see that you had treated me fairly: I could *not* see that it was a performance that the *Atlantic* ought to have declined—nor banish from my mind the reflection that the responsibility, in any case, as regards the readers of the magazine, the public, should, when it's a question of an old and honourable reputation, be left with the author himself. The editor, under such circumstances may fairly leave it to him.... These impressions were distinctly chilling as regards the production of further work. (4 Mar. 1891, *Letters* 3: 338)

Scudder, lamenting to his diary that James "did not take my rejection of his story with as much equanimity as I first thought," was conciliatory (13 Mar. 1891). He urged the author to contribute not only three more stories but also a personal remembrance of the recently deceased James Russell Lowell. All of these were duly written and accepted with polite gratitude, including assurance that even the punctuation would be "rigidly respected" (Scudder to James, 21 Oct. 1891).

During the next few years, James tried, with humiliating lack of success, to win in the theater the appreciative and lucrative audience his novels lacked. Scudder did not reestablish contact until 1895, when he again asked James for three short stories, each to run 12,000 to 15,000 words, around twenty pages, a length that was standard for the *Atlantic* but somewhat longer than most magazines encouraged. James's painful attempts to corset his muse to accommodate this conventional literary form, which he had earlier used with facility, cost him considerable personal agony and considerable irritation with Scudder. They also graphically reflected the growth of both his art and his final unwillingness to compromise it. "I will with pleasure," he wrote, "send you three short stories for the *Atlantic*—if you will permit me to remind you what I mean by 'short.' I can't, with the accumulated manner which is the result of my time of life, or maturity of means, treat a subject that I find interesting enough to be treated at all, in the brief compass of the usual snippit story of the usual magazine.... I will do my best in the three things you propose to confine myself to ... about 20 pages of the *Atlantic*, but I must ask you for a margin or an alternative if hard-pressed" (12 May 1895).

The first two "short" stories he began for Scudder eventually became novels. The day after writing Scudder, James found in his notebooks the seed of a story which he tentatively titled "The House Beautiful," about a refined mother dispossessed of a house filled with museum pieces by a philistine son and his boorish, vindictive bride. Within days the story bloomed luxuriantly in his imagination as a three-act drama, outgrowing the narrow limits of twenty pages. The same happened with his next idea, tentatively titled "The Awkward Age." After failing in what he bewailed to himself as a "tragic ... waste of labour" to contain them, he set the two pieces aside, certain that no magazine editor would take them and that he would have to "make terms for them in some other way, terms bad, terms sadding, at the best" (*Notebooks* 129–130). "The truth is," he lamented to Scudder, "I can't do the very little thing any more, and the process—the endeavor—is most expensive. ... However, you *shall* have your three stories and have them tiny. They are probably the last (*very* small ones) I shall ever do—so cherish them" (3 Sept. 1895, *Letters* 4: 18).

But James faced an economic truth that directly conflicted with his aesthetic impulse, the truth that he still needed income from magazines and that those few magazines that still asked him for anything were asking him only for single-number stories, generally of 10,000 words or less. On sitting down to make the next attempt for Scudder, he wrote: "I must now try to do the thing of 10,000 words (which there is *every* economic reason for my recovering and holding fast the trick of)" (*Notebooks* 130).

After agonizing for a month attempting with limited success a "ferocious compression" in the third story, "The Glasses," James wrote Scudder: "I am in much humiliation and distress, for though I am sending you something by this post, I am not sending you what will satisfy you. This is not, heaven knows, for want of time and labour—but because I *can't* alas, even after renewed heroic effort, keep within your limits of space. ... As I wrote you the other day, I find in my old age that I have too much manner and style, too great and invincible an instinct of completeness and of seeing things in all their relations, so that *development*, however squeezed down, becomes inevitable. ... I must candidly and cynically say that rather than worry over [the other promised stories] as I have worried over this, I shall have ... sadly to renounce the attempt. But I will *make* it once more" (4 Oct. 1895, *Letters* 4: 22).

Scudder, genuinely sympathetic to James's tribulations and worried about losing a contributor he valued highly, responded that he liked the story immensely and would publish it in a single number, despite its substantially exceeding twenty pages. He also invited James to rework one of the earlier stories into a three- or four-part serial instead of agonizing over two new stories. James expressed his "eternal gratitude" and proposed to work "The House Beautiful" into a short serial of 30,000–40,000 words. Inevitably, what was projected as a story of 12,000 words and evolved into a serial of 30,000, swelled to a novel of 70,000 words by the time Scudder ran it in seven installments in 1896 as "The Old Things" and Houghton Mifflin published it under the title *The Spoils of Poynton*. It was James's first novel since *The Tragic Muse* in 1890.

Scudder joked to his protégé Josephine Peabody that "Henry James can make his hero make a speech of 20,000 words by just looking in some peculiar way at the heroine" (10 Dec. 1896). Scudder, however, accommodated the expansion of *Spoils* at each step, praised the "delicate patterns" of the narrative, and declared himself "filled with admiration of the art which has so firmly defined conduct so evasive" (to James, 9 June 1896). James defended the expansion as necessitated by aesthetic integrity and expressed gratitude: "One has to do these things as one can (at least I have), and as one 'can' depends on the whole aesthetic life of one's donnée. I am greatly obliged to you for your patience and tolerance" (to Scudder, 21 May 1896).

Later recalling the evolution of *The Spoils of Poynton* in the preface to the New York edition, James wrote: "I found myself—as against a mere commercial austerity—beguiled and led on," while "the sole impression it made [on the editor], I woefully gathered, was that of length" (x). James's sensitivity had made his memory selective; Scudder had actively invited the novel and praised it sincerely. But as editorial negotiator between James and the public, he had indeed responded to a "commercial austerity" rooted in the resistance of even a relatively sophisticated reading public, as well as his employers, to James's later style. James, adept at defending his aesthetic integrity from editors since Howells's time, was right to resist the confinement of "magazineable" short fiction. His conflicts with Scudder and agonized failures at compression must have contributed to his return in 1896 to the novel form and liberation from the attempt at popularity which opened the way to the last great phase of his work. But at a time when most American and British magazine editors had virtually abandoned James for anything but very short potboilers, Scudder's solicitations had initiated at least five significant stories and a short novel. Both in a long series of reviews and in Houghton Mifflin's publishing councils, Scudder had also asserted that James was a consummate literary artist who had achieved permanent stature and deserved to be widely read. Unfortunately, his successors would not agree.

The *Atlantic*'s literary future must at times have looked dim to Scudder in contrast to the brilliance of its recent past, peopled by writers he knew and admired. James and Jewett, he hoped, would continue to be significant, if less frequent, contributors, despite the frictions. But Howells, Twain, and others of their generation were committed to larger magazines, and the last of the older generation that had given the *Atlantic* its early literary reputation were dying, duly memorialized in the magazine. Lowell departed in 1891. His friend and literary executor Norton proved that despite his detestation of commercial civilization, he himself had a head for business. Norton auctioned the literary remains to the New York magazines for prices up to $100 per page and book royalties up to an unheard-of 25 percent. Scudder considered himself lucky to get a fragment for a mere $50 a page. When Scudder requested a memorial essay, Norton righteously declined: "I do not propose to write anything about Mr. Lowell or to say in public anything.... I do not like this talking in public over one's dead friends" (to Scudder, Aug. 1891). But, perhaps to augment Lowell's estate, he swallowed his principles to accommodate a more lucrative offer by *Harper's Monthly* (Ballou 384–86).

Holmes, like Whittier, was proud of his early association with the "Maga" and maintained to the end a tribal loyalty that now seemed atavistic in the competitive national market that had supplanted regional publishing after the Civil War. Declining an offer of syndication from the most successful magazinist of the decade, he declared his staunch refusal to be "lured or McClured" (Lyon 123). After a brief hiatus, Holmes resumed the $4,000-a-year exclusive contract he had held with Houghton Mifflin since 1883 and in 1890 published a new series of essays entitled "Over the Teacups." But even the tough, alert old Yankee doctor's wits were clouding. Several times he spoke with Scudder about writing his autobiography. Scudder was delighted, until the doctor's son, Oliver Wendell Holmes, Jr., abruptly called to "forbid publication of any of his father's ramblings" (Ballou 390). In the gentlemanly spirit of those days, Scudder declared himself "unhesitatingly averse to acting . . . against the judgment of Dr. Holmes' family" and so forswore a valuable publishing property (to Oliver Wendell Holmes, Jr., 16 Sept. 1891).

With the two older generations fading, Scudder knew that the magazine needed to recruit a new generation. Since 1891, he had tried to hire a really capable young assistant, to add a new perspective and scout younger writers. Most of the reviewers he chose were young, including M. A. D. Howe, C. T. Copeland, G. L. Kittredge, Moody, Santayana, and Woodrow Wilson. But, as with other changes he knew were needed, he could not develop a full cadre of new writers himself. His daily work load overwhelmed him and discouraged developing new contacts. Adding to his discouragement was the plain fact that as soon as young writers such as Crane or Kipling gained some notoriety, they were commissioned not only by the older illustrated monthlies but increasingly by the immensely successful new upstarts such as *McClure's*, *Munsey's*, and *Cosmopolitan* at fees far beyond Scudder's means.

The difficulty not only of Scudder's *Atlantic* but of Houghton Mifflin's entire trade division in attracting and holding new writers in the rapidly expanding competition of the nineties was reflected in a letter from Mifflin to Scudder describing a plan to produce a new series of world classics in inexpensive formats partly to provide a sufficient volume of material to keep the company's Riverside

Press operating at capacity. Mifflin noted that this project would relieve the editorial staff "of the interminable scramble for new authors at extortionate prices." "Of course," he added, "we should not relax for a moment our efforts to secure new men and the magazine, if handled with vigor, should help us. It is simply that our sole reliance would not be upon the new, but upon the old men who by the verdict of time have been pronounced as standard writers" (7 Feb. 1898).

Mifflin's letter implies that the house, and to an extent the magazine, were forced into a high-culture niche relying on a more traditional, less popular canon because they could not compete economically for new authors and more current material. This condition had been evolving since the seventies. But another fundamental reason why the *Atlantic* failed to draw large numbers of new writers was that both Scudder, nearing sixty, and his magazine, nearing forty, possessed the virtues and limitations of late middle age. Both had been shaped by the New England culture that had spoken for conscience in politics, a specifically American literature, and the engagement of literature and writers in American life. Both still advocated these things but were cautious about new forms, applications, or extensions of them. Neither the editor nor his magazine was given to the dour, reactionary fin-de-siècle disillusion of Henry Adams or Barrett Wendell. Both were balanced in judgment and humanely tolerant, but they lacked a youthful enthusiasm for new causes and a taste for risk.

This benign, balanced, middle-aged conservatism was evident in Scudder's treatment of several younger writers of fiction and poetry, including Charles Chesnutt, Owen Wister, and Josephine Preston Peabody. Chesnutt, who had published three tales in Aldrich's *Atlantic*, wrote Houghton Mifflin in 1891 proposing publication of a book of short stories. Identifying himself for the first time as a black writer, he claimed that the book would be "the first contribution by an American of acknowledged African descent to purely imaginative literature" and the first treatment of black characters "from a closely sympathetic standpoint" (to Houghton Mifflin, summer 1891, Chesnutt 68–69). Scudder was complimentary and reaffirmed Houghton Mifflin's interest in Chesnutt's fiction but counseled waiting while developing a reputation through publishing more stories. "The place you have won," he wrote, "is an honorable one, yet as good as your work is, we question whether it has secured for you so general a recognition that a book would be at once welcomed by a large enough number to insure success" (27 Oct. 1891).

Seven years later Scudder, at the instigation of Walter Page and probably of Francis Garrison, finally endorsed publishing a book of Chesnutt's "conjur tales," local color plantation stories that reflected the cruelties of slavery, the cleverness of black survivors, and the sentimental misperceptions of whites. By that time, however, Chesnutt's interest had shifted from plantation stories to contemporary analyses of "the color line." Here again, Scudder proved timid and resistant to risk, asking postponement of a volume of "color-line" stories and predicting failure for

Chesnutt's novel "Rena Walden" (to Chesnutt, 16 Feb. 1899). A year later, Houghton Mifflin published not only *The Wife of His Youth and Other Stories of the Color Line* but also "Rena Walden," now retitled *The House behind the Cedars*, after Chesnutt had made extensive changes suggested by Scudder and others. Scudder was part of the council that made these decisions, but the real force behind these publications was again the southern progressive Walter Page, assisted by Garrison and possibly also by Bliss Perry, Page's eventual successor in the *Atlantic* chair.

Scudder's resistance to the new was also reflected in his failure to perceive and tap the real source of literary energy in the young Owen Wister. At the very beginning of his career, Wister, fired with enthusiasm for depicting western ranch life in at least a semirealistic way, submitted a story. Scudder declined it but encouraged Wister to write an essay on another topic in which he had claimed some expertise: light opera. Wister agreed. In the meantime, however, Alden of *Harper's Monthly* accepted two of Wister's stories and commissioned eight more. "They want eight stories," Wister wrote, "and their terms are so favorable to name and fame and also so liberal to a beginner that though these stories are not the kind of thing I want to do in fiction—too much adventure and too little study of character—it would have been foolish to stick at that" (to Scudder n.d.). Wister found it impossible to write on light opera when his mind and heart were absorbed in recording the immense vitality of cavalry and cowboy. Scudder, through a middle-aged lack of enthusiasm for the new, lost a young writer who would have contributed energy and variety, and Wister learned to write in a more superficial and popular style than Scudder would have demanded of him.

In his treatment of poetry, as in fiction and editorial method, Scudder tried earnestly but often with little success to understand and recognize new developments among the young. He was no reactionary like Aldrich. He advised Stedman, working for Houghton Mifflin on an anthology of American poetry, to include generous selections of young contemporaries. Poetry reviews in his *Atlantic* were written by younger reviewers, usually Howe, and reflected full awareness of the deficiencies of late Victorian verse. "It is the day of the Minor Bard," the *Atlantic* declared satirically, "whose mission is the depiction of transitory moods," particularly "that distinct quality of sadness which we are all wont to recognize as a note of our decadent century" ("Major and Minor Bards," Mar. 1895, 407). Lowell's *Last Poems* were judged to represent "an age and ... class which have passed away" and received less attention than Crane's *Black Riders*, which was criticized for its blasphemy but praised for its cleverness, freshness, spareness, and compact energy ("Six Books of Verse," Feb. 1896). Santayana's *Sonnets* had "a clear, cold beauty of form," and Garland was praised for a gritty integrity ("Major and Minor Bards," Mar. 1895).

Although Scudder believed that these new writers and forms deserved serious attention, he could not personally be enthusiastic enough about the new modes to encourage much experimentation in the *Atlantic*. He did publish early works, many of which Aldrich would have declined, by Lizette Reese, Edward Markham, Santayana, and Harriet Monroe, who were moving toward greater concreteness and unsentimental emotional directness. He preferred simplicity and directness, "good wheat bread," to elaborate elegance (to J. Peabody, 14 Feb. 1894). But the radical and disturbing newness of Crane or Garland did not appear, while *Atlantic* readers were too often fed what one reviewer called "a dinner of crumbs" in the often clever but forgettable wisps of magazine verse by middle-aged academicians such as Frank Dempster Sherman, Clinton Scollard, and Father John Tabb ("Major and Minor Bards," Mar. 1895, 413). And when Scudder had the opportunity to advise a young poet, Josephine Preston Peabody, his advice emphasized Victorian norms of beauty, sentiment, and form.

Josephine Peabody was a shy, beautiful, impoverished, and fatherless girl of nineteen when Scudder rejected her first poem. Scudder found her "bewitchingly pretty," touched by a "wistful" air that suggested "some sad tragedy" (Diary, 12 and 20 Apr. 1897). His feeling for her combined chaste infatuation with affectionate paternal concern. He raised scholarship money to send her to Radcliffe, invited her to visit often, acted as her advocate with publishers, and wrote copious letters of advice, often leavened by amusing flights of fancy. Not all his advice was conservative. He told her that her worst fault was imitation, that she must develop her own instincts and "settle these concerns for yourself . . . not merely be guided by an older friend" (Nov. 1893 and 21 Aug. 1896). But he criticized meters he found unmusical or harsh, deplored tones that seemed "hysterical" in emotional intensity, and hoped Josephine was not a Symbolist or Impressionist. He urged her to "speak out of a love of pure and beautiful things in nature" and published her more conventional work for its "fresh beauty." "My dear Josephine," he wrote, "you have given me a great deal of pleasure in the few years I have known you. I do not know if fame, ever so little, will follow . . . , but . . . many who read your verses will feel a pure air blowing across their minds" (1 Jan. 1894; 14 Feb. 1894; n.d. 1897). Scudder generously and genuinely wanted to encourage Josephine Peabody's growth as a new voice in poetry, and his advocacy really created her career. But he was so attached to the older ideas of beauty, form, and sentiment that most of his advice was of little help, and some may have been damaging to the extent it was heeded.

Scudder, then, saw the older writers falling away from the *Atlantic* and tried to develop new ones. The early advice and generous support he gave to Woodrow Wilson and Mark Howe, among others, were significant in their careers. But his advice to Chesnutt, Wister, and Peabody shows that while he encouraged them and published some of their works, his instincts were constraining rather than generative. With the benign voice of late middle age, he spoke for caution rather than innovation.

Scudder recognized a need to move the magazine toward the twentieth century but was personally attached to the nineteenth-century past. This ambivalence was epitomized in his relationship with his assistant and successor, Walter Hines Page. After Howe's resignation in March 1895 because of his chronic eye problems, the badly overburdened Scudder was again in the market for "a competent shoulder" onto which to shift part of the load. In the meantime, the aging Henry Oscar Houghton, Scudder's employer for nearly thirty years, was giving over active direction of the house to his younger partner, George Mifflin. Scudder, through some trying times, had been able to persuade Houghton to take the long view of the *Atlantic*. The magazine, he argued, justified its modest financial losses. It brought prestige to the house, drew writers, supported them with additional income, advertised the firm's list, and created a sophisticated reading public for Houghton Mifflin books and authors.

Mifflin also understood this logic, but he was less patient than Houghton and more inclined to insist on the logic of the bottom line: that each element of the firm, even each book published, justify itself in terms of cash return. By 1895, he had begun thinking of the *Atlantic* as a "problem" requiring solution. Despite the long, severe recession following the panic of 1893, Scudder had prevented further erosion, slightly increasing circulation from about 10,000 in 1890 to more than 12,500 in 1895, while making a small profit in 1893, and otherwise holding losses under $10,000 a year (*American Newspaper Annual* 1895, 1183; Ballou 450). But small losses were not a solution, and while Scudder was looking for an assistant with sound literary judgment to draw new authors, both he and Mifflin were looking also for a younger man who knew the current trends in the magazine trade and would be an energetic publicist. Inquiries in New York and a recommendation from Scudder's young protégé Woodrow Wilson led them to Walter Hines Page, who at forty had just resigned as editor of the polemical monthly the *Forum* after having raised its circulation from negligible to 30,000 and turned an annual loss of $20,000 into a profit (Ballou 450).

Mifflin was enthusiastic but left the decision mainly to Scudder. Scudder approvingly found Page "democratic, cosmopolitan, and ambitious." His force of personality and sincerity were obvious, but Scudder correctly suspected he might be impulsive. He liked Page's Johns Hopkins background in classics but worried whether his long experience as a newspaper reporter and editor before joining the *Forum* had "lowered his standard" (Diary, 16 and 26 July 1895). Page was obviously energetic, well trained in modern publishing, and progressive in his views. But was he suited to the *Atlantic* and its traditions? After visiting Page's home, Scudder concluded: "The more I saw of him, the more sure I felt of the man, sure of his integrity, of his adaptability to our ends, of a cordial relation between us" (Diary, 2 Aug. 1895). Over the next four years, Scudder and the *Atlantic* were to adapt to the strong-willed Page as much as he to them, and while the relationship continued respectful, even cordial, it was often strained by a sharp difference in editorial values. The editorial tension between them in many ways marked the fault line between nineteenth- and twentieth-century publishing.

Page began in September 1895, assigned to work with Scudder on both the *Atlantic* and the general book publications. This arrangement would continue Houghton's concept of the close reciprocation between the two and ensure Scudder's direct supervision, on which Mifflin insisted. Scudder thought Page's initial salary should be $3,000, to be increased to $5,000 when Scudder took his long-planned sabbatical. But Page immediately manifested his powerful personality by demanding $5,000, only $1,000 less than Scudder, and he proceeded with characteristic energy to justify it.

During Page's first year, Scudder was delighted with the lightening of his daily load and with Page's energetic, innovative editorial style. He began to think seriously of his European sabbatical. Page's work, however, also stirred in Scudder a disturbing ambivalence not only about Page but also about his own editing. Page had more taste for current affairs controversy than Scudder and proposed to delegate more detail work to his assistants, freeing himself to solicit and develop papers on these topics. Scudder responded that his own temperament and ideal for the *Atlantic* required considerable detail work with manuscripts and that Page should not expect a lot of free time simply to think and plan. But privately he wondered if Page was not right. "Curious it is," he wrote privately, "that I used to have the same theory and propound it to Mr. Houghton. Have I become the subject of circumstance? Do I live only from day to day?" (Diary, 21 Apr. 1896).

Scudder, then, began not only to see clear differences between himself and Page but also, at times, to feel that the *Atlantic* might need the energy and vision of the younger man, even though there was a danger of his debasing its tone from the literary to the journalistic. At moments of painful honesty, he realized that his own reticent temperament, his scholarly inclinations, and Houghton's combining the editorship of the *Atlantic* with the trade books had buried him in detail and made him less able to shape the magazine and less responsive to current affairs than he had originally intended to be. In 1894, he had admitted to Houghton that "the first year I took hold of [the *Atlantic*], I made it my most important work . . . [but now] the magazine suffers for lack of concentration on my part" and requires "something more of knocking about among men than one so necessarily tied to his desk as I can hope for" (3 Sept. 1894).

When Houghton died the week that Page began work, Scudder noted in his diary that Houghton "was a large-minded man and very far-sighted" (1 Sept. 1895). The patient Scudder now found himself working closely with two younger men impatient for immediate results. Page, he felt, had "a smoldering volcano in him," though Scudder acknowledged frankly that perhaps he himself and the firm needed more of this impatient spirit (Diary, 26 Apr. 1896). He also admired the "splendid vim" with which Mifflin took hold and pushed the business side of the magazine. Scudder, aware of trends in magazine publishing, had long tried to persuade Houghton to bolster circulation and advertising by hiring full-time publicists. Mifflin had responded by hiring the effective MacGregor Jenkins and later an assistant, William B. Parker, to promote the magazine as well as trade books. "There is no time within the last twenty years," Scudder told Page, "that the *Atlantic* might not have been commercially successful if [Mifflin's] publishing energy had been brought to the fore" (2 Nov. 1897). But Mifflin and Page's youthful impatience for results and the rise of the promotion managers, which Scudder pragmatically supported, had distinct costs to his cultural values. "I cannot resist the feeling," he noted in his diary, "that a more commercial spirit is stealing over the minds of the men [in the pow-wow], that there is a more insistent reference of all questions to the money standard. . . . [E]ach enterprise . . . must justify itself" (20 Apr. 1897).

In the spring of 1896, both Page and Mifflin became exercised over the magazine's failure to gain circulation and its continuing loss of about $10,000 a year. Scudder was defensive about his own performance and apprehensive about Page's literary values. But, as his diary revealed, he was generously ready to give the younger man scope to try his hand at the *Atlantic* problem:

> Page came to me consumed with zeal for bringing up the circulation. He accomplished that feat for the *Forum* and as I brought him here largely for that reason, I do not see why I should not take the logical step and put the fortunes of the magazine largely, indeed so far as shaping goes quite unreservedly, into his hands. I cannot resist the feeling that the magazine as it stands is all right and that the lifting power should be in the business management, but I cannot simply make Page business manager with Jenkins as his aide. So though I foresee something of a change of character in the magazine, I have come to the conclusion to turn over the initiative to Page, working with him and doing my best to preserve the literary character of the magazine. It is a painful surrender, but . . . I can surely keep Page from warping the *Atlantic* into a *Forum*. . . . O my poor *Atlantic*. (Diary, 27 Apr. 1896)

Mifflin insisted that he had confidence in Scudder's judgment and that Scudder should remain in charge. But Scudder arranged that beginning in July 1896, Page was to take the initiative in soliciting manuscripts and shaping the magazine while Scudder sifted volunteer matter and worked on book manuscripts (Diary, 7 May 1896). With both relief at the easing of his load and anxiety about the magazine, Scudder began planning his sabbatical and thinking of the direction of his own life apart from work. On the eve of his departure in June 1897 for a year in Europe, he wrote: "I hope to meet a few people, but secretly I hope somewhere on the journey to meet myself. I have been too closely occupied for a long time to give more than a passing nod to myself, and I am suspicious our acquaintance is becoming somewhat distant" (Diary, 13 June 1897).

Still nominally the *Atlantic*'s editor and deeply concerned with its well-being, Scudder kept up a volley of advice to Page both before and during his year in Europe. "When I receive a number," he wrote, "there is a tight pull at my heart strings and I go about for a day or two with an uncomfortable feeling of being lost in Europe" (9 Sept. 1897). But as his sabbatical waned and his sixtieth birthday neared, he dreaded the prospect of taking up routine office work again. Immediately on returning in July 1898, he submitted his resignation from the magazine. He could, he felt, best serve both the firm and the cause of literature by devoting himself to editing the trade books and writing the biography of Lowell to which he had committed himself. This semischolarly making of books was the work for which he was best fitted. The magazine he would give over to Page's comparative youth and energy.

On his resignation, Scudder wrote in his diary:

> It was inevitable and deep down in my mind I accept it with a certain degree of satisfaction. Nevertheless, I cannot give up the charge without real regret. I had an ideal for the magazine which I see is not the same as Page's. I think his conception of its promise may bring in more subscribers and make it more prosperous, even if at present the cost is increased, but I think it means a disturbance of the fine nature of the magazine, an undue emphasis on the more aggressive function, an ignoring of the repose which belongs to high literature. I think, moreover, that America needs as never before an insistence on the high ideals of literature and life. I do not for a minute think Page indifferent much less hostile to all this, but . . . his conduct of the magazine has lacked steadfastness and fineness of aim. . . . All of this sounds possibly hypercritical, but I am sensitive about the *Atlantic*; it is in the nature of a trust with me. (5 July 1898)

More like his nineteenth-century predecessors than his twentieth-century successors, Scudder had held for the magazine an ideal of high literary culture, both past and present. Like the *Atlantic*'s founders, he saw this literary culture as a central source of humanistic and ethical values. Like Lowell, whose portrait hung behind his desk and whose biography he would write, he took as his mission the propagation of that culture and those values, and he would not knowingly compromise his mission to buy the magazine's prosperity.

Scudder sought to preserve a place in contemporary life for the literary past, and his *Atlantic* contained not only memorials to the New England writers earlier associated with the magazine but also discussions of the authors and major texts of Western humanism. In fact, his magazine was perhaps the last to publish serious essays on the Greek and Roman writers for a nonscholarly audience. More important, his proposals to incorporate the American "classics" into the educational curriculum reflected his belief in the ethical and social value of an explicitly American literary tradition.

Scudder was attached to the literary past, but his main concern had been with contemporary literature. He had committed nearly half of his magazine to fiction and reviews, a percentage that Page would cut sharply. His aesthetic judgment had been formed in the early years of realism during the seventies, but unlike Howells's and James's aesthetic ideas, his failed to continue evolving. He was not bold in taking risk. The intensity of his conviction that literature had a moral as well as aesthetic purpose made him favor works reflecting a world of moral choice and consequence and reject works portraying a brutal environmental determinism. The moderate conservatism of his own aesthetic ideals rendered him, unlike Howells, largely unable to bring much new literature to birth among the younger writers of the nineties.

Scudder's reviews of the fiction of Howells, James, Jewett and others, however, had been very consistently supportive even at times when many others were highly critical of Howells's politics or James's style. In his editorial handling of both James and Jewett as contributors, he allowed himself in at least one instance to be the instrument of market conditions detrimental to their art. But despite his idealism, Scudder was fully conscious of the financial context of his work, and his practice throughout his lifetime was to moderate commercial pressures to the greatest extent possible. His early encouragement and, with a single major exception, his advice over a quarter-century had served Jewett well. Despite tensions, he was virtually the last American magazine editor to initiate work by Henry James through active solicitation.

Atlantic reviewing, led by Scudder himself, assisted by a distinguished group of young critics, remained strong, as did the essay. In fact, James, lamenting a decline in the quality of American magazines, commented publicly that "the *Atlantic* remains with a distinction all its own, practically the single refuge of the essay and the literary portrait.... In the *Atlantic*, the book lover, the student, and the painter standing on his own feet continue to have room to turn around" ("American Letter" 678). Other commentators reaffirmed James's impression that Scudder's *Atlantic* retained an intellectual integrity and substance lacking in other periodicals. While the *Nation* found the new *Scribner's* "a miracle of bubble blowing," it spoke of the *Atlantic*'s "old fashioned solidity of contents" and found it "heavily packed with serious matter" (*Nation*, 7 May 1891, 381; 8 Jan. 1891, 33; 3 Aug. 1893, 85). In 1895, it judged the *Century* "by no means so distinguished as [the *Atlantic*] in its mass" and applauded the *Atlantic* for giving "a basis for the optimistic conclusion that quality and not selling power may be the reason of a magazine's existence" (*Nation*, 11 July 1895, 29, and 12 Dec. 1895, 429).

This old-fashioned solidity and fidelity to high literary culture, however, came at a steep price, not only financial, but paradoxically intellectual as well. The *Atlantic*'s stagnant circulation to a degree compounded its inability to attract new writers and isolated it in a traditional high-culture niche. The magazine had drifted too far from the American cultural mainstream. Scudder's commitment to preserving the cultural past hindered him from successfully reintegrating it. But he was aware of the need to do so and began the task. The nineties saw the rise of the "Henry Adams syndrome," when many who were attached to canonical high culture retreated before the mass culture of an increasingly pluralistic and industrial society and took refuge in various forms of intellectual alienation. Scudder refused both alienation and reaction.

Scudder lacked the founders' passionate political cause and lacked also the gusto for political controversy of successors like Page. But like the founders, he believed in a literary culture engaged in contemporary social issues. He spoke for a moderately realistic literature, sometimes dealing with significant contemporary social issues. He also engaged the magazine much more actively in discussing current affairs. He particularly promoted the causes of party reform, civil service reform, and universal public education. Several commentators approvingly noticed the *Atlantic*'s increased engagement in contemporary life. One noted its "rapid strides" in taking a "foremost place . . . for the molding of public opinion," and another remarked on an increase in "very businesslike essays on current affairs" (*Literary World*, 5 Sept. 1896; *Nation*, 2 Nov. 1893, 330).

Scudder, like his magazine, had an integrity and solidity that were perhaps old-fashioned and that sometimes limited his aesthetic vision and his editorial effectiveness in the early years of progressive journalism. But he was far less quaintly antique than portrayed by some of the younger men he had generously helped. Mark Howe later painted him as "too full of sweetness and light," and Sedgwick caricatured him as a benign, befuddled old gentleman likely to lead off the magazine "with an excellent paper on the Upanishads" (154). But Scudder had foreseen the essential changes his successors, particularly Sedgwick, would make to bring the magazine closer to current publishing practices and cultural norms, including tighter editorial shaping, increased coverage of current affairs, and effective publicizing. All of these he initiated, although in the end his workload and temperament prevented him from fully realizing them.

While Scudder's kindness seemed naïveté to some, he had a clear and usually quite accurate sense of the economic realities of publishing. But while realistic, and therefore credible to his employers, he placed his commitment to "the cause of high pure literature" first. When Joseph Pulitzer sought to lure him to New York in 1886 with a very large salary increase, his sole comment in his diary was an exclamation point (Ballou 462). In the councils of Houghton Mifflin, he had argued for what he perceived as aesthetic and intellectual quality. He had labored long, often anonymously, always without self-promotion, and had treated everyone—his employers, assistants, writers new and old—with frankness and a large-hearted generosity. He had honorably fulfilled the trust he felt on taking up the editorship. But he had left to Page and others the changes that would be necessary if the magazine was to survive in the twentieth century.

Walter Hines Page as editor of the *Atlantic* in 1899 (from Burton Hendrick, *The Life and Letters of Walter H. Page* [New York: Doubleday Page, 1922]).

7
Walter Hines Page
(1 8 9 8 – 1 8 9 9)

Progressive Editing

After hiring Page in 1895, Mifflin and Scudder rapidly gave him editorial authority specifically to bring the *Atlantic* into the twentieth century: to draw younger writers and audiences, to adapt the magazine to new publishing trends, and to assure its survival by making it more commercially successful. But Scudder was sincerely committed to the magazine's traditional mission to support literary and intellectual high culture. Mifflin, while impatient to stem the *Atlantic*'s financial losses, accepted the idea that it could not afford to imitate the popular illustrated magazines but must cultivate its own modest garden. Like Scudder, he knew that its main value to his house was its reputation for literary and intellectual quality. Both Mifflin and Scudder realized that some changes were necessary, but neither wished radical change that might alienate the magazine's present readers, who demonstrated their loyalty with consistently high renewal rates. In considering Page's background and temperament, they found a record of energetic accomplishment but also values that, particularly for Scudder, raised questions about the younger man's adaptability to the *Atlantic*.

Page had been born in North Carolina in 1855 and at twenty had been awarded a prestigious scholarship to read Greek at the newly formed Johns Hopkins University. Soon growing impatient with the antiquarian niceties of Greek philology, he had become a newspaper reporter, first in St. Joseph, Missouri, later in New York and Washington. In 1883, he had returned to his native state to establish a progressive newspaper, the *State Chronicle*, that advocated Cleveland liberalism and attempted to jolt the postwar South out of its obsessive nostalgia and make it think more pragmatically of its future.

The *Chronicle*'s progressive spirit had undermined its financial condition, and when it failed in 1885, Page, wiser about the commercial constraints of publishing, sought his fortunes in the more liberal publishing climate of New York, in 1887 becoming both assistant editor and business manager of the *Forum*, a periodical of current affairs controversy, under Lorettus Sutton Metcalf. By 1891, the energetic and forceful Page had so convincingly demonstrated his aptitude for making the *Forum* respected and profitable that he had displaced Metcalf from the editor's chair. By 1895, he was ready to displace the owners. But he was less successful in his ambitions to gain financial control and resigned as editor following a failed coup to take ownership of the magazine he had so successfully resuscitated.

Page, who was forty when he joined Houghton Mifflin, was, in the words of a later *Atlantic* editor, Ellery Sedgwick, "the incarnation of those qualities we love to call American. . . . A sort of foursquareness, bluntness, it seemed to some; an uneasy, often explosive energy; a disposition to underrate fine drawn nicenesses of all sorts; ingrained Yankee common sense, checking his vaulting enthusiasm; enormous self-confidence, impatience of failure—all of these were in him; and he was besides affectionate to a fault, devoted to his country, his family, his craft—a strong, bluff, tender man" (Hendrick 1: 55–56).

Page's eight years in New York from 1887 to 1895 had been years of radical change in publishing. This revolution, which Christopher Wilson calls progressive publishing, had had a formative influence on Page's editorial style and ideology.[1] During the nineties, a recent explosion in newspaper circulation was beginning to influence strongly the entire publishing world, including high literary culture and the quality magazines. Between 1870 and 1900 newspaper circulation multiplied by a factor of six (C. Wilson 18). This journalistic boom produced a new generation of writers such as Dreiser, Crane, Kipling, and Norris, many of whom began as newspaper reporters and later moved toward an often naturalistic fiction dealing with contemporary social problems. It also reflected and fueled an immensely increased public interest in current affairs. Howells at *Harper's* felt the impact of journalism when he lamented the intrusion of a great vogue of "contemporanics" that doomed the old-fashioned, discursive literary essay and threatened to displace public interest in fiction and more permanent literature (*Literature and Life*, 1–35). An *Atlantic* article by Arthur Kimball titled "The Invasion of Journalism" (July 1900) reported that between 1872 and 1897, the number of articles on current affairs had risen 10 percent in *Harper's, Scribner's,* and the *Century*. Kimball regretted the journalistic emphasis on simplicity, directness, sensation, entertainment, celebrity, and ease of reading which were changing "our ways of speaking, writing, even thinking" (120–21).

Also in the eighties and early nineties, building on the immense increase in the new readership and influence of newspaper journalism, a host of entrepreneurial editor-publishers began creating a new wave of "magazines for the masses." These progressive publishers included Frank Munsey, Edward Bok, John Brisbane Walker, and Frank Doubleday; the archetype and initiator of this new style, however, was Samuel S. McClure, whom Page knew well. McClure's genius was to realize the publishing opportunity inherent in the fact that between 1880 and 1900 the population of the United States increased 50 percent, while national wealth doubled. Advertising boomed to sell a flood of new goods to an increasingly wealthy populace. McClure and others reasoned that large advertising revenues could be used to cover the costs of producing a magazine, including very generous authors' payments. The magazine could then be sold for 10 cents or 15 cents instead of the 35 cents charged by the *Atlantic* and other "qualities," thus vastly increasing the readership, which would in turn bring in increased advertising revenues.

Unlike Munsey and others, McClure sincerely believed, as Fields had earlier, that a popular magazine could be of high quality, though his definition of quality would not have been Scudder's, much less Henry James's. *McClure's* was well written, lively, and educationally substantive. Its appeal was to a middle-brow, middle-class, practical audience, for whom business, not intellectual development or literary culture, was the focus of life, but who were reasonably educated and intellectually curious. Perhaps conscious of the feminization of literature and literary culture frequently noted by later critics, it particularly aimed to expand male readership. McClure's editorial policy emphasized a literature of vigorous action by writers such as Kipling, Stevenson, Crane, Garland, and London; an interest in business, science, and technology; accounts of travel adventure; generous illustrations reproduced cheaply and well through the halftone process, which had displaced woodcuts; interviews with authors and other celebrities; and later, muckraking investigative reports on contemporary social institutions and problems. The emphasis was distinctly on the present, not the past; on the literature of adventure, not psychological subtlety or reflection; on human interest and personality, not intellectual analysis and book culture. Six years after starting his magazine, McClure had a circulation of 400,000, with over 200 pages of advertising per issue. *McClure's* was beating *Harper's* and the *Century*, the older, more culturally focused, 35-cent quality magazines, in the competition for readers, writers, and advertisers (Lyon 159). Before the end of the decade, McClure had also hired away *Scribner's* business manager and an *Atlantic* editor. By 1895, Page had absorbed and adapted many of these progressive publishing concepts to turn around the *Forum*, and they would inform his approach to the *Atlantic*.

Page's frustrations in academe and in the South had also left an impress on the editorial style and ideology he brought to the *Atlantic*. Page's education and early interests in literature had given him a knowledge of "the best that has been thought and said." He believed, as he wrote to Woodrow Wilson (who as president would fifteen years later appoint him ambassador to Great Britain), that "a man who proposes to write anything worthwhile should steep himself in the great English literature in order to have the genius of the race as a basis for his style and a corrective to his thought" (20 Mar. 1899). But his temperament and southern experience made him distrust too great a veneration for the past. His impatience with the minutiae of scholarship had led him to throw it over for journalism, in which he could influence current opinion on important issues. He wished to be out among the movers and shakers, not cloistered in the library or even in the editorial office. As a young man trying to take an active part in reconstructing the South, he had been frustrated by its self-defeating fixation on the past, its fatuous preference for spending its scant resources on memorials for the dead rather than on education and material betterment for the living.

As a southerner, Page seemed an unusual choice for the "apostolic succession" to the *Atlantic* editorship. That succession had fallen on several ambitious young men from the provinces, but never yet on one born a member of the southern planter class that the magazine had forty years before excoriated as barbaric, witless, and medieval. The *Atlantic*, unlike the *Century*, still had very little circulation in the South. But paradoxically, Page was more a modern believer in social progress, less a venerator of the cultural past, than many inheritors of the New England tradition at the end of the century.

The *Atlantic*'s dominant tone had never become reactionary, even under Aldrich. On the contrary, its essential tradition had remained the liberal Emersonian faith in the material, intellectual, ethical, and social progress of civilization. It had continued also Emerson's idea of the moral leadership of the American scholar and the education of a democratic nation by proponents of a socially engaged high literary culture. Scudder, while lamenting the corruption of democratic politics, retained the essential faith in cultural progress through education. In the pages of the *Atlantic* he had held the line fairly uncompromisingly for his idea of high literary culture. He had also expressed his conviction that that literary culture could still be a potent social force, and he had advocated increasing its engagement in contemporary American life through integration of American literature into public education, through realistic fiction, and through the magazine's social commentary. But his tastes and temperament had substantively limited that engagement. More important, there had been in some quarters a considerable waning of Emersonian optimism both about progress and about the role of "the cultivated classes." The magazine had for twenty-five years contained voices such as those of Arthur G. Sedgwick, Aldrich, Harriet Waters Preston, and Agnes Repplier lamenting the declining influence of the old cultural gentry first in politics and later in literature and cultural matters. Some intellectuals and writers, particularly from New England, had lapsed from the socially committed liberal idealism of the sixties into an isolated cultural conservatism.

These writers represented Santayana's "genteel tradition," namely, a life of the mind—a literature, religion and moral sensibility—that was retrospective, distrustful of the present and future, excessively refined, and entirely divorced from the progressive optimism and immense energies of American social organization and economic activity (Santayana 39–40). While Santayana attributed the separation of American literary culture from the vital realities of national life to the division of the feminine and masculine spheres of influence, subsequent observers have emphasized class and ethnicity as sources of the division. Alan Trachtenberg argues that there was in the late nineteenth century "an evolving consensus of belief that culture indeed represents a higher sphere of activity associated with class privilege and with the older Anglo-Saxon America, a sphere distinct from . . . the common life, of trade and labor" (9).

Since the eighties, the *Atlantic* had conveyed the message that some of those who cared for "the best that has been thought and said" did repudiate the present as a degradation of the Anglo-American past. They felt politically impotent and socially isolated in contemporary America. Some felt deprived even of their traditional Brahmin function as cultural educators in a nation they perceived as increasingly dominated by plutocrats and immigrants equally indifferent to culture. As Jackson Lears demonstrates, some of these custodians of culture such as Charles Eliot Norton or Barrett Wendell lived bitterly on pessimism, reminiscences, and contempt, while others found sustenance in a cult of literary aesthetics in the manner of Aldrich or, like Henry James, in exile to a more traditional society. Some of the more original reacted against the aridity of soulless mass culture by seeking refuge in older cultural forms, such as Hearn in Orientalism or Henry Adams in medievalism. A greater number, especially among women, found an alternative to modernism in a romantic or sentimental and reassuringly idealistic genteel fiction. All of these groups in one way or another sensed their own superfluity in contemporary America and increasingly immersed themselves in a high culture alienated from the American realities, of industrialism, urbanization, corporate capitalism, class polarization, immigration, and mass culture.

In sharp contrast to the alienated intellectuals of New England, the southerner Page was a pure progressive. Though he emphasized material development more than Emerson had, he shared the Emersonian beliefs that humankind was evolving inexorably toward a higher degree of civilization; that improvements in material well-being brought a higher level of culture; and that the economic, educational, scientific, and political advances made by the United States put it in the vanguard of progress. Soliciting an article supporting his own views against those of the intellectual pessimists, Page wrote: "What we should like is a record and measure of social betterment, that is to say, the most striking and specific facts which show to what extent the mass of the people in the United States has improved during the century. . . . Of course, these facts lead irreversibly to the conclusion that the cry of the alarmist is unwarranted—do they not?" (Page to

John McMaster, 6 Oct. 1896). Like the true progressive he was, Page was committed to constructive present action and a vision of a future vastly improved for all by education and technology, sheer human intelligence and energy. He possessed an indefatigable faith in himself and in the American nation. "A man who won't bet on himself," he believed, "isn't worth a damn." This confident faith in self and country gave him the power to achieve his considerable ambitions. It also made him at times insensitive to moral complexities, at times flatly chauvinistic.

Page retained faith too in the earlier Emersonian philosophy of intellectual culture as a vital force for social progress, rather than as an alternative for those who felt distaste for the present or disinherited from political and social power. He loathed what he saw as self-indulgent lamenting, pusillanimous despair, or clever cynicism among intellectuals. He opposed the alienation of culture from social issues, its removal to a genteel or academic nonutilitarian sphere. He was far less interested in praising the past than in influencing the present. Furthermore, he believed that literary culture and those who were shaped by it could exert a potent influence for the better if they concerned themselves not with antiquarian irrelevancies or carping negative criticisms but with positive approaches to the issues of their times. Accordingly, his aim in accepting the *Atlantic* position, in addition to improving the magazine's circulation, was to bridge the gap between high culture and the social, economic, and political realities of contemporary America—in Santayana's terms to reunite the two parts of the American psyche, to convince what Emerson had called the cultivated classes to exert their influence more actively in social issues, and to encourage the constructive use of literary culture for his definition of social progress.

Page's letter to Scudder defining his understanding of the position proposed by Houghton Mifflin reflects both his self-confident ambition and his editorial policy of bringing literary culture to bear on contemporary issues:

> What you want as I understand it, is editorial assistance, not routine assistance merely, ... the assistance of a man trained indeed to accurate routine ... but who also has a broad outlook on contemporaneous life, who knows a piece of literature when he sees it in the rough, and who may sometimes know when and where to look for a piece of literature before anybody else has found it....
> These things, let me say frankly, I think I could do with some measure of success.
> ... the way should be open to become, if I show the qualities that entitle me to become, one of the real forces in the institution. While there is no escape from routine work (and for the balance and discipline even of the most fertile men there ought to be no escape) I should like in whatever work I take up to have time to hold and to extend my acquaintance among men who are bringing things to pass; for in this way, I think, I can render my best service. While most men of scholarly pursuits, who know the use of literary tools concern themselves with what has happened in the past, my work has been

to know with as wide a horizon as possible, the directions and values of contemporary activity. (20 July 1895)

Thus Page served notice that he would be an editor who engaged the magazine in the social and political issues of the present. He expected not only autonomy but also scope and time to solicit actively and to keep current not just of books but of events. The focus of his editorial energies was not to be suggesting stylistic revisions but rather to be implanting ideas and soliciting contributions; the locus of his editorial activities was not to be confined to Houghton Mifflin's Park Street offices, nor to the literary clubs and salons of Boston and Cambridge that had partly circumscribed Lowell, Fields, and Aldrich's solicitations. Rather, he intended to enlarge his acquaintance among politicians, journalists, educators, and industrialists, the movers and shakers of the nation.

Page's assertion that his interests lay in the application of literary talents to contemporary affairs, rather than to literature itself, further implied a radically different conception of the purpose of the magazine from that held by *Atlantic* editors from Lowell to Scudder. At the founding of the magazine, Emerson had written in his journal, "None should go in but pieces of permanent worth" (*Journals* 14: 167). The magazine's founders, including Emerson, had intended it to carry current political commentary speaking forcefully against the slave powers. But politics had from the beginning been secondary to literature, and it remained so, despite Scudder's increase of coverage. All of the editors had felt that their highest function was to publish literature of permanent worth rather than more ephemeral reports on social conditions. While they were often frustrated at the scarcity of such literature, their essential aspiration was to create numbers that could be bound and read with intellectual profit ages hence. In fact, while the magazine's total circulation was less than 15,000 when Page officially became editor-in-chief, the Riverside Press was binding about 5,000 semiannual volumes preserving the issues in book form (*American Newspaper Annual*, 1897; Riverside Cost Books). Page's predecessors were at heart makers of books, not journalists.

Page felt that the purpose of a magazine, even the *Atlantic*, was entirely distinct from that of a book. "Every magazine paper," he reminded a potential contributor, "ought to be not only a clear-cut, pointed piece of work in itself, but it ought to have as clear and definite and pertinent a present application as possible" (to John McMaster, 26 Aug. 1896). Page edited not for the future but for the present. A magazine would be read and perhaps discarded before the next issue supplanted it. It should aim not at permanence but at relevance. It must have its influence now or not at all.

Scudder, more than any of his predecessors since Lowell, had tried to engage the *Atlantic* in contemporary social and political issues. But throughout Page's tenure there remained a tension between Scudder's essentially traditional, literary view of the magazine's purpose and Page's more progressive journalistic view. "Timeliness is a good secondary quality," Scudder cautioned Page, but "the only essential thing about an article is its intrinsic quality" (Dec. 1897). When it was apparent that Page placed greater value on currency, Scudder wrote: "You and I ought to compliment each other; your tastes and training lead you to emphasize the higher journalism, and mine make me eager to keep the magazine in the ranks of formative books that last. Each admits the worth of the other side, but nature is strong and we lean imperceptibly to one side or the other" (11 Oct. 1897).

Mifflin and Scudder had hired Page because of his spectacular resurrection of the *Forum* and because he was literate, experienced in practical publishing, enormously energetic, and progressive in his notion of how to edit a quality magazine. Scudder, however, had privately worried that Page had "a grain too much of the journalist, a grain too little of the litterateur" for the *Atlantic* (Diary, 16 July 1895, qtd. in Ballou 450). Mifflin also was cautious. Page's job was initially structured so that he would work on both the *Atlantic* and trade books under Scudder's direct supervision. In less than a year, with Mifflin's encouragement, Scudder gave Page primary responsibility for the magazine. The title of editor-in-chief did not follow until July 1898, but after July 1896 the essential influence was Page's. Page continued, however, to have responsibilities for the trade books and complained bitterly about not being able to focus all his efforts on the magazine. But despite this division of his energies and the brevity of his tenure (1895-99), Page left the lasting imprint of his aggressive personality and progressive editorial philosophy on the magazine.

Page's editorial methods were as distinct from those of previous *Atlantic* editors as were his aims. Editing was becoming a much more specialized profession than it had been. Lowell, Howells, and Aldrich had been writers who took the job partly to supplement their literary income. Scudder, a transitional figure, had begun as a writer and continued considerable writing but became an editor by profession. Page, unlike his predecessors but like most of his *Atlantic* successors, was a professional editor and publisher. Unlike previous editors, he wrote very little for the magazine himself, focusing instead on generating contributions and exerting overall editorial control. At the heart of his strenuous editorial style was the conviction that the editor should not be a passive gatekeeper but should actively shape the magazine. *Atlantic* editors had solicited more and more actively, and Scudder particularly believed in editorially shaping the magazine, although his work load and personality had restrained him. But Page controlled all phases of the editorial process, except proofreading, more forcefully than had his predecessors. His monthly issues began not in submissions but in an editorial notebook where he sketched ideas for articles and noted appropriate contributors to be solicited. Not only did he relegate the sludge pile of unsolicited manuscripts to his assistants,

Susan Francis and later William B. Parker, but, to Scudder's disapproval, he did not even review negative judgments.

The scope and method of Page's solicitations were less genteel than those of his predecessors. In the earliest years, when the magazine drew most of its material from a relatively small geographic and social sphere, Lowell had wheedled Emerson or cornered Longfellow at a Dante Society meeting and extracted a promise of a contribution. Fields broadened the scope as a polished "dining editor," successfully combining his social life with his editorial duties, exploiting both his publishing contacts and his wife's literary salon for contributions. Howells had sought further afield, but as late as 1882, Houghton and Osgood had held "*Atlantic* dinners" in which a large proportion of the magazine's contributors gathered socially. By 1896, however, the "circle" had long since dissolved, contributors were much more diverse geographically and socially, and Boston was a backwater to New York and points west. Furthermore, competition from the high-paying New York magazines—not only *Harper's* and the *Century* but also the new ten-cent magazines—necessitated aggressive solicitation and scouting for new talent.

Scudder, highly conscious of the demise or defection of the writers who had formerly given the *Atlantic* its prominence, had had to scout more actively than previous editors and had hired Page explicitly to "search for new writers" (Ballou 450). Page continued to spread the net geographically, particularly through his contacts in New York and a "collecting trip" through the South, where *Atlantic* readers and contributors had been very sparse since the war. He was less genteelly observant than his predecessors of the old-fashioned "courtesy of the trade" and more aggressive in soliciting authors associated with other houses. He contracted more contributions from professional journalists such as William Allen White in Kansas and Jacob Riis in New York. He also actively solicited those who spoke for ethnic minorities such as Abraham Cahan, W. E. B. DuBois, Booker T. Washington, and Israel Zangwill.

Page, fully aware of the magazine's financial disadvantage, made the intended contributor feel the full weight of his hearty and aggressive personality. On reading Page's letter of solicitation, many were undoubtedly surprised to find themselves in the unpleasant position of having to break a virtual commitment if they did not wish to write the article Page wanted. "Although it takes two to make an engagement," Page wrote to Woodrow Wilson, "and you, I believe, have never definitely given your assent, these [articles to be written] are so desirable and so excellent that we have been unable to look upon them in any other way than engagements" (21 Nov. 1896). Typically Page's letters of solicitation ended with a summary of the notation he wished to put in his *Atlantic* engagement book, a reminder of when the copy was due to meet the deadline, and the characteristic closing "Heartily Yours."

During his first two years, 1895–96, Page generally conferred with Scudder in developing ideas for articles, and even after Scudder began his sabbatical in July 1897, topics were discussed in the weekly Tuesday morning "pow wow" of Houghton Mifflin's editorial staff. From the start, however, Page was given scope to develop his own ideas. Having noted a topic and targeted a contributor, he wrote a solicitation not only defining in considerable detail that aspect of the subject he wished treated but also stipulating the approach to be taken and, sometimes, even suggesting the conclusions to be drawn.

One of the first major projects Page undertook in 1895 was to arrange a series on current secondary education. The general topic was Scudder's suggestion, but the editorial method was Page's. First, Page distributed to thousands of teachers and school administrators copies of a questionnaire on the quality of public education in their communities. Responses were then compiled, summarized, and forwarded to three professional educators whom Page and Scudder had selected to write the articles. Page sent with these summaries a four-page description of the project and the particular aspect of it allotted to each author. This type of journalism, actively investigating the current condition of a major American institution, eliciting audience participation, and editorially shaping the solicited essays, was entirely new to the *Atlantic*.

In addition to defining the specific topic and approach desired, Page gave even seasoned writers considerable advice about audience and style. In these matters, as in his choice of topics, Page clearly tried to bridge the gap between the traditional literary culture with which the *Atlantic* had been associated and the world of practical activity. While cautious not to alienate the magazine's traditional constituency, he considered a broader audience, especially among those active in public life, necessary for both financial success and influence.

In fact, Page recognized that the *Atlantic* had, or at least could have, several constituencies and that a proper balance of material and tone could satisfy them simultaneously. Page was also constantly aware that he had been hired by Mifflin to turn the *Atlantic* "trick." He was not concerned with maintaining a scholarly standard but with increasing circulation and extending influence. Accordingly, he kept close contact with the business office and was not squeamish about popularizing the *Atlantic*. To do this, he suggested to authors that they choose topics of wide interest and write for an audience that was "popular but cultivated."

This audience, he suggested, would be intellectually curious but not necessarily interested in history, literature, or ideas as ends in themselves. Authors must demonstrate clearly the contemporary relevance of their topics and make applications explicit. The best topics were concrete and viewed human experience directly rather than refracted through books. All abstractions were suspect. Page himself was impatient of mysticism, introspection, and excessive subtlety and believed these had no appeal to the American reader. Ernest Fenellosa, the American interpreter of the Orient, was told that his work was "too philosophical for use in a popular magazine," and Elizabeth Phelps Ward was warned that Jesus Christ was not an appropriate subject and reverence not an appropriate emotion in the *Atlantic* (Page to E. Fenellosa, 7 Jan. 1899; Page to E. S. P. Ward, 28 Sept. 1896). The Sage of Concord would have fared badly in Page's hands.

Page also put *Atlantic* authors on notice that they should not now assume a broad familiarity with traditional literary culture. "I have a feeling," Page wrote to Owen Wister in soliciting an article on James Fenimore Cooper, "that in most writing about literature, the writer takes for granted too much knowledge on the part of his readers. It may seem absurd to say that the readers of the *Atlantic* do not know ... about [Cooper, Emerson, Hawthorne, and Bryant]. But great numbers of people are now reading them for the first time, for the *Atlantic* has young readers as well as old ones" (26 Aug. 1896). Although Mifflin himself suggested publishing an article in the original French, presuming that most of his readers knew the language and that it would give the magazine a cultivated tone, Page remonstrated to Paul Shorey that "quotations from the Latin and Greek are not intelligible to one reader in twenty of the *Atlantic*" (23 June 1897). Clearly Page's intended audience was less culturally homogeneous than *Atlantic* audiences of the past, less limited to those for whom the knowledge of "the best that has been thought and said" was a major pursuit. He wanted to add to the magazine's traditional constituency another that was younger, less liberally educated, and more actively engaged in contemporary life.

Pursuing his own interests and the lead of editors such as Munsey and McClure, Page also intended to add more men to the *Atlantic* audience. The advertisements in Scudder's *Atlantic* for products like Sapolio, Royal Baking Powder, Baker's Coco, and Imperial Granum ("the Salvator for Invalids and the Aged") would have told him, had he not known already, that a very large proportion of its readership were women. The producers of Athlophoros patent medicine had targeted their advertising carefully in a prominent *Atlantic* ad declaring, "The amount of suffering there is through indiscreet marriages is not a comparison to the amount of suffering there is from Neuralgia. Ladies principally suffer and doctors are not able to grapple with the disease." Page, while willing to accommodate what he patronizingly considered feminine tastes such as romantic fiction, intended to produce a magazine whose content and style were, to his mind, more vigorously masculine.

The more masculine audience Page aimed to attract required, as he reminded contributors, a direct and concrete style. Page practiced and advocated a more strenuous, journalistic style than previously characterized the *Atlantic*, a style emphasizing information, concrete illustration, decisive judgments, and a minimum of philosophizing. "The man who would write convincingly and entertainingly of the things of our day and our time," he believed, "must write with more directness, with more clearness, with greater force" (qtd. in Mott 4: 13). Page had little use for the old discursive essay that had been the *Atlantic*'s mainstay in the days of Emerson and Holmes. He wanted information and terse argument, not lyrical inspiration or reflective ramblings. In both fiction and nonfiction, he instinctively sought clarity and force and correspondingly undervalued subtlety. When Henry James submitted a story titled "In a Cage," Page contemptuously dismissed it in his reader's report as a literary case of the emperor's new clothes. "A duller story I have never read," he fumed. "It wanders through a deep mire of affected writing and gets nowhere, tells no tale, stirs no emotion but weariness. The professional critics who mistake an indirect and round-about use of words for literary art will call it an excellent piece of work; but people who have blood in their viens will yawn and throw it down—if, indeed, they ever pick it up" (MS report 6743, qtd. in Ballou 455–56). Page's admonitions to authors about style show that he intended to edit the *Atlantic* to suit the tastes of those who had blood in their veins.

Page preferred to exert his editorial control before rather than after the submission of the manuscript both because it was more malleable then and because he preferred to work with authors rather than with the minutiae of copyediting. Characteristically impatient of detail, Page was cheerfully indifferent to small changes of stylistic proofreading, which had been an obsessive ritual since the *Atlantic* began. He was never willing to risk an author's irritation to enforce meticulous stylistic conformity. "Your good-natured revolt," against the blue pencil, he wrote Henry Fuller, "speaks well for your individuality and literary integrity, and you may be sure we will respect it" (3 Oct. 1897).

Page did not hesitate, however, to ask a contributor to rework a piece that he felt had substantively missed the mark. In suggesting revisions as in soliciting, Page was not timid about intruding his own ideas even with the most authoritative contributors. Page returned an accepted paper by Theodore Roosevelt on his reforms of the New York Police Department with the suggestion that the author add a conclusion stating that police reform was antecedent and fundamental to all municipal reform (7 July 1897). Upon receiving a paper solicited from Booker T. Washington on his Tuskeegee program combining vocational and academic education, Page returned the manuscript, asking Washington to write a conclusion "broadening the application of the principle you have worked out so as to show ... that the principle which has made a success of Tuskeegee is really the proper principle for education in the whole south without regard to race" (15 July 1896). Whether this universalization of the Tuskeegee idea of vocational education was Washington's or Page's, it duly concluded the influential article titled "The Awakening of the Negro" (Sept. 1896).

By 1897, Page had engineered a clear shift in the *Atlantic*'s character and focus. He had made commentary on contemporary American life a major focus of the magazine, overshadowing the fiction, history, historical biography, and literary criticism (i.e., the general emphasis on literary culture) that Scudder and his predecessors had considered the magazine's soul. Soon after arriving in Europe on his sabbatical, Scudder expressed regret that Page had given his two lead places to current affairs, lumped the fiction toward the back, and thereby "by implication made the literary character of the magazine subordinate" (7 Sept. 1897). The October issue brought further evidence that Page was making the tone of the magazine less literary, more journalistic. Again, Scudder hopefully but ineffectually chided Page:

> I have often said that a magazine like the *Atlantic*, while it cannot afford to be dull, can afford to have quiet, ruminating articles. An *organ* must be made up of force, but the *Atlantic* is only in part an organ, and literature is never more true than when it is serene. Moral energy is indispensible to a magazine which is to push reforms, but I confess that two or three strong reformatory papers in a number are enough, [and] that creative and critical literature should constitute the main substance....
> ... People read their magazines for pleasure, not to be knocked over by them, and I believe more and more in the doctrine of equilibrium in magazine making. (11 Oct. 1897)

Page preferred energy and sometimes controversy to equilibrium, editorial comment and factual information to literary criticism and fiction.

Scudder, emphasizing the essentially literary nature of the magazine and perhaps its close connection with Houghton Mifflin's trade division, had typically begun his issues with an installment of a serial novel. Page, pursuing the "higher journalism," characteristically led not with fiction but with his most authoritative article on American politics or social issues by writers such as E. L. Godkin, Woodrow Wilson, John Fiske, or Theodore Roosevelt. Frequently, Page's lead would respond directly to current political events. At the outbreak of the Spanish-American War, Page patriotically ordered the flag unfurled on the *Atlantic*'s cover for the first time since the Civil War and himself wrote a chauvinistic lead editorial vigorously endorsing the American action as "a necessary act of surgery for the sake of civilization" ("The War with Spain and After," June 1898, 727).

Not only in his leads but throughout the magazine, Page more than doubled the number of articles on politics, economics, and social issues. He by no means shared the genteel assumption of *Atlantic* editors since James T. Fields that the magazine's influence was primarily cultural rather than political. Like Scudder, he had a personal interest in educational reform and published a good deal on the subject, but he intended the magazine to publish frequent and timely articles on a full range of social issues. Page solicited the majority of these articles specifically to reflect his own progressive views, which cut across conventional distinctions of liberal and conservative, combining a strong nationalism and a distaste for socialism, with an advocacy of genuine reform and equal opportunity. His *Atlantic*, like that of his predecessors, reflected some distrust of majorities and by implication favored the leadership of an educated meritocracy. But it also proposed a broad range of reforms, expressed confidence in the ability of an enlightened government to solve social problems, and exuded optimism about the growing economic and political power of the nation. It continued to warn of dangers from both the socialistic left and the plutocratic right.

The populist revolt, capped by the Democratic party's nomination in 1896 of William Jennings Bryan for the presidency, brought Page's conservative side to the fore; he, in turn, brought the *Atlantic* forcefully out of its careful political neutrality with an editorial entitled "The Political Menace of the Discontented" (Oct. 1896). The article portrayed the populists as a mindless agrarian mob whose ignorance and class antagonisms had been exploited for political purposes and whose socialistic demands threatened the bases of civilized progress, namely, observance of law, the judicial system, property rights, and financial integrity. Page worked assiduously, however, to secure Prince Peter Kropotkin's *Autobiography of a Revolutionist*, which he extensively serialized in eleven *Atlantic* issues from December 1898 to September 1899. Kropotkin's American tour at the time had been arranged by Emma Goldman, and his autobiography contained classic statements of the anarchist position, including the justification and advocacy of political violence.

The *Atlantic* under Page also had a stronger reform component than at any time since the early years of Reconstruction. "It was a shock to many," Mott notes, "when the *Atlantic Monthly*, in 1898, turned to political controversy, social reform, and the exposure of corruption in government" (4: 8–9). In fact, the *Atlantic* tradition of political controversy ran back to Lowell's uncompromising attacks on slavery, Emerson's calls for emancipation, Sumner's and Douglass's radical proposals for southern Reconstruction and black rights, Howells's publication of W. D. Lloyd's searing exposure of Jay Gould, and the attacks on the Tammany Tiger, Boss Crocker, and other corrupt political beasts published by Scudder.

Page's *Atlantic* carried a wide range of strong reformist articles such as David Starr Jordan's muckraking exposure of corporate exploitation in Alaska, John Jay Chapman's "Capture of Government by Commercialism," C. F. Adams's advocacy of increased federal regulation of railways, several essays calling for the extension of municipal services and the reform of municipal government, and Jane Addams's critique of philanthropy in "The Subtle Problems of Charity." Civil service reform was again a favored cause, but Page's methods and tone were more aggressive than Scudder's. To discredit the spoils system, Page attempted to persuade friends in the State Department in Washington to draw up lists of politically appointed consuls and give detailed information on the qualifications and performance of each, this information to serve as raw material for two articles (Page to Faison, 28 Dec. 1895). Page was bringing the tactics of muckraking to the *Atlantic*, as he did again in publishing a series of eight articles on the tenement house blight by Jacob Riis, a New York reporter turned sociologist and advocate. In his reports, Riis detailed the devastating physical and psychological effects of the "repellent and disheartening" slums on the "starved lives" of the poor. He unequivocally blamed absentee landlords and speculative builders motivated by "profit without conscience" and asserted that reform could come only through passing and enforcing laws that placed human welfare above property rights.

Another significant change in Page's *Atlantic* was the appearance of ethnic writers advocating reform and affirming the value of ethnic identity. At Page's invitation, Abraham Cahan, editor of the *Jewish Daily Forward*, wrote "The Russian Jew in America" (July 1898), protesting the movement toward stricter immigration laws that several *Atlantic* writers had previously supported. Cahan also justified socialism and trade unionism as necessary means for opposing the curse of the sweatshop system. Page secured a powerful indictment by John S. Durham, a black writer, of both labor unions and employers for denying black Americans the opportunity to benefit justly by their labor. He requested and received papers from Booker T. Washington advocating the "Tuskeegee system" of education for both black and white southerners. He also solicited and published several articles by W. E. B. DuBois. African-Americans, DuBois declared in "Strivings of the Negro People" (Aug. 1897), rejected assimilation but sought removal of the "vast veil" that prevented their self-realization and the acceptance of their social, cultural, and economic equality. He protested the fragmenting of the black family and "the stain of bastardy" resulting from "two centuries of legal defilement of Negro women . . . by white whoremongers and adulterers." The black man, DuBois told the *Atlantic* audience, "does not wish to bleach his negro blood in a flood of white Americanism for he believes . . . that Negro blood has yet a message for the world" (194–98).

Page did not subscribe to Scudder's "doctrine of equilibrium in magazine making" but enjoyed controversy. After flaunting the national flag on the magazine's cover in June 1898, Page made the Spanish-American War the focus for a number of articles analyzing its impact on the nation's mission, interests, and international relationships. The controversial issue of American colonialism was particularly debated. The appearance of the flag declared Page's own stand on the war, which was hardly calculated to suit the anti-imperialist sentiments of his boss Mifflin and much of intellectual New England, who opposed the war. Following the lead of his two editorials, most essays endorsed the war as an inevitable and desirable fulfillment of the law of progress, according to which the influence of a decadent civilization such as that of Spain must be displaced by that of a more vital, more technologically and morally advanced civilization such as that of the United States. The argument bore striking similarity to the Civil War editorials predicting the inevitable triumph of the more highly evolved democratic civilization of the North over the feudal, sensualist South. Both the articles on the war and a series on

Anglo-American relations reflected Page's ethnocentric conviction that contemporary events were working out a manifest destiny for the ascendancy of English-speaking peoples, a belief that coexisted oddly with his conscious encouragement of ethnic pluralism in the *Atlantic*.

Most of the articles morally justifying the war warned of the dangers of colonialism and suggested that the moral superiority of the United States over Spain must be demonstrated in a policy prohibiting exploitation and governing in the genuine interests of the governed. Page refused to publish an article submitted by E. L. Godkin suggesting that British colonialism had resulted, and American colonialism would result, only in exploitation of the governed and in political and moral corruption of the governors. Having himself declared in an editorial that the war was "a wholesome stimulus to higher politics," Page asserted that a paper with such a "hopeless tone" would strike a "false note" in the *Atlantic*. "If we cheerfully and hopefully go to work to make the best of it we shall succeed. The only thing I am afraid of," he pointedly wrote Godkin, "is the continued estrangement of the intelligent classes who criticize and predict disaster, and the men who must take those tasks in hand" (31 Jan. 1899). Here, as elsewhere, Page asserted his own vaulting confidence in material and moral progress in contrast with what he considered the paralyzing and backward-looking pessimism of intellectual New England. Here also, he characteristically regretted the alienation between those trained in traditional high culture and the world of political power.

As Page tried to counteract this alienation by increasing the proportion of *Atlantic* articles on politics, economics, and sociology, he also proportionally reduced the papers devoted to history, biography, literary criticism, and book reviews. Page's slighting of these last two categories, the bases for a considerable part of the *Atlantic*'s reputation, caused constant conflict with Scudder. Scudder had maintained that an honest and rigorous criticism of literature was perhaps the magazine's most important cultural function. By contrast, Page contemptuously dismissed most literary criticism as "mere talkee-talkee." To his progressive temperament, literary criticism seemed destructive rather than constructive. Despite his interest in political reform, Page, like Theodore Roosevelt condemning the muckrakers, characteristically disliked a hypercritical dwelling on deficiencies. In a letter defending his deletion of what he considered a gratuitous sneer at the tastes of the American reading public, Page asserted his belief that "the present dearth in American letters is due to the abnormal development of our smart critical faculty and our lack of sympathy alike with writers and with people in the mass" (to J. E. Chamberlin, 30 Sept. 1896). The *Atlantic*, Page told Scudder with considerable justice, suffered from excessive fastidiousness. It was "too disposed to criticize every movement to liberate it" (Scudder diary, 30 Mar. 1897).

Literary critics, Page suggested, tended to be alienated intellectuals—at best superfluous, at worst destructive to a healthy literature. He cut literary criticism and book reviews by two-thirds, eliminating entirely the "Comments on New Books" section that had been Scudder's labor of love. By 1899, Page's numbers carried an average of one article on literature and sometimes no book reviews at all. Acknowledging that the *Atlantic*'s readership expected literary discussions, Page had attempted to displace the older, ponderous literary papers with a "Men and Letters" section for which he invited established writers to contribute short, informal prose pieces. The response to his solicitations was dismal and left Page wondering why American writers did not want to write. The fact was that they found the format uncongenial, a distraction from serious work. Page was soon forced to abandon the attempt. He did, however, publish major critical work by John Jay Chapman and pieces advocating new realism and ethnicity in the theater by Norman and Hutchins Hapgood, young critics whom Scudder had discouraged.

Page himself, unlike all of his predecessors, was no literary critic. Nor were his literary tastes sophisticated. He liked what had emotional impact and immediate human interest and disliked the excessively subtle, cerebral, or aesthetically refined. Aldrich had contemptuously parodied James Whitcomb Riley's folksy verse, but Page much preferred Riley to the metrically perfect maunderings and spiritual angst of Louise Chandler Moulton and others. Aldrich had considered Whitman a roaring raree-show freak; Page admitted that he sometimes could not fathom Whitman but liked his emotional force and democratic optimism.

Page's selection of both literary criticism and fiction reflected his strenuous progressive ideology as clearly as his treatment of politics did. The debate between realism and romanticism continued, but Page's values cut across these lines as they cut across the predictable political lines of liberal and conservative. In 1899, he supported *Atlantic* acceptance of "An Odyssey of the North," the first of Jack London's stories to gain a national audience. Similarly, he admired Stephen Crane's virile prose, vigorous action, and gritty realism. But the deterministic theory of naturalism, with its inclination to focus on the sordid and hopeless, was antithetical to Page's progressive optimism. His real loathing, though, was reserved not for the brutalities of naturalism but for what he considered the limp-wristed, neurotic self-indulgence of fiction featuring psychological introspection. He shared the contempt of another red-blooded progressive, Theodore Roosevelt, for the elaborate subtleties of Henry James and his effeminate followers, as he showed in his scathing report on "In a Cage."

Page explained his red-blooded critical philosophy in a letter to F. Hopkinson Smith, who had submitted a Jamesian psychological study written by a protégée, Lillie French. "[The story] is too subjective, too introspective. We wish to keep the

Atlantic utterly free from the present fashion of stories about the innermost vitals and immortal souls of meditative people. One reason why we like your work and why the public likes it so well is that it has to do with people who live out-doors—people of action, normal, wholesome, vigorous people.... It is [an] unwholesome tendency to meditation and this use of psychological studies in fiction that have brought upon us the flood of unhealthful novels" (4 Mar. 1897). To Lillie French herself he wrote, "Our feeling is very strong in favor of stories not necessarily of adventure, but certainly of action—objective rather than subjective stories. We believe that wholesomeness in literature as well as in life discourages ... the laying of emphasis on introspective tendencies. We are aware that in this feeling we run counter to a strong fashion in current fiction, but this strong fashion is itself ... an additional reason why the *Atlantic Monthly* should stand for the opposite tendency" (4 Mar. 1897).

Page was entirely sincere in saying that he personally preferred objective, action-oriented fiction and found the fiction of psychological introspection unwholesome and unconstructive. But he was also entirely aware that standing against the "strong fashion" of Jamesian psychological fiction was a financial advantage rather than the bold risk he implied. In rejecting a story by Alice Brown, he noted that "the public has begun to criticize us very sharply" for psychological stories departing from the "normal," and he confessed that he found the criticism justified (8 Sept. 1897). Basically, he knew that advocating a return to wholesome action and adventure promised considerable reward. The vogue of romance, particularly historical romance, that had sprung up in direct reaction against the morbidities of naturalism and the psychological novel was at full sway, and sales were high. R. W. Gilder at the *Century* was delighted that "the romantic has been of late warmly welcomed by contrast to the straining modern condition" (qtd. in Herbert Smith 144). The virile plots of Stevenson and Kipling were helping to swell the circulations of the new ten-cent magazines. Houghton Mifflin and the *Atlantic* could not afford Stevenson and Kipling, but lesser romancers were working a more modest financial magic even for them. In 1897, Page cheerfully wrote to Scudder of the firm's list, "the second and third rate literature booms," citing as examples several romances, including Paul Leicester Ford's *Story of an Untold Love*, which he had just finished serializing (13 Sept. 1897).

Serial fiction in Page's *Atlantic* was entirely given over to historical romance and light, sentimental, idealistic novels. Scudder had tried to preserve a place for James and Jewett, "the permanent element in American literature," and had made his compromises on serials with reluctance. Page seems to have seen serial fiction frankly as a way to raise circulation, even allowing Mifflin and other company executives to secure works they felt would be popular. The favorite of the front office was Kate Douglas Wiggin, who contributed *Penelope's Progress*, a frothy serial travelogue of three clever, spirited young American women. Mrs. Wiggin, also prized by the *Century*'s Gilder, was the *Atlantic*'s best-paid contributor at an average of $20 a page (and a high of $52 a page), twice the average of $10 paid to writers such as Francis Parkman or John Burroughs, and considerably above Henry James's last rate (Ballou 433). Other serials included wholesome, swashbuckling historical romances by Paul Leicester Ford, Gilbert Parker, and Mary Johnston, a Virginia novelist. Page's great coup was securing a second novel from Miss Johnston, whom he visited on his collecting trip through the South. It was pure Scott and water: the story of the English tobacco settlements in tidewater Virginia of the 1620s featuring a flashing-eyed, raven-haired, high-born heroine who in the first installment defends her honor against the bluff, virile hero who has just purchased her as his wife for 120 pounds of tobacco. Serialized in the *Atlantic* in 1899 as "To Have and to Hold," Johnston's novel temporarily "almost doubled" circulation (Ballou 464). This result would have elated Page, but by that time he had departed to play for bigger stakes.

In an editorial observing the *Atlantic*'s fortieth anniversary in November 1897, Page asserted that the aim of the editors had been and remained to render "a literary interpretation of American life" ("Forty Years of the *Atlantic Monthly*," 576). Judged solely from the serial fiction, the slice of American life interpreted would have been thin indeed and mainly situated in the idealized past. But serial fiction did not tell the full story either of the complete magazine, with its new emphasis on current social issues, or of its literature as a whole. Page despised Jamesian introspection as unhealthy and used historical romances as a sop to his audience's desire for entertainment. But he was also entirely in earnest about giving his readers an accurate image of contemporary American life. To accomplish this goal, he published some substantial realistic fiction but even more nonfiction reportage, including narratives of personal experience, that recorded a broad sweep of the American social environment and its impact on individual Americans.

In his editorial, Page claimed somewhat ingenuously that literature was still the *Atlantic*'s central mission, but he asserted a very broad definition of literature. "Political questions," he maintained, "are, and always have been, material for good literary work." Page was here equivocating to justify his new focus on current affairs. But he was also consciously trying to break down distinctions that he felt were harmful and to reclaim for "literature" and for the *Atlantic* a larger scope of contemporary American life—a scope he saw constrained by the expectations of formal literary fiction. Page extended the scope and realism of fictional literature in the *Atlantic*. More important, he greatly increased nonfiction narrative and description of the American scene and gave them equal status as literature. The pupose and methods of this frequently narrative nonfiction were similar to those of literary realism: a direct, objective observation of the American social environment and an analysis of its effects on its inhabitants.

Page's commitment to this form of literary journalism is reflected not only in his publishing a good deal of it but also in his determining to write, himself, a series of firsthand descriptive reports on conditions in the South, particularly on race relations and the status of black Americans. To gather material for these articles, Page toured the South in February and March of 1899. A letter he wrote to George Mifflin at this time reveals a good deal about his character and journalistic interests:

> I think I shall get three or four of the best articles I have ever written out of the trip. I talk with . . . young and old,—black, ginger cake, and white—from bishops and governors down to the little devils in rags. . . . I spent the evening at a great university reception where some of the finest young ladies of the town were cousins to the mulattoes I had seen in the afternoon. . . . [Two lawyers, one white and one black,] each told me his high regard for the other. But I saw the wives and the homes of each—a sight that neither of them ever saw or ever will see; and I talked with each of the women about the other. . . .
>
> It's all a little confusing now and then. I have lost my own identity a time or two. Several times I have checked the impulse to weep by the sudden and saving thought that if [Francis] Garrison could see these things, he'd drop dead! Both the pathos and the humor of it go beyond anything in literature. (23 Feb. 1899)

Certainly the paradoxical realities of race that Page reported in his letter went beyond anything in the *Atlantic*'s frothy serials of the period. Mary Johnston, whom Page met on the same trip, facetiously wished him success in his talks with his "niggers"; contemporary race relations clearly did not interest her as a subject for literature. But Page's definition of literature was broader, including both fiction and nonfiction.

Page was not the first to introduce nonfictional sociological reportage into the *Atlantic*, any more than he was the first to introduce political controversy. John Trowbridge and John W. DeForest had reported graphic, firsthand descriptions of the postwar South and the condition of the freedman. Howells had published sociological descriptions of New England mill towns by the Reverend J. B. Harrison, and Houghton had subsequently hired Harrison to tour the South to report on conditions there during the seventies. Howells's first works of realism had been his suburban sketches made from direct observation, and he had turned to grimmer scenes in his description of the criminal court. For twenty-five years, Lillie Wyman had contributed factual accounts of individual lives, as well as working and living conditions among industrial workers. Sociological reportage, often in the form of a personal narrative, was indeed an established form in the *Atlantic*. But, as with the political controversy to which it was related, Page increased its volume and incisiveness. He also systematically expanded the scope of both nonfiction and fiction geographically, socially, and ethnically.

Page continued to publish the fiction of local color realists, mainly women, from all sections of the country. Sarah Orne Jewett, still in her prime, contributed to Page's *Atlantic* some of her most subtle and sympathetic portraits of rural Maine women facing age or isolation with self-reliant dignity and communal kindliness. Alice French, under the pseudonym Octave Thanet, presented relatively bleak images of a rural Iowa peopled by slightly more stock figures like the hard-bitten, independent, middle-aged farm spinster who learns trust and affection through a hired laborer and his child. Kate Chopin contributed several stories of Creole life, and Mary Halleck Foote wrote of Idaho, Colorado, and California.

To these fictional accounts Page added first-person journalistic reportage on current social and economic conditions, attitudes, and manners across the nation. He himself intended to write on the South. He engaged Kansas newspaper editor William Allen White, a disciple of Howells's, to write on life in the small-town Midwest, Rollin Hartt to report on the Far West, and Alvan Sanborn to visit and describe several representative New England towns, both rural and industrial. Frank Norris starkly dramatized starvation among the war refugees in Cuba. Some of these reports were as grim and gritty as the slums of Crane's *Maggie*; none confined themselves to "the smiling aspects of life" or genteel reassurance. Significantly, when the *Atlantic* reviewed a book of fictional stories that Alvan Sanborn derived from his nonfiction reports published earlier in the magazine, the reviewer criticized their "ghastly reality" and noted that they "make their appeal as documents, horribly human, rather than as pieces of fiction. Nothing is set down with a perceptible wish to make things seem better, or indeed other, than they are" ("Comments on New Books," Mar. 1897, 423). Clearly many critics felt that fiction should idealize or try to ameliorate rather than simply report but that a higher degree of realism was acceptable in nonfiction. Page therefore often turned to nonfiction "human documents" for their greater realism and their exemption from the need to "make things seem better than they are."

Page rendered a much fuller picture of urban life than did his predecessors. Fields had published *Life in the Iron Mills*; Howells had written some bitter little urban portraits, including the one of an Irish prostitute and a drunk in the Boston criminal justice system; and Scudder had engaged some reporting on the industrial boom in Chicago. Page now published fiction with an urban setting from the Chicago realist Henry Fuller and from a young Chicago journalist named Will Payne, both protégés of Howells. But he also solicited Jane Addams, the Chicago settlement worker, and Jacob Riis, recommended by Theodore Roosevelt, for nonfiction narratives that would give his readers insight into the lives of the urban poor. "I propose," he wrote Riis, "under some such general heading as 'Out of the

Book of Humanity' to print a group of . . . articles each of which shall contain a picture of some genuine exhibition of human nature, pathetic if it happen to be so, but not necessarily so at all. There is nothing else so interesting as a genuine piece of human experience. It is this that forms . . . the basis of every really great piece of literature" (22 Aug. 1896). Riis's narratives, highly empathetic but sentimental, were not great literature. Page, however, was delighted with their direct human appeal and followed up by soliciting a major series of eight articles describing "the tenement house blight," its causes, and its effects on the urban poor.

Page expanded not only the geographic and social range but also the ethnic diversity of *Atlantic* literature in both fiction and nonfiction. Charles Chesnutt, one of the first black American writers of prose fiction, had initially been introduced to a national audience in Aldrich's *Atlantic*. Scudder had given him only cautious, limited encouragement. He found Page, however, an enthusiastically appreciative advocate (and was delighted also to discover that the new editor was a fellow Tarheel). By 1897, Chesnutt had shifted from local color plantation stories to fiction examining contemporary racial issues along the color line, stories such as "The Wife of His Youth," the narrative of an ambitious, talented light-skinned black man reclaimed at the height of his success by a moral commitment to his dark-skinned, uneducated former wife. Gilder at the *Century* and Alden at *Harper's* had rejected several color-line stories as lacking "charm or mellowness" (Chesnutt 103), which Chesnutt understood to mean that they did not like fiction dealing seriously with racial issues. Page, however, accepted two of these stories with enthusiasm and invited Chesnutt to visit. "I shall watch with great interest . . . the continuance of your work," he wrote, "if you will be good enough to permit me. When you get your long story done, I cannot help thinking that it will be a successful book if you write that as well as you write short stories, and I have thought too that a skillfully selected list of your short stories might make a book. Whenever you are in the humor to talk about these things, let me hear from you" (2 Oct. 1897, in Chesnutt 82).

Having waited six years to bring out a collection of stories and finding, at last, a genuinely appreciative editor, Chesnutt responded with elation checked by a disciplined and dignified self-reliance.

> I felt in a somewhat effusive mood the other day and I sat down to write a long letter in which I was going to tell you all about my literary plans, how long I have cherished them, and how I hope to be devoting my whole time to the literary life, etc.
>
> But it occurred to me you were a busy man and that anything I might say to you as an editor might be better said by what I should write for publication . . . and that it would be in better taste to reserve personal confidences until I might have gained your friendship and your interest by having accomplished some worthy thing. (7 Dec. 1897, in Chesnutt 85)

Page's friendly interest and his publishing influence helped substantively to create the major breakthrough in Chesnutt's career. But Houghton Mifflin's decision makers, including Scudder, were cautious and most convinced only by demonstrated success. In 1897, despite Page's invitation, influence, and assurance of success, the weekly powwow declined to publish a collection of Chesnutt's stories. Four months later, however, the critical and popular success of "The Wife of His Youth" in the *Atlantic* gave Page and Chesnutt the evidence they needed. At Page's request, a collection of Chesnutt's "conjur tales" was reconsidered and accepted for publication. Within a year, again at Page's instigation, Houghton Mifflin went a step further and accepted a collection of color-line stories. These stories, reviewers noted, were unique in contemporary American literature in presenting black characters not as occasions for pathos or humor but empathetically as fully complex and credible individuals (Chesnutt 131).

The publication of both of these collections in 1899 gave Chesnutt the confidence to abandon temporarily his successful business as a legal secretary and to commit himself full-time to writing. With Page's encouragement and Scudder's suggestions, he now revised the ending of *The House behind the Cedars*, a novel about a light-skinned young mulatto woman's moral conflict over "passing" and her choice between black and white identity. Houghton Mifflin published the novel in 1900 following an *Atlantic* article by William Dean Howells (May 1900) praising Chesnutt both as a literary artist and as an interpreter of black experience. In 1901, Houghton Mifflin brought out a controversial second novel, *The Marrow of Tradition*, about two half-sisters, one black, one white, which Howells found unnecessarily bitter. By this time, Page had established his own publishing company and was competing with Houghton Mifflin for Chesnutt's work. But it was unquestionably Page, probably assisted by Francis Garrison, who had persuaded Scudder and George Mifflin that Chesnutt's fiction was not only of high caliber but also saleable. Page had supported Chesnutt's transition to contemporary racial themes; he had helped provide both the contacts and the confidence that initiated the most productive period of Chesnutt's writing career; and he had contributed importantly to making him the first black writer of fiction to find a substantial white readership.

Page also introduced into the *Atlantic* fiction by and about Jews in such stories as Israel Zangwill's fictional account of Heine's deathbed affirmation of his Jewish identity and Abraham Cahan's story "A Ghetto Wedding" depicting the religious devotion and persecution of Jewish immigrants. But in the exploration of ethnic issues, as elsewhere, nonfiction reportage and personal narratives tended to be Page's preferred modes and to offer greater realism than fiction.

Issues of race and ethnicity regained importance in the *Atlantic* during the late nineties with new black initiatives under the leadership of Booker T. Washington and W. E. B. DuBois, the continued high tide of immigration, and increasing recognition by progressives like Page of the impact of ethnic cultures. During its first decade, the magazine had resisted political accommodation with slavery, called for rapid abolition, and after the war supported black rights to property, education, and political power. During following decades, attitudes toward race and ethnicity in the *Atlantic* ranged widely, becoming somewhat more conservative but sharing a common set of assumptions derived from Emerson by way of Spencer.

Most *Atlantic* writers during the half-century from Emerson to Page believed in a hierarchy of cultural values and levels of civilization from primitivism to the technically and morally advanced liberal Christian democracy of nineteenth-century America. This comfortable ethnocentricity was used to justify the ascendancy of the more educated, individualistic, democratic North over the feudal, sensual, aristocratic South; the manifest destiny of white civilization over the Stone Age Indian; progressive North American culture over decadent Spanish colonialism in Cuba and the Philippines; and later the democratic individualism of Anglo-American culture over the militaristic Prussian autocracy of Kaiser Wilhelm's "Huns."

The second axiom was that the status of individuals and even of cultures within the hierarchy of civilizations was not fixed but fluid and evolutionary. Individuals, no matter what their ethnic or cultural origin, could by an Emersonian exercise of will evolve beyond the values of their society. Values were, in Werner Sollor's terms, not determined by descent but developed by consent. Furthermore, whole races and cultures were constantly, if gradually, moving up the scale in an evolution partly inevitable but also aided by human effort. The decencies of civilization were not the exclusive property of any race or class but should be the aspiration of all.

The third, closely related axiom was that those at the higher levels of civilization, as "the cultivated classes" assumed themselves to be, were morally obligated to aid in the upward cultural mobility of those less developed. This assumption fostered cultural colonialism, a smug sense of moral superiority, sometimes a justification for military force. But it committed those who held it to the development and empowerment of ethnic and racial minorities as individuals and as citizens.

Page's treatment of ethnic and racial issues reflects his essential acceptance of these European-American ethnocentric axioms. Characteristic of the progressive movement, however, it also reflects an increased emphasis on social and economic upward mobility for ethnic groups, usually through assimilation. While Page clearly believed that educated Anglo-Saxons could still exert a major influence in America, he warned them that to do so, they must pay less attention to their own cultural past and much more attention to the voices of other American ethnic groups. Accordingly, Page instituted a change in the *Atlantic* canon. On the one hand, he reduced writing on traditional literary culture; on the other, he published a variety of ethnic writers, some of whom were beginning explicitly to challenge middle-class, white American assumptions about cultural hierarchy and even assimilation.

Beginning in 1896, Page commissioned an extensive series of reports on ethnic groups in American society.[2] These articles included not only analyses of political, economic, and social status but also case histories, extensive descriptions, and personal narratives. Some were filtered through a heavily ethnocentric, middle-class point of view, sometimes sympathetic, sometimes antipathetic, but generally they assumed Northern European–American cultural superiority. Certain injustices caused by white conquest and certain admirable ethnic traits were acknowledged. George Bird Grinnell in "The Wild Indian" (Jan. 1899) asserted that "civilization has brought to this Indian many hardships," including loss of freedom, disease, and alcoholism, and had "broken down many of the fine savage qualities that he once possessed" (20). But Native Americans were seen as inhabiting a mental and technological Stone Age. Mexican Americans were only a little more advanced. Authors felt that the dominant culture was responsible for trying to improve the condition of these groups, but frank questions were raised about whether the majority could ever evolve to a level of economic or educational parity with mainstream American life. German and Irish immigrants, by contrast, were considered to come from highly evolved cultures, to share many characteristic American values, to be capable of important contributions to the nation, and to be easily assimilable.

Other accounts in Page's series on ethnic America were contributed by writers who were themselves members of these groups. These sometimes narrated bitter personal experiences of racial or ethnic prejudice and exclusion and sometimes frankly challenged Anglo-American ethnocentricity. Interestingly, however, even the more militant such as DuBois generally accepted the professed Anglo-American, middle-class hierarchy of cultural values, but argued first that their ethnic group practiced these values more consistently than their WASP critics, and second that they would make unique contributions to American life consonant with the highest civilized ideals. Abraham Cahan, for instance, claimed for Russian Jewish immigrants a culture with greater respect for intellectual and spiritual values than that they found in America, and one that would considerably leaven American materialism. In 1897, Page responded enthusiastically to a proposal from DuBois to write several papers on the life of black Americans that would later become part of his first book, *The Souls of Black Folk*. True to his progressive philosophy, Page initially sought narratives that would both highlight black accomplishments and validate his concept of America as a land of progress and upward mobility for all. DuBois could, he suggested, narrate "life stories and human experiences which illustrate in a striking way the lift from the old darkness of slavery into the ambitious life of American citizenship at the end of the nineteenth century.... [T]he step from the profound indifference of ignorance to a large ambition brought about in a very brief part of a single individual life—this is matter for literature" (24 June 1897). DuBois's agenda was quite different. The essays and personal-experience narratives he submitted emphasized not the rapidity of progress but its tortuous slowness, not accomplishment but wasted talent, not opportunity but the impediments of grinding poverty and particularly "the Veil" of prejudice. Page, despite DuBois's refusal to endorse his progressive optimism, recognized racial reality, printed several papers, and encouraged further submissions.

In his seminal first paper, "The Strivings of the Negro People" (Aug. 1897), DuBois challenged European-American ethnocentricity by arguing that black Americans endorsed the values of civilized progress as fervently as anyone. DuBois refused to accept defense of these values as a justification for racial prejudice, insisting that African-Americans had their own cultural contributions to make to American civilization. "Men call the shadow prejudice," he wrote, "and learnedly explain it as the natural defense of culture against barbarism, learning against ignorance, purity against crime, the 'higher' against the 'lower' races. To which the Negro cries Amen! and swears that to so much of this strange prejudice as is founded on just homage to civilization, culture, righteousness, and progress, he humbly bows.... But before that nameless prejudice that leaps beyond all this, he stands helpless, dismayed, and well-nigh speechless" (197). The black American, DuBois asserted, wished to be a "co-worker in the kingdom of culture" so that "some day on American soil two world races may give each to each those characteristics which each so sadly lacks." "Will America be poorer," he asked, "if she replaces her brutal, dyspeptic blundering with the light-hearted but determined Negro humility, or her coarse, cruel wit with loving jovial good humor, or her 'Annie Rooney' with 'Steal Away'?" Black culture is "the sole oasis of simple faith and reverence in a dusty desert of dollars and smartness" (197–98).

Page, then, used both fiction and nonfiction to render a relatively broad and realistic view of contemporary American life. In doing so, he not only increased the *Atlantic*'s coverage of the contemporary scene but also broadened its social and ethnic perspectives. In fact, it is easily arguable that Page's magazine, though its assumptions about cultural hierarchies were clearly narrower, described a broader social and economic cross-section of American life than is found in current issues of the *New Yorker*.

As Scudder had feared, Page was making substantive changes in the *Atlantic*. But with characteristic impatience, Page continued to feel constrained by the magazine's high-culture, literary traditions and by the division of his editorial attention between the magazine and trade books. In June 1899, he received a letter from S. S.

McClure, who had just been appointed by J. P. Morgan to resurrect the bankrupt House of Harper. "I have got the earth with several things thrown in," McClure wrote ebulliently, "and I am eager to see if you don't want one or two kingdoms for yourself.... I have got four or five major generalships to give out and I regard you as the one indispensable man in the world for our enterprises at the present time" (24 June 1899). Page resigned as editor of the *Atlantic* effective August 1.

McClure's expansive offer, which included a trebling of salary from $5,000 to a princely $15,000 plus a stake in the enterprise, must, as Ellen Ballou comments, have "made Park Street seem a rabbit warren" and appealed powerfully to Page's considerable ambition (458). But Page had additional motives for resigning. First, he believed that the only financial security available to an editor was to own a portion of the publishing house. He had tried and failed to participate in ownership of the *Forum*, and there now seemed no prospects of significant ownership at Houghton Mifflin (Hendrick 1: 66). Within a year of his departure from the *Atlantic*, Page had broken with McClure and was editing his own magazine, the *World's Work*, published by Doubleday, Page and Company, of which he was vice-president and part owner.

Page's resignation from the *Atlantic* was probably motivated also by a need for autonomy. Mifflin had seldom interfered in Page's editorial conduct of the magazine, even when Page's unfurling of the flag on the *Atlantic*'s cover during the war with Spain had outraged the anti-imperialist sentiments of intellectual Boston in general and Mifflin himself in particular. In a letter to Scudder following his resignation, Page asserted that "there is no fairer man or juster than G.H.M." (2 Aug. 1899). Still, Page had apparently felt a frustrating constraint imposed by both the nature of his job and the nature of the *Atlantic* itself, a constraint which he blamed for a series of incapacitating illnesses during his last year with the magazine. In justifying his resignation to the dismayed Scudder, who now had the task of replacing him, he wrote:

> If [Bliss] Perry comes ... to edit the *Atlantic*, insist on it for God's sake that he has a chance to edit the *Atlantic* to the best of his ability, for ... I could never get a fair chance with the organization that we have here....
>
> You edited the *Atlantic* and did the book work too. In my judgment you didn't do either as well as you could have done if you had had only one to do. I have done both—in the main; and made a failure of it in comparison with what I think I could have done if I had had either task without the other.
>
> I have been unable to make a magazine that gave me any satisfaction with the necessity of acting as executive head of the office, of doing a great correspondence pertaining to the literary department in general, and of reading book mss. to boot.
>
> I'm fagged out, worked out, sucked dry, gone to seed, withered up. I am tired till the muscles of my mind ache because it is only after a long day of routine correspondence and book work that I have a chance at night to plan for the magazine; and I have not had

time to read books so as to keep fresh and little time to meet men except by neglect of the routine. (2 Aug. 1899)

But it was not just the office-bound routine and the fragmenting of his efforts that had frustrated Page. He had also felt himself constrained by the *Atlantic*'s traditions, for which Scudder had often acted as spokesman. To Scudder he claimed with characteristic hyperbole, "The proper man, if he be free, can make it not only the most powerful publication in the world, but more powerful than all others in our country put together" (2 Aug. 1899). But during his editorship Page had often muted his instinct for powerful journalism to suit the literary traditions of the magazine; he had been forced to concern himself with literary criticism, cultural history, third-rate romances, lugubrious poetry, and neurotic introspective fiction—all of which represented a distraction from his real interests: contemporary American social and economic life. When Page was free in 1900 to establish his own magazine, the *World's Work*, he announced with characteristic progressive chauvinism: "It is with the newly organized world [of twentieth-century America], its problems and even its romance that this magazine will concern itself, trying to convey the cheerful spirit of men who do things" (*World's Work*, Nov. 1900, 3). His magazine, he asserted, had "a more original aim than to thresh over old straw and call the chaff 'Literature' " (Oct. 1901, 1257). The *World's Work* was frankly journalistic, was popularly written, contained no fiction, and within a few years achieved a circulation of 100,000 (Mott 4: 783). Yet by 1932 it was defunct, while the *Atlantic* survived the depression to thrive again.

Despite his frustrations and some incompatibility of temperament with the magazine, Page had definitively left his mark. The *Atlantic*'s history had limited its malleability, but Page had gone far toward reshaping it in his own image. He had been brought in to increase circulation, and under him circulation had risen from about 10,000 in 1895 to more than 17,000 by 1899 (Ballou 453–54). Advertising revenues, which Page had encouraged and which would become increasingly crucial in supporting the *Atlantic*, had risen from around $1,600 to $2,500 a month (Ballou 453). The magazine was still losing money, partly because of increased promotion expenses, but it had clearly rebounded from its nadir and begun a recovery that proved lasting. Furthermore, Page had helped the *Atlantic* to recover from its inclination to genteel neurasthenia caused by excessive preoccupation with literary culture and the past.

Several years later, Page's successor, Bliss Perry, wrote Page that "no one who has not seen something of its inside history can appreciate how great a debt the *Atlantic* owes to you for breathing into it the breath of life.... If it had not been for your impatient energy in getting the magazine out of the ruts, the grass would be growing over it today" (1 Feb. 1904). Perry did not exaggerate much. Though Page had not "Forumized" the *Atlantic*, he had made it less bookish, scholarly, and retrospective; increased the pluralism of its voices and perspectives; and brought it into closer contact with current American conditions and social issues. He had shown successors ways to combine literary culture with journalistic reporting and analysis of contemporary American life. In doing so, he established the essential editorial direction of the magazine in the twentieth century.

Bliss Perry, *Atlantic* editor, 1899 to 1909. By permission of the Boston Athenaeum.

8

Bliss Perry

(1 8 9 9 – 1 9 0 9)

Liberal Humanist in the Progressive Era

In the wake of Page's sudden resignation to take dominion over a kingdom or two for McClure, Mifflin called on the faithful Scudder, still the firm's chief literary adviser, to find a successor. Though only one previous editor had been a Harvard graduate, one of Scudder's first impulses was to cull a list from the Harvard College alumni directory, including the names of A. Lawrence Lowell and the novelist Arthur S. Hardy. Mifflin was delighted with the prospect of another Lowell in the succession, but this one declined, as did Hardy. Scudder next shuttled to New York to interview Henry Dwight Sedgwick, gentleman lawyer and conservative defender of gentry culture, Houghton Mifflin author, and older brother of later editor Ellery Sedgwick. Scudder knew and liked the elder Sedgwick's commitment to literary high culture but admitted doubts about "his competence as a man of the day"— doubts that quickly proved well founded. Sedgwick worried that his mother-in-law would object to his moving to Boston, that every respectable family needed a lawyer to manage its affairs, and that "he loved books but after all he was not very fond of work and really he should not know how to take hold" (Scudder diary, 14 July 1899).

Having narrowly escaped Sedgwick, Scudder was running low on ideas when MacGregor Jenkins, the *Atlantic*'s young business manager, recommended a fellow Williams graduate, Bliss Perry, a thirty-nine-year-old professor of English and American literature at Princeton. Perry was the son of Williams professor of economics Arthur Latham Perry, whom Scudder, as a trustee of Williams, had only a month before voted to dismiss for writing an "insolent," divisive book about the college, but this did not prejudice Scudder. The younger Perry, as was his summer custom, had disappeared into the woods of northern Vermont on a fishing trip but on reemerging found Jenkins sitting on his rooming house porch and then proposing a wholly unexpected turn in his life. Interested, but conscious of his lack of editorial experience, Perry agreed to an interview with Scudder, which proved decisive.

Many years later, Perry recalled Scudder as "a unique idealist," "a strange compound of dreamer, 'projector,' and literary hack" with a quasi-religious loyalty to the moderately mercenary firm of Houghton Mifflin and a quixotic conviction that "every hour of hack work [was] a permanent contribution to the development of American culture and character" (*Gladly Teach* 165–66). Perry's later cynicism about commercial publishing, reflected in this description, resulted largely from his *Atlantic* editorship. At the time of the interview, however, Scudder proselytized Perry with his own cultural evangelism and convinced him that as *Atlantic* editor and literary adviser to the house he would exercise a more potent good influence on national literary culture and render a broader public service than he could as a teacher.

Perry was by nature and background an inheritor of the New England cultural tradition of liberal humanism and therefore susceptible to this type of idealism about cultural service. He soon accepted. Scudder was relieved, but mildly worried about the *Atlantic*'s fate. "Though it does not impress me as the ideal arrangement," he confessed to himself, "the event may set at rest my vague doubts. Perry has had good training in literature. He has been pushed forward to better and better positions so that those nearest him have plainly valued him. He is a serious, religious-minded fellow and has no doubt lots of work in him. . . . How much initiative he has, I don't know" (Diary, 5 Aug. 1899). Scudder's perceptions were largely accurate. In Page, he had lost a dynamic and pragmatic professional editor, self-confidently committed to progressive journalism and a broader audience, and to Scudder's dismay quite willing to sacrifice the *Atlantic*'s high cultural traditions in literature, literary criticism, and history. In Perry, he had hired a capable, broad-minded, and principled humanist whose training was in literature, not journalism, and whose initiative would be blunted by a frequent conflict between his own high-culture instincts and the requirements of commercial publishing.

The progressive Page had been impatient to jettison much of the *Atlantic*'s baggage of high culture to gain present-day impact and broader influence. Perry, the liberal humanist, believed that intellectual culture should be engaged in contemporary issues. He was also pragmatic enough to recognize the commercial case for giving attention to current events and to acknowledge the essential rightness of Page's editorial direction. Perry later claimed that he learned more about editing from his friend Edward Bok, editor of the immensely popular *Ladies' Home Journal*, than from the likes of Gilder and Alden, aging editors of "quality" literary monthlies. A comparison of Perry's *Atlantic* with Scudder's shows a 5 percent reduction in fiction and a sharp increase in articles on politics and social issues, from about 5 percent to nearly 15 percent. But while Perry followed Page's progressive trend toward "contemporanics," he was more reluctant to acknowledge literary criticism worthless or the cultural past defunct. He restored reviews and criticism (16 percent) as well as biography and history (18 percent) to about the same levels as in Scudder's *Atlantic*.

Bliss Perry came from a line of Yankee teachers, Brahminic neither in social prestige nor in wealth but in culture and social function. He grew up in the small, rural Massachusetts community of Williamstown as a lanky, loose-jointed American boy who loved baseball and fishing, the natural democracy of sports and the woods. But he also learned early a moral seriousness, social responsibility, and respect for the life of the mind. Throughout his life he thought of himself as a product of old New England: sincere, relatively unsophisticated, democratic, unpretentiously informal but gentlemanly in manners, an American of simple principles who admired plain living and high thinking. Later experiences—including graduate education in Germany, wide travel, teaching at Williams, Princeton, and finally Harvard, as well as a ten-year stint in Boston publishing—added intellectual complexity, a habit of gentle irony, and a broader awareness of contemporary social realities but did not blur the main outlines of character and values.

Perry represented a new adaptation of the old tradition of liberal Yankee humanism, blending conscience, intellectual tolerance, individualism, respect for reason, social responsibility, and a commitment to both high culture and democratic ideals (Brooks, *Indian Summer* 506). He characterized himself as an idealist and believed that America was a nation of idealists. But unlike the exponents of genteel idealism, he refused to be merely retrospective, ethnocentric, or cynical about the direction of American culture. In one *Atlantic* essay, noting the immense population shift that made Boston currently two-thirds Catholic, he commented: "Far better these immigrants as raw material for Democracy's wholesome task than that exhausted strain of Puritan stock which lives querulously in the cities or grows vile in the hill towns" ("Whittier," Dec. 1907, 856). In another *Atlantic* piece, he castigated the sophisticated, intellectual cynicism typified by Henry Adams and reasserted the need for simplicity of life and manners and vigorous work ("Indifferentism," Sept. 1903, 329–38). Sharing some of Page's progressive optimism but more genuinely attached to humanistic culture, Perry sought both to preserve that culture as a continuing source of values and to keep it in contact with American social realities.

Preserving humanistic culture, making literature clarify and illumine the contemporary world, had been Perry's profession in colleges for more than ten years before he moved into the small third-floor study at 4 Park Street to begin work as the *Atlantic*'s seventh editor in August 1899. But although his purpose, as Scudder had suggested, would be largely the same, he found commercial publishing a very different world than academe, one in which he was unable to feel as confident or comfortable. In fact, he remained in close contact with the academic world until he returned to it full time in 1909 after nearly ten years of editing. During his first year, his new editorship had to share his energies with a full teaching commitment at Princeton. Monday and Tuesday were spent at Park Street, Wednesday through Sunday with students, colleagues, and family at Princeton. In 1900, he settled full time into the *Atlantic* and a home in Cambridge, but by 1904 he was writing a book on Whitman and developing a lecture series for Harvard. These efforts led to an offer of Lowell's old chair in literature at Harvard and half-time employment there from 1906 through 1909, when he resumed full-time teaching duties.

In Lowell's *Atlantic* days, splitting time between academe and editing had not been ideal but was not unusual because the editor's job was less active and competitive and his salary relatively modest. But the great expansion in publishing since the fifties, and particularly the advent of the mass-circulation magazines in the mid-nineties, had brought increasing competition for audiences, writers, and profits and the expansion of the editor's function not only as solicitor but as generator of topics and shaper of contributions. As a result, magazine editing, like many other professions, had become much more specialized. It had passed from academics and writers to professional magazine editors like Page or the immensely successful editors of new popular magazines such as Edward Bok of *Ladies' Home Journal* or George Horace Lorimer of the *Saturday Evening Post*, who were paid $15,000 and more to keep their fingers on the pulse of the American middle-class reading public. The *Atlantic*, of course, was not even turning a profit, so Mifflin was naturally reluctant to commit a fully competitive editorial salary to it. On Scudder's death in February 1902, he further economized by appointing Perry editor-in-chief of the trade division in addition to his *Atlantic* duties, at Scudder's old salary of $6,000 (Houghton Mifflin Private Journal, 1896–1908). Unquestionably, the *Atlantic* suffered from Perry's lack of experience as well as from the three-way division of his time and intellectual energy between the magazine, trade books, and teaching. In structuring its editorial position, the magazine was not to catch up to the trade until it became independent of Houghton Mifflin in 1908 and gained a full-time editor and publisher, each with assistants.

Perry, as an academic in the increasingly professionalized publishing field, had a different approach to editing than most of his contemporaries. Academic training, fair-mindedness, and disparate demands on his time combined to make him a less aggressive, less coercive editor than Page or most contemporaries. Page had helped to create the trend in progressive publishing toward centralized control of a magazine by an editor who generated and shaped material. Perry followed the older, more passive style, leaving more initiative to the writer. He was never either as clear in his vision of what he wished the *Atlantic* to be or as dynamic in shaping it as

Page. He did project editorial plans, most notably for some challenging series on civil rights and business ethics, but the coherence of his planning slacked after 1903. The pace and breadth of his solicitations, never great, slacked too. In soliciting, also, he was less coercive than Page in defining either the topic or the approach. Even in editing manuscripts, he urged writers to treat comments as suggestions over which their own decision was final. He insisted that editorials and book reviews be either signed or initialed so that they would represent the views of individuals, not the vatic utterances of the *Atlantic*. But some of what the *Atlantic* lost in energy and coherence as a result of Perry's less aggressive or authoritarian editorial style, it made up in diversity of view.

Because of his multiple responsibilities, Perry was given a younger assistant for *Atlantic* work. Rushed, lacking editorial confidence, and egalitarian by nature, he tended to rely too heavily on these associates. During the chaotic transition after Page's departure, with Perry in Princeton most of the week, the affairs of the magazine were handled mainly by the twenty-eight-year-old William B. Parker, a pattern that set a precedent. Perry must have been grateful for Parker's efficiency, and Parker enjoyed his new authority after Page's tight rein. Parker not only acted as first reader for submissions but wrote most correspondence, edited manuscripts, solicited authors, made up issues, even proposed editorial programs and traveled to meet with major contributors.

Parker was decisive and efficient and at times could be a sensitive editor. In one case, Parker not only encouraged a young immigrant medical student to write his autobiography but took pains to console him and ensure continuance of medical treatment as he wasted from tuberculosis (Parker to Nathan Babad, 1900). He also cultivated some good younger writers, mostly Harvard acquaintances, including William Vaughn Moody, Norman and Hutchins Hapgood, Will Payne, Norman Duncan, and Trumbull Stickney. But Parker's correspondence and relationships, even with friends, often reflected a youthfully officious or pedantic tone. In accepting one of Jack London's first stories, he wrote the author that for the byline "we venture to suggest the use of the more frequent form of the Christian name—John seeming to us better suited than Jack to literary purposes" (10 Oct. 1899). He also often made the mistake of sanguinely encouraging authors to develop their work or laboriously to revise it, even lavishly praising the result, but finally refusing publication with a brief statement that it would be commercially unprofitable. This was not the stuff of long-term editorial relationships.

When Parker was transferred to the trade division in 1902, Ferris Greenslet became Perry's *Atlantic* assistant. Greenslet, then in his late twenties and later to become longtime editor-in-chief of the firm's trade books, had a Ph.D. in English literature from Columbia, where he had imbibed the orthodox literary tastes of Aldrich's protégé George Woodberry. Greenslet had a smoother touch with authors than Parker, but his tastes seemed limited by an odd combination of high literary convention and commercial prudence, and he provided little balance to Perry's own inclination to the academic.

When Greenslet followed Parker to the trade division in 1907, MacGregor Jenkins was frequently called on to assist Perry, who was now teaching half-time in addition to serving as editor-in-chief of both the magazine and trade books. As the magazine's business and advertising manager since 1893, Jenkins had long been an increasingly significant presence, energetically placing paid and unpaid promotions of the *Atlantic* in newspapers nationwide, soliciting advertising for the magazine, promoting newsstand sales, targeting and soliciting prospective readers such as teachers, and working tirelessly to persuade the editors to shed the magazine's highbrow image and address a broader audience. Jenkins was resolutely middlebrow, a voice of the mass market and the *Saturday Evening Post* influential in the inner councils of the *Atlantic*. Like Page, and later Ellery Sedgwick, to both of whom he was a trusted lieutenant, Jenkins was committed to reducing the gap between "high" and popular culture. He expressed contempt for "Literature with a Large L," aesthetically self-conscious literature, excessively subtle or intellectual. The only justifications for literature were entertainment and "interpretation." Its merits could be judged by how simply and directly it accomplished these goals for a maximum number of readers. Real literature was written not by precious, professional "literary persons," self-serious about their bogus "art" (and demanding large payments), but by plain people with a vital experience to tell. Literary criticism and talk about aesthetics were mostly "empty silliness."

Jenkins had originally proposed Perry for the editorship and played a central role in the negotiations. On Perry's arrival Jenkins had secured him a room in his own boardinghouse and been not only a genial friend but also a collegial guide to the mysteries of magazine publishing in general and Houghton Mifflin in particular. Throughout Perry's editorship, Jenkins's influence was often direct. In pursuit of newsstand sales, especially to the younger, less literary male reader, Jenkins proposed a series on outdoor sports, to which Perry, an avid dry-fly fisherman, contributed an article entitled "Fishing with a Worm." Jenkins's particular bête noire, the incarnation of Literature with a Large L, was Henry James. Jenkins and Page shared a loathing for James. In the midst of a Jenkins campaign to convince the American News Service that the *Atlantic* was not highbrow but written for red-blooded Americans, neophyte editor Perry printed a story by James that the business manager felt completely shattered his credibility. The distraught Jenkins came to Perry "with actual tears in his eyes," begging him not to print another infernal "sinker" by James (Perry, *Gladly Teach* 176, 178).

From beginning to end of his editorship, Perry was ambivalent about the nature of the magazine's mission and audience and about his responsibilities as editor. His academic background, personal taste, and high-culture instincts told him that his function was to publish James and the best of contemporary literature, pursue an honest and vigorous literary criticism, encourage discussion of the canonical authors of Western humanism, and sustain a high intellectual level of free debate on political and social issues. Nevertheless, like Page, he was impatient with the split between high literary and intellectual culture and the broader currents of American life. He sincerely wished to make humanistic culture more engaged in the present. His ideological commitment to bridging the culture gap was further complicated by the economic influence of his business manager and his publisher and by his observation of competing magazines. All of these told him that simply to pursue the *Atlantic*'s old high-culture line would put it under the sod and that substantive concessions to middlebrow mass culture were necessary. To Page, as to Perry's successor Sedgwick, such concessions were progress, giving the magazine greater influence. But to Perry, they often warred with his instincts, worried his conscience, and in the end led him back to academe feeling a slight bitterness about his years in commercial publishing.

Perry's quandary about his audience and editorial judgments is reflected in a letter written to Henry James early in his editorship accepting James's proposal to write some "literary papers" for the *Atlantic*. Page would have flatly rejected the proposal; Perry accepted it with private misgivings based on Jenkins's recent analysis of the subscription list. He cautioned James:

> I am tempted to add a word of suggestion about the new audience which the *Atlantic* is reaching nowadays. More than half of its circulation—which has been growing rapidly of late—is now west of the Mississippi, and there are more subscribers in Wisconsin than in any state except Massachusetts. I confess that I am not very certain about the temper of this audience, but I know it differs markedly from the old *Atlantic* circle of readers. The nuances of "Maude Evelyn" [a recently accepted story by James]—to take a current illustration—will be quite lost upon a great many of our subscribers who are losing their heads over "To Have and to Hold" [the immensely popular serial romance that Page had contracted from Mary Johnston]. That cannot be helped, I suppose, and it ought not and will not prevent our printing an occasional story that is too subtle and delicate for "the general." But I think it will be well for you to bear these new conditions in mind when you are mulling over the subjects and possible modes of treatment of the papers which you may from time to time do for us. Please don't think we are sufficiently "journalized" to prefer coarser work to finer work—and naturally you would not do coarse work if you could—but it does seem to me essential to the effectiveness of an *Atlantic* paper nowadays that it should be constructed upon as simple and strong lines as possible. (31 Oct. 1899)

Perry would seek a different balance than Page had, a balance he hoped would retain more of the old magazine and include occasional pieces by James. But he knew too, because Jenkins and others kept reminding him, that he had to aim at a broader, more diverse, less intellectual, belletristic, and liberally educated audience. In sanguine, public moments he rejoiced in the democratization of his audience, noting as evidence of success that "a subscription to the *Atlantic* is apparently no longer as it once was said to be in certain newly settled communities—a sufficient evidence of one's social standing . . . , a badge of respectability" ("A Readable Proposition," Jan. 1905, 1–2). But in delivering the message to authors, he frequently lamented having an audience that preferred Mary Johnston to Henry James, did not know a "sposa" from a "trattoria," and refused to read poetry not immediately transparent (Perry to Mrs. Stetson-Channing, 25 Aug. 1899).

Ellen Ballou has claimed that "Perry, more than any of his predecessors, deferred to the prejudices and preferences of his Gentle Readers" (465). Certainly he was editor at a time when commercial mass culture had become increasingly dominant, and he was under more pressure from the culture at large, and from his publisher, to popularize. Probably there was more conflict between his personal tastes and what he published than with any of his predecessors. Unquestionably he did accept material, particularly in fiction, that he knew to be second- or third-rate because it would be successful with a larger audience, and conversely both he and his assistants rejected fiction they knew to be of high quality because it would have little appeal. This commercial pragmatism did not sit easily on Perry's high-culture conscience and eventually soured him on the publishing profession.

Perry, however, had in him the old New England starch of principle and an ability to adapt it to the present. In some contexts he was as willing as any of his predecessors to lead rather than follow his readership—even, as Emerson had hoped, to defy the public and follow his own conscience. In editorials, he directly criticized some *Atlantic* readers for intellectual intolerance. In making up issues, he balanced more popular material with more intellectually subtle literary or historical discussions, including James's, that he knew would appeal to relatively few. He was also willing to raise unpopular political and social issues, such as the disenfranchisement of blacks and colonization in the Philippines. On these issues he presented an impressive range of views, and he himself took clear, principled, controversial stands. In soliciting political discussions, he indicated "the desirability of allowing full and free discussion of all views and doctrines whether or not unpopular for the moment" (James Bryce to Perry, 13 Dec. 1901, summarizing Perry's directives to him).

Perry made clear both his resistance and his capitulation to his audience in editorial addresses in January of each year. The tone of these was amiable and sometimes genteel, but Perry's characteristic principled earnestness, mirrored in his conduct of the magazine, lay beneath. He ridiculed those dour persons who directed "streams of sorrowful correspondence" to the editor after each issue condemning the magazine because an article offended their taste or convictions. The *Atlantic*, Perry maintained, was edited not for sectarians who sought constant affirmation of their own creeds but for the intellectually vigorous who wished to hear a range of rationally argued views ("On Reading the *Atlantic* Cheerfully," Jan. 1902, 1–4).

In "Catering for the Public" (Jan. 1904), however, Perry acknowledged that while the *Atlantic* editor was "no vulgar caterer to the public in general," leaving that to the "yellow journal and the corner saloon," he was like the landlord of a boarding house dependent on the tastes of his boarders, which were frequently not his own. "Does anybody suppose," he quipped, "that Mr. Munsey's favorite reading is the Munsey Storiettes? Does 'the sound of the swashbuckler swashing on his buckler' seem less humorous to the editors who encourage it than it does to Mr. Howells who has laid aside his editorial armor and can smile at the weaknesses of his former fellow warriors? Do the peaceful editors of the 'Outlook' really thrill with those stern praises of fighting men and fighting machines which adorn its secularized pages? Or does the talented conductor of 'The Ladies' Home Journal' really . . . ? No, he cannot" (3). Perry's humorous irony reflected an uncomfortable sense of hypocrisy that haunted him often during his editorship.

In no field did Perry cater so flagrantly, with such conflict between his personal tastes and editorial choices, as in his selection of fiction, particularly the serial novels. In no field did the business office feel so free to tread on editorial prerogatives, since book as well as serial rights were involved and popular fiction was the most lucrative part of the trade market. In Perry's serials, therefore, the sound of the swashbuckler was heard often, as were the sounds of sighs and wedding marches. In fiction, as elsewhere, he tried for a balance, but undeniably there was more of Mary Johnston than of Henry James. Did Bliss Perry really print *Atlantic* serials with a clear conscience, much less a pride in contributing to "the permanent element in American literature"? No, he did not.[1]

Perry's performance should be judged in context, and the literary context of his years at the *Atlantic* was bleak. Howells, looking back over the fiction of the first decade of the twentieth century, commented that "there never was a more imbecile time, perhaps," and Larzer Ziff has called it the dreariest decade in American letters (qtd. in John 253). Early in the decade, particularly, the imbecility was in large part caused by an extraordinary seduction of many writers by the vogue of historical romance. The quality of these works varied widely, but James had judged the entire genre "fatally cheap" (Cary, *Jewett* 152). Instead of the complexities of Jamesian psychological realism or the depressing brutalities of urban, industrial America reflected by the naturalists, it offered readers not only a plot but an escape into an earlier time of simpler problems and clearer moral values, often a kind of Anglo-Saxon, American golden age.

Authors were strongly encouraged to write romances by editors and publishers, who shared their hopes of cashing in on a swelling mass-publishing market. Younger writers such as Ellen Glasgow and Upton Sinclair, who were later to distinguish themselves in an extremely different direction, were co-opted by the lure of this market. Charles Chesnutt, hoping to support his family while he wrote serious fiction, tried and failed to publish two romances. Even well-established writers who had had reasonable success in the realistic or local color modes succumbed to the temptation. Howells lamented the defection of his realist protégé Henry Fuller to romance. Page, by contrast, anticipated and fueled the market, persuading Joel Chandler Harris and others to write romances. As noted, even Sarah Orne Jewett allowed herself to be inveigled into joining the romantic reaction by Scudder and Charles Dudley Warner, a leader of the revolt against realism. A flood tide of romances by these and other authors came across Perry's desk, while Mifflin, Jenkins, and other publishers celebrated soaring sales of similar literary commodities.

Perry's tastes in literature were considerably more sophisticated than Page's and more modern than Scudder's. His book on Whitman was the first full-scale critical biography, and while not adulatory, it clearly asserted that Whitman was the most original and important American poet to date. Called on to commemorate the centennials of the New England Olympians, he nonetheless knew, as Scudder had not, that Longfellow, Lowell, Holmes, and Whittier were secondary or tertiary figures already beginning to fade. Of the old New England writers, he valued Hawthorne, Emerson, and Thoreau most highly; he considered that persuading Houghton Mifflin to publish the journals of Emerson and Thoreau was his most significant editorial accomplishment. Of contemporary novelists, he was certain that James was the one whose reputation would remain solidest, followed by Howells. Perry's own fiction, including an early novel dealing with racial issues, realistically reflected contemporary social conditions and was praised by Brander Matthews for having "the flavor of American life" (Matthews to Perry, 5 Aug. 1898).

If Perry knew good literature from high-grade pulp, he also received an early object lesson in the power of pulp. Before leaving, Page had contracted Mary Johnston's romance of colonial Virginia *To Have and To Hold* as an *Atlantic* serial for 1900. Perry sardonically recalled that Page and the elated Mac Jenkins knew that they had a blockbuster on their hands when they found the typists borrowing galleys to read at lunch hour (*Gladly Teach* 175). As installments came in from Johnston, W. B. Parker was kept busy heading off absurdities in letters that were restrained versions of Twain's essay on romantic implausibilities in the novels of Cooper: was it credible that the hero would turn pirate? how could one know from footprints that a pursuer was ten feet behind the pursued? But as the installments came out, sales of the magazine soared (though most of the gain proved temporary); on publication as a book, *To Have and To Hold* rapidly sold an astronomical 240,000 copies (Francis Garrison to George Mifflin, 21 Aug. 1900). Later, Johnston's romance was twice made into a movie and in turn inspired another young southern woman, Margaret Mitchell, who would use it as a model to produce an even bigger blockbuster, *Gone with the Wind*.

While *To Have and To Hold* was enjoying immense sales, Perry was negotiating for his next serial and as a neophyte was receiving considerable advice and active pressure from Mifflin, Jenkins, Scudder, and others at Houghton Mifflin. Howells, apparently released from his exclusive contract with *Harper's*, offered a short serial, but Perry begged off, saying he could not use it any time soon (Francis Garrison to Mifflin, 17 Aug. 1900). When Henry James submitted the outline of a new novel, probably either *The Sacred Fount* or *The Ambassadors*, Perry expressed interest, asking the price and production schedule but saying that he must wait to review material already solicited by Page. "Furthermore," he added, "we must reckon more or less upon the passing taste of the American public. Right now people are quite daft, as you know, over the American historical romance, and incline to be suspicious of anything else. This makes us hesitate—I wish it did not!—to engage a serial from your hand in spite of the convincing plot that you have already submitted. It may be that it will be best to do so. Yet our uncertainty is so great that I cannot feel comfortable without laying the matter thus frankly before you" (to J. B. Pinker, 20 Dec. 1899; to Henry James, 13 Dec. 1899 and 14 Mar. 1900). Perry knew the historical romance for the light, transitory, commercial product it was, as he knew the aesthetic integrity and permanence of James. But he was also aware not only of the appetite of his readers but more immediately of the pressures from Houghton Mifflin's management, who saw the prospect of unprecedented book sales. Despite a bad conscience, he could not in this case finally face down his readers and publishers.

Who were the authors whose serials Perry awaited and, in the event, published in preference to those of Howells and James? One was Sarah Orne Jewett, whom Mifflin and Scudder had been courting for a romance. Her romance of the American Revolution, *The Tory Lover*, serialized by Perry in 1901, was her last major work before she suffered a concussion and permanent brain damage by being thrown from a carriage in 1902. While Perry would have defended this and the other romances he published as "good of their kind," he certainly knew that it was a kind on which Miss Jewett's particular talents were largely wasted. But in puffing it for promotion, Perry called it "the most important piece of work which Miss Jewett has ever attempted," a claim that must have had a bitter, hollow ring of irony for him (Perry to W. S. Moody, editor of the *Bookbuyer*, 5 Sept. 1900).

A second author whose works were preferred to those of Howells and James was Kate Douglas Wiggin, whose short serial "Penelope's Irish Adventures" also ran in 1901. Perry, heavily prodded by Albert Houghton, solicited Wiggin, a proven Houghton Mifflin literary property and soon to be author of *Rebecca of Sunnybrook Farm*, and declared the result "simply delicious." Kate Wiggin wrote her own press notices for the promotion department, but Perry also obligingly wrote a puff that characterized this bit of pink cotton candy as "a most brilliant and attractive piece of work" (Perry to W. S. Moody, 5 Sept. 1900).

The serialization of Mary Johnston's second romance, *Audrey*, reflected even more clearly the heavy hand of management in initiating serials at the beginning of Perry's editorship. Hoping for a second *To Have and To Hold*, the firm rapidly dispatched Albert Houghton to Warm Springs, Virginia, to court Mary Johnston for her next book with the instructions to "get the goods" without going over $7,500 for serial rights or a 15 percent royalty on the book (Francis Garrison to Albert Houghton, 7 Sept. 1900). Perry had virtually nothing to do with contracting the serial, which was purchased sight unseen, but he was left to sustain the nervous author through its completion. Mary Johnston, who required constant editorial reassurance, despite her immense success, had sometimes suspected that *To Have* was "the veriest trash that ever escaped a waste-paper basket." Now she lamented that she wished *Audrey* were better, "but with only a woman's allowance of grey matter, plus sickness and trouble . . . , it is the best I have been able to do" (to Perry, 18 Dec. 1899 and 22 Oct. 1901). Perry obligingly reassured her that it was an artistic success. Certainly Houghton Mifflin expected the book to be a commercial success; they planned a first edition of 125,000, of which 100,000 were already on order before publication, and arranged retailing partly through department stores such as Macy's, Bloomingdale's, and Wanamaker's (Garrison to Mifflin, 1 Mar. 1902).

By the beginning of 1902, however, Perry was complaining to Page of being terminally sick of historical romances. Page characteristically acknowledged that he too had had his fill but that publishing was a matter of selling books, not of personal taste (Page to Perry, 1 Jan. 1902). To his credit, Perry was not as cynical about literature as Page, and he sought to jettison the historical romance fad earlier than editors such as Gilder and *Scribner's* Burlingame. Having surfeited on cream puffs while catering to his readers and employers, he now rejected a series of romances written by authors such as Florence Converse, Henry Fuller, and Upton Sinclair, who, like Page, belatedly hoped to cash in on the literary fad.

By 1902, then, Perry was seeking more realistic fiction having contemporary settings and characters. Here again, however, he felt obliged to cater to certain constraining prejudices in his readers. Like Page, he perceived that the chief prejudice of both men and women, genteel and progressive, was against fiction that was merely depressing, that weighed down rather than inspiring the reader. Readers wanted optimism, hope of moral salvation, and preferably a touch of humor. Closely related to this desire for optimism was the genteel rejection of the "unpleasant" or excessively graphic.

Even the old New England local color fiction, with its Calvinistic sense of fate, seemed now too gray and bleak for the increasingly broad middle-class audience Perry projected. As he observed to Alice Brown:

> The present day readers of the *Atlantic* do not particularly care for the somber New England story with its touch of renunciation or tragedy. That particular vein in human nature has yielded rich ore for fiction. . . . Nevertheless, I honestly believe that to most of the persons whom we are endeavoring to persuade to renew their subscriptions to the magazine, this mine seems exhausted—a dark and dismal hole in the ground with clammy water standing in the bottom. As a New Englander myself and a lover of the New England short story, I could hope that you would continue forever to write stories like "The Herb Doctor," but in my capacity of purchasing agent and salesman to the general public, I hold with the *Century* people that "goods of another pattern" are being worn more now. . . . Come in some time and let me join my lamentation with yours. (18 Jan. 1906)

Clearly Perry felt a touch of contempt for his role as "purchasing agent," but he continued to play it, and to let his assistants play it with even less reference to aesthetic integrity than he made. It is unfair to suggest that Perry allowed only optimistic, sentimental pieties into *Atlantic* fiction. But he was hypersensitive to his publishers and readers and usually maintained a conservative balance of optimism. "Unluckily," he wrote rejecting a friend's story, "we have accumulated without knowing it a good many stories that end tragically, and we have been trying for several weeks past to correct our blunder by sending back a good many tempting things which are open to this special and temporary objection." Following Jenkins's advice to get some red-blooded sport into the magazine in this strenuous Roosevelt era, Perry with conscious irony proposed that the friend renounce tragedy and try a "big game story." "I will not go as far as our friends on the *Youth's Companion*, who will order a writer to manufacture a story containing a big bull moose, which must be shot in the last paragraph by the young hero," he continued, "—but all the same we really need something of that sort" (to Max Foster, 14 Mar. 1900). The objection to tragedy was more than temporary, and the characteristic self-parody reflected Perry's continued discomfort at subverting the literary quality he was supposed to be upholding.

Perry's younger assistants, Parker and Greenslet, seemed to feel no such irony and express no such guilt. Many of their rejections of fiction, which must have been at least reviewed by Perry, seem especially cynical because they acknowledge, even enthusiastically praise, the quality of the work but complacently reject it in the end solely because its vision seems too dark to be commercially attractive. In declining "The Law of Life," Jack London's classic story of an old Eskimo left to die, Parker wrote: "We have heartily liked the vigor of it and the breadth of treatment with which you have written it. But the subject is forbidding—in fact seems to us depressing, and so the excellent craftsmanship of it has not changed our mind" (3 May 1900). Kate Chopin's story "The Demon" was similarly rejected, despite its "excellent craftsmanship," because "the sad note seems to us too much accented" (Parker to Kate Chopin, 16 Jan. 1900).

Clearly Perry and his assistants at times knowingly sacrificed the quality and integrity of the literary work in the *Atlantic*. They rejected some work they knew to be of substantive value and accepted, even proposed, hack work of greater commercial appeal. These hypocrisies did not, however, preclude the publication of some good fiction or in all cases limit *Atlantic* fiction solely to "the smiling aspects of life." Perry did genuinely seek a balance in his fiction rather than total suppression of the tragic or disturbing, and he did grow somewhat more assertive in following his own tastes. After rapidly sickening of the historical romance, he solicited the Chicago realist Robert Herrick for a contemporary serial. Herrick produced one of his best novels, *The Common Lot*, a story of a young architect who sells his soul for profit by building a shoddy tenement that burns down, killing its inhabitants. Perry found this "a strong piece of work . . . calculated to make a deep impression upon the reader" and serialized it in 1904 (to Herrick, 21 Sept. 1903).

Perry's admiration of Herrick's work was genuine, but the rewards he could offer were modest, especially compared with the remuneration frequently offered by other editors for the more popular, romantic-formula fiction that dominated the market at the turn of the century. Perry's editorial budget from Houghton Mifflin was simple. He was allotted $1,440 to fill 144 pages. Once a month, he met with the firm's treasurer, James Murray Kay, a portly, "rubicund Scot," to render accounts. Any proposal to pay over $10 per page aroused Kay's disapproval and insinuations that the editor was unjustifiably wasting partners' profits, unless the work in question could be demonstrated to bring concrete benefits in the form of higher circulation or a profitable book manuscript (Perry, *Gladly Teach* 181). Kay and George Mifflin were persuaded by *To Have and To Hold* that Mary Johnston was a paying property, and while she had received $3,500, or about $17 a page, for the serial rights of *To Have and To Hold*, she was offered $7,500, more than $30 per page, for *Audrey* (Ballou 422 and Garrison to A. F. Houghton, 7 Sept. 1900). This was still less than the $10,000 offered Miss Johnston by a New York magazine (the *Century* regularly paid $5,000 or more), but very considerably more than the $1,200 (about $10 per page) offered Herrick or even the $2,200–$2,500 offered Sarah Orne Jewett. As Perry later noted, the scale of values in the firm's powwows was commercial, not aesthetic. "Professors of Literature might rate *The Country of the Pointed Firs* much higher than *Rebecca of Sunnybrook Farm*, but if one of these works sold ten times as many copies as the other, that settled the question of the relative importance of the two authors" (*Gladly Teach* 182). In this point of view, the firm simply reflected the market. An editor was hard pressed to resist both.

One defense that Perry had against a market and readership that promoted mediocre fiction at high cost to his editorial budget and conscience was to reduce the amount of fiction in the magazine. He did moderately curtail the proportion of fiction from about 35 percent during Scudder's time to slightly less than 30 percent, sometimes by omitting the traditional serial novel. Since Lowell's day, the magazine had constantly featured one serial, and during the editorships of Howells and Aldrich it often carried two. But Scudder and Page, dissatisfied with available novels, had begun experimenting with options, and Perry followed their lead. In 1903 and again in 1906, Perry could find no satisfactory serial fiction and determined to publish none at all rather than run one of the romances or sentimental domestic stories submitted in abundance. Some of the space thereby created was given to nonfiction serials—most of them of high quality, most cheaper than fiction—which during the decade included an autobiography by the early *Atlantic* contributor John Trowbridge, Edith Wharton's "Second Motor Flight through France," Ruskin's letters to Charles Eliot Norton, and Thoreau's journals. They included also Page's "Autobiography of a Southerner," containing frank discussions of current racial issues, and J. O. Fagin's muckraking "Confessions of a Railroad Signalman." Both of these last demonstrated again that *Atlantic* nonfiction was not only cheaper than fiction but often freer to deal with controversial issues.

Perry did publish some quality fiction from both established writers and a promising group of younger authors. Unfortunately many of the former contributed seldom because they could command higher fees in New York, while several of the latter, after their careers were launched, left because they found another publisher who paid better or showed more consistent, less conditional enthusiasm for their work.

The *Atlantic* payment policy continued to be to refuse direct competition with New York for established writers but to rely on the editor's solicitations and the magazine's literary reputation to draw authors. Perry was habitually frank about this restriction. "We have never," he wrote in returning a piece for which he would not meet the price, "made the slightest attempt to compete with the illustrated magazines in rate of payment.... We are quite aware, of course, that almost every *Atlantic* contributor makes a pecuniary sacrifice in writing for it, and we cannot urge anyone to accept rates which are far below the price which most of our authors can secure elsewhere" (to Edith Wyatt, 10 Feb. 1906). Still, several established authors wanted to continue to appear in the *Atlantic* occasionally, and with some financial compromise on both sides, they contributed good fiction. Perry acknowledged to George Washington Cable that "we are quite aware that by keeping to a prudent policy we lose many contributions which we should be glad to secure," but he finagled $1,000 from Kay to secure Cable's three-part serial, "Bylow Hill," nearly as much as Herrick had received for a novel three times longer (27 Feb. 1901).

In 1903, Edith Wharton, like Cable a *Scribner's* author, sent a story and scolded Perry: "Why have you never asked me for a story for the *Atlantic*? I am tired of waiting.... My usual price for a short story is $500 but I know that the *Atlantic* does not pay as high prices as the illustrated magazines and I shall be quite satisfied with this . . . first because I have always thought it an honor to appear in the *Atlantic* and secondly because I believe it is always advantageous to a writer to get a fresh audience" (9 Nov. 1903). Perry picked up some excellent fiction from this desire among major writers to maintain exposure to the *Atlantic* audience, including stories by Howells, Owen Wister, and James.

More important, Perry's *Atlantic* also gave some early exposure and support to several new writers, some of whose contributions went beyond the fiction of popular entertainment or genteel self-insulation. Perry was not an aggressive solicitor of young talent; his assistant Parker was aggressive but sometimes inept. But the magazine, finally free from the shadow of the Olympians, now gave more evidence of supporting a younger generation of writers than at any time since Howells's editorship.

Jack London's relationship with Perry's *Atlantic* demonstrates the recognition that the magazine gave new writers, styles, and ideas as well as the financial and philosophical limits of that support. It shows that while the editor's judgments were by modern standards limited, neither Perry nor his magazine can be dismissed as merely genteel, addicted to either neurasthenic fiction or sentimentally idealistic, politically safe ideas. Once again, it demonstrates too that this tolerance was broader in nonfiction than in fiction.

During the chaos of Page's departure, he and Parker had accepted a story of the Yukon called "An Odyssey of the North," which the editors found "vigorous" and "essentially healthy" (Parker to London, 24 July 1899). The acceptance and the commendatory wording reflected Page's taste for a strenuous, "masculine" literature. It was Jack London's first publication for a national audience. He expressed his neophyte's satisfaction to his friend Cloudsley Johns, noting that the *Atlantic* editors "seem nice . . . and I understand that they pay well" (24 Aug. 1899, London 1: 106). Houghton Mifflin, with Perry and Scudder participating actively, soon accepted the young Californian's first book of stories, *The Son of the Wolf*, which brought him national critical recognition though modest sales of about 2,500 copies in the first year, earning London $400 (Ballou 482).

London, who was destitute, prolific, and ambitious, sent manuscripts everywhere, and after the publication of his book, he began to meet with success. But for a short time it looked as if the *Atlantic* and Houghton Mifflin would be his major publishers. In 1900, however, Perry and Parker rejected three stories, including "The Law of Life," which they found too grimly depressing. London sent the latter story to *McClure's*, which published it, paid him well indeed, and offered him a generous advance on his next book, a policy Mifflin disapproved. A combination of genteel squeamishness and financial conservatism had lost the firm a rising star. On learning of the loss, Parker wrote London a sympathetic letter apologizing that the house had not understood how desperate his financial situation was, admiring

McClure's "hearty generosity," and hoping that London had "now left behind the rougher road" (14 Mar. 1901).

In terms of finances and recognition, London clearly had left behind the rougher road. While beginning to be widely published in mass-circulation magazines, London, with Perry and Parker's encouragement, continued to submit work to the *Atlantic*, which accepted several more pieces over the next three years. Perry took pains to seek London out on a trip to California and to include his work prominently in an all-California issue of the *Atlantic*. The lead of the California issue asserted that "the creative ability displayed by Mr. London is a most encouraging sign, indicative of the prevalent desire among the majority of western writers to avoid ... 'the musty grip of the past' " (Herbert Bashford, "The Literary Development of the Pacific Coast," July 1903, 8).

As London became increasingly involved in labor issues and radical politics, he continued to submit manuscripts to the *Atlantic*, but now nonfiction rather than the fiction, for which he was getting better prices elsewhere. In 1903, he sent a strongly pro-union labor piece titled "The Scab." The article condemned scabbing as a Darwinian displacement of the weak by the strong, caused by an immoral, barbaric capitalism that refused just payment of labor and created competition among workers for survival. Perry expressed "lurking editorial doubts as to the soundness of your conclusions" but had no intention of limiting *Atlantic* debate on social issues to what he or most of his readers already believed. He found the piece "thoroughly interesting" and printed it in January 1904 in a series on business ethics.

London's next submission, titled "Revolution," sympathetically represented the ideology of what London claimed was a substantial internal radical force seeking the overthrow of the United States government. This time Perry balked:

> Our objection to it is based not at all upon the ideas that are expressed, but upon the fact that it does not seem to us that you have chosen the right style of talk for an *Atlantic* audience. Forgive me for saying that many passages of the paper read precisely like editorials in one of the Hearst papers. These editorials are very ably and brilliantly adapted to the kind of people who read Hearst papers, but it is not the style of address which we can profitably adopt in the *Atlantic*.
>
> I know that you will forgive this unasked criticism, for I do not wish to take refuge behind the conventional editorial formula in your case. (25 May 1905)

London's reply indicated that while he interpreted Perry's rejection as a case of class-based cultural conflict, he recognized the differences in intellectual style as real. "Thank you for your kind rejection of May 25," he wrote. "Now this is not sarcastic at all and I am thanking you for the best and most genuine rejection I ever received in all my life" (31 May 1905, London 1: 487).

London went on to become immensely popular, writing mainly for a high-paying mass market, among other things as a Hearst reporter. This work may have damaged his writing less than producing exclusively for the "quality" periodicals would have done. It is certain, however, that the *Atlantic* editors had recognized his power when he was unknown, helped expose him to a national audience, and shown themselves open to much of his style and thought. Perry had rejected as excessively depressing, though powerful, a story of an old man literally cast to the wolves when he became an economic burden to his tribe. But he had also paradoxically accepted a direct indictment of American capitalism as a wolfish, unjust, and barbarous system forcing the strong to survive by destroying the weak on a massive scale. Certainly he could have expected "The Scab" to be more disturbing to middle-class sensibilities than the death of an old Eskimo. But once again he demonstrated that *Atlantic* editors were more willing to engage a broader spectrum of disturbing realities in nonfiction than they often were in fiction. They may have been sensitive to their readers' distaste for depressing fiction, but as humanists they were committed to a substantial, though not full, diversity of views.

This greater latitude in nonfiction was again demonstrated in the *Atlantic*'s response to another poor but ambitious new writer, Theodore Dreiser. Dreiser had submitted several poems and stories without success. But when he began to submit nonfiction reportage, rejection slips turned into encouraging notes, Parker visited him to solicit work, and Perry finally accepted an article on social conditions in the mill town of Fall River, Massachusetts. Poor like London, Dreiser was paid on acceptance as he requested. But in preparing the manuscript for publication, the editors discovered that Dreiser had defrauded them. "We find," Perry wrote in cold anger, "that considerable portions of your paper have been taken almost verbatim from an article in *The Forum* for November 1894. We enclose a copy of parallel passages in order to remind you unmistakably of the extent to which you have used this article. . . . We do not think it necessary to use many words in characterizing this deception which has been practiced upon us" (22 Dec. 1900, in Ballou 478).

Perry's relationship with another young writer, Mary Austin, was much more productive. Austin, later to become a national advocate of Indian-Hispanic culture and of women's rights, was then a teacher living in relative poverty in the deserts of southern California. She described herself to Perry as "a small, plain brown woman with too much hair, always a little sick and always busy about the fields and the mesas" (25 Nov. 1902, Fink 110). In her isolation, she began recording her observations of desert life and the Mexican-Indian culture. Early in 1900, she compiled a list of magazines she wished to write for, ranked in order of their literary excellence. The *Atlantic* was at the top. Perry, finding the subject, observations, and writing fresh, enthusiastically accepted the first paper and asked for more. After publishing several, he suggested that Austin think of a book. On receiving a large batch of manuscripts in 1902, he contracted to print several pieces serially in the *Atlantic* and persuaded Houghton Mifflin to bring out the collection, titled *The Land of Little Rain*.

For Mary Austin, the receipt of Perry's letter announcing this acceptance was an exhilarating and perhaps fearsome moment. Her life took a decisive turn. She committed herself to writing, subsequently left her family for a Carmel artists' colony, lived a life of bohemian intellectualism in New York, and finally settled in Santa Fe, meanwhile writing on everything from women's independence for the *Ladies' Home Journal* to politics for the *Nation*. Perry's editorial relationship with Mary Austin was never as generative as, for instance, Howells's with James or Boyesen, but he had recognized her promise, separated her work from the mountains of unsolicited manuscripts, praised it generously, spoken for preserving its integrity, convinced her that sympathetic writing about Mexican-Indian culture was of interest to Anglo-American readers, and helped her negotiate the perilous beginnings of a literary career.

Perry's record in prose literature, then, shows modest accomplishments against a background of compromise with his audience's tastes and his publisher's economic interests. This same pattern holds in his treatment of poetry. In defending his own record, Perry noted with justice that it was "a dull decade for American poetry," as in fiction (*Gladly Teach* 176). Even the contemporary editors and poets, anticipating the modernists who would soon pillory them, acknowledged the triviality, the lack of vigor or conviction in contemporary verse. R. W. Gilder, poet and editor of the *Century*, who probably published more watery genteel verse than any other major editor, declared in an *Atlantic* poem the need for a potent new poetic voice:

> Above the pretty songs of schools
> (Not of music made but rules),
> Above the panic rush for gold
> And emptinesses manifold....
>
> ("A New Poet," June 1905, 748)

Perry, who appreciated Whitman's extroverted vigor and love of the world, complained that genuine poets were on strike and that their places had been taken by versifying "scabs" intent on picking up checks for "telling us all about their little emotions with . . . tiresome particularity." Like Gilder, Perry waited for a forceful and heroic figure ("A Readable Proposition," Jan. 1905, 2). Whitman was far closer to Perry's model for this figure than either Longfellow or Tennyson. But certainly neither Gilder nor Perry would have recognized the robust idealist to whom they looked for the resurrection of poetry in Eliot or Pound a decade later.

While waiting for the Messiah, Perry gave modest support to his prophets. The fundamental problem, as always, was that poetry had a very limited readership, especially in magazines, and even that small readership was quickly reduced if a poem looked long or complex. Perry allowed himself to be convinced by the conventional editorial wisdom that no one would read a magazine poem that was not fairly transparent on first reading. This general guideline accounted for the frequent appearance of the classical quatrains and witty epigrammatic "bitcherell" of the Jesuit Father John Tabb. It accounted too for Perry's rejection of Edwin Arlington Robinson's poem "Aunt Imogen."

Perry did, however, publish Robinson's "Calverley's" and support with reservations the publication of his second book, *Captain Craig*. The manuscript report suggested serious aesthetic and commercial problems but also recognized occasional brilliance that was worth supporting for further development: "A volume of obscure verse, often eccentric and prosaic in character but with flashes of genius occasionally. It is the work of an interesting man, who is thought by his friends to be capable of real poetical accomplishment. They admit, however, the grave faults of this Ms volume. . . . The only ground of acceptance is the faith of Robinson's friends and the possibility of a more popular book later" (Manuscript Report 9502, Ballou 487–88).

Perry's support for another young aspirant to the position of redeemer of American poetry, William Vaughn Moody, was somewhat stronger, though still qualified by concessions to his readership. Scudder had commissioned reviews from this idealistic son of an Illinois steamboat captain, and in 1898 Page had published Moody's first poem to reach a national audience. But by the beginning of Perry's editorship in 1899, Moody was frustrated by the *Atlantic*'s standard of poetic lucidity, which he felt unrealistic, limiting, and destructive. As he wrote to his Harvard acquaintance Parker:

> I despair of attaining the standard of perspicacity set up by the *Atlantic*; indeed it seems to me that to do so with imaginative symbols is to set them to a work for which they were never intended. . . . [I] regret that the *Atlantic* has not seen its way to adopting a more liberal attitude toward verse. It has been in the past the only one of the monthlies whose standards were not hopelessly conventional and I feel under correction that it could exert a wide and happy influence upon the future of American literature by laying stress upon positive rather than negative qualities in the verse manuscript submitted to it, by weighing an ounce of charm and power against an ounce of obscurity or imperfect finish. (17 Nov. 1899)

Parker characteristically stonewalled Moody's accusations, replying preciously that "every one who loves the *Atlantic* would be sorry to have it thought that the noise of the marketplace should rise so high in its rooms as to frighten the shy children of the muses" (8 Dec. 1899). Precisely that noise echoed in his rejection of several poems by another Harvard acquaintance, Trumbull Stickney, who was to die within months of a brain tumor. Stickney's poems, Parker regretted, had "too little of the trumpet and drum about them to be most suitable for magazine use" (to Trumbull Stickney, 1 June 1904).

Perry was franker in admitting to Moody that the editors' demands for clarity catered to their readers' refusal to strain their faculties on magazine verse. Moody's reply acknowledged the difficulty of the editor's position: "It was really at that same public (O vague Many-headedness, inscrutable, sitting upon thy hoard!) that I was grumbling, not the Editors of the *Atlantic Monthly*, who, of course must charm it and flute to it somewhat in the way it likes or be devoured by it and rendered quite incapable of fluting at all! So it comes back, does it not, to the sad truth—against which I rise in puny periodic revolt—that only by accident can poetry be at once worthy and marketable" (6 Dec. 1899).

Despite the many-headed monster's indifference to poetry, Perry did substantively support Moody on several occasions. Perhaps shamed by Moody's accurate criticisms, Perry soon published the poet's most enduring lyric poems, "On a Soldier Fallen in the Philippines" and "Ode in Time of Hesitation," the latter especially both long and complex. Perry was in complete sympathy with Moody's protests in these poems against the corruption of American ideals of justice and respect for individuals by the colonization of the Philippines and with his basic affirmation of those ideals themselves. He seemed to see in Moody the high-minded and vital exponent of American values he hoped would revive American poetry. In late 1900, he proposed that Moody assemble a volume of lyrics and strongly supported its publication by Houghton Mifflin. He also arranged a sympathetic review of the book by Rollo Ogden, noting that it contained "a few poems... which seem to me of very great promise" (to Rollo Ogden, 2 May 1901). During the remaining years of Perry's editorship and Moody's brief life, Moody turned to drama and submitted almost nothing. Perry did, however, publish "Three American Poets of To-Day" (Sept. 1906), an article by May Sinclair affirming that E. A. Robinson, Robinson's friend Ridgely Torrence, and Moody were the major hopes of American poetry.

After 1902, Perry grew increasingly discouraged with the poetry available to him. His solution, as with serial fiction, was to reduce the amount he published rather than to publish quantities of the type of mediocre verse and humorous doggerel carried by the New York monthlies. The average number of poems fell from four to two or three per issue, about half written by women, half by men. Besides lack of quality, another motive for this reduction in quantity may have been economy. Treasurer Kay was confounded by the logic of paying $25 or $30 for a sonnet to fill a third of a page when the same fee would fill three solid pages of prose. Even the editor, though less relentlessly utilitarian, may have wanted to use his limited budget elsewhere. At the end of his tenure, Perry, like his predecessors, could honestly claim that he avoided the trivial norm of most magazine verse, took some risks to feature important poems or introduce new poets, and published works by poets such as Ridgely Torrence, P. E. More, Paul Dunbar, Moody, Josephine Peabody, Louise Guiney, Edith Thomas, Harriet Monroe, and Lizette

Reese that was better in general, despite a tight budget, than the poetry in other American monthlies.

But Moody had articulated exactly the problems which prevented the *Atlantic*, like other quality magazines, from giving American poets sustained support to experiment and develop: an acquiescence to its readers' intolerance of obscurity, a negative insistence on orthodoxy of form, and a lack of compensating positive enthusiasm for poetic force. These proscriptions would limit the *Atlantic*'s encouragement of poetry well into the twentieth century, despite isolated accomplishments, and would inhibit the magazine from responding to the resurrection Perry had awaited.

If Perry sometimes compromised his own judgment to accommodate his audience in selecting transparent poetry and popular serials, he stood his Yankee humanist, high-culture ground a good deal more firmly in the fields of book reviewing, literary criticism, and discussions of humanistic culture, as well as in social issues and politics.

Perry later admitted to overestimating his readers' interest in literary analysis and intellectual history; unlike Page, however, he insisted, against commercial pressures, on both the value of these discussions and their centrality to the *Atlantic*. Like all of his predecessors before Page, he saw the *Atlantic* as essentially a literary magazine, believing, like them, that literature was an important source of moral value.

More than the fiction, the reviews and essays on literary culture distinguished Perry's *Atlantic*, as they had Scudder's, from other contemporary magazines. It was these and not the fiction that caused Edith Wharton to write: "I cannot tell you how much praise I think you deserve for maintaining the tradition of what a good magazine should be in the face of our howling mob of critics and readers; and I hope that the *Atlantic* will long continue to nurse its little flame of sweetness and light in the chaotic darkness of American 'literary' conditions" (8 Aug. n.y.). For Perry, as for Lowell and Scudder, the Arnoldian mission to preserve the sweetness and light of humanistic tradition and maintain a high standard for contemporary literary and intellectual culture was central. But despite its high-culture emphasis, criticism in Perry's magazine was neither mainly retrospective nor insensitive to American cultural diversity.

Perry, like Wharton, Henry James, and others, condemned the widespread commercial corruption of American literary reviewing during this period.[2] In the new era of advertising and mass marketing, the genial promotional spirit of James T. Fields had triumphed. Promotional staffs at Houghton Mifflin as elsewhere were expanding more rapidly than editorial staffs. Their job was to generate and distribute universal enthusiastic praise of their firm's books, often reprinted verbatim in newspapers and magazines. Magazines and newspapers, which now lived increasingly on advertising revenues, had become very sensitive to the interests of advertising clients, and in the quality magazines publishing houses were primary advertisers who provided large amounts of income. Partly for this reason and partly because reviews were not popular with most readers, *Harper's*, *Scribner's*, and the *Century* dropped virtually all reviewing. Perry clearly felt these commercial pressures, as well as the pressure to free more space for current events. But unlike many editors of his day, he continued to publish reviews that kept readers abreast of current books, resisted commercial influence, and raised useful questions about literary quality.

Perry committed about 8 percent of his magazine to book reviews and another 8 percent to literary discussion, only slightly less than Howells and Scudder, who had made these a major focus of their magazine. Most books were discussed in group reviews of works in such categories as fiction, politics, science, economics, biography, and art, while one or two major works were often selected for separate articles. For group reviews, Perry asked an expert to select six to twelve of the best recent books and "give the layman a fair idea of the progress made in that field of literature" (to W. R. Thayer, 22 Sept. 1904). Reviewers and literary critics included Alice Meynell, Henry James, Henry Boynton, Harriet Preston, Mark Howe, Mary Moss, H. H. Brownell, Edmund Gosse, Louise Guiney, Christian Gauss, Talcott Williams, William James, and Royall Cortissoz.

Perry sustained a high, though not perfect, record for integrity in *Atlantic* reviews. He did request that the still-living Harriet Spofford be spared the judgment that she had failed to achieve her early promise. When Harriet Preston wrote a strong condemnation of Howells, based partly on an old but virulent personal feud, Perry wavered over whether to publish it. Miss Preston was intransigent. Howells, she said, was provincial, half-taught, intolerant, dictatorial, and dogmatic—not the great reformer he pretended but an obstructionist who needed deflation (to Perry, 7 Nov. 1902). Perry sent the piece to Howells with an offer to suppress it. But Howells replied adamantly that he had never sought to control reviews of his books and begged Perry to publish the article so that he should not seem to do so now (12 Nov. 1902). Perry also worried about criticism of James in the same article. But when the editor finally published the piece unaltered, James reassured Perry that his "sensibilities have resisted the shock . . . quite adequately unscathed" and that he had found it "as stupid as it is spritely" (23 Jan. 1903).

Aside from these isolated cases and the plug for Moody, Perry held to the principle of not intervening. Unlike in the past, reviewers generally were given total freedom in selecting the works they wished to review, thus removing the editor's ability to steer books to a sympathetic (or unsympathetic) reviewer. Also, reviews were either signed or initialed, making their judgments specifically those of the author, not, as before, subject to editorial modification. The acid test of reviewing integrity was that even Houghton Mifflin books received no special prominence and were often either omitted from reviews altogether or criticized. In fact, two *Atlantic* serial romances, Johnston's *Audrey* and Mary Austin's *Isidro*, were briefly dismissed as light, sometimes entertaining, but improbable fictions, while Kate Wiggin's works were justly assigned to that "pleasant class" of books requiring no discussion, quickly read, quickly forgotten.[3]

As these reviews show, the standards held by *Atlantic* criticism were considerably higher than those achieved by much of its serial fiction. Gilder's *Century*, for instance, in addition to frankly favoring "sentimentalists and romanticists" in its fiction, continued in sporadic comments on books after 1900 to welcome the escapist, the romantic, and the genial in literature. The *Atlantic*, by contrast, reflected a rapid reaction against the new romanticism (John 253, 255). In March 1901, Perry ran a stinging satire by Charles Loomis titled "How to Write a Novel for the Masses," accusing those writing and publishing historical romances of a cynical commercialism that mixed trite melodrama with cheap public fascination about the life-styles of the rich and famous. Certainly the irony of this article's appearing while the *Atlantic* itself was serializing historical romances was not lost on Perry. The *Atlantic* was doing essentially what it accused the mass-market publishers of doing.

It has been a cliché of modern cultural and literary criticism that Boston culture, generally typified by the *Atlantic*, continued long into the twentieth century to suffer from a fixation on its own past. H. G. Wells was one of the first to sound this theme when he alleged in *The Future in America* (1906) that Boston since 1875 had died from the neck up and cared only for collecting its own musty intellectual memorabilia (226–36). e. e. cummings hit the same note in describing "the Cambridge ladies who live in furnished souls" and "believe in Christ and Longfellow, both dead."

In the early nineties, Scudder indeed had seen Emerson, Thoreau, Hawthorne, Lowell, Holmes, Whittier, and Longfellow as the foundation stones on which to build a national literature and proposed that they be integrated into public education as a source of national values. Scudder had shared this judgment of their literary merit with most of national literary opinion at the time, as he had shared ambivalence over Whitman's value as a poet (Mott 4, 128–31). But by the 1900s, only a decade or two after the deaths of the Olympians, a major reevaluation was apparent in the magazine that had most identified itself with them. Centenaries of Longfellow and Hawthorne were duly observed, as was the fiftieth anniversary of the *Atlantic* itself in November 1907. Perry also ran literary reminiscences of midcentury by the artist, journalist, and diplomat W. J. Stillman and by T. W. Higginson, whose professed object was to act as an antidote to the eulogistic histories by making the Olympians more life-sized and human.

But a clear sorting was taking place. Emerson, despite jokes about his vatic obscurity, survived a rigorous reevaluation by John J. Chapman, who found in Emerson an inspiration for his own moral individualism and defiance of commercial culture. Emerson was still cited by several *Atlantic* writers as a source of values for the contemporary world, and three articles marked his centenary in 1903. Perry, believing Thoreau of lasting importance, ran his *Journals* in a long serial during 1905–6, and persuaded Houghton Mifflin to publish them complete. Perry also asserted his own faith in the enduring significance of Hawthorne's work. He noted, however, that not only literary values but "the very basis of literary judgments . . . seem to be shifting in our contemporary civilization," and therefore it was impossible to tell whether Hawthorne would speak to readers of the year 2000 ("The Centenary of Hawthorne," Aug. 1904, 196). Perry and several *Atlantic* writers affirmed too the genius and endurance of Whitman. Mark Howe, reviewing Perry's book, called Whitman, "the most original and suggestive poetic figure since Wordsworth" and the one American poet most sure to be read one hundred or five hundred years hence ("The Spell of Whitman," Dec. 1906, 854).

For the rest of the nineteenth-century New Englanders, however, despite his role as spokesman for their publisher and sometimes official centennial eulogist, Perry foresaw at the least a severe winnowing of their work. "The tide," he noted later, "was already running against most of them" only a decade or two after their deaths (*Gladly Teach* 187). Of Longfellow he predicted that while held in contempt by academics and clever young men, he would continue to appeal to those who had always been his audience: schoolteachers, country ministers, and children ("The Centenary of Longfellow," Mar. 1907). Whittier, he noted, had breathed life into "the accepted moralities, the familiar religious formulas of his day" but created "no novel world for the spirit of man" ("Whittier for To-Day," Dec. 1907, 857). His "songs of labor" would be incomprehensible to workers under current industrial conditions. Whittier, Perry asserted, had been "everlastingly right" in condemning racial injustice and in supporting universal peace, both issues still potently relevant, but he suspected that if any of Whittier's work survived it would be his simple, nondogmatic hymns.

In the new decade Holmes was seldom mentioned in the *Atlantic* he had helped to found and support for forty years. Aldrich received occasional compliments and a kind eulogy but seemed largely forgotten even before his death in 1907. When Houghton Mifflin editors approached Henry James proposing that he follow his 1892 *Atlantic* reminiscence of Lowell with a full biography, James declined, saying that neither Lowell's work nor his life was rich enough to justify another biography (to Houghton Mifflin, 29 Dec. 1902). Lowell, Holmes, Whittier, and Longfellow, wrote Josephine Daskum in a May 1901 *Atlantic* article, "The Distinction of Our Poetry," "represent an offshoot of the English school, whose members, our types of scholarship and culture, transmitted to us the forms and conventions" of Western humanism. They were a useful stage in our evolution, Daskum suggested, but they wrote few lasting poems and fail both the modern and the national standards for a genuine American poet. Lowell had written in a hymn that "time makes ancient good uncouth." The American qualities, in subject matter, character, language, and idea, that his generation of New England writers had worked to achieve were now taken for granted by those following, who condemned their predecessors as obstacles to further progress.

Ancestor worship of the New England writers was not, then, a habit either of Perry or of his *Atlantic*. "That New England should have lost whatever ascendency she once possessed," Perry affirmed, "is not a matter of prime importance" (*Park Street Papers* 189). Contrary to the modernists' claims, Whitman was, in fact, more the poet regnant than Longfellow. But while not overrating the recent provincial past, Perry and his magazine were clearly sympathetic to the larger Western humanistic tradition from which the New England writers had derived and which, according to Daskum, they transmitted to America. This allegiance to the traditional Western canon did not, however, prevent a generous and surprisingly modern recognition of major contemporary writers, both American and European. In fact, *Atlantic* literary essays of this period suggested that a knowledge of the past spurred interest in contemporary literature and considerably aided in distinguishing between first- and third-rate. The magazine's interests in first-rate literature, past and present, were soon to decline together.

Perry's *Atlantic* was one of the last public forums in America for discussion of major works and figures of Western humanism outside an academic context. Here the intellectually curious lawyer or housewife, the small-town minister, teacher, or farmer, could read intelligently written commentary intended for a general, educated audience on the life and works of Chaucer, Castiglione, Dante, Petrarch, Grotius, Shakespeare, Cervantes, Johnson, Voltaire, Herbert, Hazlitt, Walpole, Austen, Scott, Schiller, Keats, Byron, Wordsworth, Hugo, Trollope, Carlyle, Arnold, and Zola. Perry even accepted, with hesitation, some papers on Eastern traditions, although, as he noted with regret, "we have had to abandon papers on Greek and Roman literature" because they interested such a small audience (to P. E. More, 6 June 1906 in Ballou 468). Ten years later the major English, French, German, Spanish, and Italian writers had almost universally been banished by mass culture to the college classroom and the academic journal, as the classical writers had already been permanently banished. Eighty years later college professors, citing tenable arguments for cultural pluralism, would quarrel over whether these writers should be ejected from the classroom. By then, even their names would already be unrecognizable to legions of college graduates, who nevertheless would know a great deal about the ephemeral celebrities of commercial mass culture.

Perry's *Atlantic* did not, however, slight the present for the past. Book reviews covered current production, and full critical essays were fairly balanced between major writers of the past and of the present. The magazine did continue the unfortunate policy, compounded of genteel delicacy and commercial opportunism, of printing major evaluations of an author's work only on his or her death. But Perry broke this policy more often than his predecessors. Full critical reviews were given to several currently publishing Continental authors, including Anatole France, the German dramatist Hauptmann, the critic Brunetière, and Mallarmé. Among British writers, Hardy near the dispirited end of his career, Conrad near the beginning of his, and the middle-aged Shaw were judged the major figures who would last.

Perry's *Atlantic* gave distinguished recognition and high critical praise among American authors to men and women in about equal numbers, and among only three or four men so honored one was an African-American and one a Russian Jewish immigrant. The women who received high critical praise were Edith Wharton, Alice Brown, and Sarah Orne Jewett, all of whom also had serials in Perry's *Atlantic*. Of the men, Henry James was rated by W. C. Brownell just below the greatest British novelists. He was praised for his unrelenting intelligence and resistance to commercialism but somewhat paradoxically was criticized for a later style forbidding in its complexity even to the sophisticated reader ("Henry James," Apr. 1905).

In 1900, Howells proposed and Perry accepted an evaluation of Charles Chesnutt's fiction to date, all of it published by Houghton Mifflin, much having appeared in the *Atlantic*. Howells affirmed Chesnutt's works to date admirable by any standard, black or white, and asserted that if he continued to resist "cheap success . . . one of the places at the top is open to him" ("Charles Chesnutt's Stories," May 1900, 701). In "Libin, a New Interpreter of East Side Life" (Mar. 1903), Charles Rice praised the work of a Russian Jewish immigrant who published in the socialist Yiddish daily the *Forward*. The author asserted that Libin's sketches, directly observed from life in the tenements of East Side New York, were both more sophisticated and more honest than the work of conventional American novelists. "It is high time that American fiction wake up and interpret . . . the American reality with its various foreign ingredients and stratifications" (260).

Reflecting Perry's old ideals of Yankee humanism, *Atlantic* literary criticism tried both to keep alive the traditional humanistic canon of the past and to recognize contemporary achievement of high quality in diverse forms. It does not support the prevalent view that "after 1890, the older literary establishment became much more narrowly elitist and reactionary" while in the process of being displaced by commercial mass culture (Brodhead 476).

Toward popular culture itself, the *Atlantic* was often critical but not reactionary or closed-minded. In a systematic attempt to assess current popular culture, Perry planned a long series of articles from Rollin Hartt and others on amusement parks, dime museums, burlesque, popular novels, baseball, and similar topics. Predictably, some *Atlantic* writers regretted the popular American mania, manifested in national expositions as elsewhere, for amusement and entertainment instead of reflection and learning. But Rollin Hartt's article "The Amusement Park" (May 1907) noted approvingly that this new phenomenon "was not founded for the culture of decorum . . . [but] for the culture of wild hilarity" and "expresses joyousness, sings it, shouts it, a hundred times screeches it" (669, 677). Comic strips, another new phenomenon, were roundly condemned for their racist stereotyping, utter disrespect for decency and beauty, and childish slapstick brutality, but the form itself was said to have potential if artists had the courage to resist easy, low humor (Ralph Bergengren, "The Humor of the Colored Supplement," Aug. 1906, 269–73). Likewise, the best-seller phenomenon was lamented and satirized. But the point was also made that mass publishing gave large circulation to good work as well as pulp and that, if adequately educated, "the mass of mankind is sound at heart" in literature as in other things (Edward Fuller, "Real Forces in Literature," Feb. 1903, 270–74). Even the dime novels mass distributed by Erastus Beadle, whom Charles Eliot Norton had unsuccessfully tried to convince to try dime Shakespeares, were admitted to be absurdly melodramatic but defended as good entertainment and healthy fantasies for boys. Perry's *Atlantic* often criticized popular culture for intellectual lassitude or moral shabbiness but also often respected it as a source of pleasure and sometimes of learning.

Like the literary and cultural criticism, the social and political commentary in Perry's *Atlantic* also fails to support the charge that high culture became predominantly elitist and reactionary. Certainly reactionary lamentations—cultural, literary, and political—had been heard in the *Atlantic* even before Aldrich's time. Those that continued under Perry had as their primary target the corrupting influence of industrial capitalism on both cultural and political values. Certainly also there was an overt, general resistance to commercial mass culture, even as that culture was influencing the *Atlantic*'s selection of literature. But the dominant note in Perry's social and political commentary was new applications of the liberal Yankee humanism of the old cultural elite. It was principled, highly critical of America's departures from its professed liberal ideals, and still moderately optimistic that a specifically American form of high culture could serve a vital social function and was not inevitably incompatible with political democracy. This old Yankee humanism also included, more than in Lowell's day, a limited but clear sensitivity to the claims of racial and ethnic minorities.

Perry wasted no time lamenting with the dispossessed gentry for a vanishing preindustrial, small-town America. But he did believe that certain of the old liberal ideals of Yankee humanism could provide guidance in the present and future. He was also less convinced of the blessings of industrial capitalism than Page and less blind to the costs. His ideals made him less pragmatic, more morally sensitive. In an *Atlantic* editorial, Perry noted that the magazine's office at 4 Park Street was symbolically "somewhat apart from the insane whirl which is miscalled 'progress,'" looking out as it did over Saint-Gaudens's Civil War memorial to Robert Gould Shaw and the black Massachusetts regiment on Boston Common and haunted by the honest ghosts of dead abolitionists. The *Atlantic*, he pointedly noted, had been established "before the days of 'commercial invasions' and 'world records' and 'Anglo-Saxon domination'" and could not be "indifferent to human liberty, or be persuaded that commercial supremacy is the noblest ideal of an American citizen" ("Number 4 Park Street," Jan. 1903, 1–5).

Perry's editorship corresponded with the era of muckraking, a critical reevaluation of the excesses of the gilded age and the rise of corporate America. His *Atlantic* entered often into this reevaluation, mainly by measuring contemporary institutions against the traditional Yankee humanistic ideals. Materialism, the overvaluation of property rights relative to human rights, and corruption by ownership was as much a target now as in Emerson and Thoreau's day. Since the end of Howells's editorship, the *Atlantic* had carried warnings against the unchecked growth of corporate power and great personal wealth. Hostility toward corporate influence became a frequent theme in Perry's magazine and came from conservative and liberal alike. The reactionary Henry Dwight Sedgwick, lamenting the passing of the old gentry type, noted how American character and leadership had declined from Washington and Adams to McKinley. The new type produced by corporate, industrial America was a "mechanical, soulless engine" lacking principle and conviction. By the year 1961, he predicted, America would be ruled by an imperial president who had begun, like Edison or Ford, as an inventor/entrepreneur, had put together a vast conglomerate corporation, and ruled over a Senate of chief executives representing smaller corporations. The senators' major source of interest and information would be a stock ticker in the Senate chamber ("The New American Type," Apr. 1904; "The American Coup d'Etat of 1961," Nov. 1904).

Sedgwick's antagonism toward corporate power was matched from more democratic and optimistic sources. The old-fashioned liberal T. W. Higginson inveighed against "the aristocracy of the dollar" that polarized classes. But unlike many of his surviving peers, he maintained a vague Emersonian faith that cultural and educational progress would eventually displace the aristocracy of the millionaire with the ascendancy of the enlightened millions ("The Aristocracy of the Dollar," Oct. 1903). Rollo Ogden of the *New York Evening Post*, identifying himself only as "an Emersonian Democrat," declared that "men of superior and soulless wealth . . . are the greater flouters as well as corrupters of democracy—our really dangerous classes." The great task facing the nation was to throw off the tyranny of the plutocracy by using government regulation of corporations and above all the power to tax ("Notes on the Reaction," Sept. 1901, 421).

Corporate capitalism was accused not only of polarizing and pauperizing Americans, corrupting politicians, subverting principles, and supplanting the ideal of public service with the principle of the public trough but also with rotting the individual soul and the culture at large. In reviewing "Old Gorgon Graham," an admiring portrait of a gruff but shrewd captain of industry written and serialized in the *Saturday Evening Post* by its new editor George Lorimer, Mary Moss felt appalled at the popular admiration for a life of disciplined work, profit, and success entirely devoid of human joy or sympathy ("Significant Tendencies in Current Fiction," May 1905, 694). H. D. Sedgwick, anticipating Santayana's critique of the genteel tradition, noted that under industrial capitalism all energy was absorbed in pursuing material profit while religion, emotion, literature, philosophy, and intellectual culture were dismissed as effeminate ("Certain Aspects of America," July 1902). D. G. Phillips's serial "The Common Lot" demonstrated how the profit motive sapped the moral will. And several writers described how the lure of mass circulation and large profits compromised the intellectual and aesthetic integrity of editors and writers alike, a fact that could have been illustrated from the magazine's own fiction.

While Perry himself had strong, relatively liberal views on economic and political issues, he did not attempt to make the *Atlantic* an organ for his own opinions, any more than Aldrich had limited it to his conservatism. In the Yankee humanistic tradition, he believed that the magazine should express a broad range of rationally argued views, taking an editorial stand only on critical, nonpartisan issues of moral principle such as civil rights and the colonization of the Philippines. Despite the range of views, however, Perry's *Atlantic* clearly reflected a consensus that corporate capitalism and the accumulation of great personal fortunes had caused serious economic, social, political, and cultural damage and that controls were necessary. The debate on solutions was broad and prominently included not only federal regulation of trusts, corporate taxes, and personal income taxes but also unionization and even nationalization of industries.

Several commentators, including Talcott Williams in "The Anthracite Coal Crisis" (Apr. 1900) and Charles Bullock in "Trusts and Public Policy" (June 1901), suggested that between big business and big unions, the former was now far more dangerous. Articles including London's "Scab" and William Ripley's "Race Factors in Labor Unions" (Mar. 1904) endorsed unions as necessary not only to oppose the power of the trusts and prevent disastrous wage collapse but also to provide the immigrant with some security and experience in democratic governance.

Perry also promoted a serious analysis and debate of socialism. H. G. Wells's contention that Boston had been intellectually moribund since 1875 was controverted by Perry's enthusiastic interest in serializing Wells's sympathetic explanation of socialist ideology, "A Plain Account of Socialism," which Perry felt contained "some very brilliant writing" (Perry to Paul Reynolds, 6 Apr. 1907). A last-minute inability to publish simultaneously with an English periodical canceled the series, but Perry solicited essays explaining and advocating socialism by the labor economist John Graham Brooks, including "A Socialist Programme" (May 1906) and "Recent Socialist Literature" (Feb. 1907). Brooks, like several other *Atlantic* commentators, noted that socialism was gaining force from widespread moral revulsion at the injustices of competitive capitalism. He condemned profit making as thievery, indicted employers as "parasites sucking from the life blood" of workers, predicted failure for regulatory efforts, asserted the need to nationalize major industries, and called for "a generous field for collectivist experimenting" ("Literature" 281, 283).

In politics, as in social and economic commentary, Perry's *Atlantic* presented a range of views, the median of which was a moderate, principled liberalism. The *Atlantic*'s range, however, had limits. It was one thing to propose socialist evolution as Brooks had, but another to endorse political violence. Perry respectfully turned down not only London's "Revolution" but also an offered contribution by the "Queen of Anarchists," Emma Goldman, earlier jailed for planning the 1892 assassination attempt on the industrialist Henry Clay Frick. Still, after the assassination of McKinley by the anarchist Leon Czolgosz, who claimed to have been inspired by Goldman, Perry wrote an editorial explicitly condemning repressive reaction against anarchists and other political dissidents ("The Death of the President," Oct. 1901).

While Page had broken the nonpartisan policy to denounce the Populist threat of W. J. Bryan in an unsigned article, Perry returned to signed articles by representatives of both parties. But his *Atlantic* also continued the deep distrust of all parties that the mugwumps had inherited from the Emersonian traditions of moral individualism and the politics of principle. The latter-day crusader for Emersonian idealism, John J. Chapman, quixotically advocated political leadership by "moral bosses" with no party organizations. Though Chapman would soon break with Theodore Roosevelt over the latter's compromises with the Republican party, he endorsed him in 1900 as a moral rough rider over political corruption ("Between Elections," Jan. 1900).

After Roosevelt had held the presidency awhile, however, an anonymous satire by Rollo Ogden lampooned him for violently denouncing his opponents while coolly stealing their ideas and pointedly reminded him that political parties are capable of any treachery ("Alciphron," "Letters to Literary Statesmen," Mar. 1905). The satire so angered Roosevelt and his staff that the offending pages were removed from the White House copy of the *Atlantic*, and the officious Henry Cabot Lodge, who seemed to feel that the *Atlantic* was a local organ that should be obedient to his bidding, protested to Mifflin. Perry, honorable soul that he was, submitted his resignation in case his publisher had either lost confidence in him or intended to interfere. Mifflin was a fraternity brother of Roosevelt's at Harvard's Porcellion Club and had hosted the president on a visit to Houghton Mifflin's offices. But his response, as with Page's flag-waving during the Spanish-American War, showed that while he might exert pressure to serialize more popular fiction, he adhered strictly to a gentlemanly code of noninterference on political or ideological issues. He expressed complete support for Perry and asked him to continue. Perry, however, on his own initiative, canceled further satires in Ogden's series—fortunately for Mifflin, since the target of the next was to have been Henry Cabot Lodge, whose arrogance Perry loathed (Ballou 472).

Though he relented after the fact with Ogden's satire, Perry clearly did not back away from controversy that might discomfort not only the gentle reader but also the rough rider in the White House, particularly when the issue involved fundamental principles. United States policy in Cuba and the Philippines was such an issue. Page had applauded the "progress of civilization" in the American displacement of decadent Spain and had blunted criticism of United States policy. Perry ran about ten articles representing virtually every view. But he was personally deeply opposed both to war and to colonialism and made his views felt in his selections and editorials. In a March 1901 editorial, "Give the Country the Facts," he accused the government of deliberately withholding the truth about the Philippine situation from the American public, perhaps to mask a forcible annexation that would transgress American ideals of liberty and self-government. By 1902, he was deploring Roosevelt's Philippine policy as a subjugation of "a weaker people who are struggling ... for that independence which we once claimed as an inalienable right for ourselves." Despite hypocritical and racist paternalism, the government was pursuing its own economic advantage at the expense of the helpless and was trading American principles of liberty and equality under law for commercial supremacy ("On Keeping the Fourth of July," July 1902, 4).

Perry was a life member of the American Peace Society and later a trustee of the World Peace Foundation. While he did not feel justified in using the *Atlantic* as a lobbying organ, some of his editorials criticized militaristic nationalism in the United States, and he published several articles on the world peace movement. The *Atlantic*, while insisting that it represented explicitly American values in literature, politics, and social policy, had periodically made serious attempts to keep its readers informed of literary, social, and political developments in Europe and the rest of the world. Perry, despite apparent isolationist indifference on the part of most readers, placed greater emphasis on international material than did most of his contemporaries, increasing articles on foreign affairs and instituting regular letters reporting cultural and political news from England, Germany, France, Italy, Mexico, and Japan.

Perry's willingness to challenge his readers, his contemporary applications of old-fashioned New England conscience, and his sympathy with the humanistic liberalism of the early *Atlantic* manifested themselves not only in his treatment of Philippine colonization and world peace but also in his attention to racial and ethnic issues. Despite the progressive spirit of the time, the nation had comfortably acquiesced in the failure of Reconstruction and allowed the wholesale suppression of black constitutional rights, often through violence, in return for southern white political cooperation. Perry, haunted, as he had suggested, by the ghosts of old abolitionists in his editorial office, felt an obligation to expose the comfortable deceit and support "the old-fashioned American doctrine of political equality irrespective of race, color, or station" (Perry, "Reconstruction and Disenfranchisement," Oct. 1901, 435). Accordingly, his most extensive editorial program was a series of about fifteen contributions in 1901 and 1902, first on the failure of Reconstruction, then on disenfranchisement and related racial issues.

Characteristically, Perry solicited a wide range of views, including southern apologists such as Thomas Nelson Page as well as black leaders such as Washington and DuBois. Clearly, however, Perry summarized the consensus in an October 1901 editorial. Reconstruction, he declared, was an utter failure which had given way to a kind of colonial "government by force" in which, exactly as in the Philippines, Anglo-Saxons suppressed the political rights of a subject race ("Reconstruction and Disenfranchisement," 435). Nor was the North much more just than the South, Perry suggested, except in permitting the black vote.

The current status of black Americans was most graphically summarized by several black writers. Perry, for whom the Shaw memorial that he viewed from his editorial window embodied a heroic ideal, published a bitter poem by Paul Dunbar asserting that Shaw and his troops had died for nothing, since the present condition of blacks was essentially unchanged from slavery ("Robert Gould Shaw," Oct. 1900, 488). A black northern lawyer, Edward Wilson, in an elegant, sardonic satire titled "The Joys of Being a Negro" (Feb. 1906), imagined responding to a promotional invitation to visit an aristocratic southern hotel. The vacation, he noted, would require most of his life savings; he could not ride the Pullman car; and when he arrived, management and staff would be "gorgonized" by his color and immediately eject him. In an even more somber vein, W. E. B. DuBois characterized the whole South as "an armed camp for intimidating black folk" and predicted bloody revolt if the suppression continued ("Of the Training of Black Men," Sept. 1902, 296).

In articulating a consensus about solutions, Perry asserted that while enfranchising freedmen in the Constitution had thus far failed to produce effective representation, genuine black political empowerment was essential. Significantly, he did not rule out educational qualifications for voting or holding office, but he insisted that, if instituted, any such qualifications must be applied with absolute equality to blacks and whites, and there must be strong, immediate commitment to universal education. The difficult solutions, then, were "labor and education, and mutual understanding and unimagined patience, [leading] to the goal of full political privilege" ("Reconstruction and Disenfranchisement," Oct. 1901, 436). DuBois argued for federal assistance in the form of a new, expanded Freedman's Bureau which was to be "a great school of protective citizenship" including employment and legal aid offices for blacks, black school systems, and black banks ("The Freedman's Bureau," Mar. 1901). Booker T. Washington's proposals emphasizing technical education and economic self-help rather than political action and social equality were represented but were balanced by criticisms from other black writers. Edward Wilson ridiculed Washington's gradualism, and DuBois initiated his famous challenge to Washington by submitting a specific reply to Washington's Tuskeegee program titled "Of the Training of Black Men" (Sept. 1902), which Perry ran as a lead article. Here DuBois argued for not just trade schools but full intellectual higher education to prepare black Americans to solve problems of social and economic advancement and to develop in them a "higher individualism." Intellectually educated black Americans, DuBois said, would soon "give the world new points of view" (297).

Although Perry rejected the populist, Hearstian style of journalism, the voices and images of America in his *Atlantic* were not limited to upper-middle-class Anglo-Saxon Protestant culture, nor did the magazine protect readers from criticisms of that culture. Even in fiction, where Perry and his assistants were most genteel, there were clear indications that many younger writers were abandoning the drawing rooms of the well-to-do for the streets and tenements. There was a trace of trendy silliness in a number of declined manuscripts from young Harvard men who had been skulking around New York's Syrian quarter or the tenements of Hell's Kitchen in search of a story packed with pathos and "human interest." But there was also a clear sense that the most vital, new material of American literature lay in the lives of the immigrants and the poor.

Perry and Parker, while cautious, encouraged and accepted for publication writing on these themes by several younger writers. These included descriptions of the Bowery and of ghetto theater by Hutchins Hapgood, Nathan Babad's autobiography of his immigration experience, tales of Middle Eastern immigrants by Norman Douglas and of poor Jews by I. K. Friedman, one of the socialist Ernest Poole's first stories of urban poverty, and Mary Austin's admiring sketches of Mexican and Indian life. Perry also continued Page's series on the contributions of ethnic groups to national life, including a lead article entitled "The Social Disability of the Jew" (Apr. 1908), by a Jewish spokesman, Edwin Kuh, directly addressing the issue of anti-Semitism. Furthermore, at this time when immigration was rising from a half million a year to its all-time peak of over 1.2 million a year, and 70 percent of the populations of Boston and New York were either immigrants or the children of immigrants, most articles on immigration in Perry's *Atlantic* advocated a relatively liberal policy (Green 103). Perry commissioned an article—timed to influence congressional debate on immigration—that viewed continued large-scale influx from southern and eastern Europe as both inevitable and desirable. The author criticized Americans for placing the blame for their own social problems on the newer immigrants and assured readers that the new immigrants, like the Germans and Irish before them and the English earlier, would become upwardly mobile and assimilated into the American whole (Kate Claghorn, "Our Immigrants and Ourselves," Oct. 1900).

The decades around the turn of the twentieth century, with the high tide of immigration and with colonialism and international power rising in both England and America, saw a sharp upsurge in popular theories of Anglo-Saxon superiority and manifest destiny. Because of its traditional convictions about cultural hierarchy and the leadership of an educated elite, the *Atlantic* was vulnerable to these ideas, although it also held counteracting traditions of individualism and respect for personal and political rights, regardless of race or culture. Particularly since Aldrich's time, in discussions of immigration, Indian affairs, and later the Spanish-American War, ideas of Anglo-Saxon leadership and responsibility—the white man's burden—had been implied if not stated. Perry did not suppress all discussion of these ideas, but in several editorials he did explicitly condemn them, holding up the old humanistic ideals of respect for the rights and abilities of individuals regardless of ethnic category, self-determination, political democracy, and the repudiation of racial prejudice. He also published some sharp criticisms of Anglo-American culture, especially its arrogant assumption of superiority.

In his first editorial Perry noted that the magazine's traditions predated and opposed modern ideas of "Anglo-Saxon domination" (*Park Street Papers* 14). He admired and defended civilized decency, altruism, intellect, a desire for learning, and self-discipline but asserted that these were exclusive to no race and that racism transgressed all of them. "Intelligence, virtue and force of character," he claimed, "are not the endowment of the Anglo-Saxon exclusively" ("Reconstruction and Disenfranchisement," Oct. 1901, 437). In fact, the arrogant assumption that they were, he argued, was responsible for the violent and immoral suppression of the Philippinos abroad and black Americans at home. This explicit criticism of American racism came from several sources in Perry's *Atlantic*. Edward Wilson spoke scathingly of the "self-exalted Aryan who, if American, thinks himself nearing the limits of perfection . . . constantly telling himself that he is the climax of civilization" ("Joys," Feb. 1906, 246). DuBois, addressing the white reader directly, asserted the intellectual equality of blacks and spoke of the "moral crookedness" of white society ("Training of Black Men," Sept. 1902, 296).

Related criticisms were voiced in other contexts. Charles Rice in his article "Libin" (Feb. 1903) argued that most Russian Jews had a stronger literary tradition and better aesthetic sense than most college-educated Americans, or indeed than most magazine editors. A Chinese boycott of American goods was justified as a reaction against the racist American exclusion of Chinese immigration (John Foster, "The Chinese Boycott," Jan. 1906).

One of Perry's earliest editorial decisions was his acceptance of an autobiographical series written by a young Yankton Sioux woman, Zitkala-Sa (Gertrude Bonnin), later founder of the National Council of American Indians and a prominent activist for Indian rights.[4] The three-part series (Jan.–Mar. 1900), which narrated her mother's hatred of the white race, her own voluntary departure from home with educational missionaries, and her Quaker schooling in Indiana, was a bitter record of victimization and alienation from her own culture. Describing her initial terror and lasting loathing of the palefaces with glassy blue eyes, she accused them of destroying her natural religious faith and freedom and supplanting these with sterile "white man's papers." Liberal white Christians, she concluded, feel arrogantly righteous for "educating" Indian children, but "few there are who question whether real life or long-lasting death lies beneath this semblance of civilization" ("Indian Teacher," Mar. 1900, 386). Although he knew that he had a sizable missionary audience that might well take offense, Perry, far from trying to blunt the criticism, heartily encouraged Zitkala-Sa to expand the series into a full autobiography, offering his editorial assistance at her convenience. She began, then temporarily abandoned the project, though not without publishing another paper, "Why I Am a Pagan" (Dec. 1902), celebrating her return to her native animism and denouncing the "bigoted creed" of white Christianity.

Contrary to the facile assumptions of much modernist criticism about the genteel tradition, Perry's *Atlantic* did not speak in a polite Anglo-Saxon monotone. His concept of America was inclusive; he sincerely condemned curtailment of political rights or cultural recognition for ethnic groups, and he actively raised issues important to them. Except in fiction, Perry did not, as Ellen Ballou suggests, take as his main mission the protection of the "gentle reader" from controversy or disturbance. Nor, as critics of the quality magazines have asserted, did his *Atlantic* systematically shield white middle-class culture from criticism.

Clearly Perry and his magazine sometimes consciously capitulated both to genteel squeamishness and to the lure of popular commercial success in the selection of serial fiction, and to a lesser degree in the choice of short stories and poetry. Like other editors, Perry felt that his readers of fiction, most of whom he suspected were female, were more fastidious than readers of nonfiction. He also seems to have calculated that printing widely acceptable popular fiction would enable him to carry other material for smaller groups of readers. At a time when other magazines had dropped reviews as risky to advertising and all criticism as commercially marginal, he maintained more extensive reviews of contemporary books than did the editor of any other general periodical, and his *Atlantic* was almost certainly the last general periodical which welcomed extensive discussions of the canonical texts and authors of the Western tradition before these were relegated to the academy.

Aware of the growing taste for what Howells, lamenting the slighting of fiction for current affairs, had called "contemporanics," Perry continued Page's emphasis on social issues, politics, and economics. His selection of topics, writers, and approaches, however, was grounded essentially in his own principled, liberal Yankee humanism. One tenet of these principles was intellectual tolerance for a broad range of ideas, and both in his selection and occasionally in editorials he challenged readers to exercise that tolerance. Following both his own idealism and the tendencies of the time, he published a good many criticisms of the destructive economic, social, and cultural effects of unrestrained corporate capitalism, especially of the trusts and large personal fortunes. His coverage of the aftermath of the Spanish-American War represented the whole spectrum of opinion, but the majority, including his own editorials, resolutely opposed colonialism as a violation of American principles. At a time when most Americans, and most magazine editors, were willing to acquiesce in the systematic suppression of black rights and aspirations, Perry had developed a long series of papers, many solicited from black writers, condemning that suppression and advocating specific remedies, including genuine political power. These papers particularly, as well as many papers on economics, ethnic groups, and the Philippine situation, questioned middle-class American moral pretensions and raised fundamental and uncomfortable issues of social and economic justice in the United States.

Partly because of the popularity of serials such as *To Have and To Hold* in 1900 and *The Helpmate* in 1907, partly also because of the increase in "contemporanics," Perry's *Atlantic* extended the modest but clear circulation gains achieved under Page, reporting a circulation exceeding 22,500 for 1902 and maintaining a steady monthly circulation of 20,000 or more (*American Newspaper Annual* 1902, 1152). Certainly the circulation increase was also attributable to the promotional exertions of MacGregor Jenkins, who by Perry's editorship had geared up the magazine's publicity apparatus to mail 20,000–25,000 annual letters soliciting new subscriptions; to target special populations, including teachers, librarians, and even Chicagoans; to advertise the magazine in 250 newspapers nationwide; to mail summaries of major articles to hundreds of newpapers every month in advance of *Atlantic* publication to whet the appetite of potential readers; and to build newsstand circulation through the American News Service (Houghton Mifflin Advertising Journals and Riverside Press Cost Books). Better still from Mifflin's point of view, the tenacious Kay had kept costs down: the magazine went from a loss of nearly $10,000 in 1901 to a slight profit of between $2,000 and $8,000 in all but one year between 1903 and 1908 (Ballou 464).

By 1908, however, both Mifflin and Perry had decided on a change of course. Perry had never developed the evangelical idealism about the publishing business that Scudder had used to persuade him into the editorship. The pressure to publish fiction that his academic training told him was third-rate, the public's coolness to those editorial projects he valued most such as discussions of canonical authors and of racial issues, the intellectual intolerance of some readers, the constant need to determine when to cater and when to resist, the haggling with Kay over authors' fees—all increased his cynicism about editorial work. In the meantime, he had kept his contacts with academe, producing two critical books and a lecture series for Harvard. By 1905, Harvard's President Eliot had determined to add him to the faculty and offered him the prestigious chair in literature previously held by Ticknor, Longfellow, and Lowell. A return to teaching appealed to Perry, but he felt committed to his editorship at least until a successor could be found. Thereafter Perry had a foot in each camp, teaching half-time while continuing to edit the *Atlantic* and Houghton Mifflin's trade books. During Perry's awkward period of straddling academe and editing, his attention to the *Atlantic* inevitably suffered.

The problem was finally resolved when in January 1908 Mifflin received an offer from Ellery Sedgwick, younger brother of Henry Dwight Sedgwick and a former protégé of both Scudder and Page, to buy the magazine. Sedgwick, at thirty-six, had spent the past six years in a variety of editorial jobs in the progressive publishing world of New York and now wished to put together a small company to realize his ambition, apparently conceived as a college sophomore, to become the *Atlantic*'s publisher and editor. Mifflin, like Houghton before him, had turned down several offers for the magazine. During the 1880s Houghton had rejected, among others, an offer from the millionaire publicist, later owner and editor of *Cosmopolitan*, John Brisbane Walker, who wanted to "move it to New York, fill it with pictures, and thus make it a genuine threat to its three rivals" (Ballou 375). In 1901, Mifflin had turned aside a proposal made anonymously through Page (perhaps acting on Sedgwick's behalf), commenting dryly that "curiously enough the magazine is not for sale, but perhaps that is lucky for the fellow who might like to buy it!" (to Page, 6 May 1901, in Ballou 464). Despite its long stagnancy in circulation and profitability, Mifflin had felt that the magazine continued to feed the firm's list of authors and contribute to its literary prestige.

In 1908, both the situation and the proposal were different. Houghton Mifflin was restructuring itself from a partnership into a corporation, an opportune time to reconsider a financially marginal operation. More important, the contract that Mifflin negotiated with Sedgwick stipulated that the new Atlantic Monthly Company was to buy the magazine for $50,000—with $35,000 in cash and $15,000 in Atlantic Monthly Company stock to be held by Houghton Mifflin. Francis Garrison explained to Oswald Villard, the *Nation*'s new editor, that because the house still owned "a minority block of stock with special advisory powers, it really remains with us, if no longer of us" (10 Apr. 1908, in Ballou 494–95). The Riverside Press would continue to print the magazine, editorial offices would remain at 4 Park Street, and the new management would continue to steer authors toward Houghton Mifflin. Or so Mifflin believed.

If Mifflin really wished to retain the magazine as a feeder for the firm, he would have done better to listen to another proposal. On learning of Sedgwick's offer, Perry had alerted Mark Howe, who had held hopes of eventually securing the *Atlantic* editorship ever since his brief apprenticeship to Scudder had been frustratingly ended by chronic eye strain. Apparently their plan was for Perry to propose that the firm keep the magazine and have Howe succeed him as editor, perhaps with Perry acting as part-time literary adviser. When the agreement with Sedgwick was struck, Perry wrote Howe: "I want to tell you again that it is a deep regret to me that a certain bubble burst.... But... as soon as [Mifflin] began to reflect upon the possibility of a sale, the idea went to his head" (3 Apr. 1908). At any rate, Howe was out, Sedgwick was in. Within ten years Sedgwick, completing the progressive changes initiated by Page, had transformed the *Atlantic* into a highly competitive magazine with a circulation near 100,000, moved out of Park Street, and shifted the highly lucrative printing contract from Houghton Mifflin's Riverside Press to a printing company of which he became a director and shareholder. He had also hired Howe as chief editor of a new book-publishing enterprise, Atlantic Monthly Books, that competed directly with Houghton Mifflin.

Sedgwick intended from the beginning to edit the *Atlantic* himself, but he persuaded Perry to remain for a year while he established editorial contacts and, with MacGregor Jenkins, who was now employed by the Atlantic Monthly Company, laid a firm foundation on the business and promotional side. The year was not a happy one for Perry. One of Sedgwick's first editorial mandates manifested his intention to introduce substantive changes that would make the magazine more profitably popular. He initially limited articles on literary or biographical history to one per issue and then declared a moratorium on them altogether. Perry found himself explaining with some embarrassment to old contributors such as T. W. Higginson that the magazine could no longer afford discussions of literary or political theory. A second editorial mandate was to limit all contributions to a maximum of ten pages. When Perry relented in this Procrustean task to accept what he felt was some particularly incisive literary criticism, Sedgwick and Mac-Gregor Jenkins, whose editorial influence was now strengthened, wore long, solemn faces for a week. "Despair rules at 4 Park Street," Perry confessed to W. R. Thayer, "and it is all my fault" (16 Nov. 1908).

Perry's release came in August 1909, when he began full-time teaching at Harvard, where he carried on the tradition of a "noble Yankee humanism... its ethical delicacy and its tolerant candor, together with its steadfast faith in the goodness of men" (Brooks, *Indian Summer* 506–7). He had foreseen the return since 1905. It had become clear that his ideal for the *Atlantic*, including a commitment to maintain humanistic discussions of literature and history, was incompatible with the new management. His return to the academy, the last bastion of such discussions, where the audience was largely captive and where intellectual, aesthetic, and moral judgments could be made without direct reference to how widely they would sell, was in part a welcomed relief. His deepest instincts had often been frustratingly at odds with commercial publishing, while Sedgwick's would prove positively serendipitous. Perry was "willing enough," he said with a touch of defensiveness, "to let a younger and far better journalist take his turn in conducting the campaign" (*Gladly Teach* 198).

But the other part of the truth was that Perry had often felt the exhilaration of the campaign. If he had not, like Lowell, been ambivalent about giving up his "old man of the sea," he would have accepted President Eliot's offer in 1905, rather than trying for four years to be both scholar and editorial man of action. Like the old liberal humanists whose values he inherited, he believed in the need for American scholars to enact their values in the world. While frequently frustrated, he had worked out a balance between compromise and resistance that had both modestly sustained the *Atlantic* in an era of booming commercial mass culture and found new applications for the best values of the Yankee humanism for which the magazine had long stood.

The *Atlantic* itself was about to enter a new avatar. Sedgwick, whose editorship was to last nearly thirty years, would complete the fusion begun by Page of the magazine's besieged tradition of literary/intellectual high culture with the progressive journalism, with strong emphasis on the latter. In doing so, he would pump circulation from 17,000 to a peak of more than 135,000. This evolutionary adaptation was necessary to the magazine's survival, or at least its success, in the new, more commercial, journalistic, mass-culture publishing environment of the early twentieth century. While the *Atlantic* continued to represent, and even self-consciously appeal to, a distinct cultural minority, the sharp increases in circulation and in social and political reportage brought it, both for better and for worse, closer to the commercial mainstream of American culture. The profit motive continued to be a potent democratizing cultural force.

Lowell, Emerson, Holmes, Higginson, and other members of the New England cultural elite who had sustained the early *Atlantic* had hoped that the magazine would serve as one means to establish high literary and intellectual culture as a major influence on mainstream American culture, including moral and social as well as literary values. They had held sanguine hopes that their Yankee humanism would foster the development of a serious American literature and intellectual scholarship, setting aesthetic and ethical standards that would win wide national acceptance. For several decades they had succeeded in exerting a potent influence, partly through the *Atlantic*. From the beginning, their *Atlantic* had contributed to the development of Americanism in literature. While valuing European culture, it had promoted a belief that American literary and social values were different from the European. Lowell and Fields had exercised an editorial taste for the indigenous that strongly fostered regionalism and early realism, including the women's local color tradition.

The Yankee humanists believed also in reasoned intellectual examination of both new ideas and established institutions. Their *Atlantic* was sometimes sharply critical of religious dogma and was progressive in introducing new ideas such as Darwinian evolution and raising controversial issues such as the status of women. They believed too in the engagement of the writer and scholar in social issues and the application of moral conscience to politics. Their *Atlantic* had spoken forcefully and effectively for the abolition of slavery, and later it asserted federal responsibility for the social welfare as well as the civil and political rights of the freedman. These positions, later acknowledged to be, as Perry put it, "everlastingly right," were at the time the views of a relatively small minority, many of them members of the New England cultural elite.

But from near the beginning, the canon, standards, and ideologies of the Yankee cultural elite represented in the *Atlantic* had been modified and democratized by both commercial and cultural forces. While some expressed ambivalence toward these forces, most generally welcomed rather than resisted them in a moderate form, at least until the 1880s, when the older generation of New England humanists were displaced by a less secure younger generation. There was little resistance, for instance, and in fact much support for both Fields and Howells, each of whom represented a form of democratization. Fields, anticipating many techniques of modern commercial publishing, had significantly extended the distribution, readership, and influence of the *Atlantic* and other works of Yankee culture. But he had also diluted literary criticism and introduced more popular fiction, domestic essays, and reportage. Howells, whose early career demonstrated the New Englanders' support for literary talent of diverse geographic and social origins, had maintained their essential faith in literature as an important source of national moral value. But he had also carried their nascent realism considerably further and actively sought to further democratize, geographically and socially, both the profession of authorship and the readership for serious literature. He had done this in the *Atlantic* partly through very early support and frequent publication of writers including H. H. Boyesen, John DeForest, Henry James, Sarah Orne Jewett, Bret Harte, Mary Noailles Murfree, Mark Twain, and Constance Fenimore Woolson.

By contrast, Aldrich during the eighties had grown alarmed at the pace of cultural and social change and what he perceived as the threatened marginalization of traditional high culture by democratic mass culture. His *Atlantic* reflected the decline from the expansive cultural optimism of the Yankee humanists of the fifties and sixties to the onset of the conservative, defensive cultural gloom of the genteel tradition in the eighties. He maintained the magazine's liberal tradition of debate and its critical support for Howellsian realism. But he gave new emphasis to cultural hierarchies, the conventions of literary form, and an ideal of purely aesthetic pleasure. As reflected in his contempt for both Walt Whitman and James Whitcomb Riley, Aldrich resisted literary populism. While himself an able negotiator in the literary marketplace, he condemned commercial mass culture and defended the idea of a noncommercial aesthetic, as reflected in his continuing to publish the novels of Henry James at a time when James's work had largely failed to make the transition to higher-circulation, illustrated magazines. Scudder, like Aldrich, used the *Atlantic* in an Arnoldian attempt to conserve and propagate the high culture of the past. In particular, he sought to enshrine the works of the Yankee humanists who had established the magazine in the educational curriculum and in the public mind as classical American texts. Under Scudder and Aldrich, the *Atlantic* had tacitly accepted a niche as a commercially marginal but culturally honest exponent of a high literary culture that was still influential but was itself threatened.

Scudder, however, had looked forward as well as back. While personally committed to preserving the literary past, he had seen the need for more active reportage on current social and political issues and had felt the economic pressure for more popular fiction and more aggressive commercial promotion of the magazine, the essential elements of the progressive publishing movement that was creating new mass-circulation magazines in the nineties. His assistant and successor Page, who had never accepted the *Atlantic*'s marginal cultural or commercial status, instituted these reforms, which were to be carried much further in the early twentieth century by Sedgwick. Page, motivated by both economics and ideology, had intentionally tried to bridge Santayana's cultural gap by breaking down distinctions between high and popular culture, between genteel tradition and aggressive commercial enterprise, and between literature and journalism. One result of Page's increased emphasis on contemporary social conditions and reportage and his deemphasis on traditional literary form was his early publication of and support for several important new writers. Many of these writers, including Charles Chesnutt, Booker T. Washington, W. E. B. DuBois, Abraham Cahan, Jacob Riis, and Jack London, raised issues of class, race, and ethnicity from new perspectives.

Perry, more attached to literary tradition than was Page, attempted his own synthesis of past and present; literature and commerce; Yankee humanism, genteel tradition, and progressive journalism. Sometimes this synthesis seemed a painful straddling. Perry published some mediocre but popular serial romances with a bad conscience and salved his conscience by publishing papers on canonical works that no longer had a significant nonacademic audience. But Perry and his *Atlantic* demonstrated also that the old liberal Yankee humanism was still potent enough both to contribute to the new progressive ideology and to condemn its chauvinistic blind spots and excesses. Perry, acting on the Emersonian principle that "culture" should free individuals from a narrowly self-interested ethnic or nationalist view, followed Page in publishing representatives of American pluralism, including Zitkala-Sa, Mary Austin, and DuBois, several of them sharply critical of white American middle-class culture. He continued Page's emphasis on economics and politics but extended coverage to include some fundamental socialist critiques and went beyond Page in reporting on foreign cultures and the international peace movement. His *Atlantic* also honorably represented the old politics of principle and conscience by conspicuously raising the unpopular issues of black social and political status and by forcing open debate on and editorial opposition to the popular policy of United States colonialism.

Perry had a more modest view than did Lowell or Scudder of the potential influence of the *Atlantic*, of its Yankee humanist tradition, and, more generally, of high literary culture. All of the *Atlantic*'s editors had known that high literary culture was a minority culture. But while Lowell, Fields, and Howells, each in his own way, hoped that it could shape the national culture or establish widely recognized standards of literary and ethical value, Scudder, Page, and Perry had seen that high literary culture was itself being transformed and would have to adapt to retain any influence.

The truth was that since Fields's time the traditions represented by the *Atlantic* had been increasingly altered, both for better and for worse, by the pressures of the marketplace, democratic ideology, democratic journalism, and the new values of each generation that succeeded to the editorship. Much was gone or fading fast: the reputations of most Olympians, nonacademic discussion of the Western literary and historical canon, a belief in the literary artist as an articulator of affirmative national ideals, the faith that literature could be a major source of national social and moral values, even of universal truths. By the early twentieth century, the modified remnant of high culture, including the *Atlantic*, lacked the authority earlier editors had assumed. Americans had always ridiculed self-appointed nabobs of culture, but now such competing pressures as ethnic pluralism and the homogenization of commercially driven, mass culture made them increasingly resistant to the old idea of a hierarchy of cultural values and increasingly inclined to cultural relativism, all trends that would grow through the twentieth century.

But the *Atlantic*, despite a long dip in circulation, had survived, and would continue to survive, the decline in prestige and authority of the old New England literary culture through a strategic blend of adaptation and resistance. It had survived and adapted partly because each generation of editors had brought new truths and because its cultural tradition was more open to these new truths, broader, less brittle and exclusionary, than many later critics claimed. It had survived because while failing to establish wide acceptance of its own standards, it had entered into a dialectic with mainstream culture that benefited both. It had received from that mainstream a moderation of its cultural elitism and bookish tendency and a fuller engagement in the democratic life of the nation. It had offered to that mainstream one model of respect for intellectual inquiry, for literature and history as sources of understanding and values, for the application of conscience and moral principle to politics, and for the criticism of mass culture.

In the future, it would be one cultural voice among a great many—but a distinct voice. It would continue to provide a means for writers of serious fiction and poetry to develop an audience and a market, a stimulus to intellectual reflection and aesthetic pleasure, a source of public exposure to new ideas, a platform for a high level of political and social debate representing diverse views, and often a useful critique of the assumptions and pieties of mass culture.

Notes

Introduction

1. Buell's "Appendix. Vital Statistics: A Quantitative Analysis of Authorship as a Profession in New England" (375–99) is very useful in gaining a clear sense of both the patterns and the diversity in the backgrounds of the New England authors.

2. For a full discussion of the concept of progressive journalism, see Christopher Wilson's *Labor of Words* 40–62.

3. Van Wyck Brooks's essay "Highbrow and Lowbrow" in *America's Coming of Age* (1915) examines a split in American culture very similar to that defined by Santayana. Brooks describes a highbrow American literary culture based on "transcendental theory" out of touch with a society operating on lowbrow "catchpenny realities."

1. Founding

1. Buell's survey of New England literary history reminds us that Boston's literary ascendency even within New England was relatively recent in 1857 (23–55). During the early Republican period, the New Haven–Hartford axis in the lower Connecticut Valley had been the dominant voice. Evidence of the Boston-Connecticut rivalry persisted. Buell quotes a statement in the early *Atlantic* that "there are no poets known to exist" in Connecticut, "unless it be that well-paid band who write the rhymed puffs of cheap garments and cosmetics" (34, quoting F. Sheldon, "The Pleiades of Connecticut," Feb. 1865, 187).

2. Historians of publishing generally assume three to five readers per copy of a magazine in the nineteenth century. Brodhead, for example, assumes five in estimating the *Century's* readership (472).

3. Mott's sketch of the *Atlantic* gives a balanced evaluation of the magazine's early regionalism (2: 495–98).

2. Lowell

1. Lowell's editorial staff consisted only of himself, Underwood, and an apparently infallible proofreader, a Mr. Nichols. By contrast, the current *Atlantic* editorial staff, which produces a slightly shorter although much more varied magazine, numbers twenty-nine, not including ten contributing editors.

2. Levine argues in his book *Highbrow/Lowbrow* that there was an increasing division toward the end of the nineteenth century between highbrow and lowbrow culture.

3. For an early example from the *Atlantic* itself of the facile dismissal of the New England renaissance poets as essentially imitative of European traditions, see Daskum (696–702).

3. Fields

1. Josephine Donovan (38–49) gives a full documentation of Annie Fields's relationship with and assistance to women authors from Harriet Beecher Stowe to Sarah Orne Jewett and Willa Cather.

2. For characteristic portraits of the South in *Atlantic* literature, see Holmes's "Ministers Plenipotentiary," Mar. 1864; Lowell's second series of "Biglow Papers," Jan. 1862–May 1866; and Theodore Winthrop's "Sacryssa Myllesses," Sept. 1861.

4. Howells

1. By far the most comprehensive account of *Scribner's/Century* is Arthur John's excellent book *The Best Years of the Century*. The comparison below between the contents of the *Atlantic* and those of *Scribner's* is based mainly on John's analysis of *Scribner's* and *Harper's* (43–45). I have used the issues of February, May, August, and November 1880 to parallel his comparison. Robert Scholnick's article "J. G. Holland and the 'Religion of Civilization' in Mid-Nineteenth Century America" (*American Studies* 27 [Spring 1986]: 55–79) contains a sympathetic and perceptive analysis of *Scribner's* founder and founding.

2. One of Sedgwick's patrician articles attacking General Benjamin Butler, a populist Democratic candidate for governor of Massachusetts, and later presidential nominee of the Greenback Labor party, was derisively quoted by Butler in his campaign speeches to win votes by standing against the white-gloved Yankee elite.

5. Aldrich

1. See Ballou 354–55 for various recollections of Aldrich as editor, and Parrington, C. Samuels, and Tomsich for a broader analysis of his thought and career.

2. In *The Problem of Boston* Martin Green gives a graphic description and thoughtful analysis of what he believes to be the weakening, corruption, and trivializing of intellectual culture in Boston during the second half of the nineteenth century.

3. Pressmen and male compositors averaged about $50 per month, while more specialized male proofreaders and artists might earn $75 or even $100 per month. Wages for women were listed in separate accounts and were generally little more than half the wages of a man doing the same job. A female compositor or proofreader might average $30 per month. An average *Atlantic* writer, male or female, would have to publish a ten-page paper every month to make between $75 and $100. (Houghton Mifflin Payroll Books: 1876–1880, Harvard)

4. For Scudder's reviews of Howells, see "Review of *Dr. Breen's Practice*," Jan. 1882, 129; "Review of *A Modern Instance*," Nov. 1882, 709; "James, Crawford, and Howells," June 1886, 856–57; and *A Hazard of New Fortunes* in "New York in Recent Fiction," Apr. 1890, 563–66.

5. For further analysis of James's relationship with the *Atlantic* from the editorship of Fields to that of Bliss Perry, see Ellery Sedgwick, "Henry James and the *Atlantic Monthly*: Editorial Perspectives on James' Friction with the Market," *Studies in Bibliography* 45 (1992):

311–32. This article documents the importance of the American magazine market, and the *Atlantic* in particular, to the first thirty years of James's career, his attempt and ultimate failure to place major works in the New York illustrated magazines, his continued reliance on the *Atlantic*, and the increasing commercial pressure during the rise of progressive journalism in the nineties to limit his access even to the *Atlantic*.

6. For a discussion of the ideal of an organic society, see the chapters "Scholars in Politics" and "Economics for an Organic Society" in John Tomsich's *Genteel Endeavor*.

7. Lillie Wyman's *Atlantic* articles during the editorships of Howells, Aldrich, and Scudder represent early examples of the kind of reportage on the social consequences of industrialism that gained prominence near the turn of the century after the publication of Jacob Riis's *How the Other Half Lives* (1890). Her articles for Aldrich were "Studies of Factory Life," July 1888, 16–29; "Among the Women," Sept. 1888, 315–21; and "Black Listing at Fall River," Nov. 1888, 605–12.

6. Scudder

1. Biographical accounts of Scudder are scarce. The best sources are Ballou 102–7; Higginson, "Scudder"; and Allen.

2. For a sample of the characteristic positions of Scudder's *Atlantic* on education, see G. S. Hall, "The Case of the Public School," Mar. 1896.

3. Scudder's major comments on the role of literature in education are in "Authorship in America," June 1883; "The Primer in Literature," Sept. 1892; and "The Educational Law of Reading and Writing," Feb. 1894.

4. For these responses to the manifestos of Howells and Garland, see Scudder, "Mr. Howells' Literary Creed," Oct. 1891, 566; Charles Minor Thompson, "Hamlin Garland," Dec. 1895, 840–44; and Paul Shorey, "The Present Condition of Literary Production," Aug. 1896, 156–68.

5. For further discussion of Jewett's editorial relationship with Scudder, see Ellery Sedgwick's "Horace Scudder and Sarah Orne Jewett: Market Forces in Publishing in the 1890s," *American Periodicals*, Fall 1992.

7. Page

1. For an account of the progressive publishing movement, see Wilson 40–62.

2. Articles in Page's series on ethnic groups included W. C. Merwin, "The Irish" (Mar. 1896), and Josiah Flynt, "The German and German-American" (Nov. 1896); W. E. B. DuBois, "The Strivings of the Negro People" (Aug. 1897); William Leighton, "The Greaser" (June 1899); Abraham Cahan, "The Russian Jew in America" (July 1898); and George Bird Grinnell, "The Wild Indian" (Jan. 1899).

8. Perry

1. For a comparative examination of R. W. Gilder's selection of serials for the *Century* after 1900, see John 253–54. The succession of sentimental domestic novels, historical romances, and adventure stories was essentially similar to Perry's, but longer and more unrelieved.

2. For contemporary criticism of reviewing practices, including those described in the following paragraph, see, for instance, Bliss Perry, "Literary Criticism in American Periodi-

cals," *Yale Review*, July 1914, 635–55; Henry James, "The Lesson of Balzac," *Atlantic*, Aug. 1905, 166–80; Charles Minor Thompson, "Honest Literary Criticism," *Atlantic*, July 1908, 179–90.

3. These books are reviewed in H. W. Boynton, "Literature and Fiction," May 1902, 706–7; Mary Moss, "Notes on New Novels," Jan. 1906, 49; and Harry James Smith, "Some Recent Novels," July 1907, 133.

4. The three autobiographical articles by Zitkala-Sa were "Impressions of an Indian Childhood" (Jan. 1900), "The School Days of an Indian Girl" (Feb. 1900), and "An Indian Teacher among Indians" (Mar. 1900).

Works Cited

Unless otherwise specified, all references in the text to unpublished correspondence refer to manuscript materials in the Houghton Library of Harvard University. The Houghton Library holds the major collections of the papers of James Russell Lowell, William Dean Howells, Thomas Bailey Aldrich, Horace Elisha Scudder, Walter Hines Page, and Bliss Perry, as well as extensive archives of the publishing firms of Ticknor and Fields and the Houghton Mifflin Company. Most of these collections are separately indexed. Most references to works published in the *Atlantic Monthly* are cited in the text, giving author, title, and date of publication. All references to published works in the text and here in "Works Cited" that are not otherwise specified refer to works in the *Atlantic Monthly*. The *Atlantic* has been indexed with listings by both author and title in *The Atlantic Index* (Boston: Houghton Mifflin, 1889), covering the years 1857 through 1888 (volumes 1–62) and *The Atlantic Index: Supplement, 1889–1901* (Boston: Houghton Mifflin, 1903) covering volumes 63–88.

Aldrich, Thomas Bailey. *The Poems of Thomas Bailey Aldrich*. Boston: Houghton Mifflin, 1907.
Allen, Alexander. "Horace Elisha Scudder." Apr. 1903.
American Newspaper Annual. Philadelphia: N. W. Ayer, 1895–1909.
Andrews, William. *The Literary Career of Charles W. Chesnutt*. Baton Rouge: Louisiana State UP, 1980.
Anesko, Michael. *Friction with the Market*. New York: Oxford UP, 1986.
Atlantic Monthly Archives. Boston: Atlantic Monthly Co.
Austin, James C. *Fields of the Atlantic Monthly: Letters to an Editor, 1861–1870*. San Marino, CA: Huntington Library, 1953.
Bagby, George. "Editorial Table." *Southern Literary Messenger* Dec. 1857.
Ballou, Ellen. *The Building of the House: Houghton Mifflin's Formative Years*. Boston: Houghton Mifflin, 1970.
Bishop, William H. "Authors at Home." *Critic* 8 Aug. 1885.
Brill, Leonard. "Thomas Wentworth Higginson and the *Atlantic Monthly*." Diss. U of Minnesota, 1968.
Brodhead, Richard. "Literature and Culture." *Columbia Literary History of the United States*. Gen. ed. Emory Elliot. New York: Columbia UP, 1988. 467–81.
Brooks, Van Wyck. *The Flowering of New England*. New York: E. P. Dutton, 1936.
———. *New England: Indian Summer, 1865–1915*. New York: E. P. Dutton, 1940.

Works Cited

Buell, Lawrence. *New England Literary Culture: From Revolution through Renaissance.* New York: Cambridge UP, 1986.
Butler, Robert E. "William Dean Howells as Editor of the *Atlantic Monthly*." Diss. Rutgers U, 1950.
Cady, Edwin. *The Gentleman in America.* Syracuse: Syracuse UP, 1949.
———. *The Road to Realism: The Early Years (1837–1885) of William Dean Howells.* Syracuse: Syracuse UP, 1956.
Cary, Richard. *The Genteel Circle: Bayard Taylor and His Friends.* Ithaca: Cornell UP, 1952.
———. *Mary N. Murfree.* New York: Twayne, 1967.
———. *Sarah Orne Jewett.* New York: Twayne, 1962.
Charvat, William. *Literary Publishing in America: 1790–1850.* Philadelphia: U of Pennsylvania P, 1959.
———. *The Profession of Authorship in America.* Columbus: Ohio State UP, 1968.
Chesnutt, Helen. *Charles Wadell Chesnutt.* Chapel Hill: U of North Carolina P, 1953.
Coultrap-McQuinn, Susan. *Doing Literary Business: American Women Writers in the Nineteenth Century.* Chapel Hill: U of North Carolina P, 1990.
Cyganowski, Carol. *Magazine Editors and Professional Authors in Nineteenth-Century America: The Genteel Tradition and the American Dream.* New York: Garland, 1988.
Daskum, Josephine. "The Distinction of Our Poetry." May 1901.
Dickinson, Emily. *Letters of Emily Dickinson.* Ed. Mabel Loomis Todd. New York: Harper, 1931.
Donovan, Josephine. *New England Local Color: A Woman's Tradition.* New York: Frederick Ungar, 1983.
Douglas, Ann. *The Feminization of American Culture.* New York: Knopf, 1977.
Duberman, Martin. *James Russell Lowell.* Boston: Beacon Press, 1966.
Dupree, A. Hunter. *Asa Gray.* Cambridge: Harvard UP, 1959.
Elliot, Emory, gen. ed. *Columbia Literary History of the United States.* New York: Columbia UP, 1988.
Emerson, Edward. *Early Years of the Saturday Club, 1855–1870.* Boston: Houghton Mifflin, 1918.
Emerson, Ralph Waldo. "The American Scholar." *Works of Ralph Waldo Emerson.* Ed. Edward Emerson. Boston: Houghton Mifflin, 1903. 1: 81–116.
———. "Culture." Mar. 1860.
———. *The Journals of Ralph Waldo Emerson.* Vols. 5, 9, 14. Ed. Susan Smith, and Harrison Hayford. Cambridge: Harvard UP, 1978–82. 16 vols.
———. *Letters of Ralph Waldo Emerson.* Vol. 5. Ed. Ralph Rusk. New York: Columbia UP, 1939. 6 vols.
Eppard, Phillip, and George Montiero. *A Guide to the Atlantic Monthly Contributor's Club.* Boston: G. K. Hall, 1983.
Exman, Eugene. *The House of Harper.* New York: Harper and Row, 1967.
Ferguson, Alfred. *E. R. Sill: The Twilight Poet.* The Hague: Martinus, 1955.
Fields, Annie. *Life and Letters of Harriet Beecher Stowe.* Boston: Houghton Mifflin, 1898.
Fields, James T. *Yesterdays with Authors.* Boston: J. R. Osgood, 1872.
Fink, Augusta. *I, Mary.* Tucson: U of Arizona P, 1983.
Gilman, Arthur. "Atlantic Dinners and Diners." Nov. 1907.
Glasrud, Clarence. *H. H. Boyesen.* Northfield, Minn.: Norwegian-American Historical Assn., 1963.
Green, Martin. *The Problem of Boston.* New York: W. W. Norton, 1966.

Works Cited

Greenslet, Ferris. *Thomas Bailey Aldrich*. Boston: Houghton Mifflin, 1908.
———. *Under the Bridge*. Boston: Houghton Mifflin, 1943.
Hall, David. "The Victorian Connection." *American Quarterly* 27 (Dec. 1975): 561–74.
Harlow, Virginia. *Thomas Sergeant Perry*. Durham: Duke UP, 1950.
Hendrick, Burton. *The Life and Letters of Walter Hines Page*. Vol. 1. New York: Doubleday Page, 1922. 3 vols.
Higginson, Mary T. *Thomas Wentworth Higginson: The Story of His Life*. Boston: Houghton Mifflin, 1914.
Higginson, Thomas Wentworth. "Americanism in Literature." Jan. 1870.
———. *Cheerful Yesterdays*. Boston: Houghton Mifflin, 1898.
———. "Horace Elisha Scudder." *Proceedings of the American Academy of Arts and Sciences* 37 (May 1902): 657–61.
———. *Letters and Journals of Thomas W. Higginson*. Ed. Mary Thacher Higginson. Boston: Houghton Mifflin, 1921. New York: DaCapo Press, 1969.
Holmes, Oliver Wendell. "The Professor at the Breakfast Table." Jan.–Dec. 1859.
Howe, Daniel. "American Victorianism as a Culture." *American Quarterly* 27 (Dec. 1975): 507–52.
Howe, Mark DeWolfe. *The Atlantic Monthly and Its Makers*. Boston: Atlantic Monthly Press, 1919.
Howells, Mildred. *Life in Letters of William Dean Howells*. 2 vols. Garden City, NY: Doubleday Doran, 1928.
Howells, William Dean. *Editor's Study: A Comprehensive Edition of W. D. Howells' Column*. Ed. James Simpson. Troy, NY: Whitston, 1983.
———. "Henry James." *Century* Nov. 1882.
———. *Literary Friends and Acquaintances*. New York: Harper, 1900.
———. *Literature and Life*. New York: Harper, 1902.
———. *My Literary Passions*. New York: Harper, 1895.
———. "Recollections of an *Atlantic* Editorship." Nov. 1907.
———. *Selected Letters of William Dean Howells*. Ed. George Arms and Christopher Lohman. 4 vols. Boston: Twayne, 1979.
James, Henry. "American Letter." *Literature* 2 (11 June 1898): 678.
———. *The Complete Notebooks*. Ed. Leon Edel and Lyall Powers. New York: Oxford UP, 1987.
———. *Letters of Henry James*. Ed. Leon Edel. 4 vols. Cambridge: Harvard UP, 1975–84.
———. "An Open Letter to Mr. Howells." *North American Review* Apr. 1912. Also qtd. in *Letters* 1: 268–69.
———. *The Spoils of Poynton*. New York: Scribner's, 1908.
Jenkins, MacGregor. *Literature with a Large L*. Boston: Houghton Mifflin, 1919.
Jewett, Sarah Orne. *Letters of Sarah Orne Jewett*. Ed. Annie Fields. Boston: Houghton Mifflin, 1911.
———. *Sarah Orne Jewett Letters*. Ed. Richard Cary. Waterville, ME: Colby Coll. P, 1956.
John, Arthur. *The Best Years of the Century*. Urbana: U of Illinois P, 1981.
Lears, T. J. Jackson. *No Place of Grace: Antimodernism and the Transformation of American Culture, 1880–1920*. New York: Pantheon, 1981.
Levine, Lawrence. *Highbrow/Lowbrow: The Emergence of Cultural Hierarchy in America*. Cambridge: Harvard UP, 1988.
London, Jack. *The Letters of Jack London*. Vol. 1. Ed. Earl Labor et al. Palo Alto: Stanford UP, 1988. 2 vols.

Works Cited

Lowell, James Russell. *Letters of James Russell Lowell.* Ed. Charles Eliot Norton. New York: Harper, 1894.

——. "Nationality in Literature." *North American Review* 69 (July 1849): 196–215.

——. *New Letters of James Russell Lowell.* Ed. Mark D. Howe. New York: Harper, 1932.

Lynn, Kenneth. *William Dean Howells: An American Life.* New York: Harcourt Brace Jovanovich, 1970.

Lyon, Peter. *Success Story: S. S. McClure.* New York: Scribner's, 1963.

McMahon, Helen. *Criticism of Fiction: A Study of Trends in the Atlantic Monthly, 1857–1898.* New York: Bookman Associates, 1973.

Matthiessen, F. O. *Sarah Orne Jewett.* Boston: Houghton Mifflin, 1929.

Mitchell, Robert. "American Life as Reflected in the *Atlantic Monthly*: 1857–1881." Diss. Harvard U, 1950.

Morse, John. *The Life and Letters of Oliver Wendell Holmes.* 2 vols. Boston: Houghton Mifflin, 1896.

Mott, Frank Luther. *A History of American Magazines.* Vols. 2–4. Cambridge: Harvard UP, 1939–68. 5 vols.

Norton, Charles Eliot. "The Launching of the Magazine." Nov. 1907.

Oberndorf, Clarence. *The Psychiatric Novels of Oliver Wendell Holmes.* New York, 1946.

Oviatt, Edwin. "J. W. DeForest in New Haven." *New York Times* Sat. Supp. 17 Dec. 1898.

Parker, William B. *Edward Rowland Sill: His Life and Work.* Boston: Houghton Mifflin, 1915.

Parrington, Vernon. *Main Currents in American Thought.* 2 vols. New York: Harcourt Brace, 1927.

Pattee, Fred. *The Development of the Short Story.* New York, Harper, 1923.

Perry, Bliss. *And Gladly Teach.* Boston: Houghton Mifflin, 1935.

——. "The Editor Who Never Was the Editor." Nov. 1907.

——. *Park Street Papers.* Boston: Houghton Mifflin, 1908.

Persons, Stowe. *The Decline of American Gentility.* New York: Columbia UP, 1973.

Peterson, Theodore. *Magazines in the Twentieth Century.* Urbana: U of Illinois P, 1964.

Pierce, Zina Fay. "Cooperative Housekeeping." Nov. 1868–Mar. 1869.

Rideing, William H. "Boston Letter." *Critic* 18 Dec. 1886.

Samuels, Charles. *Thomas Bailey Aldrich.* New York: Twayne, 1965.

Samuels, Ernest. *Henry Adams.* Cambridge: Harvard UP, 1989.

Santayana, George. "The Genteel Tradition in American Philosophy." *The Genteel Tradition: Nine Essays.* By Santayana. Cambridge: Harvard UP, 1967.

Scholnick, Robert. *Edmund Clarence Stedman.* New York: Twayne, 1977.

——. "Whitman and the Magazines: Some Documentary Evidence." *American Literature* 44 (May 1972): 222–46.

Scudder, Horace Elisha. *Henry Oscar Houghton: A Biographical Outline.* Cambridge, MA: Houghton Mifflin, 1897.

——. *James Russell Lowell: A Biography.* Boston: Houghton Mifflin, 1901.

Sedgwick, Ellery. *The Happy Profession.* Boston: Little, Brown, 1946.

Smith, Gail. "A Study of Prose Fiction in the *Atlantic Monthly* and *Harper's New Monthly Magazine*: 1857–1861." Diss. Texas A&M U, 1974.

Smith, Henry Nash. *Democracy and the Novel.* New York: Oxford UP, 1978.

Smith, Herbert. *Richard Watson Gilder.* New York: Twayne, 1970.

Sollors, Werner. *Beyond Ethnicity.* New York: Oxford UP, 1986.

Stowe, Harriet Beecher. "The Chimney Corner." Jan. 1865–Sept. 1866.

Taylor, Bayard. *Unpublished Letters of Bayard Taylor.* Ed. John Schultz. San Marino, CA: Huntington, 1937.
Tebbel, John. *A History of Book Publishing in the United States.* Vol. 1. New York: R. R. Bowker, 1972. 2 vols.
Thoreau, Henry David. *The Correspondence of Henry David Thoreau.* Ed. Walter Harding and Carl Bode. New York: New York UP, 1958.
———. *The Journal of Henry David Thoreau.* Ed. Bradford Torrey and Francis Allen. Vols. 5 and 10. Boston: Houghton Mifflin, 1906.
———. *Life in the Maine Woods.* Ed. Joseph Moldenhauer. Princeton: Princeton UP, 1972.
Tomsich, John. *A Genteel Endeavor: American Culture and Politics in the Gilded Age.* Palo Alto: Stanford UP, 1971.
Trachtenberg, Alan. *The Incorporation of America: Culture and Society in the Gilded Age.* New York: Hill and Wang, 1982.
Trowbridge, John. "The Author of Quabbin." Jan. 1895.
———. "An Early Contributor's Recollections." Nov. 1907.
Tryon, Warren S. *Parnassus Corner: A Life of James T. Fields.* Boston: Houghton Mifflin, 1963.
Turner, Arlin. *George Washington Cable: A Biography.* Durham: Duke UP, 1956.
Tuttle, Donald. "Thomas Bailey Aldrich's Editorship of the *Atlantic Monthly.*" Diss. Western Reserve U, 1939.
Twain, Mark. *Mark Twain–Howells Letters: 1872–1910.* Vol. 1. Ed. F. Anderson, W. Gibson, and H. N. Smith. Cambridge: Harvard UP, 1960. 2 vols.
Underwood, Francis. *James Russell Lowell: The Poet and the Man.* Boston: Lee and Shepard, 1893.
Wellek, René. *A History of Modern Criticism: The Later Nineteenth Century.* New Haven: Yale UP, 1965.
Wells, Anna. *Dear Preceptor.* Boston: Houghton Mifflin, 1963.
Wells, H. G. *The Future of America.* New York: Harper, 1906.
Wilson, Christopher. *The Labor of Words: Literary Professionalism in the Progressive Era.* Athens: U of Georgia P, 1985.
Wilson, Edmund. *Patriotic Gore: Studies in the Literature of the American Civil War.* New York: Oxford UP, 1962.
Wilson, Forest. *Crusader in Crinoline: The Life of Harriet Beecher Stowe.* Philadelphia: J. B. Lippincott, 1941.
Winter, William. *Old Friends.* New York: Moffatt, Tard, 1909.
Woodress, James, ed. *Essays: Mostly on Periodical Publishing in America.* Durham: Duke UP, 1973.
Wright, Paul. "The Boston Publishing Community, 1830–1860: A Case Study in Professionalization." Paper at American Studies Association, Minneapolis, 27–29 Sept. 1979.
Ziff, Larzer. *The American 1890s: The Life and Times of a Lost Generation.* New York: Viking, 1966.

Index

Adams, Charles Francis, 215; *Atlantic* endorses for President, 154; reform journalism in *Atlantic*, 157, 258
Adams, Henry, 249
Addams, Jane: critique of philanthropy, 258; in Page's *Atlantic*, 265; Scudder rejects, 215
Advertising: aimed at teachers, 217; aimed at women, 255; of *Atlantic* in newspapers, 150; effect on book reviews, 296–97; in Fields's *Atlantic*, 82; under Page, 272; rates in *Atlantic*, 130
Agassiz, Louis, 23; in Fields's *Atlantic*, 87, 100
Alcott, Louisa May, 93
Alden, Henry Mills: 217, 276; editorial license, 171; friendship with Scudder, 204; rejects Chesnutt's fiction, 266; salary, 206; secures Wister for *Harper's*, 236
Aldrich, Thomas Bailey, 249; accomplishments as editor, 199; aestheticism of, 169, 184; American authors poll, 165; authors solicited by, 176; background of, 164; contents of his *Atlantic*, 182; contrast with Howells, 159; contrast with Scudder, 201–2; cultural conservatism of, 11–13, 162, 169, 172, 185; described, 165; dislike of self-revelation, 184; editorial license, 171; editorial methods, 170–77; editorial policy, 11–14; edits *Every Saturday*, 165; enthusiasm for Boston, 165–66; forced to resign, 198; forty-four when appointed, 203; genteel tradition and, 161, 315–16; Howells rejects, 149; Lillie Wyman and, 321; literary judgment, 169; New York writers and, 165; office at 4 Park Street, 170; publishes in *Harper's, Century*, 180; regular contributors under, 175; reputation of, 165, 299; reviews for *Atlantic*, 88; salary, 167; Scudder and, 205; Scudder jokes by, 228; social life, 166–68; *Story of a Bad Boy*, 169
Allen, Francis, rejected as assistant editor, 212
American News Service, 311; Jenkins negotiates with, 280

Anonymity of early authors, 36
Antislavery movement: *Atlantic* founding and, 29, 33; diversity of, 23
Arnold, Matthew: *Atlantic* shares cultural mission, 12, 181–83; criticizes *Atlantic*'s nationalism, 52
Atlantic: advocates American literature, 11, 35; advocates reform, 10; bound into volumes, 251; competition with other magazines, 11, 12; cover, 35; cultural nationalism of, 10; distribution of, 81; economic pressure to diversify, 9, 317; ethnocentrism in, 268; first issue described, 34–38; founding, 3–4, 29; high culture and, 3, 129, 242, 315–17; named by Holmes, 34; national scope of, 10; New England regionalism of, 10; overview of first fifty years, 9–19, 314–18; price, 39, 247; profit and loss (1890s), 206, 238, 240; profit and loss (1901–1908), 311; profit and loss under Page, 272; progressivism of, 17; religious liberalism of, 10; sale to Ticknor and Fields, 64. *See also* entries under editors
Atlantic, changes in. *See* under editor, accomplishments
Atlantic Monthly Company buys *Atlantic* in 1908, 312
Austin, Mary, 308, 316; criticized in *Atlantic*, 298; Perry and, 292–93

Babad, Nathan, immigrant autobiography of, 308
Babbitt, Irving, Scudder publishes, 214
Bankroft, George: on Lincoln, 103; on manifest destiny, 106
Bellamy, Edward, Scudder solicits, 224
Bishop, W. H.: serials for Aldrich, 192; writes on New York for Howells, 150
Bok, Edward, 15, 247, 278; Perry learns editing from, 276
Book reviews: under Aldrich, 188–91; under Fields, 72, 87–88; under Howells, 119–20, 152–

Index

Book reviews (*cont.*)
53; increase under Perry, 277; under Lowell, 37, 53, 55, 56; under Page, 260–62; under Perry, 296–301; Perry's criticism of, 321; under Scudder, 220–23, 242; Scudder writes, 208. *See also* Literary criticism
Booth, Edwin, friendship with Aldrich, 169
Boston: Aldrich prefers to New York, 166; criticism of, literary culture, 320; as cultural center, 21; in gilded age, 163; as publishing center in 1860s, 77
Boston writers. *See* Yankee humanists
Boyesen, H. H., 315; Howells's editorial treatment of, 144–45
Boynton, Henry, 297
Bradford, Gamaliel, 212
Brooks, John G., on socialism, 305
Brown, Alice, 301; Page rejects story by, 262
Brownell, H. H., "Abraham Lincoln," 94
Brownell, W. C., on Henry James, 301
Bryan, William Jenning, Page opposes populism of, 258
Buell, Lawrence, on New England cultural elite, 4–5
Bullock, Charles, on labor and capital, 304
Burroughs, John, 263; rate of payment, 178

Cable, George Washington: *John March, Southerner,* 224; serialized in *Atlantic,* 289
Cahan, Abraham, 259, 267, 316; on Jews, 269; Page solicits, 253
Canon: *Atlantic* and, 3, 11, 12–13; decline of western, 317; Scudder on American, 218; Scudder's attempt to preserve, 213–14, 241; western classics under Aldrich, 183; western classics under Perry, 300
Carman, Bliss: assists Scudder, 212; reviewed, 222
Carter, Robert, founds *Pioneer* with Lowell, 28
Cather, Willa, friendship with Annie Fields, 320
Catherwood, Mary H., serials by, 225
Century Magazine, 248, 287; circulation exceeds 200,000, 177; compared to *McClure's,* 247; critiqued by *Nation,* 242; cuts book reviews, 297; decline of, 15; endorses romantic fiction, 298; increase in current affairs, 246; payments to authors, 178, 180; poetry in, 293; prizes work by Kate Wiggin, 263; publishes *Bostonians,* 194; rate of payment, 288; supports civil service reform, 197. *See also* Gilder; Holland; and *Scribner's* (*Century*)
Chapman, John Jay, 214; criticizes Aldrich, 172; on Emerson, 298; in Page's *Atlantic,* 258, 261; opposes political parties, 305; protests Scudder's editing, 209
Charvat, William: on Fields's promotions, 87; on publishing history, 2
Cheesebro, Caroline, 93

Chesnutt, Charles, 316; Aldrich publishes stories by, 176; Howells's article on, 301; Page advocates publishing, 266–67; Scudder and, 235–36; tries to publish romances, 284
Child, Lydia Maria, fictional portrayal of South, 94
Chopin, Kate, 219; in Page's *Atlantic,* 265; rejected as depressing, 287; Scudder reviews, 223; Scudder urges to write novel, 227
Circulation (*Atlantic*): boosted by *To Have and to Hold,* 263; decline in 1870, 109–10; decline under Aldrich, 177; decline under Howells, 127, 158; in 1857–60, 39–40; in 1898, 251; under Fields, 81; under Page, 272; Page and Mifflin try to raise, 240; under Perry, 311; under Scudder, 238; under Sedgwick, 313, 314
Civil service reform, *Atlantic* endorses, 13–14, 196
Civil War: as cultural progress, 100–101; literature of, in *Atlantic,* 93–95; reportage on, 85
Clarke, James Freeman, 23; essays on religion, 99–100
Cleveland, Grover, Scudder supports, 216
Clough, Arthur Hugh, "Amours de Voyage," 50
Conrad, Joseph, *Atlantic* criticism on, 301
Contributors' Club: Howells initiates, 114, 132, 152–53; Sill contributes often, 187
Converse, Florence, fiction rejected, 286
Cooke, Rose Terry, 93; in Lowell's *Atlantic,* 37, 56; Lowell's editorial treatment of, 55
Copeland, Charles, 212, 220; review of Garland, 222; review of *Tess,* 222
Cortissoz, Royal, 212, 297
Cosmopolitan, Howells's editorship, 159
Craddock, Charles. *See* Mary Noailles Murfree
Crane, Stephen: *Black Riders* reviewed, 236; Page approves, 261
Crane, Walter, "Why Socialism Appeals to Artists," 217
Crawford, Francis Marion: Aldrich loses, 192, 197–98; Scudder and, 224
Critic: on Aldrich's *Atlantic,* 181; American authors poll, 165; satirizes James, 194
Current affairs. *See* Politics

Dana, Charles, 177; publishes stories by James, 194
Darwinism: in Fields's *Atlantic,* 100; in Lowell's *Atlantic,* 10, 61, 315
Daskum, Josephine, on New England poets, 299
Davis, Rebecca Harding: "A Story of Today," 96; Fields's editorial treatment of, 96–97; friendship with Annie Fields, 92–93; on *Galaxy,* 77; "Life in the Iron Mills," 96
DeForest, John W., 315; Fields and, 98; Howells's editorial treatment of, 145; reportage on Reconstruction, 85, 264
Deland, Margaret, 226

330

Index

Denison, J. H., 217
Dial, 27, 50
Dickens, Charles, and Fields, 88, 91
Dickinson, Emily: Aldrich's criticism of, 185; as *Atlantic* reader, 40; Higginson and, 79
Dobson, Austin, exchanges reviewing favors, 189
Doubleday, Frank, 247
Douglas, Norman, 308
Douglass, Frederick, essays on Reconstruction, 104
Dreiser, Theodore, plagiarism by, 292
DuBois, W.E.B., 316; criticizes Anglo ethnocentrism, 309; "Of the Training of Black Men," 308; in Page's *Atlantic*, 269–70; Page solicits, 253, 259; proposes new Reconstruction, 307–8
Dunbar, Paul, 295; "Robert Gould Shaw," 307
Duncan, Norman, 279
Durham, John, 259

Economic issues. *See* Politics
Editors: cultural significance of, 1; influence on writers, 2. *See also* names of individual editors of *Atlantic*
Education: under Page, 254; under Scudder, 217–19, 321; universal education advocated, 105
Eggleston, George Cary, trades reviewing favors, 189–90
Eliot, Charles, 215; "The New Education," 86–87; rejected by Aldrich, 198
Emancipation, Lowell and Emerson advocate, 101
Emerson, Edwin, 212
Emerson, Ralph Waldo, 22, 282, 298; accepts Lowell's editing, 46; advocates emancipation, 101–2; advocates National Academy, 107; "American Civilization," 87; "American Scholar," 26, 51; "Aspects of Culture," 107; asserts *Nation's* superiority, 76; Civil War poems, 93–94; contributes to *Atlantic*, 36, 58; cultural nationalism of, 7, 51; on democracy, 6, 25; on editing, 1; founding of *Atlantic* and, 29, 31; helps Lowell retain editorship, 65; hopes for *Atlantic*, 314; interest in magazines, 28; *Journals* published, 284; leadership of cultural elite, 25; on moral basis of politics, 61; payments to, 46; poetry, 89; progressive movement and, 249; in Scudder's canon, 219; sees magazine as book, 251; supports Lowell as editor, 31; war as cultural progress, 100–101
England, attitudes toward, under Fields, 92
Essay: change in style under Fields, 83; under Lowell, 50

Fagin, J. O., "Confessions of a Signalman," 289
Fawcett, Edgar, antipathy for Howells, 138
Fenellosa, Ernest, 254

Fiction: under Aldrich, 182–83; 191–95; *Atlantic* compared to *Scribner's*, 128; decline of New England, 286–87; in early *Atlantic* and *Harper's*, 38–39; under Fields, 88–93; under Howells, 133–46; influence of journalism on, 246; under Lowell, 36, 52–57; more genteel than nonfiction, 292; nostalgia in postwar period, 95; under Page, 262–67; under Perry, 283–93; under Scudder, 223–36, 241–42; serials under Page, 262–63; serials under Perry, 283–86; short story supplanting serial, 226–27. *See also* Novels; Realism
Fields, Annie, 23, 72, 179; and Aldrich, 167; companion to Jewett, 227–28; friendships with women authors, 320; influence, 92
Fields, James T., 23, 257; accomplishments, 110–11; active editorial solicitation, 77; background, 70; compared to Aldrich, 199; death, 163; democratizing influence of, 315; editorial policies, 73–88; ends anonymity, 83; forty-four when editor, 203; hires Aldrich, 165; hopes for *Atlantic*, 317; influence on literature, 69, 73, 85; literary judgment, 72, 88–89; manipulates book reviews, 87–88; popularization of *Atlantic*, 70, 81–82; promotes "Atlantic circle," 9, 22, 74–75; promotes nonfiction reportage, 83; publicity, 71, 83; reputation for liberality, 71; retirement, 110; solicits *Our Old Home*, 85–86
Fiske, John, 215; on Herbert Spencer, 100; Howells's editorial treatment of, 146–47; Page and, 257; writes on science for Howells, 137, 152
Foote, Mary Halleck, 265
Ford, Paul Leichester: Scudder advises, 208; serial by, 225; *Story of an Untold Love*, 262–63
Forum, 240; Dreiser plagiarizes, 292; Page edits, 238
France, Anatol, 301
Francis, Susan, 175, 176, 198, 212; on Aldrich, 170; assists Fields, 78; assists Page, 253; assists Scudder, 208; censors Hardy, 172; proofreading by, 209; salary, 206
Freeman, Mary E. W. *See* Mary E. Wilkins
French, Alice, 265
French, Lillie, 261–62
Friedman, I. K., 308
Fuller, Henry: Page and, 256, 265; rejected, 286; tries romantic fiction, 284

Galaxy: New York's alternative to *Atlantic*, 77; solicits James, 140
Garland, Hamlin: poetry of, 236, 237; reviews of, 221, 222, 321
Garrison, Francis (Houghton's financial assistant), 177, 235; on sale of *Atlantic*, 312
Gauss, Christian, 297
Genteel tradition, 310; *Atlantic* and, 11, 248–49; attitude toward James, 193

Index

Gibbs, Herbert, assists Scudder, 208, 211, 212

Gilder, Richard Watson, 217, 224, 276; on *Bostonians*, 194; editorial license, 171; rejects Chesnutt's work, 266; and romantic fiction, 286; salary, 206; seeks the "new poet," 293; selection of serials, 321; welcomes revival of romance, 262

Gildersleeve, Basil, 214

Glasgow, Ellen, 283

Godkin, Edwin Lawrence, 215; criticism of gilded age, 191; Page rejects antiwar article by, 260; writes for Page, 257

Godwin, Parke: break with Lowell, 47; criticizes Buchanan, 62; political editorials by, 36

Goldman, Emma, 258; Perry rejects, 305

Grant, U. S., 104–5; *Atlantic* reluctantly supports, 154

Gray, Asa, 210; defends Darwin in *Atlantic*, 23, 61

Greenslet, Ferris, 287; assists Perry, 279–80

Grinnell, George Bird, on Native Americans, 269

Guiney, Louise, 295

Hale, Edward Everett: on freedmen, 104; *New England Boyhood*, 213

Hamilton, Gail: Fields recruits, 75; suit against Fields, 76, 109

Hapgood, Hutchins: on the Bowery, 308; writes for Page, 261

Hapgood, Norman, 279; Scudder declines reviews by, 220; writes for Page, 261

Hardy, Arthur: Aldrich loses, 192; declines editorship, 275

Hardy, Thomas: reviewed, 222, 301; serials for Aldrich, 192

Harper, Fletcher, retains editorial control, 38

Harper's Monthly: Alden as editor, 171; avoids religion and politics, 58; book reviews in, 152, 297; cancels DeForests *Miss Ravenel*, 145; circulation (1850–1860), 39; compared with *Atlantic* (1857), 38; compared with *McClure's*, 247; competes with *Atlantic*, 76, 177; decline of, 152; *Every Saturday* to compete with, 165; Fields and Longfellow in, 135; founding of, 29–30; Hearn breaks with, 214; Howe declines offer from, 212; Howells champions realism at, 188, 219; increases American fiction, 130; increases current affairs, 246; payments to authors, 180, 234; and Reconstruction, 136; rejects Woodberry, 188. *See also* Alden, Henry Mills

Harris, Joel Chandler, 284

Harris, W. T., on black education, 217

Harrison, Rev. J. B., social reportage in *Atlantic*, 148

Hart, Albert B., 215

Harte, Bret, 315; protests rate of payment, 130–31

Hartt, Rollin: in Page's *Atlantic*, 265; on popular culture, 301–2

Hawthorne, Nathaniel, 22, 284; death, 91; Fields advises, 74; Fields and "Dolliver Romance," 89–91; on Lincoln, 102; *Our Old Home*, 85–86; Perry's judgment of, 299; posthumous publications, 91; in Scudder's canon, 219

Hayes, Rutherford B., 154

Hayne, Paul, 42, 136

Hearn, Lafcadio, 249; Scudder and, 214

Herrick, Robert, *The Common Lot* serialized, 288

Higginson, Thomas Wentworth, 24, 313; advocates democratic culture, 107–8; assistant to Fields, 78; *Atlantic* founding and, 29; "Cheerful Yesterdays," 213; criticism of book reviews, 87–88; criticism of plutocracy, 303; on cultural mission, 4; cultural nationalism of, 7, 107–8; on freedmen, 104; hopes for *Atlantic*, 314; influence on reviewing, 88; "Leaves from an Officer's Journal," 85; "Letter to a Young Contributor," 78–79; objects to Lowell's editing, 47; "Oldport" stories, 95; reminiscences by, 298; reviews Emerson, 88; reviews for Aldrich, 189; on Scudder, 210; on slave revolts, 101; support for women writers, 78–79; on women's issues, 99

Holland, Josiah Gilbert, 129, 227; founds *Scribner's*, 127; on Howells in *Scribner's*, 131; solicits James, 140

Holmes, Oliver Wendell, Sr., 23, 298; on Aldrich, 166; Aldrich's *Atlantic*, 186; *Atlantic* founding and, 29; "Autocrat of the Breakfast Table," 36; on Civil War, 93; criticism of religion, 96; cultural nationalism of, 52; *Elsie Venner* ("Professor's Story"), 96; *Guardian Angel*, 96; hopes for *Atlantic*, 314; Howells and, 133–34; Lowell's *Atlantic*, 58–59; on New England cultural elite, 4–5; rate of payment, 178; reputation of, 50, 284, 299; Scudder's *Atlantic*, 234; supports publishing Byron article, 108; on writing for the *Atlantic*, 181

Houghton, Albert, 285–86

Houghton, Henry Oscar, 211, 238; buys *Atlantic* from Osgood, 125; characterized, 126; confidence in Scudder, 205; death of, 239; disapproves unsigned editorials, 152; discourages partisanship, 216; dissatisfaction with Aldrich, 177, 197–98; ends partnership with Osgood, 157; opposes competition, 11; plans workingman's magazine, 155; promotes *Atlantic* dinners, 133; protests criticism of firm's books, 220; prototype for Howells's Lapham, 126; reluctance to influence editor, 177; seeks assistant to Scudder, 212; selects Aldrich, 165; strategy for authors' payments, 177–78; values James, 195

Houghton Mifflin, 205, 276; *Atlantic*'s contributions to, 238; becoming more commercial, 240; books criticized in *Atlantic*, 297; contract with Holmes, 234; copyrights on canonical writers, 213, 218; difficulty drawing young writers, 234; expands promotional staff, 296; influences Perry as editor, 285, 288; James's novels at, 230; loses Crawford, 224; marketing of Johnston's *Audrey*, 286; Page's frustration with, 271–72; Perry as trade editor for, 278, 312; publishes Chesnutt, 235–36, 267; publishes Jewett, 228; publishes London, 290; publishes Moody, 295; publishes romances in 1890s, 262; restructuring in 1908, 312; Scudder edits series for, 208; Scudder's influence on, 243; sets Perry's editorial budget, 288

Hovey, Richard, 222

Howe, Julia Ward, "Battle Hymn of the Republic," 93–94

Howe, Mark, 237, 297; as assistant to Scudder, 212; eyesight fails, 212; hopes to edit *Atlantic*, 313; resigns, 238; reviews for Scudder, 220; reviews of poetry, 236; on Scudder, 243; Scudder assists, 209; on Whitman, 299

Howells, William Dean, 192, 193, 284, 290, 293; *A Chance Acquaintance*, 123–24; on Aldrich, 168; ambiguity about Boston, 115–24; as assistant editor, 117–25; assumes editorship, 124; *Atlantic* circle and, 48, 114; *Atlantic* criticism of, 321; as *Atlantic* reader, 41; on book reviews, 11; Boston clubs and, 124; censorship by, 143, 148–51; changes *Atlantic* format, 152; on Chesnutt, 267, 301; compared to Aldrich, 199; conflict with Higginson, 134; contract with *Harper's*, 223; decline of Olympians and, 134; democratizing influence of, 315; distaste for English fiction, 135; editorial methods, 144, 151–52; at *Harper's*, 219; hired by Fields as assistant, 79–80; hopes for *Atlantic*, 317; influences Aldrich's *Atlantic*, 175–76; influences on his editorship, 131–32; on impact of journalism, 246; intellectual growth as editor, 113; James and, 117, 122; leaves *Nation* for *Atlantic*, 115; loses Cable to Scribner's, 138; Lowell and, 32, 48, 116; makes *Atlantic* fully national, 135–36; New England authors and, 137; New York authors and, 136–37; Perry and, 284, 285; "Police Report" as realism, 147; pragmatic nature, 113, 117; promotes social reportage, 147–48, 155–56; publishes Stowe's Byron article, 109; rate of payment, 178; realism in early contributions, 122–24; refuses to suppress criticism, 297; reportage by, 264; resigns editorship, 157; reviews of Twain's works, 142; salary, 115, 124, 157; on scarcity of fiction (1900–1910), 283; Scudder and, 221, 242; Scudder reviews, 190–91, 220–21; secures ambassadorship for Lowell, 125; sees self as democratic westerner, 124; solicits older Boston authors, 133; southern writers and, 136; "Suburban Sketches," 98, 123; thirty-four when editor, 203; tries to expand readership, 150; *virginibus maxim* and, 150–51; western writers, 136; younger authors and, 122, 135–48

Illustration: in *Atlantic* and *Harper's*, 38; Houghton rejects, 129; Osgood proposes, Fields opposes, 82

Immigration, articles on, under Perry, 308–9

Jackson, Helen Hunt, 180; Aldrich rejects *Ramona*, 184; rate of payment, 179; suggests Aldrich overedits, 173; support for Edith Thomas, 186

James, Henry, Jr., 221, 249, 283, 290, 315–16; Aldrich and, 164, 165, 192–94, 199; *American*, 139–40; in American authors poll, 165; *Atlantic* evaluation of, 301; competition for his work, 140; criticized by Preston, 297; difficulty with brevity, 231–32; early stories in *Atlantic*, 97–98; *Europeans*, 140; Fields's editorial treatment of, 97–98; on historical romance, 283; Howells's editorial treatment, 138–40; Jenkins begs Perry to reject, 280; Page and, 256, 261; Perry, 281, 284; play of *Daisy Miller*, 193; *Portrait of a Lady*, 140; praises *Atlantic*, 242; *Princess Casamassima*, 194; proposes serial to Perry, 285; "The Pupil" rejected, 230–31; rate of payment, 140, 178, 194; relationship with *Atlantic*, 320–21; Scudder and, 205, 230, 242; in Scudder's *Atlantic*, 219; Scudder reviews, 221; *Spoils of Poynton*, 231–32; submits manuscripts for others, 174; on *Tory Lover*, 229; *Tragic Muse*, 195, 224, 230

James, Henry, Sr., 23; series on marriage, 87

James, William, 297

Jenkins, MacGregor (business manager for *Atlantic*), 16, 224; advocates "red-blooded" fiction, 287; approves *To Have and to Hold*, 284; increased influence, 313; Perry and, 275, 280, 285; promotes *Atlantic*, 240, 311; tries to change image, 280

Jewett, John (publisher), 29

Jewett, Sarah Orne, 219, 301, 315; accepts Aldrich's editing, 173; Aldrich's *Atlantic*, 193; Annie Fields and, 93, 320; *Country of the Pointed Firs*, 228–29; Howells's editorial treatment of, 146; Page's *Atlantic*, 265; rate of payment, 179, 288; Scudder and, 204, 205, 209, 227–30, 321; Scudder publishes early stories, 204; Scudder reviews, 223; serial for Aldrich, 192; *The Tory Lover*, 229–30, 285; tries romantic fiction, 284

Johnson, Andrew, 103–4

Johnston, Mary, 264, 283; *Audrey* criticized in *Atlantic*, 298; rate of payment, 288; serial romances by, 286; *To Have and to Hold*, 229, 263, 284, 281–82, 311

Jordan, David Starr, 258

Index

Kay, James Murray, 311; constraint of Perry, 288; on payments for poetry, 295; warns of libel, 215
Kennan, George, 215
Kipling, Rudyard, 262; Norton praises *Ballads*, 223
Kirk, Sophia, 220
Kittredge, George Lyman, 234
Knickerbocker Magazine: and Boston authors, 27; regionalism of, 43
Krockow, Countess Lida, 220
Kropotkin, Prince Peter, Page publishes *Autobiography*, 258
Kuh, Edwin, 308

Ladies Home Journal, 283; Mary Austin writes for, 293
Larcom, Lucy, 93; suggests Aldrich overedits, 173
Lathrop, George Parsons: applies for editorship, 165; conflict with Howells, 144; serials for Aldrich, 192
Liberator, 27
Libin (Yiddish writer), realistic fiction of, praised, 301
Lincoln, Abraham: Fields's *Atlantic* on, 102; Lowell on, 63–64
Literary criticism: under Aldrich, 182, 183; under Page, 260–62; under Perry, 296–301; under Scudder, 219–23. *See also* Book reviews
Lloyd, Henry Demerest: on Jay Gould, 197; reform journalism in *Atlantic*, 157
Lodge, Henry Cabot, protests to Mifflin, 305–6
London, Jack, 316; "Law of Life," 287; Page on, 261; Parker suggests name change, 279; in Perry's *Atlantic*, 290–91; "The Scab," 304
Longfellow, Henry W., 22, 298, 300; Aldrich and, 166; *Atlantic* reviews of, 87–88; founding of *Atlantic*, 31; poetry in *Atlantic*, 89; rate of payment, 75; reputation fades, 284, 299; in Scudder's canon, 219
Loomis, Charles, 298
Lorimer, George, 278; *Old Gorgon Graham*, 304
Lowell, A. Lawrence, declines editorship, 275
Lowell, James Russell, 22, 298; accepts Aldrich's editing, 173; accomplishments as editor, 67; advocates emancipation, 101–2; Aldrich and, 166; background, 31–33; "Biglow Papers," 101; on book reviews, 11; cultural nationalism and, 7, 51–52; as editor, 45–67; editorial policies, 34–38, 49–53; editorial prerogative, 47; editorial staff under, 319; encourages Underwood, 30; Fields as publisher and, 65–66; founding of *Atlantic*, 31–32; founds *Pioneer*, 28; generosity to younger writers, 47–48; hopes for *Atlantic*, 314, 316; Houghton loses poems, 179; Howells and, 48–49, 116; intellectual tolerance, 61; James's recollection of, 231, 299; *Last Poems* reviewed, 236; literary judgment, 53–57; "Memorium Positae R G S," 94; opposes slavery, 32–33, 47; poetry in *Atlantic*, 89; political essays for Fields, 101; posthumous publications, 234; religious controversy and, 59–61; reputation fades, 284; resigns editorship, 66; salary, 34; satire on didactic literature, 55; in Scudder's canon, 219; sees magazine as book, 251; selected as editor, 31–33; thirty-eight when editor, 203; western canon and, 50; as Yankee humanist, 33
Lowell, Percival, 214
Ludlow, J. M., advocates cooperative production, 217

Macmillan Company, publishes Crawford, 198, 224
Magazines: competing with *Atlantic*, 76–77, 158, 192–93, 234, 235, 289; contrasted with book, 202; profession of authorship, 26
Manifest destiny, postwar visions of, 105–6
Markham, Edward, 237
Mason, Alfred, criticism of laissez-faire, 156
Matthews, Brander, 284
McClure, S. S., 15, 177; editorial policies, 247; hires Page from *Atlantic*, 271; uses advertising to cut price, 247
McClure's, 14; competes with "quality" magazines, 247; gains London as contributor, 290–91
McKinley, William, 303
Merwin, H. C., 215; attack on Tammany, 215; on Whitman, 222
Metcalf, Lorettus, Page displaces, 246
Meynell, Alice, 297
Mifflin, George, 171, 220, 224, 254, 255, 259–60, 264, 267, 288; and *Atlantic* "problem," 238; considers sale of *Atlantic*, 311–13; disapproves advances, 290; enthusiasm for romantic fiction, 229; hires MacGregor Jenkins, 240; Page and, 271; Perry and, 285, 305–6; proposes series of classics, 235; seeks Page's replacement, 275; sees *Tragic Muse* as liability, 230; strategy for *Atlantic*, 245; supports Perry in controversy, 305–6
Miller, Joachim, on writing for the *Atlantic*, 181
Mitchell, D. G., *Dr. Johns*, 95
Monroe, Harriet, 237, 295
Moody, William Vaughn: Parker and, 279; Perry and, 294–95; reviews for Scudder, 220
More, Paul Elmer, 295; Scudder publishes, 214
Moss, Mary, review of novel by Lorimer, 304
Moulton, Louise Chandler: Aldrich criticizes morbidity of, 185; Page deplores poetry of, 261
Munsey, Frank, 247, 283
Murfree, Mary Noailles (Charles Egbert Craddock), 219, 315; Howells and, 136; serials for Aldrich, 192

Nation: on Aldrich's *Atlantic*, 181, 183; circulation, 182; comments on *Atlantic* in 1890s, 242; competes with *Atlantic*, 76; on poetry of 1880s, 188

Naturalism: Page's dislike for, 261; Scudder's dislike for, 225

New England cultural elite. *See* Yankee humanists

New England Magazine, edited by Edwin Buckingham, 28

New England regionalism: in *Atlantic*, 37, 42; Howells on, 43

New England writers: not socioeconomic elite, 5; Perry's *Atlantic*, 298

New Humanists, 213–14

New York writers, and early *Atlantic*, 42

Nichols, George (proofreader for *Atlantic*), 65, 319

Norris, Frank, 265

North Atlantic Review, 50; circulation, 27; published by Fields, 87; Scudder contributes, 204

Norton, Charles Eliot, 22, 183, 289; alienation from American culture, 249; declines reviewing due to low pay, 178; as Lowell's literary executor, 234; proposes dime Shakespeares, 302; reviews for Lowell, 37; views on democracy, 25

Novel: *Atlantic* criticizes romantic, 298; Perry's reduction in serials, 288–89; revival of romantic, 192, 223, 224–25, 262–63, 283–85; Scudder on decline of serial, 226–27; serials under Aldrich, 192; serials under Scudder, 223. *See also* Fiction.

Ogden, Rollo: criticism of plutocracy, 303; reviews Moody's poetry, 295; satire on Roosevelt, 305–6

Oliphant, Margaret: accepts Aldrich's editing, 173; serials for Aldrich, 192

O'Reilly, John Boyle, 168

Osgood, James, 168; becomes Fields's partner, 108; becomes publisher of *Atlantic*, 125; buys out Fields, 110; changes *Atlantic* format, 152; liberal payments to authors, 130

Page, Thomas Nelson, 215; accepts London story, 290; accomplishments as editor, 272–73, 316; advocates civil service reform, 258; advocates publishing Chesnutt, 235; "Autobiography of a Southerner," 289; background of, 245; brokers proposed sale, 312; contracts *To Have and to Hold*, 284; contrasted with Scudder, 243; critical of Scudder, 213; dislikes literary criticism, 219, 260; dislikes psychological fiction, 17, 261–62; editorial activism, 251–53; editorial judgment, 250–52; editorial methods, 239, 252–70; editorial policy, 14–19; edits *Forum*, 246; emphasis on current affairs, 251; encourages romantic fiction, 225, 284, 286; favors journalistic style, 255; founds *World's Work*, 272; given control over *Atlantic*, 240, 252; idea of magazine, 202; increases ethnic pluralism, 266–70, 321; increases nonfiction reportage, 263; interest in educational reform, 257; interest in race relations, 264; learns progressive publishing, 246; literary tastes of, 261–62; on marketability of romance, 225; politics of, compared to Perry, 302; politics under, 18, 256–60; as professional editor, 252; progressive journalism of, 14, 215; progressive views of, 248–50; reform journalism under, 258; resigns editorship, 271, 275; salary, 239, 271; as Scudder's assistant, 238; Scudder's evaluation of, 238, 252; seeks change in high culture, 317; series on ethnicity, 269, 321; Spanish-American War and, 257, 259–60, 306; trade books and, 239, 252

Palmer, G. H., 207

Parker, Gilbert: Scudder advises, 208; serial by, 225

Parker, William B., 240, 290; assists Page, 253; assists Perry, 279; declines "Law of Life," 287; edits *To Have and to Hold*, 284; Moody and, 294

Parkman, Francis, rate of payment, 263

Parsons, G. F., on class conflict, 197

Parton, James: Fields recruits, 75; Howells on, 84; new magazine journalism and, 83–84; series on spoils system, 105

Payments to authors: under Aldrich, 177–80; competition and trade courtesy, 131; competition in 1870s, 130–31, 135; in 1890s, 263; under Fields, 75; to Harte, 141; Houghton's conservatism, 130; under Howells, 130–31; to James, 140; to Jewett in 1890s, 228; under Lowell, 46; under Perry, 288–89; for poetry, 46, 75, 130, 295; on publication, 180; set by business office, 177; under Scudder, 223; to Twain, 141

Payne, Will, 265, 279

Peabody, Josephine, 233, 235, 295; Scudder assists, 209, 237

Perry, Bliss, 236, 271; accomplishments as editor, 293, 310–11, 316; appointed trade book editor, 278; background of, 275–77; compared to Gilder, 321; compared to Page as editor, 278–79, 281–82; compared to Scudder, 276–77; credits Page, 272; criticizes Anglo ethnocentrism, 309; criticizes Roosevelt's policy, 306; cultural mission of, 296; editorial addresses to readers, 282–83; editorial methods, 278; editorial policy, 14–19; ethnic pluralism and, 302, 306; literary judgment of, 284, 287, 293; on McKinley assassination, 305; on poetry, 17, 293–94, 299; political views of, 302–4, 306; reaction against romances, 286; resists commercial influence, 296–97; returns to teaching, 312–14; salary, 278; Scudder advises, 205; sees change in high culture, 317; Yankee humanism of, 14

335

Index

Perry, T. S., reviews for Howells, 137, 152
Phelps, Elizabeth Stuart, 177; on Fields, 92; moralizing of, 226; serials for Aldrich, 192
Phillips, David G., "The Common Lot," 304
Phillips, Moses: *Atlantic* founding and, 3, 30–31; death of, 64; influence on *Atlantic*, 46, 49–50; religious controversy and, 59; supports Lowell's politics, 63
Pierce, Zina, 93; "Cooperative Housekeeping," 99
Pioneer, 28, 50
Poetry: under Aldrich, 185–88; in *Atlantic*, 17; under Fields, 89; under Lowell, 37; payments for, 46, 75, 130, 295; under Perry, 302–8; under Scudder, 236
Politics: under Aldrich, 182, 196–97; class conflict, 13, 156, 196–97; in early Harper's, 39; under Fields, 98, 100–107; under Howells, 153–57; London on, in the *Atlantic*, 291–92; under Lowell, 36, 61–64; in original prospectus, 35; under Page, 256–60; under Perry, 18, 277, 283, 293–96; under Scudder, 214–17, 243
Poole, Ernest, stories by, 308
Popular culture, *Atlantic* comment on, 301–2
Powderly, Terrance, Aldrich solicits, 197
Preston, Harriet Waters: criticizes Howells, 297; reviews for Aldrich, 189
Progressive publishing, defined, 246
Proofreading: Nichols and, 65, 319; Page's indifference to, 252, 256; payment for, 178
Pulitzer, Joseph, Scudder declines offer by, 243
Putnam's Magazine: and Boston authors, 27; ceases publication, 39, 76

Quincy, Edmund, advocates civil disobedience, 62

Race: in Fields's *Atlantic*, 104; in Page's *Atlantic*, 266–70; in Perry's *Atlantic*, 307–9
Reade, Charles: *Griffith Gaunt* serialized, 91; praises early *Atlantic*, 41
Readership: appeal to teachers, 217; of *Atlantic* and Hearst papers, 291; attempts to expand, 15, 83, 132, 254–55, 280, 315; averages five per copy, 319; of early *Atlantic*, 40–41; of early *Harper's*, 40; Howells's perception of, 149–52; influence of, on magazine, 57; influence of lyceum system on, 40; influence of newspapers on, 246–47; less culturally homogeneous, 255; limited for poetry, 293–94; Moody's lament of, 295; Perry warns James of change in, 281–82; in south, 248; stability of, 41; uninterested in classics, 300
Realism: under Aldrich, 183, 188; *Atlantic* and, 10, 192, 314–15; criticized by Warner and Repplier, 191; under Fields, 95; in Howells's early reviews, 120–22; Howells's editorial support for, 114, 132–33, 138; Libin's, praised, 301; Lowell's taste for, and limits, 53–57; and nonfiction reportage, 147–48; relation to reportage, 84, 263–64; under Scudder, 219–23; Scudder on, 147–48, 190–91, 220–21. *See also* under individual editors; Fiction; Novel
Reconstruction: in Fields's *Atlantic*, 100, 103–5; in Perry's *Atlantic*, 307; reportage on, 85; Sumner on, 103
Reese, Lizette, 237, 296
Reform journalism, 258
Religion: under Fields, 99; Holmes's criticism of, 59, 96; under Lowell, 57–60
Repplier, Agnes, 248; critical of realism, 191
Republican party, 10, 14, 104–5; *Atlantic* breaks with, 196; Howells's relationship to, 154; Lowell criticizes, 63
Reviews. *See* Book reviews
Reynolds, Paul, 212
Rice, Charles: on Libin, 301; on Russian Jews, 309
Riis, Jacob, in Page's *Atlantic*, 253, 258–59, 265–66, 316
Riley, James W.: Aldrich parodies, 184; Aldrich's dislike of, 315; Page enjoys, 261
Ripley, William, "Race Factors in Labor Unions," 304
Riverside Magazine for Young People, 204, 227
Riverside Press: loses *Atlantic*, 313; prints *Atlantic*, 312
Rives, Amalie, Aldrich and, 171–72, 174
Robinson, Edwin Arlington, 294
Roosevelt, Theodore, 215, 257; advocates civil service, 216; Chapman endorses, 305; distaste for James's fiction, 261; Ogden satirizes, 305; Page influences article by, 256; recommends Riis, 265
Royce, Josiah, 214

Salary: editorial, *see* individual editors; of writers and skilled workers, 178, 320
Sanborn, Alvin, 265
Santayana, George, 236, 237; on cultural division, 15, 18, 214, 316; on genteel tradition, 248–49; reviews for Scudder, 220
Schurz, Carl, 215
Science: under Aldrich, 182; under Fields, 99–100; under Lowell, 60–61
Scollard, Clinton, 237
Scribner's (*Century*): book reviews in, 152; censorship, 171; circulation, 127; compared to *Atlantic*, 127–29; compared to *Harper's*, 320; reconstruction, 136
Scribner's Magazine, 224; competition with *Atlantic*, 289–90; critiqued by *Nation*, 242; cuts book reviews, 297; increase in current affairs, 246; romantic fiction and, 286
Scudder, Horace Elisha, 265, 267, 270, 284, 290, 312; accomplishments as editor, 241–43; advo-

336

cates high literary culture, 248; background of, 201–5; biography of, 321; canonizes older *Atlantic* authors, 13, 213; compared to other editors, 199, 201–2; contrasts self with Page, 239–41; corresponds with Hans Andersen, 204; criticizes Page for controversy, 257; cultural mission of, 12, 204, 206, 241, 315; death of, 278; denounces party politics, 216; editorial advice, 208–9; editorial policy, 11–14, 207–9, 213; fifty-two when editor, 203; friendship with Howells, 210; Henry James and, 230–33; hopes for *Atlantic*, 316; illnesses of, 211–12; increases current affairs, 251; influences Aldrich's *Atlantic*, 176; interest in education, 217–18; on literary canon, 218–19; on literary education, 321; literary ethics, 225; literary judgment, 190–91; on marketability of romance, 225; on moral basis of politics, 216; observes change in fiction, 225; Perry describes, 276; reading as editor, 207–8; realism and, 13, 190–91, 220–21; relationship with Houghton, 204–6; relationship with Page, 239–41, 252, 257, 271–72; requests assistance, 212; resigns as editor, 241; reviews American fiction, 220; reviews for Aldrich, 189; reviews Howells's novels, 190–91, 320; reviews James, 93, 194, 195; sabbatical in 1897, 240; salary, 206; seeks Page's replacement, 275–76; serial form and, 227–28; stands in for Aldrich, 198; trade editor for Houghton, 165; travel as editor, 207; work load, 206, 209–11; writes "Comment on New Books," 208; younger writers and, 209, 234–37

Sedgwick, Arthur George, 248; attacks on Benjamin Butler, 320; political views of, 154–56; writes on politics for Howells, 152

Sedgwick, Ellery, 215, 281; critical of Scudder, 207, 213, 243; description of Page, 246; editorial guidelines for Perry, 313; editorial policy, 14–19; editorship of, 314; Jenkins and, 280; offers to buy *Atlantic*, 312; Scudder assists, 209

Sedgwick, Henry Dwight, 214; critic of corporate capitalism, 303–4; declines editorship, 275

Shaw, George Bernard, 301

Shepherd, Edwin, 216

Sherman, Frank Dempster, 237

Shorey, Paul, 255

Sill, Edward Roland, 172, 185–87; accepts Aldrich's editing, 173; pleads to use pseudonym, 187–88; on writing for the *Atlantic*, 180

Sinclair, May, on American poetry, 295

Sinclair, Upton, 283, 286

Slavery, *Atlantic* opposition to, 61–64, 101–2

Smith, Azariah (Houghton's director of advertising), 189, 206

Smith, F. Hopkinson, 261

Socialism, in Scudder's *Atlantic*, 217

South, in *Atlantic* literature, 94–95, 320

Southern Literary Messenger: denounces *Atlantic*, 42, 62; regionalism of, 43

Southern writers, and early *Atlantic*, 42

Spanish-American war: Page supports, 257, 259; Perry's *Atlantic* and, 306

Spofford, Harriet, 297

Sprague, Charles, on Darwinism, 100

Stedman, Edmund C., 185–86, 212, 236; reviews for *Atlantic*, 88

Stevenson, R. L., 262

Stickney, Trumbull, 279; Parker rejects, 294

Stillman, W. J., reminiscences by, 298

Stockton, Frank, and Scudder, 204, 205, 224

Stoddard, Richard H.: resentment of Boston authors, 137; reviews for *Atlantic*, 88

Stowe, Harriet Beecher, 23–24; Byron article scandal, 109; "Chimney Corner," 86, 99; founding of *Atlantic*, 30; friendship with Annie Fields, 92, 320; Lowell's editorial treatment of, 36, 54–55; "Minister's Wooing," 96; "Oldtown Fireside Stories," 95; popularity of, 50; proposes "women's department," 86

Sumner, Charles, 86; manifest destiny, 106; Reconstruction plan in *Atlantic*, 103–4

Tabb, Father John, 237, 294

Taylor, Bayard, 165, 210; "Byways of Europe," 85; reviews for *Atlantic*, 88

Thanet, Octave, Page's *Atlantic*, 156, 265

Thaxter, Celia: friendship with Annie Fields, 92; "Isle of Shoals," 96

Thayer, William Roscoe, 212

Thomas, Edith, 185–86, 295

Thompson, Charles Minor: review of Garland, 222; review of Twain, 221; reviews for Scudder, 220

Thoreau, Henry David, 87; Fields recruits, 74–75; Journals published by Perry, 284, 289, 299; Lowell's editorial treatment of, 59–60

Ticknor, Howard: becomes assistant editor, 65; Fields's dislike of, 78; forced out of business, 108

Ticknor, William: death of, 91; forms partnership with Fields, 71

Ticknor and Fields: buys *Atlantic*, 64; dominates New England publishing, 74; emphasis on literature, 89; publishes *Atlantic*, 23

Torrence, Ridgely, 295

Trade courtesy, 131

Travel literature, under Fields, 85

Trent, W. P., 214

Trowbridge, John: autobiography, 289; Lowell's *Atlantic*, 37; reportage on Reconstruction, 85, 264

Turner, Frederick Jackson, 220

Twain, Mark, 223, 315; on Aldrich, 168; on *Atlantic* readership, 142; Howells rejects religious

Index

Twain, Mark (*cont.*)
satire, 149; Howells's editorial treatment, 140–44; *Old Times on the Mississippi*, 141–42; Parton recommends, 84; reviews of, 221; Whittier dinner speech, 141

Underwood, Francis, 45–46, 319; applies for editorship, 165; assistant to Lowell, 34; *Atlantic* founding and, 3, 29; loses bid for *Atlantic*, 64–65; solicits in England, 34

Villard, Oswald, 312

Walker, John Brisbane, 247; proposes to buy *Atlantic*, 312
Ward, Elizabeth, 255
Warner, Charles Dudley: critical of realism, 191; distrusts organized labor, 155; promotes romantic fiction, 284; rate of payment, 178; urges Jewett to write romance, 229
Washington, Booker, 307–8, 316; Page influences article by, 256; in Page's *Atlantic*, 253, 256, 259, 267
Wasson, David, 23, 99; cultural nationalism of, 52
Waters, Harriet Preston: criticism of Howells, 138; reviews for Scudder, 220; series on classics, 214
Wells, H. G.: criticism of Boston, 298; Perry seeks to serialize, 304
Wendell, Barrett, 249
Wharton, Edith, 301; Howells publishes, 137; praises *Atlantic*, 296; rate of payment, 289–90; writes for Perry, 289–90
Whipple, Edwin Percy, 23, 87; condemns Andrew Johnson, 103–4; founding of *Atlantic*, 31; reviews for Lowell, 37
White, Richard Grant, 171, 172, 174
White, William Allen, in Page's *Atlantic*, 253, 265
Whitman, Walt, 300; on Aldrich, 164; Aldrich's dislike of, 184, 315; in American authors poll, 165; comment on, in Perry's *Atlantic*, 298–99; comment on, in Scudder's *Atlantic*, 221–22; Howells on, 137; *Leaves of Grass* reviewed, 190; Lowell censors, 54; Page approves of, 261; Perry's admiration for, 278, 284, 293; submissions to Fields, 89
Whittier, John Greenleaf, 23, 89, 298; accepts Lowell's editing, 46; in Aldrich's *Atlantic*, 186; Howells and, 133; Whittier in Scudder's canon, 219; reputation fades, 284, 299; requests review article, 87
Wiggin, Kate Douglas: in *Atlantic* reviews, 298; moralizing of, 226; *Penelope's Progress*, 263; Perry serializes, 285–86; Scudder advises, 208
Wilkins, Mary E., 219; contract with *Harper's*, 223–24; Scudder advises, 227; Scudder reviews, 223
Williams, Talcott, 297; on labor and capital, 304
Wilson, Edward: criticizes Anglo ethnocentrism, 309; "The Joys of Being a Negro," 307–8
Wilson, Henry, advocates reform Republicanism, 105
Wilson, Woodrow, 215, 237; encouraged by Scudder, 198; Page and, 247, 253, 257; recommends Page as editor, 238; reviews for Scudder, 220; Scudder assists, 209
Winthrop, Theodore, "Life in the Open Air," 85
Wister, Owen, 255, 290; Scudder and, 235, 236
Women's issues, in Fields's *Atlantic*, 99
Women writers: in *Atlantic*, 10; in Lowell's *Atlantic*, 36, 55–57; in Fields's *Atlantic*, 86, 92–97; in Howells's *Atlantic*, 145–46; of poetry under Aldrich, 186; rates of payment, 179
Woodberry, George Edward, 185, 191, 279; Aldrich influences reviews by, 189; and Aldrich's resignation, 198–99; Aldrich supports, 177, 188; friendship with Aldrich, 169; rate of payment, 178; reviews for Scudder, 220
Woolson, Constance, 315; on writing for the *Atlantic*, 180
Wyman, Lillie Chase: defends unionism, 197; reportage on industrialism by, 147, 264, 321

Yankee humanism: *Atlantic* and, 314–15; belief in cultural progress, 98–99; canon and, 7; cultural democracy and, 6–7; defined, 4–9; democracy and, 102–3; Howe and, 212; Lowell as representative of, 31–33; opposes industrial capitalism, 13, 303–4; Perry as representative of, 276–77, 301, 302, 313; politics of, 5–6, 7–8; views on democracy, 6, 25
Yankee humanists: American cultural nationalism and, 7, 24; background of, 4; British ties of, 25; as cultural minority, 9, 196; cultural mission of, 4, 8, 24, 107; diversity of, 8–9, 22; on high culture and democracy, 107–8; Howells and, 132; opposition to slavery, 26; political activism of, 8, 26; tolerance valued by, 9, 57
Youth's Companion: Howe and, 212; "red-blooded" fiction and, 287

Zangwill, Israel, 253, 267
Zitkala-Sa (Gertrude Bonnin), 316; autobiography of, in *Atlantic*, 310, 322

www.ingramcontent.com/pod-product-compliance
Lightning Source LLC
Chambersburg PA
CBHW031704230426
43668CB00006B/105